Christian Apologetics as Cross-Cultural Dialogue

Christian Apologetics as Cross-Cultural Dialogue

BENNO VAN DEN TOREN

t&t clark

BT
1103
.T67
2011

Published by T&T Clark International
A Continuum Imprint
The Tower Building, 11 York Road, London SE1 7NX
80 Maiden Lane, Suite 704, New York, NY 10038

www.continuumbooks.com

All rights reserved. No part of this publication may be reproduced or transmitted in any form or by any means, electronic or mechanical, including photocopying, recording or any information storage or retrieval system, without permission in writing from the publishers.

© Benno van den Toren, 2011

Benno van den Toren has asserted his right under the Copyright, Designs and Patents Act, 1988, to be identified as the Author of this work.

British Library Cataloguing-in-Publication Data
A catalogue record for this book is available from the British Library

ISBN: 978-0-567-05276-6 (hardback)
978-0-567-16916-7 (paperback)

Typeset by Fakenham Prepress Solutions, Fakenham, Norfolk NR21 8NN
Printed and bound in India

Unless otherwise indicated, all Scripture quotations are from the New Revised Standard Version Bible: Anglicized Edition, copyright 1989, 1995, Division of Christian Education of the National Council of the Churches of Christ in the United States of America. Used by permission. All rights reserved.

[B]ut in your hearts sanctify Christ as Lord. Always be ready to make your defence to anyone who demands from you an account of the hope that is in you (1Pe 3:15)

Do not be conformed to this world, but be transformed by the renewing of your minds, so that you may discern what is the will of God – what is good and acceptable and perfect. (Ro 12:2)

For Berdine

TABLE OF CONTENTS

PREFACE

This study seeks to understand the nature and possibilities of Christian apologetic witness in a multicultural world. This may be the greatest challenge and opportunity to communicate the Good News of Jesus Christ since the beginning of the modern era. For the last two centuries Christian apologists have invested most of their energy in relating the Christian faith to the modern mind. Currently the appeal of modern rationality is fading rapidly. The task of the apologist has not necessarily become easier, for in many quarters the brick wall of scientific rationalism has been replaced by cultural relativism that seems more like the wall of a bouncy castle: it gives in, but always changes shape without giving way. Postmodern "tolerance" leaves room for a variety of religious and cultural perspectives, yet excludes any claim to a universal Gospel.

Apologists have, at the same time, become aware that they need to address a multiplicity of audiences. In our "global village", modernism and postmodernism are just two cultural options among many – often vibrant – alternatives such as Islam and Buddhism. In this new environment, many of the older apologetic models have become obsolete, because they are answering questions that many are no longer asking and which have never been the most important questions outside the Western world. Rather than an apologetic witness that addresses a purportedly universal rationality, we need "local" or "audience-sensitive apologetics" that take the particular culturally embedded outlooks of the changing audiences into account.

Missiologists have done much work understanding how the Gospel should be proclaimed to culturally varied audiences, yet few of these reflections have been brought to bear on the apologetic task. This study aims to do just that. It explores whether and how apologetic witness is possible in a world in which every truth claim is made within a culturally embedded context. In doing so, it effectively presents a different approach to understanding apologetic witness. Apologetics should not ask how the Gospel can be justified over and against a supposedly universal rationality, whether through evidentialist, rationalist, or presuppositionalist argumentation. Instead, apologetics should always be understood as cross-cultural dialogue and more precisely as a dialogue aimed at persuasion. Because both dialogue partners argue from culturally embedded frameworks, apologetics should ask whether and how it is possible to engage in true dialogue and develop persuasive arguments for the Christian message across such cultural barriers.

This study offers an analysis of the postmodern challenge to apologetics, a development of a Christian anthropology and theory of knowledge as the basis for a truly Christian apologetic, and reflections on the nature of culture and cross-cultural communication. These different threads are thoroughly intertwined, and only when seen together can the strength and practice of the Christian alternative be fully appreciated. Modernism, postmodernism and the Christian worldview are all-encompassing conceptions of reality and life. As with a cobweb, you cannot remove one thread without weakening the whole. Yet some readers may be most interested in one or two of the different constituent elements of the argument. The "outline of the argument" in the first chapter will help them to find the sections that may be most interesting to them. Those who might be interested in using this study as a textbook for advanced courses in apologetics in a multicultural world could concentrate on Chapters 4 to 8, which present a positive sketch of Christian apologetics as cross-cultural persuasion.

A study covering such a wide field is never possible without the extensive use of the research and reflections of others in the different areas treated. The specific contribution of this study lies more in the integration and interweaving of the constituent threads of the argument rather than in any of these threads individually. The study seeks to make its specific contribution in the combination of a cultural and a theological analysis of the contemporary crisis of apologetics, in the bringing together of theological anthropology and Christian epistemology, and in the linking of the theory and practice of Christian apologetics. Because of the necessarily multidisciplinary nature of the project, I am sure that there will be many areas in which significant improvement is possible, and I hope that readers will consider these reflections an invitation to further dialogue on a work in progress rather than a fortress to be attacked or defended.

The debate on the end of modernism and the possibility of moving beyond it colours many contemporary theological debates, even if the talk about postmodernism is slightly less prevalent than a decade ago. Some readers will feel that I have ceded too much to conceptual relativism and to multiculturalism as an ideology. Others may feel that I continue to defend too many modern values. However, this study in apologetics should not be read as a middle course, but rather as an alternative course based on a Christian theological anthropology and on a Christian epistemology – and it should be judged in that light.

Some of the theological and epistemological explorations may at first seem relatively abstract, but they have been driven by practical experiences of apologetic dialogue with many different people of varying religious and cultural backgrounds. My experiences as a student worker in the Netherlands, as a missionary in Africa, and as an expatriate in North America and England have provided the principal motivation for embarking on this project. These varied experiences have made me feel that many of the older models for apologetics remain theoretical constructs based on epistemological presuppositions with limited value for everyday apologetic witness. The explorations in this study are driven by the desire to understand what is actually happening when apologetic dialogue takes place and when people are, in the process, persuaded of the truth of the Gospel. Conversely, it shows that serious engagement with theological, epistemological and cultural studies can bring a new depth and realism to the apologetic witness of the Christian community.

This study is part of a much longer pilgrimage and a wider project. It began with a doctoral thesis (1995) on the nature of Christian apologetics in dialogue with Barth and postmodernism. Many of the ideas on the contextual and culturally embedded nature of Christian praxis and witness were developed during the eight years I lived and taught in the Central African Republic. Recently, I published *A Pocket Guide to Christian Belief* (Oxford: Lion, 2009) in which I aim at introducing outsiders to the Christian world and life, encouraging them to seek to understand this world on its own terms rather than in terms of other world-views, whether they be modern, postmodern or other. In *Reasons for my Hope: Responding to non-Christian Friends* (Oxford: Monarch, 2010) I sought to give a practical introduction to dialogical apologetics for a Western European audience.

Both postmodernism and cultural anthropology have pointed out that all human reflection is culturally located. I will argue that this does not exclude the confidence of the Christian community that in Christ they encounter the Creator of the universe and are therefore gripped by a truth that by far surpasses their cultural location. However, the cultural embeddedness of all reflection does mean that I will often use "we" in the development of the argument, referring to the reflective community of which I form a part and from which and for which I reason. I do not suppose that all readers will automatically feel included in this "we". It is rather an invitation to further dialogue between people reflecting from different perspectives and rooted in different traditions.

Most of the sources I use are in English. Where I use German, French and Dutch authors in the original edition, I refer both to the original edition and to a translation, if one has been available. A special remark is needed concerning Karl Barth. Though he is often known as a critic of the apologetic enterprise, I believe that his criticism is directed particularly against the apologetics of the modern era that wanted to "build" the truth of the Gospel on a presupposedly universal foundation to which all human beings have equal access. I often refer to him, for I consider his reflections on the nature of revelation, salvation and theology crucial for the development of a properly Christian apologetics and of particular relevance in a postmodern and multicultural context. In order to facilitate looking up the references in his *Kirchliche Dogmatik* or *Church Dogmatics*, I do not refer to the year of publication of the respective volumes, but rather to the volume numbers as "*KD* IV/3: 121; trans. *CD* IV/3: 109", etc.

In venturing into a number of disciplines, I have been greatly helped by many guides and I am grateful to those who have read parts of the manuscript and whose comments have deepened my reflections and spared me poor judgement. I would like to mention particularly Paul Helm, Charles Ringma, John Stackhouse, Jack Robinson and Peter Verbaan. Shortly before his untimely death, Stanley Grenz made important comments on earlier drafts of the theological anthropology developed in Chapter 4. I am particularly grateful to Faculté de Théologie Evangélique de Bangui and to the Mission Deputees of the Christian Reformed Churches in the Netherlands, who allowed me a year of study-leave, as well as to Regent College, Vancouver, which welcomed me as scholar-in-residence in the year 2002–2003. During that year I was able to undertake a significant part of the research leading to this publication. Because I have been writing in a foreign language, I am hugely indebted to the many people who have helped me to improve my English – particularly to Hilary Schroeder and Theodora Robinson. I am grateful to Dominic Done and Derk van den Toren for their help with the bibliographical references and index.

A shorter version of Chapter 7 of this book has been published in the *Evangelical Quarterly* as "Challenges and Possibilities of Inter-religious and Cross-cultural Apologetic Persuasion" (82/1, January 2010, pp. 42–64). I am grateful for the permission to re-publish the material.

I am especially grateful to Berdine who has been my closest friend in the many cultural contexts in which we have lived together. Her sensitivity to the integrity of others guards me from believing too easily that I have understood other cultures when there is always more to explore. Her companionship while moving around has been a basis from which to explore other cultures in all their strangeness and to build friendships across three continents. Above all, I want to thank our God who continues to amaze me with the greatness of the gift of his Son who speaks in so many ways to the deepest needs of so many worlds.

Chapter 1

TWO CONVERGING CHALLENGES FOR CHRISTIAN APOLOGETIC WITNESS

1.1 Two converging challenges

A postmodern audience

I met Sharon on a long-distance bus from London to Paris. She was a typical cosmopolitan young woman. Originally from Australia, she had been working for a few months in England and was now taking some time to travel the European mainland. A long bus journey like this is actually an ideal occasion for apologetic dialogue. The eight hours give you all the time needed for careful listening and provide prolonged pauses for reflection. At the same time fellow travellers are completely new to each other and know that they will probably never meet again, which creates the sort of situation in which people can open up and be honest with each other and with themselves.

Sharon's initial criticisms of the Christian faith were quite recognizable and related to the critical and scientific attitude many of us have absorbed by growing up in the modern world. "I just cannot believe in God in an age of science knowing that the theory of evolution has shown belief in God to be an obsolete superstition." Further on, though, her attitude towards religion seemed to be less negative. She actually valued the sacredness of nature as seen by the Australian Aboriginals, for it served the protection of nature better than modern day materialism. Notwithstanding her evolutionary ideas, she could not accept the policy of the survival of the fittest, which had exterminated the Tasmanian Aboriginals and decimated their Australian brothers and sisters. She saw in this a lack of respect, which is due to each human being because of the divine spark they all share – an idea she valued in Hinduism. She also liked the Hindu notion of reincarnation, which helped her face death. She didn't really interpret reincarnation in the Eastern way, though, for she didn't consider human suffering as a rightful and purifying punishment for evil done in former lives. She rather kept to the Christian ideal that human suffering should be prevented and relieved.

Sharon was happy to extend her openness and tolerance of all sorts of religious ideas to Christianity, too. "It's fine for me that you and some of my friends are

Christians. Actually, I think it's great that you are so driven by your convictions and that it gives meaning to your life. I think it is great as a truth for you, but I don't feel that it is true for me, too. What annoys me in so many Christians is that they cannot leave others free in their convictions and always try to convince them. I hope you can respect me for making different choices in life. Finally it's personal what we believe, isn't it?"

This type of reaction is well known to many who desire to share their faith with Europeans and North Americans who don't know Jesus Christ. It shows how radically the situation in which the Christian community finds itself has changed over the last few decades. From the beginning of the modern era until recently, the Christian faith has been under heavy attack for being backward, obscurantist, non-scientific and not in accordance with right reason. Christian apologetics was heavily involved in the defence of the truth and rationality of the Christian faith. Nowadays the opposition from science still has some sort of plausibility, but generally all sorts of religious beliefs can count on a new openness and tolerance. This gives the Christian faith a host of new opportunities and, equally, new challenges.

The challenges are particularly felt in Christian apologetics, for where the Christian faith and religions in general can count on a new tolerance, Christian *apologetics* cannot. Traditional apologetics seems obsolete and of place. It seems *obsolete*, as most people are no longer asking that their convictions be rational or true in the traditional sense. People do not even expect their beliefs to be coherent as the eclectic hotchpotch of Sharon's ideas shows. In fact, Christian apologetics itself is in need of a defence, because the new tolerance for religion goes together with an allergy to everything that sounds like a claim of universal truth.

Traditional apologetics, moreover, seems *out of place*. It is not so much that many of the older arguments have been refuted, but that it addresses questions that most of the people it encounters are no longer asking or have never asked. The modern mindset, which provided the background of these questions, is crumbling. Moreover, in this process we discover that the modern mindset cannot and never could realistically claim to reflect a universal pattern of thinking. It seems justified to speak of a crisis of apologetics. Yet, it may be a crisis that, just as with a medical crisis, cannot only bring death, but also healing and the promise of new strength.

A non-Western audience

The challenge to apologetics encountered in those who can be labelled "postmodern" has a parallel in the non-Western parts of the world. For a number of years, I have been teaching Christian apologetics to students in the Central African Republic, in "Beafrika", or the heart of Africa, as the Central Africans call their own country. In this context it is apparent from the start that the critical questions asked by those outside the Church from a perspective of African Traditional Religion (questions from outside the Church that are often shared by those inside, just as in the West) are radically different than what I was used to. My students will tell that they find it difficult to answer those who reject the Christian faith because they feel that going to a traditional healer is much more effective for obtaining healing and protection from evil curses, than praying to the God of the Bible. There are so many stories in their own families and lives, about seeking for help from traditional healers and healing being instantaneous and miraculous. There are as many stories of those who went to their pastor and were prayed for, but advised to remain patient and to accept that God will heal in his own time. So, which religion is better?

Others will reject the Christian faith as the religion of white people. As a Westerner this reproach seems at first sight easy to answer: Jesus was, after all, a Jew and the Gospel is addressed to all people. Yet, it is a problem that touches many Africans in what is most crucial to their identity. In Africa, the extended family and the clan are traditionally the most important points of reference when making important decisions. Religion is a communal affair and exists for the flourishing and harmony of the community – the community of both the living and the deceased.[1] A religion that comes from outside and harms the community and the ancestors is thus a contradiction in itself. That is one of the reasons why for many Africans it is easier to *add* another religion to their traditional one than to break with the religion of their ancestors. The reproach that Christianity is the whites' religion goes emotionally even deeper because it automatically relates the Christian faith to the colonial powers. The deep resentment against past colonial oppression and today's neo-colonial international relationships are carried over to the Christian faith. Answering the reproach that Christianity is the whites' religion demands, therefore, an engagement with the wider search for a modern African identity and for an African Christian identity.

Some of the typical Western questions – for example, concerning the relationship of religion and science – may be asked, for Africa is more and more a part of our global culture. However, these questions do not grow by themselves on Africa soil. On average, typical Western or typical modern questions do not loom large. People do not find it that difficult to believe in a Creator and in creation, in miracles and in divine revelations. These beliefs are most natural to them. In this situation, Western apologetic textbooks are strangely out of place and basically ignored as irrelevant, both because of the questions they deal with and because of their one-sided intellectual approach. This intellectualist approach seems totally inappropriate in relation to the emotional load and existential urgency these questions have, dealing with cultural identity and with the need to face the daily dangers of illnesses and spells. It is not that the Christian faith is not in need of a defence and a justification. Many of the first theological publications by twentieth

1 For more on this issue, see §4.4, pp. 110f.

century Africans are precisely dealing with the question of identity: how does the God of Christ relate to our past and to the God of our ancestors and how can we be both African and Christian?[2] So, these theological writings are dealing with one of the prime apologetic questions in contemporary Africa, but not under the classic rubric of "apologetics".

Converging challenges

Exchanges with Christians living in other continents and cultures have shown me that a case for the lack of relevance of Western apologetics could equally be made from a Hindu, Buddhist or Muslim culture or from Latin America (cf. Dyrness 1982: 13f; Netland 1988). The same could be said concerning the large sections of Western society that do not share the secularized modern consciousness.[3] In many of these contexts some sort of alternative apologetic witness has been developed, though not always under the label of apologetics. Yet, the challenge and promise this entails for Western style apologetics is much less perceived and debated than the challenge perceived from the side of postmodernism. However, both challenges are closely related, for the discovery that all of our thinking and reasoning is culturally embedded fuels postmodern relativist attitudes towards reason and truth. Inversely, the postmodern sensitivity to the cultural conditioning of our reasoning may contribute to the development of Christian apologetics that can speak to different cultural worlds. From both angles we are pointed to a limitation of the type of apologetics that Western Christians have developed since the Enlightenment. Modern apologetics perceives itself as giving a general defence of the Christian faith based on perceptions and standards of reasoning that all sound and rational human beings supposedly share. Under the developments of postmodernism and the increasing realization that our world is multicultural, we need to ask what form apologetics should take in the light of these developments. What is even more disconcerting: is this apologetic project that aims to give a justification of the Gospel not doomed to failure from the start, when there are no shared convictions, from which to start the argument, and when we cannot fall back on shared argumentative procedures?

From a number of quarters different apologists have been proposing new approaches to apologetics that are more congenial to our postmodern and multi-cultural world: "postliberal apologetics" (Handspicker 1991–1992), "postmodern

2 For an analysis of African theology along those lines, see Kwame Bediako (1992).

3 Ronald Potter's perception with regards to North America maybe somewhat overstated, but is a healthy corrective: "Many of us have tended to overestimate the pervasiveness and cognitive sovereignty of so-called secularized modern consciousness. [...] Accordingly, virtually the only persons who represent so-called modern man and woman are those within the intellectual community" (1995: 179; cf. also Hexham, Rost & Morehead (eds) 2004; Johnson, Payne & Wilson 2008).

apologetics" (Murphy 1996), "humble apologetics" (Stackhouse 2002), "narrative apologetics" (Clark 1993b), "dialogical apologetics" (Clark 1993a), "person-centered apologetics" (Brent & Chismar 1984), "holistic apologetics" (cf. Hexham, Rost & Morehead (eds.) 2004), "ad hoc apologetics" (Lindbeck 1984), "contextualized apologetics" (Johnson, Payne & Wilson 2008; Netland 1988), "local apologetics" (McGrath 1992: 11), "global apologetics",[4] and even "unapologetic apologetics" (Placher 1989). Though there has been a strong call that apologetics should move beyond the models inherited from the Western Enlightenment, there has been little sustained and systematic study into the theological and philosophical foundations of such form of apologetic witness. This study aims to contribute to precisely these questions out of the conviction that this will help place newer contextualized ventures on a stronger footing. As such it aims to enrich the *method and practice* of Christian apologetic witness and dialogue that addresses people with respect to their different cultural and personal convictions, experiences, projects, biases and patterns of reasoning.

In the process, we will argue that this new context invites us to understand all apologetic dialogue as cross-cultural persuasion. Rather than aiming for universally valid arguments for the truth of the Christian faith, the Christian apologist should take the cultural embeddedness of both parties in the dialogue into account. Such an approach does justice to the cultured nature of all human existence. It reflects furthermore the particular nature of the Christian faith itself, which believes that the one God has revealed Himself in one particular context, yet in view of blessing all the nations through Abraham and Jesus Christ.

This approach to apologetics as cross-cultural dialogue will not only be crucial for engaging postmodern and non-Western audiences. It will also prove fruitful in reaching the modern Western world. Many classical apologetic approaches have started from the presupposition that the modern Western understanding of rationality represents a universal criterion in the light of which the truth of Christianity can be judged. In the process it has conceded too much and is constantly tempted to adapt Christianity to what modern reason find acceptable. Modernity itself is a particular cultural phenomenon that needs to be relativized. "The Christian community, no matter where it finds itself, is always in a cross-cultural, frontier situation; it is always on the boundary between faith and unbelief." (Bevans 2002: 123) Modern rationality should be judged in the light of the Gospel rather than the reverse and Christian apologetics to modern culture should equally be understood as cross-cultural dialogue.

We will continue this introductory chapter with a wider sketch of the different elements of the postmodern ethos in relation to the reality of life in a multicultural world and the challenges it poses to the apologist (§1.2). Next, we will give a preliminary answer to the question why in fact the development of a new

4 Cf. the "Global Apologetics and Mission" ministry founded by Philip Johnson.

apologetic is necessary. If apologetics has become obsolete and even heavily criticized, why not simply abandon apologetics and limit ourselves to the proclamation of the Gospel in other forms or even entirely give up proclamation? (§1.3) The theological and cultural reasons for continuing with a Christian apologetic witness form the basis for a new definition of apologetics, which is at the same time faithful to the Christian Scriptures and adequate to our pluralist and postmodern world (§1.4). In the fifth section, we will give a general sketch of the outline for the argument in this study. The argument contains a number of different elements: a critical analysis of modern apologetics in the light of postmodern sensitivities, thoughts on cross-cultural communication, reflections on Christian anthropology and epistemology, and an introduction to the theory and practice of Christian apologetics. The outline of the argument gives an overview of how these elements intertwine and form together one single argument for a contextual and dialogical Christian apologetic witness for our increasingly postmodern and multicultural world (§1.5).

1.2 The postmodern challenge to Christian Apologetics

The elusiveness and pervasiveness of the postmodern

Insofar as the current crisis of Christian apologetics is related to postmodernism, it is part of a larger crisis of Western culture (in the West and equally in those areas in the South and the East where Western culture is a dominant force). This culture is shaking on its foundations. Everywhere we see signs that the great Enlightenment project, which shaped the ideals of the culture we call "modern", seems to have failed. In a "dialectic of the Enlightenment" (Horkheimer & Adorno 1969; trans. 2002), we see that the Enlightenment ideals of "freedom, equality, and brotherhood" have been turned upside down in new forms of oppression and enslavement.

The Enlightenment considered this new freedom, equality, and brotherhood to be possible on the basis of a new knowledge starting from reason and general human experience alone. Yet this promise of knowledge was never fulfilled. It instead deteriorated into an overkill of information unable to direct our lives, into a profound relativism and into new ways of manipulation through the knowledge elite in the sectors of media and marketing.

All this is not to deny the value of the new freedoms, the new science and technology, and the new opportunities that modernity brought. It shows, however, that modernity is not as strong as it used to be, even not as strong of a danger for the Church. The Enlightenment project seems to carry in itself the seeds of its own destruction. It is this crisis of modernity, which brings more and more thinkers from different origins to critical reflection on the philosophical and ideological foundations of modern culture as formed by the Enlightenment. It is this questioning and crisis, which gave rise to a whole conglomeration of ideas and thinkers that can be labelled "postmodern".

The description of the changes distinguishing one cultural era from another is always a very complex task and more so when we are still in the midst of the development. It is too early yet to say with an author like T.C. Oden that the modern era has passed away (1995: 21; cf. Mohler 1995: 83). It is equally too early to say what the distinguishing characteristics of the new era will be, particularly because we are witnessing a number of contradictory developments. Outside Western Europe and North America, the resurgence and force of traditional religious perspectives on life show the vitality of these alternatives to modernity. Yet, in the same regions, we see a seemingly irrepressible progress of modern economics, technology, and media and the changes in life perspectives that accompany them. In the West, the ideology of the Enlightenment is waning, particularly among intellectuals and the ideals of the Enlightenment are crumbling on a much wider scale. Yet in social and economic perspective modernity as the fruit of capitalism and industrialized technology is stronger than ever (Guinness 1994: 330).

So far, the postmodern itself does not present a clear alternative to modernity. It can not, in the first place because postmodern*ity* as a cultural phenomenon and many strands postmodern*ism* as a conglomerate of intellectual ideas are negative to any worldview or system of thought that could present itself as a comprehensive alternative for modernity. As a cultural phenomenon, it is characterized by the fragmentation of the worldview of the postmodern citizen who is no longer able and maybe even no longer wishes to harmonize and integrate his experience of different fragments of life (Finkielkraut 1987: 107ff; trans. 1988: 111ff). A person may, all at the same time, think as a materialist in relation to science, as a romanticist in relation to art, as an idealist in relation to politics, and as a Christian or Hindu in relation to death.

A second reason why postmodernism, at this moment, cannot yet provide a clear alternative to modernism is the vagueness of the concept itself. "*Post*modernism" itself is a negative term indicating a departure from the modern ideals, worldview and culture, but without any positive content. Therefore, the concept itself is more apt to indicate a transition than a goal. As Mark C. Taylor states: "Postmodernism, which is not simply an additional epoch or era following modernism, is inseparably bound to the modern" (1992: 12). No postmodernist can completely break with this culture. A good case can be made for the analysis that the modern ideals and modern institutions themselves itself generated postmodernism (Lyotard 1979: 63ff; trans. 1984: 37ff; cf. Allen 1989: 6; Edgar 1995: 363f), which is in some of its forms rightly labelled as ultra-modernism (Oden 1995: 26). Each expression of postmodernism retains some aspect of modernity, and it is exactly this that makes a debate between different conceptions of postmodernism possible. What needs to be preserved and what should definitely be renounced?[5]

Why not then abandon completely the concepts of postmodernity and postmodernism for being equally broad as vague? The reason is that we simply need the word to indicate the departure from the ways of thinking developed in the modern period (Murphy 1996: 105). The scope of the change implies the possibility to give many interpretations concerning the origin and essence of the changes and even more concerning the solutions to be proposed. The profoundness of the change serves to underline the urgency that the apologist addresses this new situation. The vagueness of the concept, however, necessitates a further clarification of the problems that are actually involved when asking what situation the Christian apologist should address.

The ethos of postmodernity and apologetics

The profoundness and the comprehensiveness of the changes related to postmodernism are such that the challenges it addresses to the Church and to its traditional apologetic endeavour are possibly greater than any cultural change since the dawning of the modern era itself. It brings a host of new opportunities as well as new obstacles to the apologetic witness of Christ, both in terms of the content and in terms of the method of Christian witness. Like modernity, postmodernity itself needs to be evaluated: is it first and foremost an enemy, maybe even worse than the modernity it criticizes? Or is it basically an ally to be welcomed? Or are modernism and postmodernism equally foreign to the Christian faith and worldview, each with their particular obstacles and opportunities?[6] One of the goals of this study will be to give such an evaluation and analysis of where to welcome and where to resist postmodernity.

This type of critical evaluation of postmodernity is as difficult as it is relevant, because Christians, be they liberal or more conservative, never exist in a bomb shelter far from their culture. Culture is like the air they breathe; it can either

5 The many-sidedness of the concept is further related to the fact that modern culture itself can be equally described according to its different aspects and from different perspectives: from the perspective of architecture, literary theory, the history of art, of the media, of politics, sociology, philosophy, epistemology, anthropology, science, theology, etc.. From each of these different angles the relationship between the modern and the postmodern will be determined differently. See for an overview (which does not include postmodern theology, though), Bertens 1995.

6 These different approaches are all present in the fine collection of texts presented at the 1994 Wheaton Theology Conference (Phillips & Okholm (eds) 1995); and in the collection edited in the same year by David S. Dockery (1995). In the first collection William Lane Craig represents the position which sees postmodernity first and foremost as a danger (1995: 75–97, cf. Richardson 1995: 53–66); in contrast, Phillip Kenneson is an example of those who have a much more welcoming attitude (1995: 155–170). Many others evaluate postmodernity basically as a mixture of blessing and curse.

strengthen or slowly poison them while they are hardly aware. Evangelicalism was critical, but at the same time a child of early modern culture (Grenz 1995: 96) and contemporary evangelicalism seems particularly prone to succumb to many of the postmodern trends.[7] A proper apologetic response will never be possible without an answer to the question of where our participation in this culture is a strength and where it becomes a disguised trap. Evaluation is desperately needed, otherwise our involvement with postmodernity will just be the involvement of a younger generation taking leave of the modernity of their old-fashioned parents and mentors. What we need is a theological and a thoroughly Christian engagement, equally critical of the modern and the postmodern.

In terms of the content of Christian apologetics, postmodernity offers a whole series of new opportunities. In the West, for centuries modernism in its atheistic and in its religious forms has been the most vital alternative to the Christian faith. The Enlightenment project has been so enchanting and promising, that many theologians and apologists saw a thorough adaptation to modernity as the adequate response. This adaptation they considered not only to be the way to make Christianity survive, but even as the natural thing to do in the face of the ring of truth and morality of the modern ideals of knowledge and freedom. Now this once most vital alternative is close to bankruptcy and the Church seems most robust where it managed to resist its enchantment.[8] Christian apologists encounter a new openness and undreamed of opportunities as they try to explain the faith and at the same time respond to their culture's search for new orientations.[9] This crumbling of modernity, which has taken several centuries before showing itself fully, should at the same time alert the contemporary apologist not to cede too easily to the enchantment and the seemingly obvious truths of postmodernism. As they say, "He who marries the spirit of this age will find himself a widower in the next" (cf. Veith 1994: 218).

Postmodern challenges to the method of modern apologetics

Postmodernity's greatest challenges to apologetics, however, do not seem to be in terms of the *content* of what is to be defended and justified, but more in terms of the *method* of apologetic justification. At the same time as discovering new

---

7 The profound influence of modernity on contemporary evangelical thinking and practice has been analysed for example by Oswald Guinness (1983), David Wells (1993), Douglas Webster (1995), and Gene Edward Veith Jr. (1994: 210–216).

8 As Carl F.H. Henry notes perceptively: "In any event, modernity's heady dismissal of the Christian heritage as sealed firmly in the past, through its identification in terms of the 'middle ages,' has now positioned modernity in the same unenviable role, and with more propriety" (1995: 51).

9 As is also observed by Allen (1989: 6) and Oden (1995: 30).

openings for the Gospel, the traditional methods of Christian apologetics, or more precisely of the type of apologetics that grew out of the Enlightenment, seem to be out of place. In this section we will give a more general overview of the wider *ethos of postmodernity*, which is present even where the idea of postmodernity might not be known.[10] The wider postmodern ethos is of interest to the Christian apologist because it takes the world to be its audience, not just some academic subculture. Yet *postmodernism* – as referring to postmodern reflection and philosophy – will interest us in the next chapter, for postmodernism helps us to understand the deeper challenges involved in the cultural change to the postmodern ethos.

The traditional apologetic method is out of place in the postmodern world, first of all, as it relates to *truth*. The apologetics of the pre-modern and the modern period were predominantly concerned with the question of truth. Nowadays people such as Sharon are not so concerned with the truth of what they believe; they are more concerned about its relevance, its pragmatic value.

Related to the question of truth is, second, a devaluation of *reason*. Contrary to modernity, postmodernity does not value reason as a means of knowing the truth. Reason is particularly valued for its pragmatic value and the managerial capacities of reason are most valued, particularly in managing economy and society and in managing the human psyche. However, reason is not valued much and is even mistrusted in regard to its capacity to know the ultimate truth, to discover absolute values and to choose a goal for life.

The negligence of the question of truth is also related to a whole new way postmodernity uses and understands *language*, which forms the third challenge to traditional apologetics. In the Western cultural tradition language has, for a long time, been understood as serving in the first place to reflect an objective reality that exists independently from our language. Using anthropological and linguistic research, postmodernism has brought a revolution in the understanding of language. Language is rather understood as a series of acts in which the human subject expresses himself and orders his world.[11] These philosophical ideas reflect a feeling pervading the whole of Western society: modern television and the Internet create the illusion that we can invent a reality according to our own wishes. In the Churches we observe a similar explosion of expressions like "the narrative of Scripture" and "our dreams of the new world to come".[12] Traditional

10 I borrowed this distinction between *ethos* and *ideas* from Grenz (1996: 11).

11 On the importance for the understanding of language for the postmodern ethos, see Lyotard (1979: 20–24; trans. 1984: 9–11). A crucial development towards the creative understanding of language has been the act-oriented concept of language developed by J.L. Austin (f. ex. 1962).

12 As three popular theologians in three different traditions with this stress on the creative character of Christian theological language may be noted the German theologian Gerd Thiessen, who is well-known fro his analysis of the New Testament community with sociological instruments (1999); the retelling of the Scriptures by the Dutch Reformed pastor Nico ter Linde (f. ex. 1996; trans. 1999); and the Anglican Priest Don Cupitt, the main force behind the "Sea of Faith movement" (1984).

apologetics were very much concerned with the "evidence" to show that Christian beliefs correspond to an objective reality independent of our beliefs. In a postmodern context no longer concerned with objectivity, these traditional apologetics, even more than being considered false, seem to be out of place, redundant and no longer able to provoke any serious interest.[13]

Closely related to the linguistic revolution is a fourth change diminishing the adequacy and aptness of classical modern apologetics. Postmodernity has brought and provoked a renewed attention to the concept of *tradition*. Against the individualism of the Enlightenment, there is a new realization that human beings never consider questions of truth on their own, but always as a part of a community, a culture and a tradition. This tradition provides a certain perspective on reality and the plausibility structures with which reality and other people are approached and understood.[14] The fact that human reasoning, argumentation and justification always takes place within the bounds of a tradition – or there where two traditions meet – provides another challenge to classical apologetics. Since classical Christian apologetics tried to answer the Enlightenment's objections and search for universally valuable arguments, it most often tried to develop an argument from universally recognized or recognizable truths (McGrath 1992: 10). The postmodern stress on the dependency of human rationality on tradition and culture challenges Christian apologists to develop forms of apologetic reasoning that take differences between audiences, with different forms of thought seriously. At the same time, it opens up new possibilities to liberate apologetic reflection from the hegemony of Western forms of thought to answer equally the questions and preoccupations of Christians and non-Christians alike on other continents and in other traditions.

A fifth major challenge to Christian apologetics resides in the fact that this revaluation of tradition by many postmodern thinkers and in our culture at large is predominantly interpreted in a thoroughly relativist and pluralist fashion. This paralysing *relativism*, particularly in regard to religion and morality, but often much wider in relation to all of human knowledge, is a pervading feature of postmodern

13 The traditional science-like approach to apologetics is made explicit in the classical study of Alan Richardson: "Since we live in an age which has been taught to submit every claim to knowledge to the test of scientific method, no approach on the part of Christian apologists to the modern mind is likely to be effective which does not demonstrate the ability of our theological knowledge successfully to undergo that test and so to justify itself at the bar of rational scientific inquiry" (1947: 7). A well-known and widespread example is the "evidence that demands a verdict" approach of the 1970s and 1980s of Josh McDowell (1979; 1981). A recent example is the more informal description by R.C. Sproul, John Gerstner & Arthur Lindsley (1984: 16): "As a science, it [Apologetics] it is the putting together of the data common to all Christians in a scientific whole."

14 This stress on the indispensability of tradition for human knowledge is all the more remarkable, considering the variety of perspectives from which it has been argued for. From a history and philosophy of science perspective, we can f. ex. mention Michael Polanyi (1962) and Thomas Kuhn (1996), from a sociology of knowledge perspective f. ex. Peter L. Berger & Thomas Luckmann (1967: 3–30).

society. In contrast to modern scepticism this postmodern relativism takes the form of *pluralism* in regard to religion, worldview and morality. As many other crucial terms in the debate, we will need to define both scepticism and pluralism carefully. It is, after all, exactly because the different camps coin the crucial terms differently, that they can easily misunderstand and misrepresent the language of the opposite party (Stout 1987: 18–22). Here, pluralism is used to indicate the position, which says that many religions and worldviews can have their own equally valuable perspectives on reality, even if they are mutually exclusive. This pluralism should be distinguished from scepticism, which is a modern phenomenon. The typical sceptic will want to refrain from any particular conviction or commitment where universally valid knowledge cannot be secured either through rational reflection, empirical observation or moral and religious experience.[15] Postmoderns, however, are most often pluralists and do not abandon what they cannot prove. They accept that even contradictory ideas can be equally valuable.[16]

A last and sixth major change towards postmodernity that makes traditional apologetics out of place is the *fragmentation* of culture, human thinking and human identity. The French philosopher Lyotard could describe postmodernism as the end of the "great stories" or "metanarratives", the end of the all-comprehensive views of history and reality to explain and give direction to the whole of human life (Lyotard 1986: 41–60; trans. 1992: 23–27; cf. Lyotard 1979: xxiii; trans. 1984: 7; Grenz 1996: 44). Most people we meet – particularly the young and urbanized – are no longer experiencing the world in one coherent and integrated manner. They combine a number of different and even incoherent perspectives, as is illustrated with the example of Sharon in the beginning of this chapter. Sharon's inconsistencies do not by themselves make her postmodern. As we shall see, the whole Enlightenment project already suffered from basic inner contradictions (§3.5). What makes her postmodern is that she does not seem to be bothered at all by these inconsistencies and the accompanying fragmentation of her worldview, but accepts them as a fact of life.[17]

15 Modernism, starting with René Descartes, was characterized by its search for absolute indubitable truth and every thing, which could not be clearly known, was not worth believing. So religion should be either firmly grounded in a universally acceptable apologetic or be abandoned. We should remain sceptic or agnostic about those areas of life, for which such a universal starting point cannot be found (1637). *Scepticism* therefore, though much older, squares well with a modern epistemology. See for an analysis of this characteristic of modernity: Newbigin 1995: 20ff; Murphy & McClendon 1989: 192f; see further §2.1.

16 This *pluralism* in the ideological sense should be distinguished from the descriptive use of the word simply to indicate the fact that nowadays we live in a pluralist society with a number of different competing religions and worldviews. Pluralism in the ideological sense is characteristic of postmodernism and maintains that within this pluralistic society one can never defend one religion or worldview as true in distinction from the others. See for this distinction: Newbigin 1989: 14; Carson 1996: 13–22.

17 This fragmentation and the corresponding search for identity or "home" is very perceptively analysed by Pico Iyer (2000).

The observation that all human thinking is influenced by particular cultural traditions of thought, is not new for all apologists. An important stream of apologetics, notably from reformed roots and as exemplified by Edward John Carnell, has, for a long time, seen the worldview-based presupposition in human thinking, and conceived apologetics primarily as a comparison and confrontation of worldviews (1959; cf. Lewis 1976: 176–284).[18] Yet this approach becomes difficult if a coherent worldview is no longer valued. To my remark that the extinction of the Aboriginals, which Sharon deplored, was a natural consequence of the theory of evolution as she shared it, she responded by referring to some element of Hindu anthropology. The incoherence did not seem to bother her in the least. The fragmented identity produced by a fragmented society reflects itself in people who behave like chameleons who put up different appearances not because they are dishonest, but because all of this is a part of themselves (§2.3).

The need for an apology of apologetics in our contemporary culture in transition

In a modern context, the Christian faith was deeply in need of an apologetic defence, but the criticism did not extend to apologetics itself. Apologetics itself did actually go very well together with the modern plausibility structure, for if Christianity wants to gain a hearing, the acceptable way is through apologetics. And this apologetics should of course be in accordance with Enlightenment rationality.

In a postmodern context the cards are shuffled in a completely different way. Contrary to modernity, postmodernity leaves room for an extreme variety of religious and other convictions. Yet, within a postmodern context the attitude towards apologetics is the opposite of what it used to be. The six changes listed from a modern to a postmodern culture show that in this changing world traditional apologetics is in many ways out of place: it simply does not relate to the predispositions encountered and the questions asked. The challenge goes even deeper, because it is not only traditional apologetics that seems redundant, apologetics itself is under fire and in need of an apology. In this context, apologetics seems no longer *needed* to defend ones own position, because you chose your religious tradition for other reasons than its rationality or objective truth. Apologetics seems to be no longer *possible*, because all human reasoning and arguing is considered culturally dependent. Apologetics is equally no longer morally *acceptable*, because pluralism has become the politically correct attitude. One characteristic of many forms of postmodernism is the consideration of any

18 For a critical evaluation of other types of "worldview-apologetics", see §7.6.

claim of absolute truth as a tool of oppression against those who do not agree with you.[19]

This criticism of apologetics could, of course, put the whole apologetic effort in disarray and not only in its traditional forms. It might be that apologetics itself is a phenomenon of the foregone modern area and that the Church would better refrain from it than cling to what is dying and revive what is obsolete. The question whether there is a need for Christian apologetics will be answered in the next section and the question whether Christian apologetics is at all possible will retain our attention for most of this study. At the end of this whole study, we will return to the question of the moral (un)acceptability of apologetics (§8.2).

The change from modernity to postmodernity being thus mapped out, it becomes clear that the Christian apologist should reckon with a double challenge, as both streams are present in our culture. We live in a transition era and we do not even know where this transition will bring us. It seems that in the areas of science and technology, the modern worldview is still dominant, expressed in a naturalist worldview, while in the area of the humanities and the arts conceptual relativism is the dominant force.[20] In fact, most people we meet are not just typically modern or typically postmodern, but they themselves mix aspects of both approaches of reality in different areas of their lives. They can be realist and naturalist in regard to science and conceptual relativist as they think about their marriage, friendships or political stance. The fact that they can live fragmented lives is in itself more postmodern, but in specific areas they continue to live according to modern ideals. What is more, many people can easily change from one stance to another, because they breathe the air of both scepticism and pluralism, without taking any personal position. In practice, postmodernism, though permitting commitments to one particular worldview, easily ends in a paralysing inability to personal commitment or investment in any set position, for it equally respects all positions at once (Middleton & Walsh 1995b: 55ff). This is the situation to which Christian apologists need to witness in order to share their message – and not only they, but also all those who recognize that this society is in profound crisis.

---

19 The French philosopher Michel Foucault made a project exposing the oppression in the Western ideas of sexuality, of insanity and of criminality. In this way he has made some of the most thorough analyses of the exercise of power through ideas; f. ex. Foucault (1975; trans. 1977; cf. Grenz 1996: 124–138). The African philosopher V.Y. Mudimbe has used the same type of analysis to show how the Western discourse about Africa was an expression and tool of Western power over Africa (1988). It is not necessary to agree with all Foucault's conclusions, to learn from his detection of the oppressive character of certain ideas we consider "true". Middleton and Walsh argue that the message of the cross of Jesus is actually subversive to all human power structures and thereby open up a profound line of apologetic response, which we will explore later (1995a, see further §8.2).

20 See concerning the sciences: Plantinga 1992: 297–300.

1.3 The urgency of Christian apologetics

In this section I aim to give a preliminary defence of the need of Christian apologetics as an essential component to all Christian witness and as particularly urgent in a postmodern and multicultural world. This defence is at the same time a preliminary exploration in order to arrive at a definition of Christian apologetics in the next section (§1.4). In order to arrive at a properly Christian understanding and definition two opposite pitfalls need to be avoided. In the first place we need to avoid working with too *broad* a definition so that we would continue talking about apologetics in a postmodern context while emptying the idea of apologetics from its essential content. The opposite pitfall of apologetics would be to choose too *narrow* a definition with again two possible consequences. On the one hand, we could throw away the baby of apologetics while emptying the bathtub of ill-conceived conceptions of apologetics. On the other hand, we could feel obliged to defend too narrow a conception of apologetics, because we feel we cannot do away with apologetics. Anxious not to lose the baby of apologetics, we refrain from changing the dirty bath water of ill-conceived conceptions. One of the reasons traditional apologetics continues to be defended is that many see relativism and irrationality as the only alternatives and shrink from these consequences, and rightly so.[21]

To avoid both pitfalls, I will develop a theological argument for the need and legitimacy of apologetic witness. To be true to the Gospel, its proclamation would in the first place need to claim an objective referent for the truth of its message, it would, second, need to hold on to the universal validity of its message and, third, appeal to human beings as reasonable. The objective reference does not necessarily imply a direct correspondence between our words and the reality they refer to. The appeal to human beings as rational should also not be taken as narrowly rationalistic, for human beings are so much more than reasonable. Yet, these three elements – (1) a claim to an objective referent for the truth of the Gospel; (2) the universal claim it addresses to all people; and (3) its appeal to the human intellect – are both necessary and sufficient to speak in a valid way of Christian apologetics.

---

21 An example of the first mistake is Karl Barth's general criticism of apologetics in general, when in fact his critical arguments count only against the specific form of apologetics developed in the Enlightenment (see §3.2). An example of the second mistake can be found in the defence of classical apologetics by Sproul, Gerstner & Lindsley (1984). The authors rightly defend the biblical basis for the practice of apologetics, but identify apologetics automatically as a certain form of classical apologetics, without asking if *this* type of apologetics is necessary according to Scripture. For other examples, see §2.1.

The objective reference of the affirmations of faith and theology

Let us first consider the claim that expressions of faith and theological statements refer to an objective "extra-linguistic" truth: a truth beyond the reality of the language of our statements and beliefs. In relation to postmodern analysis of language in general and also of religious language, it is important to note that it rightly has pointed to the variety of functions human expressions can perform. Religious affirmations equally perform different functions. The central Christian affirmation "Jesus Christ is Lord", for example, performs first of all a doxological function because it glorifies Jesus (cf. Van den Brink 1993: 31). The same affirmation performs an expressive function because it expresses certain feelings towards Jesus. It has a prescriptive function because it calls us to certain acts and attitudes – namely those showing obedience to his Lordship. It functions as an obligation, because the speaker obliges himself through this statement to certain attitudes and acts. Finally, religious affirmations have also a descriptive, ontological or a "constative" function, because they make truth-claims concerning a certain state of affairs that exists in a reality, which supersedes the language of theology and religious belief.[22]

The fact that religious affirmations describe or imply a certain state of affairs is not, therefore, their only function. At the same time, the plurality of functions of religious language does not imply that the descriptive or constative function does not matter very much. Keeping an eye on the different functions religious language performs, actually helps us to keep the right balance. It helps on the one hand not to limit the function of religious affirmations to describing what is true or what is not, and on the other not devalue the importance of religious affirmations as truth-claims (Van den Brink 1993: 31f).

In relation to the Christian faith it is actually very difficult, if not impossible, to value the non-descriptive functions of religious language, if it is not first of all a valuable description. When I confess as a believer and a theologian "Jesus Christ is Lord", the expression of praise, reverence, prescription and obligation would not make much sense if it is not first of all a description of a state of affairs that is real, independent of my recognition. It is not necessary that we know this reality unclouded or uninfluenced by any cultural or other human factors, nor that we should grasp it in an unhistorical way, nor that we could never be mistaken. Yet it supposes that our religious language refers to an "extralinguistic" reality that exists primary to and independent of our linguistic affirmations. As Newbigin

22 The four last functions of language (also labelled: constative, expressive, prescriptive and commissive) are taken from Vincent Brümmer (1981: 17–25), who adapted a former classification by Austin. The aim here is not so much to provide an exhaustive analysis of the functions of theological language, but just to point to the variety of functions and the indispensability of the descriptive function.

underlines rightly (Newbigin 1994: 75; cf. Newbigin 1996; Achtemeier 1994: 355):

> we are not speaking of a mere cognitive exercise. We are speaking of that act of atonement wrought in Jesus through which we are brought into a loving obedience to the will of God as is exercised through all human and cosmic history. [...] It is of the essence of the Christian faith that this story is the true story.

Postmodern theologians tend to stress the performative character of religious utterances (f. ex. Lindbeck 1984: 65; see further §2.2). Some central religious utterances indeed create new situations. When I confess Christ as Lord, this creates a correspondence between Christ and me, which would not be the same without my actual confession. Yet this performative function cannot stand on its own, but presupposes the reality of the Lordship of Christ, which I come to recognize. This Christian confession recognizes that Christ has been given all the power in heaven and on earth.

Christianity, along with many other religions, believes itself to be a response to a reality, which precedes and exists independently of the religious response. The question whether or not these beliefs are true, in relation to that reality, becomes inevitable (Griffiths 1991: 9–12). Perhaps we can imagine a religion that is consciously completely performative: it considers the whole religious reality as resulting from the dispositions of human beings, from the new community they themselves create, from the hope they themselves generate and that makes them change their circumstances. Some postmodern forms of Christianity tend to lean in this direction. However, even these believers should at least make some implicit truth-claims, for example about what human beings could possibly achieve. Yet, much more important, such a completely performative understanding of religion is incompatible with the central tenets of the Christian faith. The Christian faith affirms and supposes in all its convictions a God who was the Creator, before any human being could think of Him. The Christian faith affirms that human beings cannot save themselves, but that God stooped down to save them, before they asked.[23] The Christian faith hopes for a future, which completely transcends human possibilities. The Christian faith affirms that the goal of the human being is that he does not remain imprisoned in his own possibilities, but that he should love, enjoy and glorify God forever.[24]

The Christian faith thus presupposes a *realist* understanding of its central religious convictions. Yet it does not necessarily imply a direct correspondence

---

23 See for an analysis of why this implies theological realism: Thiemann 1985: 1ff; Wright 1990: 65–125.

24 For the contrast between the Christian faith and Buddhism in this respect, see: Williams 2002: 56–60, 69–71.

between our concepts and the reality they refer to; an understanding of religious language in terms of *critical realism* will be sufficient to guard this essential link with an objective reality beyond our linguistic expressions.[25]

The Gospel lays a claim to all human beings

Even when we believe that our religious convictions have an objective referent, it is still conceivable that they are only of interest to me or my community and that I lack positive reasons to share them with others. Or I might share my convictions, but without any claim that, as far as I am concerned, others ought to be interested. This becomes apparent when we consider the character of religious adherence in a polytheistic universe. In such a religious universe, I may relate to one or a number of gods and even pledge my allegiance to one god, yet in recognition that there are many other gods to whom others may adhere. I may address myself to a particular god, because he or she is specialized in the area in which I need special help, be it in commerce, love, war or health. I may pledge allegiance to the gods of my community, country, city or state because they are considered to have power in our region and over our community. I may pledge allegiance to it because as our civil religion, our loyalty to it is an essential part of the unity of our state or community. I may even pledge allegiance to a god to which I feel personally attracted, as in the mystery religions that were influential in the classical world at the beginning of the Christian era (Grant 1986: 54–61). In all these cases, my adherence and belief in no way exclude that I accept it is proper for others to adhere to their own gods, according to the community to which they belong, the special needs they have or the attraction they may feel to certain gods.

It is easy to see that the postmodern universe parallels in an important respect the polytheist's universe. Both agree that there is no one unifying principle to the world and that beyond the gods that each of us chooses, there is only chaos. Someone's choice of gods is a matter of social adherence, felt needs, and personal inclination, as is the question of the ideals for which one lives and the resources to which one turns for strength and help. In both universes, there is also no need to limit oneself to one god or religion. It would not be wise to limit ourselves from other resources we might need or to deny the worth of other values worth pursuing. In the final analysis, it is not the gods who choose us but the human individual or the community that chooses its gods, in accordance with its own

25 "Realism" will be used for the conception that in some ways our human language and ideas, if true, can correspond to some objective reality, which exists independent from our knowledge of this reality. "Critical realism" is the form of realism, which holds that there need not be an exact correspondence between our human concepts and some objective entities, but that our human words and sentences can still adequately approach and express the nature of an objective reality existing independent of our minds (Flew 1984: 81, 299f; McGrath 1998a: 154–164; Torrance 1982: 169–196).

interests and needs. In that sense a polytheistic religion is by nature anthropocentric, centred on the human community or individual.

This is radically different in the Christian universe. Christianity is, first of all, monotheistic, for we believe in one Creator of the universe. Because there is only one Creator, who created the universe out of nothing, the universe is unified in principle. This shows that the difference between monotheism and polytheism is not simply a quantitative one, differing on how many gods there are. It is a qualitative difference concerning the nature of the entire universe and the world of the divine (Manaranche 1985: 12).

In the Judeo-Christian tradition the Creator is both the origin and the goal of creation. Human beings are created to be His people and to live in communion with Him. If they do not live with Him, they miss the goal for which they are created and their existence thereby becomes inverted and a contradiction within itself. It is in a continuous risk to fall into non-existence. Their Creator is furthermore their Judge and at the end of time all human beings will need to give an account of their lives to their Creator (Ac 17:31). In Christ, He is also their Saviour and Lord. Jesus is the only name, by which they can be saved (Ac 4:12). He is the only way that leads to salvation from their inverted existence; in Him they find the fullness of life (Jn 14:6). He is the Lord, who reigns over the entire universe and there is no Lord besides him that can compete with Him (1Co 8:6) and if lesser powers claim to be lord next to Him, they need to be rejected as deceivers, which can only enslave humanity. All these basic Christian convictions join in stressing the "only one". There is only one Creator, Judge and Goal of life; there is only one Saviour and Lord; there is only one Giver of life. By its very nature, the Gospel therefore lays a claim on every human being.[26]

God addresses the human intellect

The Christian faith thus presupposes an "extra-linguistic" truth – a truth that refers to a reality beyond the world we ourselves create with our language. It is about the Lordship of Christ, who as Lord of heaven and earth is equally Lord of non-Christians. However, the truth of the Gospel is, in itself, not enough to show the urgency of Christian apologetics. This recognition could be combined with a pure fideism. Fideism distinguishes itself from relativism, scepticism and pluralism, in that it understands the Christian faith (or the truth of any other religious belief it is applied to) as objectively true in distinction from other religions. Yet it states that human beings accept the truth of the Christian faith in a manner that passes by the ordinary use of the intellect – for example, by a direct act of the Holy Spirit. Accepting Christ is called an act of faith, precisely because

26 Christians side in this respect with all those religions that believe their religious insights or message to be of salvific importance for all people (Griffiths 1988: 16).

human reason is not involved in any real way. In that case, proclamation of the Gospel would still be urgent, but without apologetics.

Fideism is thus incompatible with the dominant forms of both modernism and postmodernism. It is incompatible with modernism because of its retreat from rational justification. It is incompatible with the main streams of postmodernism, because it holds on to an objective reference for religious belief. Yet in answer to both modernism and postmodernism, it has been used as an apologetic strategy, sometimes on an academic level, but much more on a popular level. It can be a flight from the hard intellectual questions that intellectual criticisms of the faith raise. More positively, it can be understood as self-defence for Christians who simply cannot understand why their neighbours do not believe what they know to be true. Yet for a positive justification of the faith fideism is of little value. Moreover, this fideistic understanding of faith is contrary to the central tenets of the Christian and biblical understanding of the human being. The explanation of this thesis forms the third step of this defence of the legitimacy and importance of apologetics for all Christian proclamation.

For a first defence of the need to address the human intellect, we can refer to the biblical commandment to answer those who ask for a reason for the hope we have (1Pe 3:15). It is important to note here that this is not an isolated exhortation in one of the lesser-known New Testament epistles, but that it expresses a central biblical concern. The centrality of this concern is clear both from the example of the writers of Scripture themselves and on a more basic level because it follows directly from the biblical understanding of the human being.

The wide presence of apologetic argumentation in Scripture often goes unrecognized when too narrow a definition of apologetics is used. When, for example, in the line of an Enlightenment epistemology apologetics is considered as the search to defend the Christian faith on the basis of universally recognized premises or universally accessible evidence (see §2.1), apologetics is easily identified with a certain brand of natural theology. In that case the biblical evidence for apologetics is limited to Romans 1 and 2, Acts 17 and some other classical references (f. ex. Sproul, Gerstner & Lindsley 1984: 39–63). When apologetics is conceived in the much wider sense as the intellectual justification of the truth and the relevance of the Christian faith, as developed in this study (§1.4), Scripture is packed with apologetics.

Consider for example the Gospels, which are often considered "proclamation" and therefore non-apologetic. Why should they be non-apologetic "because" of being proclamation? In a larger perspective on apologetics, each of the Gospels has its proper apologetic agenda directed to its proper audience, even when mainly written for an audience of those who were already Christians. Matthew is trying to show his Jewish audience that Jesus is the one accomplishing Old Testament expectations. Luke makes clear that he has done thorough research and that his recollection of events is thus highly reliable. Mark has recently been read as an "apology for the cross", to deal with "the shameful way in which the object of Christian faith and subject of Christian proclamation died" (Gundry 1993: 1). In reading the Gospel of John, one is struck by the centrality of the concepts of witness and testimony and their reliability. The Gospel furthermore gives special attention to the signs Jesus performed, which were written down precisely so that the reader might be convinced "that Jesus is the Messiah, the Son of God" (Jn 20:31; cf. Vanhoozer 1999: 142). "Scripture on the whole is more inclined to persuade us of the truth of things than to expect us to 'believe seven impossible things before breakfast'" (Goldingay 1994: 121).[27]

To show that the Christian faith implies the need of an intellectual defence and justification as part of Christian proclamation, we cannot only point to biblical practice, but more fundamentally to the Christian understanding of the human being. Christian theologians debate among themselves whether human beings are most fundamentally characterized as *relational* beings or rather by their *rational* faculties, their will, or both (f. ex. J. O'Donovan 1986). However, when we consider the basic relations characterizing human beings, this opposition between the rational and the relational is not as radical as it appears. After all, the most fundamental relationship at the heart of the human constitution is a very specific one – namely, his covenant relationship with God and his fellow human beings. Stones and rabbits also exist in a relationship with God who is their Creator, with other stones and rabbits, and with the rest of creation, but as far as we know they are not created for a covenant relationship as a relationship in which free love can grow. A distinguishing feature of the biblical language concerning the human being is that he is a "respondable" being, invited to respond to God's gracious offer to be His covenant partner (Berkhof, 1985: 182; trans. 1990: 186f). As respondable or responsive, he is also considered respons*ible* and accountable for the way he handles this marvellous offer. This accountability is explicit in the creation story and developed in the whole history of the covenant, both of which are marked by commandments accompanied by blessings and promises (f. ex. Gn 2:15-17; Dt 30:15-20). The accountability is presupposed in the idea of a commandment itself and in the idea of God as Judge. Human beings relate to God in a way that they are considered accountable to Him for their acts and way of life.

This human accountability, so characteristic of the human being created for the covenant, presupposes with other things that humanity has some degree of free will and the ability to critical reflection. The free will is presupposed in the fact that it is human choices that are judged. Yet free will on its own isn't sufficient for responsible behaviour. If human beings were free but unable to have and to give reasons for their choices and actions, their choices would be arbitrary. Accountability supposes the possibility of accounting for and giving reasons to be evaluated as sound or unsound. That said, intelligence on its own

27 For the variation of apologetics in Scripture according to the envisaged audience, see further Bruce (1977) and Dulles (1971: 1–21).

would equally be insufficient to consider the human being responsible. It is conceivable that his ratiocination could not follow other than logically or physically necessary laws. In this case, like a computer, he could not be considered responsible for his "conclusions" and, like a robot, he could not be accountable for his "deeds". In those instances, we look to the programmer or the designer as the one responsible. It is thus precisely the combination of free will and ratiocination, which accounts for accountability. In the rest of this study the term "intellect" will normally be used to indicate these two elements at once, free will and intelligence or reason.[28]

Human beings are not just accountable for their actions and attitudes, but equally for their beliefs – particularly their beliefs concerning God and His actions towards men. It is these beliefs that are normally at the basis of human behaviour. As Bernard Adeney rightly notes: "Our lived morality is a result of the way we perceive reality. People usually act in relation to their interpretation of the way the world really is, far more than from a set of beliefs or principles" (1995: 86). This is why, according to the biblical creation narrative, God had to judge the first human beings for listening to the serpent more than to Him (Gn 3; cf. Mk 3:28-30; Mt 10:11-15; 11:20-24). God can hold human beings accountable in His judgement, because He does the same in the revelation of Himself. In all his revelation He speaks to us as beings that have the capacity and the responsibility to direct our will to the good and to distinguish in our thinking truth from untruth. These faculties are essential to being human and therefore unalienable and even present in human beings fallen in sin. As we will argue later in §4.5, the fact that sinners use these faculties against God, and that their will is bound and their intellect clouded by sin, does not mean that these faculties are no longer present. When God addresses Himself to sinners in his Word, He addresses human beings who are essentially responsible but whose responsibility cannot function appropriately because their will and intellect are bound by sin, ignorance, untruth and

28 This relationship between the creation of humanity with a view to his participation in God's covenant on the one hand and his rationality on the other hand was clearly perceived Karl Barth, notwithstanding his general criticism of apologetics, which we will consider later. Barth considers the human being essentially as "rational being" or "Vernunftwesen" and this is, for him, a theological statement (*KD* III/2: 502; trans. *CD* III/2: 419). It is directly related to the creation of humankind in the image of God, which Barth understands as a consequence of the creation of the human being to be God's and his neighbour's covenant-partner. The fact is that the human being finds himself in a very specific relationship with God, in a relationship established by the fact that God speaks to him with his Word. Therefore God created him with the possibility of being addressed by God and that capacity is the origin of his constitution as "rational being" (p. 507; trans. p. 422). Barth does not use the term "reason" or "Vernunft" as a human faculty in isolation to other aspects of human existence, but in a comprehensive sense as indication of the manner of human existence (p. 503; trans. p. 419). The human constitution as rational being includes not just his perceiving and thinking (pp. 478ff; trans. pp. 399ff), but equally his willing and desiring (pp. 487ff; trans. pp. 406ff). The fact that Barth did not conclude from this anthropology to the importance of apologetics is related to the actualist character of his anthropology, to which we will return in §3.4.

want of freedom. However, God does not address Himself to sinners to *violate* their freedom and responsibility again, as happens through sin, but instead to *restore* them in their freedom and responsibility (cf. Torrance 1992: xi–xiii). This is why the Gospel and grace are never forced on people, but offered and acclaimed to be accepted or rejected.

When the Christian community addresses the world with the proclamation of the Gospel, this proclamation of the Church is an expression of the Word of God, wherein God Himself addresses human beings (cf. Barth *KD* I/2: 831ff; trans. *CD* I/2: 743ff). In this proclamation, therefore, the Church should reflect the way in which God Himself addresses human beings. God does not address us in a way that violates our responsibility, but in a way that respects it and offers a possibility for human freedom to flourish again, within the only relationship that brings true freedom: obedience to God. This specific character of the relationship between God and men is the most profound reason why a fideistic understanding of the character of the Christian faith is unacceptable. This is the reason that all proclamation of the Gospel and all dialogue between the Church and those who don't count themselves among its members should be apologetic in character. It should address itself to the human intellect and thus address man as a responsible being, even if it does not *exclusively* address the intellect and is not exclusively apologetic, knowing that the human being is so much more than intelligence alone. Through the apologetic character of Christian proclamation, it addresses its audience as a responsible audience, and it opens up the possibility that the listeners are liberated to accept their responsibility anew and start exercising it. This way of giving an account of the faith presupposes the accountability of the listener.

In contrast, when we do not give an account of our faith, when we do not give appropriate reasons to accept the reliability of this message, we do not give non-Christians the possibility to react as responsible beings. Maybe we can draw them in through other ways, but the resulting convictions would be like those you develop in people through advertising, propaganda or manipulation. For the proper functioning of advertising and propaganda it is sufficient that people have a certain idea concerning a product or a political party; it does not really matter if they arrive at their conclusion in a responsible way, as long as they vote or buy according to the wish of the advertisers. That is why propaganda and advertising can be so manipulative and even consciously deceptive. If we use these methods in the proclamation of the Gospel, we do not treat our audience with the same respect as God does.

Objections and a clarifications

When stating that evangelism should always address the human intellect and thus should always be in part apologetic, an objection immediately comes to mind. This defence of apologetics might be well argued, but seems to be far removed from reality. Of course we know of exceptional conversions, like the one of C.S. Lewis or, more recently, the former British Buddhist Paul Williams, in which intellectual deliberation seems to be crucial (Lewis 1955b; Green & Hooper 1988; Williams 2002). Yet in most cases, it seems that many people simply follow in the faith of their parents or become Christians (or lose their faith!) without being able to account for the reasons guiding them in making this choice. They continue or start believing under the pressure of what is or becomes "plausible" in the social context to which they belong (cf. §7.1). They become or remain believers because of a psychological need for fellowship, for security, for identity or because of a religious need for meaning or for forgiveness of sin (Sire 1994: 27–90). Against those who denounce Christianity as "wishful" thinking, it should be clear that a belief is not automatically disqualified because it answers certain needs (Küng 1978: 343–346; trans. 1981: 299–302; cf. McGrath 1990: 102). Yet in this context it is important to clarify the relationship between, on the one hand, such desires and needs that push us towards or away from certain beliefs and from the faith, and, on the other, the reasons we have to accept certain beliefs.

It is indeed true that such desires and needs push us to change or keep us stable in our convictions. The problem with all these forces, though, is that they do not legitimize themselves. When a strong social structure of what is culturally plausible makes me say goodbye to the Christian faith, this step is not legitimized by these plausibility structures, which brought it about. When we look to our deepest religious drives, we find on the one hand a deep yearning for God, which is characteristic for each human being, and on the other hand a sinful desire to fill this yearning with what is not God (§4.4). A person finds herself as a responsible being in this field of force, which constitutes her existence. She acts responsibly if she chooses with good reason between the different forces and desires, when she yields to some which are noble and beneficial and when she struggles to master others because she is conscious that they do not lead her to what is true and good.

The strength of social, psychological and cultural factors in the formation of our identity and decisions has important consequences for Christian apologetics. An apologetic, which does not account for the compelling drives of human existence, social, sociological, cultural and religious, does not address real human beings, but abstract conceptions. Such an apologetic is therefore powerless. Christian apologetics should deal with these forces not in order to manipulate people, but to help them deal responsibly with all the inner drives and outer forces they encounter. In this field of force, Christian apologetics will help search for the true and the good and discern on valuable grounds between truth and falsehood, between drives that lead to freedom and fulfilment and those that lead to destruction. A good apologist, therefore, can never neglect the field of social, psychological, cultural and religious forces and pressures in which each individual finds himself in his proper way. Yet a good apology will try to surmount this field of different forces and help the human being to stop being controlled by his surroundings and his inner drives and become a responsible being that searches for the right direction he can give to all this.[29]

The need for an intellectual defence in a postmodern world

The psychological, social and cultural factors that make people accept a certain worldview and certain values have received much attention – particularly in our postmodern culture – and the role of rational reflection has diminished accordingly and seems even to have become negligible. Biblical anthropology shows that this attention for these psychological, social, and cultural factors is a

29 The defence for the need and urgency of Christian apologetics in this section is, of course, preliminary. First of all here it is only argued that the Christian faith and anthropology imply the *need* for intellectual justification. It is not yet clear if such an intellectual justification is actually *possible*. Maybe a Christian faith without a claim to objective truth and an appeal to the intellect is incoherent, but for a confirmed relativist this could only mean that Christianity itself is incoherent and should be given up in a postmodern context. In that respect this apology for apologetics needs include the defence, that even after considering postmodern insights in the cultural relativity of all human thinking, a claim to truth and intellectual justification of our truth-claims are still possible. This might also answer those who would feel that the new definition of apologetics to be developed later already "threw out the baby with the bath water" and that this amounts to what they might call "irrational apologetics" and therefore no apologetics at all (as would be implied in criticisms such as in Sproul, Gerstner & Lindsley 1984: 13–15) On the other hand there might be those who feel that the outmoded reference to truth and justification in the definition shows that the postmodern crisis has not really been fathomed. Only actual exchange with postmodern criticism and its evaluation can bring the clarity needed.

Second, this defence of the need and urgency of apologetics depends partly on the Christian anthropology developed later in this book as a further basis for Christian apologetics. Wouldn't this stress on the significance of intellectual justification imply the clearly unbiblical idea that the intelligent are closer to the kingdom than less educated people? In the rest of the study we will discover that trust, the moral posture of the knowing subject (§8.1), are as important as intelligence and that the importance of recognizing the trustworthiness of witnesses (§5.4) shows that recognizing the truth of the Gospel could more appropriately be said to demand "wisdom" than simply "intelligence". To other questions we will explicitly return: in what sense can we really speak about the responsibility of the human being, to whom we address the Gospel, when we know that he lost his freedom, when he chooses to live without God? (See §8.1.) What should we in this respect think of small children and the mentally handicapped? (See §4.5.) And doesn't this understanding of the basic relationship between God and humankind go contrary to the biblical idea of faith as an attitude of trust in the word of God? (See Chapter 5.) These questions should wait, for in many ways the different parts of the argument, which follows, impinge mutually on each other, and everything cannot be said at once.

wholesome correction, particularly when compared with the rationalistic stages of the early Enlightenment. The human being was then considered as an individual in isolation from his history and community and as a thinking substance isolated from his body and his emotions. Influenced by the early Enlightenment, Christian apologetics could easily get a rationalistic bend.

These days, though, the balance has tipped to the other extreme. In this context the Church and particularly the apologist have the responsibility to resist the pressure of our culture in the opposite direction. She has this responsibility because of the image of the human person the Scriptures show us. She also has this responsibility for the sake of the people she meets. If it would indeed be possible to give a watertight description of human thinking in terms of its causes, social, psychological, cultural, physical, or other,[30] this would have grave consequences. First, it becomes irrational to suppose that our human reflection is in any way concerned with truth because truth is not a decisive element in these psychological and social factors. Second, in such a situation it is indeed no longer possible to speak in a real sense of people being responsible for their ideas. Yet, when people are no longer responsible for their ideas, they become the victim of those ideas and the latter will imprison them. The feeling that people are the victims of their own ideas, not being able to have any real influence on them, is indeed widespread in our postmodern society, even where people aren't in any way philosophically educated. This is evident from both sides in the dialogue between Christians and non-Christians: "I believe, for that's the way I was raised"; "I would want to be a believer, but I cannot, for that's not how I was raised". It is only when a person starts accepting – even if it is only partially – her responsibility for her convictions, that she can distance herself from her inherited convictions and can start seeking other ways.

In an apologetic dialogue people are challenged to believe with reason. They are challenged to give reasons for their own convictions and they are challenged to ponder, as responsible people, the reasons for other beliefs. They are challenged to test critically what drives their lives. This is what makes it possible to reject the "victim" role. In this respect, giving an account of the faith is therefore not only a *condition* to helping people accept the liberating Gospel, but also giving a reasoned account is itself *part* of this liberation. It liberates human thinking from the imprisonment by settled convictions and from cultural, social or psychological compulsion.

30 This idea itself is fact very hard to prove and "dogmatic" in the pejorative sense. Cultural relativism is itself very much a product of the historical, social and cultural constellation in which we find ourselves (McGrath 1990: 85).

1.4 A DEFINITION OF CHRISTIAN APOLOGETICS IN RELATION TO REAL LIFE

The preliminary reflections on the truth-claims implied in the Christian faith and on the Christian understanding of the human being can serve as the basis to formulate a theologically informed definition of apologetics. As already pointed out, this definition should be narrow enough to conserve what seems is to apologetics (the reference to truth and to intellectual reflection) and wide enough not to preclude beforehand a thorough exchange with postmodern criticisms of classical apologetics. We therefore propose the following definition:

> Christian apologetics is the scholarly reflection on Christian apologetic witness and dialogue[31] as the intellectual justification of the truth and relevance of the Christian faith.

Some elements of the definition need further clarification. First of all, in talking about "apologetic witness and dialogue" this definition of apologetics aims to keep the whole endeavour close to *real life* (Clark 1993a: viiff). The apologist witnesses and dialogues with real human beings. Traditional apologetics often worked with the idea of a supposed universal rationality (see §2.1). This idea of a universal rationality, which the apologist should address, is actually an abstraction and tends to make apologetics an arid enterprise, which only appeals to a certain type of personality and in fact only to those in a Western context. Christian apologetics should address the human being as a whole, as a social, emotional, religious and cultural entity, with certain drives and living in a specific context.

Second, within this wider context of witness and dialogue apologetics does not become a concept that covers everything, but deals specifically with *intellectual justification*. The definition should not presuppose too narrow an understanding of how intellectual justification is possible. By concentrating on intellectual justification, apologetics views real life and the concrete witness of the Gospel under one specific angle, analysing one aspect if this relationship, which it abstracts, but without isolating it from real life. As in general science, *ab*straction should never be *ex*traction. Psychology abstracts the psychological processes from human

31 In this definition a distinction is made between "apologetics" as a theological discipline and "apologetic witness and dialogue" as the primary activity which this discipline studies. Both should be carefully distinguished. Like a book of homiletics or a study in the methods of evangelism, this study is not primarily written so that it might itself address non-Christians or Christians who are struggling with doubt. Though they might profit from it, this study is primarily conceived as a study in the academic discipline of apologetics. This discipline exists to undertake research into the possibility and character of Christian apologetics and on specific apologetic themes, to understand apologetics, and to help the Church to perform better in her apologetic witness and dialogue.

existence, from other aspects like his biological or social existence. Yet it can never extract the psyche from its biological or social context or it would be dead or at least no longer the human psyche.

Third, as intellectual justification, Christian apologetics should not only be concerned with the truth, but also with the *relevance* of the Christian faith. As we saw, postmodern people are no so much interested in truth as in relevance and pragmatic value. Showing the need people have for Christ and the Christian faith may be an important way in which to create new openings for the question of its truth (McGrath 1992: 226f).

The need for showing the relevance is even more important considering the overkill of information so characteristic of our media-driven society. We can only interest ourselves in a very limited number of ideas we meet through the media and the incredible variety of people we meet. I know that many people have been discussing the question of whether purported UFOs visiting earth from elsewhere are real or products of human imagination. Yet I do not see how the answer to this question would be of significance for my life and, therefore, I have never been interested enough to even read any of the vast literature relating to the subject. There are innumerable smaller and bigger sects proclaiming to know the final truth about life, yet in my experience they are so weird they are not worth considering.

As Christians we have to recognize that for many postmodern people Christian faith falls in exactly the same category. To reach them, we need to show that this faith is highly relevant to their lives, and in our own lives we need both to show its relevance and to give it at least some plausibility. The question of the relevance of the Christian faith has been neglected in modern apologetics, partly because of the misconception that the search for objective truth should be as disinterested as possible. Yet, when Jesus and the apostles proclaimed their message, they were not just delivering some "new teaching" that might be of interest to the professional Athenian philosophers (Ac 17:19); they were teaching the Gospel, "the Good News", which was good because it answered the deepest needs of those who were lost (Mt 4:23; Ac 17:18).[32] The greatest apologists in the history of the Church, like Augustine and Blaise Pascal, followed in their footsteps by commending the Gospel for its characteristic of answering the deepest human needs, where all alternatives have failed. According to Pascal, apologetics needs to make the Christian religion attractive.

> Make her [the Christian religion] attractive, making good people wish it would be true and subsequently show that it is true. (Pascal, *Pensées*: no. 12).

Finally, this definition of apologetics limits itself consciously to *Christian* apologetics and Christian witness and dialogue. Our most profound reasons for being

32 Cf. also 1Pe 3:15, the key-verse that commands Christians to engage in apologetic dialogue, which links the reasoned defence directly to its relevance: the Christian hope.

involved in apologetic dialogue are not based on some supposedly universal epistemology or some supposedly universal conception of religion, which, I believe, is impossible to obtain. It is based on our understanding of the God we meet in Christ. Not only the content, but also the character of this apologetic witness and dialogue should be profoundly Christian, for it should reflect its specific message and relates to human beings whose most inner beings we believe to be revealed in the Scriptures, even for those who do not yet recognize this.

1.5 An outline of the argument

If a theological argument were like a detective story, outlining the argument at the beginning would be like giving away the plot. However, outlining the argument is more like drawing a map inviting the reader to start the actual discovery of the area. Or it is like an overall construction sketch – knowing it will only hold together when the constituent parts are well designed in detail and are properly linked. As an outline, it will contain a certain number of abstractions and technical expressions which can only be explained in their due place.

An important limitation of the current apologetic engagement with postmodernism and cultural pluralism is that, in what has been done, the Christian theological appreciation of these phenomena only plays a minor role. However, such an analysis is most important, if we want to remain faithful to our proper subject, which is the knowledge of God in Christ and the understanding of the human person as thinking subject, as revealed in this mirror. This is part of our recognition of the lordship of Christ over all our life and of taking "every thought captive to obey Christ" (2Co 10:5). Such a specific theological approach is in fact encouraged by a major line of postmodern analysis, which stresses the proper integrity of particular approaches to reality and which encourages us also to respect the integrity of the particular Christian understanding of postmodernism, multiculturalism, and of the apologetic task itself (see Chapter 2). It is in fact from such a theological perspective that some major insights are gained towards the integration of the historical, anthropological and epistemological analyses of postmodernism and multiculturalism and towards their practical implications for a Christian apologetics that touches real life.

A theological understanding of the crisis

The first need is the integration of philosophical and theological analysis. Philosophical reflection in the area of linguistics, epistemology, culture and science has taken the lead in introducing new and postmodern perspectives to our understanding of human knowledge. When apologists interacted with these developments they did little theological analysis: what do all these changes actually look like when we view them from the perspective of God's relationship with us and with his world? In order to react to all those developments in a way that is truly Christian such theological analysis is most needed: should these changes be seen as deceiving and leading us away from the Gospel, or as liberating us from the shackles of the Enlightenment? Or is it a bit of both?

It is with these questions in mind that we will analyse – in Chapter 2 – the implications and impact of the change from modernity to postmodernity for Christian apologetics. These changes can be analysed along three main axes. In the first place, along the epistemological axis there is a departure from the universalist foundationalism of modernity, characterized by a search for a foundation of human knowledge, which is universally and directly accessible and thus indubitable. Second, along the linguistic axis, the idea is challenged that there is a basic universal language in which other languages can be translated and which reflects a universal human rationality. Third, along the anthropological axis, a departure can be noted from modern individualism in the idea that human beings and their thinking can only be understood against the background of the tradition and the community of which they are a part. For all these reasons we should depart from the apologetics of the modern era characterized by a universalist foundationalist epistemology, by the idea of a universal language and rationality, and by individualism. These ideas made the belief in a divine revelation at one specific moment in history and entrusted to the historically embodied community of the Church so difficult to defend in the modern context.

However, the more basic reasons for departing from the Enlightenment Christian apologetics are not these developments in linguistics, the philosophy of science or cultural anthropology. From a Christian perspective most weight should be given to a theological and properly Christian analysis of modernity and modern apologetics. In Chapter 3, we will argue that the decisive divide between the Gospel of the Enlightenment and the Gospel of Jesus is not epistemological, as often supposed, but anthropological. The idea of a universal rationality, which human beings posses by virtue of being human and which can be used as a foundation for our reception of any knowledge from God, is a direct corollary of the Enlightenment quest for autonomy. This most basic modern quest for autonomy is opposed to the Christian recognition of finitude and sin. It also opposes grace and the divine goal for human existence, and should therefore be rejected by Christians who know that true freedom can only be found in Christ. A Christian understanding of the change from modernity to postmodernity thus demands not only that the gap between philosophical reflection and theology be crossed, but also that epistemological and anthropological reflection be joined.

This theological evaluation of the Enlightenment shows, at the same time, that the most influential forms of postmodernism are not as radical a departure from the Enlightenment as they conceive themselves to be. Anthropologically, the human quest for autonomy is as strong as ever; indeed, now it does not just reject revelation and tradition as impinging upon it, but even the idea of a universal and objective truth is conceived as being oppressive. Because mainstream postmodernism rejects a return to divine revelation, tradition and grace out of hand as a solution for the bankruptcy of the modern autonomous quest for truth, it places itself in an equally self-destructive position as modernism. Postmodernism recognizes the impossibility of the Enlightenment quest and yet refuses the only valuable alternative for finding real meaning and truth.

Christian anthropology and epistemology

Because modernism and important expressions of postmodernism share a common quest for human autonomy, a thoroughly Christian alternative can never be developed without reference to the alternative Christian understanding of the human being, to which we will turn in Chapter 4. Here, the biblical understanding of the human being as the image of God proves particularly helpful. First of all, it places the human being squarely within creation and thereby overcomes the subject–object dichotomy at the basis of modern scepticism and still virulent in postmodern relativism. It is in indwelling creation that the truth of creation opens up to humanity. As the image of God, the individual is, second, inextricably linked to his or her community, and human knowledge therefore always has a communal and cultural coefficient. Yet because of the priority of the third relationship that is constitutive of humanness, the relationship with God, human beings are not defenceless victims of their community but can distance themselves critically from it.

Regarding this third relationship, we will analyse the implications of the biblical idea of the human beings as created not for autonomy but for a life in loving relationship with their Creator. As such, each human being has a fundamental orientation towards God, an inner yearning, which only God can fulfil. They can only flourish and find true freedom in a loving relationship with God. Yet having fallen into sin, the human being seeks fulfilment in an autonomous way in disobedience to God. Since this search contradicts his created constitution, his deepest yearning will necessarily remain unfulfilled and his will becomes enslaved. Since he rejects the only possible centre for his existence, his life becomes self-contradictory and fragmented. The fragmentation of the human identity and the resulting fragmentation of human cultures, on which postmodernism majors, therefore turns out to be congruent with a Christian understanding of humanity.

The ontological status of the human being as dependent on God's gracious self-giving is reflected in the Christian understanding of human knowledge. The Christian understanding of the place of human beings within creation implies they can only have viable knowledge of creation if they give up a desire for absolute mastery and control, and learn to entrust themselves to the creation of which they are a part and on which they depend. In order to obtain viable knowledge, they will equally need to depart from the individualist myth and accept their place within an epistemic community and tradition, yet without surrendering themselves to it. In order to obtain a viable knowledge of God they will need to accept their place before God and accept God's gracious revelation of His aim for them. As human beings in general can only fully flourish in opening themselves up to God and grace, the human intellect can only flourish when it starts with trusting the creation (of which they are a part), trusting God's self-revelation (to which they are directed) and trusting the community that is shaped by this revelation. Before reason can nourish faith, faith should nourish reason. If it is not biblical faith that nourishes reason, some other less rational perspective will automatically take its place. In that respect a Christian understanding of human knowledge agrees with the postmodern criticism of modern apologetics: we cannot begin our argumentation on the basis of a universally recognized or directly accessible foundation of human knowledge, nor on a given universal rationality or language.

Critical realism and tradition-dependent discovery

At this point, the apologist will wish to raise a legitimate concern, a concern that she actually shares with most modern thinkers. If there is no universal starting point for human reasoning, how can we actually know that our ideas about reality are not just subjective linguistic constructs without any objective basis? And how can we ever argue with those who start from basically different conceptions? Both questions were shown to be crucial to the Christian faith (§1.3).

In the fifth chapter we will concentrate on the first question. We will argue that the objective reference of the faith is not in any way conditional upon a universal human pre-understanding; it is dependent on the objectivity of God Himself and the objectivity of his self-revelation. This objectivity of God's self-revelation shows itself by breaking through our finite and sinful preconceptions about Him. Theology shows its objective orientation in so far as it seeks to scrutinize all preconceived and subjective ideas about God, and align them with the reality it encounters in Scripture and supremely in Jesus Christ. We will discover illuminative parallels with twentieth-century philosophy of science, which has shown that science proceeds in the same way. When some forms of modern idealism and postmodernism constructivism believe that the human mind can order the whole reality according to its own liking and preconceptions, they grossly overestimate the human powers. Science and the Christian faith show reality to be too hard for this inflated human ego.

The practice of contextual and dialogical apologetics

The role of culture in apologetic witness has, from the beginning, been a major train of thought underlying the explorations of postmodernism, anthropology and epistemology. In the sixth and seventh chapter the questions relating to the role of culture gain the centre stage. Because all our own thinking and attitudes and those of our audience are deeply embedded in particular traditions and cultures and reflect a particular worldview, all apologetic witness therefore needs to be culture-sensitive. We need to explore, in detail, in what way it is contextual and in what way it is determined by its own universal message and by our shared though fragmented human nature.

Before we can engage with the apologetic question of how persuasion across cultural barriers is possible, we will need to address the preliminary question of how understanding and communication across such barriers is possible. We will discover that we can be confronted with other ways of thinking which impinge on ours in ways similar to those that show us to be in touch with an objective "extra-linguistic" reality independent of our own minds: we encounter radically different structures of understanding and reflection that have integrity of their own. These realities impose themselves on us rather than us being able to impose our conceptual structures on others and their cultures. In the process of a search for mutual understanding, our language is shown to have the capacity to acquire and express new meanings previously undreamed of, thereby offering the possibility of cross-cultural communication.

Is it possible not only to communicate the Gospel to people with entirely different frameworks of reference, but also to persuade them of its truth and relevance? The notion of "persuasion" recognizes that across cultural boundaries no conclusive argumentation is possible, for such argumentation is only possible against the backdrop of a shared conceptual structure. It furthermore recognizes the many non-intellectual factors that come into play: allegiances, loyalty to a community, and deep desires and fears. Yet the idea of persuasion implies, at the same time, that valid indicators can be found that point to the truthfulness of one conceptual scheme in comparison to another and to the veracity of the understanding of reality that is opened up to us in Christ. In the seventh chapter we explore some principal aspects of such cross-cultural apologetic dialogue. We will argue that this is possible when we present the illuminating power of the Gospel as a whole. We will review the use of so-called points of contact in apologetics and show that it is possible to exploit these in a culturally sensitive way, thus avoiding the pitfalls of the use of such points of contact characteristic for classical modern apologetics. We will furthermore explore how anomalies and tensions in worldviews and cultures can be valid pointers to Christ. Finally, we will point to the Christian community as a hermeneutic of the Gospel and an alternative plausibility structure that can give initial plausibility to people for whom it represents, initially, an entirely alien world. All this opens up the possibility of a form of apologetic dialogue that recognizes the tradition- and culture-dependent nature of the mindset of both dialogue partners. At the same time, it challenges people to be self-critical and liberates them for a valuable encounter with an extra-linguistic reality and universal truth that engages everyone.

So, Christian apologetics should be holistic in the sense that it views human beings as part of traditions and communities. To be fully Christian, both in content and method, apologetics should equally address *the person as a whole*. Thus in Chapter 8 we explore what it means for Christian apologetics that it dialogues with concrete historical people with their social and historical bonds, with their reason and will, with their inner drives, and with all the personal or communal experiences that mark them. Knowing the force of inner drives, fears, bonds and past experiences, the apologist should be attentive and address them with the good news. Knowing the way the will of a human being often directs his mind, the apologist will also address the question of conversion and a change of the will. Yet, the apologist should not manipulate these drives, needs and fears, but help the other to sift through them in a responsible way in order to distinguish what leads to truth and life from what conceals and destroys. In this way the postmodern interest in relevance, rather than truth, is met and yet by showing at the same time that the only way to be relevant is not to avoid the question of truth. Neglecting the truth of our lives is self-destructive; neglecting the truth of Christ is missing the most relevant message ever proclaimed.

We conclude that the different characteristics of an apologetics that is fully Christian, and at the same time addresses the challenges posed by a postmodern and multicultural world, should reflect the manner in which God encounters us in Jesus Christ. In Christ we meet a God who defies our tendency to create our own gods and religious universes by entering our world in his incarnation. In Christ God makes us discover who we really are, including the aspects of our being that we would rather cover up. Christ's cross and resurrection are the crisis and continual interrogation of all human cultures, in religious, secular or Christian forms. Through the cross the sinful bias, both personal and incarnate in our religions, worldviews and cultures, are exposed, yet exactly thereby Christ will liberate all that is good in order that it finds fulfilment in Him.

Chapter 2

POSTMODERN CRITICISM OF MODERN WESTERN APOLOGETICS

Christians do not live in a culture-free shelter and the rise of postmodern culture has therefore greatly influenced both the way Christians perceive themselves and the way in which they are perceived by non-Christians who share the same habitat. Under the influence of the postmodern ethos the *particularity* of the Christian religion over other religions is considered much less of a problem than it used to be just a few decades ago. Under the conditions of modernity, Christians were under constant pressure to align their Christian faith to generally accepted religious ideas, psychological values or political programmes. Now there is a new appreciation of the particularity of Christian faith and spirituality (Phillips & Okholm (eds) 1996: 11f). Those considering themselves as non-Christians are less appalled by, and even positively attracted to, Christianity's particularity – by what distinguishes it from modernity, as the interest in Eastern Orthodox and ancient Celtic forms of Christianity show. At the same time many Christians are more reticent to express themselves concerning the *truth* of their convictions than they would have been before.[1] In this respect postmodern religion is coloured by the rise of virtual reality, created by the age of television and the Internet: people can create their personal virtual worlds, aided by what they find while surfing the net or zapping through 20 to 200 TV channels. The particularity of these individual worlds has become possible thanks to their being virtual.

Both the renewed attention for the particularity of the Christian faith and the diminishing attention for its truth are theologically reflected in theological currents, which label themselves as postmodern. As a consequence postmodern theologians criticize classical modern apologetics when the latter envisage defending the truth of Christianity according to general standards of rationality. In the first chapter, we saw how multiculturalism and the postmodern ethos have made classical modern apologetics unappealing, unconvincing and redundant. In

1 As noted by Phillips & Okholm (1996: 8). These observations concerning the mainline churches and evangelical groups in North America seem to me equally true for Western European churches. For an academically formulated example of a diminishing attention for the question of truth, see Kenneson (1995).

this chapter, we will see how classical modern apologetics are equally under fire from developments in theology that are inspired by the philosophical, anthropological and linguistic turn that mark the change towards postmodernism.

The wider aim of this second chapter will be to give a more detailed analysis of the challenge postmodernism poses to traditional methods of Christian apologetics that have developed since the Enlightenment. We need to listen carefully to avoid hasty answers. Sometimes, apologists suffer from a desire to give fast-food answers, which may seem reassuring to the Christian community. Yet, if unfair and inadequate, these answers are futile and even counterproductive for real apologetic interaction.

We will analyse the consequences of the postmodern criticism for apologetics along three main axes, which will concern us for the major part of this chapter: the understanding of knowledge (§2.1); of language (§2.2); and of the human being in relationship to society (§2.3).[2] In the final section, we will draw our main conclusions for the development of a Christian apologetics after modernity. In this evaluation, we will attend to the challenge that postmodern relativism poses for apologetic witness. We will also note the need for a specifically theological approach to the question of the character of Christian apologetics – an approach that digs deeper than the analysis that linguistics, epistemology and philosophical anthropology can provide (§2.4).

As the analysis unfolds, we will keep four questions in mind that are of central importance for contemporary apologetics. The first question is: how does the postmodern criticism of modernity help us in the formulation of a Christian apology against modernity? This question remains important, knowing that modernity is waning but far from dead, and the modern conception of science, for example, is still easily appealed to in the critical questioning of the Christian faith.[3]

The second question concerns the characteristics of the postmodern mind we want to touch in a contemporary apology for the Gospel: what are its strengths and weaknesses? (What are the points of contact for our witness and what are the main barriers to overcome?)

The third question relates to how the postmodern criticism of apologetics may help us to face the challenge of developing a model of cross-cultural apologetics that can dialogue with the many religious and ideological alternatives the Christian faith encounters in our global and multicultural world. We will see how the postmodern criticism of the idea of the need for a universal and neutral starting point for human reasoning opens up vistas of apologetics that are

2 In their seminal article "Distinguishing Modern and Postmodern Theologies" (1989), Murphy & McClendon point out how these three axes are crucial for analysing the dimensions of the change from modernism to postmodernism, particularly regarding theology (and thus apologetics).

3 As exemplified by Richard Dawkins (2006). Nickey Gumbel (1994) mentions science as one of the seven objections to the Christian Faith most frequently raised during Alpha-courses.

culturally sensitive and no longer presuppose that both dialogue partners submit to a modern rationality.

The fourth question is the most technical and yet the most far-reaching in its implications: if modern apologetics has been too much indebted to the presuppositions of modernity, in what way does the criticism of modernity help to develop a Christian apologetics that has an approach more faithful to itself? We should, of course, avoid as much as possible a new bondage to postmodern patterns of thought. Yet, the debate between modernism and postmodernism itself will help us to discover the mutual weaknesses of both positions. In this way, we may discover how Christian apologists can develop their own patterns of reasoning – neither modern, nor postmodern – true to their own subject matter, true to the reality revealed in Christ, and true to the people with whom they share the Gospel, whose condition is most profoundly revealed by their Creator.

2.1 Criticism of foundationalist apologetics

Modern foundationalist epistemology

One of the recurrent themes in the postmodern criticisms of modern thought and of modern theology and apologetics is the criticism of the foundationalism of modern theology.[4] Put crudely, foundationalism wants to justify human knowledge by giving it a solid foundation or basis. This idea has a ring of truth partly derived from day-to-day experience. When we doubt an idea, we may go back to a more basic idea we are sure about in order to reconstruct our ideas from there. When I am trying to solve a mathematical problem and I do not agree with a colleague or a fellow student, we can go backwards until we find more "basic" ideas on which we agree and check our derivations from there. When we do not agree on the nature of a car problem, we can go back to more "fundamental" observations about its constituent parts to review together what we can induce from there (Sosa 1980: 3–25).

Foundationalists consider these and other examples of how, in case of doubt, we look for more fundamental and surer ideas as paradigmatic for human knowledge in general. Alvin Plantinga explains the basic structure that defines an epistemology as foundationalist with the idea of a *noetic structure*. According to his definition, "A person's noetic structure is the set of propositions he believes, together with certain epistemic relations that hold among him and these propositions" (Plantinga 1983: 48). The epistemological foundationalist says that

4 See for the criticism of foundationalism by postmodern theologians for example the representatives of the so-called "postliberal theology" (Lindbeck 1984: 129; Thiemann 1985: 9–46; Placher 1989: 24–38), who can rightly be considered "postmodern" (Murphy & McClendon 1989: 205–208); cf. also the work of John Thiel (1994: 192f).

to be solid and sound, a person's noetic structure or the totality of his convictions should be constructed according to the analogy of a *building*. Within the noetic structure we should thus be able to make a distinction between basic and non-basic beliefs, the basic beliefs forming the foundation. To be sound, the basic beliefs should be properly basic – that is, be acceptable as part of the foundation of the edifice of our knowledge. Non-basic beliefs are only justified as far as their certainty or probability can be constructed upon or derived from the foundation. For example, when I want to be justified in my belief in a certain physical law, I need to be able to *found* or *ground* it on empirical evidence following proper rules of induction (cf. Plantinga 1983: 47–59; 1993a: 84–86; Clark 1990: 32–136).

Variations are possible within the general foundationalist structure of knowledge, depending on answers to these questions: Which beliefs are to be admitted as properly basic and thus as a part of the foundation? What rules of derivation or inference are acceptable to found the non-basic beliefs on this foundation? The philosophers of the Enlightenment, followed by a high number of theologians from the same period, form a major sub-group of foundationalist thinking when they state that only those beliefs that can be directly known by all sound rational beings can be properly basic. The idea that human perceptions and reasoning should follow universal laws is one of the persistent traits of modernity.[5] We will therefore qualify the foundationalism of the Enlightenment and modernity as *universalist foundationalism*. Within this Enlightenment group of foundationalists, the differences of opinion relate mainly to the question of what propositions are, in this way, universally acceptable or accessible and thus properly basic. Should we limit properly basic beliefs to self-evident rational truths, as the rationalists say? Or should it be the data of universally accessible empirical perception, as empiricists defend? Or should it be the Kantian perception of the phenomenological world cast in the mould of the universal structures of the human mind?

Modern foundationalist apologetics

The attraction of this universalist foundationalist model of knowledge for modern man and particularly for the apologist easily comes to mind. First of all, foundationalism itself aims to avoid all circularity in reasoning. As in a building, where the construction is supported in one direction – from the bottom to the top – justification can only occur in one direction. One should always move towards beliefs

5 As A.O. Lovejoy states: "[A]nything of which the intelligibility, verifiability, or actual affirmation is limited to men of a special age, race, temperament, tradition or condition is [in and of itself] without truth or value, or at all events without importance to a reasonable man" (*Essays in the History of Ideas*, New York, 1960, p. 173; cited in Geertz 1993: 34f). In the same way modernity wanted to base morality on some universal characteristics of human nature (MacIntyre 1985: 51f).

that are more foundational. This universalist foundationalist epistemology seems to open up the possibility – maybe the *only* possibility – to defend and acclaim the truth of the Gospel in a non-circular way and in a way accessible to everyone.[6]

The universalist criterion was, second, particularly attractive in seventeenth-century Europe which, since the Reformation, had gone through terrible religious wars. This universalist foundationalist epistemology seemed to promise the possibility of a universal knowledge, morality, religion and culture that people from different traditional backgrounds could share. This promise of a universal knowledge, culture and value-system continues to be attractive in our contemporary world divided by cultural abysses, and ethnic and religious hatred and wars.

Third, the attraction of this model is clear in relation to the Enlightenment preference for doubt over belief. Following Descartes, who choose to doubt methodologically every belief he could in order to arrive at certain knowledge, Enlightenment thinkers in general preferred to doubt everything that is not entirely certain.[7] This preference for doubt has become a presupposition so basic to our culture that it feels natural to most people. If everything that can be doubted should be doubted, the promise of knowledge founded on a universally indubitable basis is most welcome.

In the tradition of modern universalist foundationalism, modern theologians sought a universal foundation that could form the basis of a universally justifiable apologetic theology. Parallel to the rationalist epistemology there exists a rationalist apologetics – starting from rational principles evident to the human mind, as in Descartes' version of the ontological proof for the existence of

---

6 Mark Wallace has shown that the analysis of the foundationalism of modern liberal theology by Lindbeck and other postliberal theologians is seriously obscured by the fact that they talk about foundationalism in two different degrees, without clearly distinguishing them. "The Yale theologians seem to be saying two things here. When they speak of foundationalism in the strong sense, they criticise liberals for 'grounding' theological claims on general philosophical foundations that 'control' the Christian subject matter. Yet they also understand foundationalism in a weaker sense as the attempt to display 'common ground' or experiential 'structures' to which theological claims are correlated in order to be made intelligible to moderns. [...] What is even more problematic (and indeed ironic) about the Yale notion of foundationalism is that in its 'strong' version it does not apply to most of these theologians under question" (1987: 163). Yet, as Placher perceptively remarks: "Nevertheless, the revisionists' own polemics sometimes seem to justify – at least in part – the charges of their opponents. They deny that they are foundationalists, yet they often reject Barth – and Frei – as methodologically misguided from the start. They dismiss "fideism". Yet they do not make it clear to me what is wrong with Barth and Frei – not merely in detail, but in fundamental starting point – unless it is the lack of a philosophical 'foundation'" (1985: 411; cf. Tilley 1988: 87).

7 Cf. Descartes' own statement of this principle: "More especially did I reflect in each matter that came before me as to anything which could make it subject to suspicion or doubt, and gave occasion for mistake, and I rooted out of my mind all the errors which might have formerly crept in. [...] to provide myself with good grounds of assurance, and to reject the quicksand and mud in order to find the rock or clay" (1983: 125). For more on the historical influence of the idea of "doubt as the way to certainty", see Newbigin (1995: 16–28).

God (*Le Discours de la Méthode*: IV). In the tradition of empiricist epistemology, modern theologians sought empirical arguments for an Intelligent Designer, exemplified in a classical way by William Paley's defence of the existence of the watchmaker from creation, which resembles a super-watch (1802). After Kant attacked the traditional arguments for the existence of God together with the rationalist and empiricist epistemologies, he proposed his own universal "proof" stating that God is the necessary prerequisite for the universal reality of human morality (1788: II, IV, 254–264). Mainstream post-Kantian liberal theology followed Schleiermacher in his apologetic program to base Christian theology in universal religious experience, in Schleiermacher's case on the "consciousness of being absolutely dependent" (Schleiermacher 1989 [1830]: 12ff).[8]

The persuasiveness of the universalist foundationalist model of human knowledge becomes clear when we see that it is followed equally both by liberal theologians and by more conservative apologists. This shows how profoundly universalist foundationalism became part of the "plausibility structures" of modern culture. In systematic theology, evangelical theologians generally used the more general foundationalist model, but in opposition to liberal theology they continued stressing the fact that not general experience, but only the Word of God in Scripture can be the proper foundation for our knowledge of God. Yet, in apologetics evangelical apologists generally share the wider cultural conviction that the search for a universally acceptable foundation of human knowledge is the only possibility for a rational defence of the faith. Religious experience is less popular as a foundation because one recognizes with Paul the "noetic influence of sin", the fact that human sin deteriorates religious experience (cf. Ro 1:18ff). Yet, when Norman Geisler starts with an irrefutable logical axiom to continue later with the universally accessible historical reality of Scripture and Jesus, he follows the universalist foundationalist pattern (1976: 8f; cf. Sproul, Gerstner & Lindsley 1984: 99ff; Clark 1990: 47–53). The same is true of Stuart Hackett's use of a transcendental argument (1957; cf. Topping 1991). The pattern is equally recognizable in varieties of so-called "evidentialist" apologetics that tries to build an argument on the basis of historic evidences considered to be equally accessible to all serious inquirers (f. ex. Montgomery 1978; McDowell 1981; see further §5.4). Even the profound scepticism towards traditional apologetics in the presuppositionalist apologetics of Conrnelius van Til starts from the same foundationalist presupposition. Van Til's observation that there is no neutral common ground between Christians and non-Christians may be right, but the fact that he concludes automatically that

8 Schleiermacher is the main representative of what the postliberal theologian Lindbeck calls, "experiential expressivism" – his indication of the modern/liberal theological stream that in line with modern foundationalism wants to found the Christian faith on universal religious experience (Lindbeck 1984: 16).

therefore the knowledge of a non-Christian may not be used in an apologetic argument betrays a universalist foundationalist bias (1967; see further §8.1). In the same way philosophical scepticism is a natural companion of a universalist foundationalist epistemology: it is exactly because human knowledge should be scrutinized according to its very strict criteria, that some conclude to a largely or even absolute sceptical stance.[9]

Of course, the degree and manner in which liberal theology and evangelical and other apologetics have succumbed to universalist foundationalism, differ. Anticipating a later conclusion, we can already note that universalist foundationalism and the Christian faith – with its starting point in the unique historical revelation of God in Jesus Christ – are in fact fundamentally incompatible (see §5.3). As a result, liberal theologians and evangelical apologists are, as a matter of fact, trying to combine two incongruent perspectives. This search itself will thus necessarily lead to inconsistencies, not being fully Christian and at the same time not completely succumbing to a universalist foundationalist perspective of knowledge. Thus liberal theology is not characterized by succumbing completely to modernity, as sometimes suggested, but more by the ideal of reconciling the Christian and the modern perspective. However, this ideal to reconcile these two perspectives is unattainable, because being Christian itself limits the possibility of being completely modern.

One example of such an incongruent amalgam is the whole quest for the historical Jesus so characteristic of nineteenth-century liberal theology and apologetics. In using historical methods that are supposedly universally acceptable, the quest for the historical Jesus searches a universally acceptable foundation. Yet in using a historical person as a basis for the Christian faith, they stick to Christianity's particular starting point, provoking the problem central to Christian Enlightenment theology: How can a particular historical person establish a universal religion? A second example of this amalgam, so popular in recent evangelical apologetics, is the conception of Christian defence as the comparison and evaluation of different religious and non-religious worldviews. For shorthand, let us call them "worldview apologists". Of course, the attention to worldview perspectives shows a basic anti-modern understanding of knowledge as never being worldview-neutral. Yet the search of Harold Netland (1991), Ronald H. Nash (1992) and others for worldview-independent criteria for judging different worldviews seems to be reminiscent of the modern search for a universally shared

---

9 Cf. Plantinga's analysis: "So classical foundationalism fails. This fact has been widely celebrated (sometimes with a sort of foolish extravagance); it has also been widely hailed as requiring a rejection of all epistemology, or even of all traditional philosophy, or even of the idea of *truth* itself. [...] These intemperate reactions to the demise of foundationalism betray an agreement with it on a deep level: agreement that the only security or warrant for our beliefs must arise by way of evidential relationship to beliefs that are certain: self-evident or about our own mental states" (1993a: 85; cf. Murphy & McClendon 1989: 192).

starting point for human knowledge.[10] The question of whether or not we can manage without such criteria remains to be seen (see further §2.4; §7.6).

Postmodern criticism

Postmodern philosophers and postmodern theologians following in their footsteps have found universalist foundationalism deficient for several reasons. Four of these are particularly worth considering.

A first objection to this form of foundationalism is directly related to the fact that even the philosophers themselves do not hold on to their position most of the time when they are not philosophizing. According to Enlightenment foundationalism, most of what we consider in general to be reliable knowledge should be counted as irrational and unjustified. Plantinga mentions the following examples: "there are enduring physical objects", "there are persons distinct from myself", "The world has existed for more than five minutes" (1983: 59). If we could not hold these beliefs rationally, or even if we were only allowed to hold them as strongly as justified by our understanding of the force of the complex arguments supporting them, our lives would be unliveable. Not only in their daily lives, but also in their own philosophizing, modernist philosophers accept many beliefs that, according to their universalist foundationalism, should be dismissed out of hand. An important example to which we will return later is their reliance on the testimony of their fellow inquirers (see further §5.4).

A second objection to Enlightenment foundationalism has a more historical character. Modern philosophers debated, for some two hundred to three hundred years, the question: what should count as a universally acceptable foundation for general knowledge, ethics and culture? Should we start with what is evident to reason or would we do better to start with what is evident to the senses? Should we start with the Kantian transcendental analysis of the human mind? If some foundation were directly universally acceptable or accessible, it should not be that difficult to find; yet neither Enlightenment philosophy nor modern liberal theology has come up with a universally accepted proposal. Alisdair MacIntyre's judgement of the history of modern ethics seems equally justified for modern philosophy and liberal theology (1988: 334f; cf. 1985):

> [T]he history of attempts to construct a morality for tradition-free individuals [...] has in its outcome [...] been a history of continuously unresolved disputes, so that there emerges no uncontested and incontestable account of what tradition-independent morality consists in and consequently no

10 Walsh & Middleton are more true to the facts when they recognize that even the criteria to evaluate worldviews are "world view dependent" (1984: 37).

> neutral set of criteria by means of which the claims of rival and contending claims might be adjudicated. [...] The most cogent reasons that we have for believing that the hope of tradition-independent rational universality is an illusion derive from the history of that project.

As the postliberal theologian George Lindbeck states, the quest for a universal religious core experience was equally unsuccessful, or the experience was generalized and emptied from its content to such a degree that "the assertion of commonality becomes logically and empirically vacuous" (1984: 32).

A third objection to universalist foundationalism is that within this model the relationship between experience, especially religious experience, and the worldview to which it relates, can only be conceptualized in one direction: the experience is the foundation that carries the superstructure, and not the reverse. Historical and anthropological studies, however, show that the relationship between worldview and experience is a lot more complex, and that the more dominant influence is from the worldview to the experience rather than the reverse (Griffiths 1988: 407). All our experience, and particularly our religious and moral experience, is culture-dependent. The majesty of the world that surrounds us will evoke a different experience in a Christian, an adherent of African Traditional Religions, a Hindu or an atheist. The same people would be likewise impressed differently when confronted with death or the opportunity to meet Jesus of Nazareth.

The fourth and last major objection to Enlightenment foundationalism is fairly technical, but no less important. It states that this position is self-referentially incoherent in the sense that this epistemology itself is irrational, according to the criterion the model itself sets for rationality. Enlightenment foundationalism formulates an extremely strict criterion for the rationality of beliefs. Its basic conviction states that to be rational a belief should either belong to the universally acceptable or accessible foundation of the building of human knowledge, or should be built on this foundation according to proper rules of inference (themselves being part of the foundation). Yet, according to the way this criterion limits rational knowledge, the basic conviction of Enlightenment foundationalism itself is not rational. After all, this basic conviction itself is not universally directly acceptable or accessible, nor can it be derived from other beliefs that are properly foundational.[11]

11 The argument follows the same structure as the final refutation of logical positivism of the twentieth century. It showed that the logical positivist criterion for what can be known in fact excludes logical positivism itself from the domain of knowledge and characterizes it as a mere human opinion without adequate justification. For a more technical formulation of the argument, see Plantinga (1983: 59–63).

Christian apologetics beyond universalist foundationalism

At first sight, the demise of foundationalism is extremely disconcerting, for it seems to imply a relativist position with regard to human knowledge in general and, more particularly, it seems to herald the end of all Christian apologetics. Within the modern concept of knowledge this fear is wholly understandable, for if one sticks to its basic model of knowledge, the denouncement of a universal basis indeed implies a relativist conclusion. No building can be stronger than its foundation and without a strong foundation thus not only apologetics, but even the Christian faith itself loses ground and stability. Since the Enlightenment, the link between apologetics and foundationalism feels so natural that someone like Lindbeck can make sweeping statements like: "Postliberals are bound to be sceptical, not about missions, but about apologetics and foundations" (1984: 129).[12] Yet William Placher seems right in reminding us that apologetic dialogue only necessitates a common ground between two dialogue partners and not necessarily a universally acceptable common ground (1985: 106ff). The possibilities this opens up will need to be explored.

It is the anxiety of the relativist alternative, which seems (more than any other force) able to explain why Christian apologists cannot draw their conclusions from the collapse of foundationalism. That said, two alternatives to universalist foundationalism should be considered in order to show that the relativist conclusion does not follow if we abandon the basic premise of modern universalist foundationalism.

First of all, we could retain the basic foundationalist model but enlarge the number of beliefs we would be willing to call properly basic, not limiting them to what is universally directly acceptable or accessible. This is the road Plantinga and the larger school of "reformed epistemologists" follow, drawing from John Calvin and the "common sense" epistemology of the Scottish philosopher Thomas Reid (1710–1796). Thus Plantinga defends that, for example, belief in God can be considered as "properly basic". Like beliefs in other persons and beliefs we receive from reliable witness it does not require further evidence, but can function as part of the foundation of a healthy noetic structure. For Christians themselves the gain seems immediately clear, as they are anew justified in believing in God or in the witness of Scripture even when a further foundation is lacking. If we allow, along with Plantinga, that we have valid reasons to defend these beliefs as properly basic to those who do not share them, the model also opens up possibilities for apologetic dialogue. The gains and limitations of such an adapted foundationalism will be explored more fully later (§5.2).

A second alternative is not to adapt the foundationalism itself, but to give up

12 Yet at other moments Lindbeck leaves more scope for nuance, for the possibility of an "ad hoc apologetic" (1984: 129, 131).

the entire idea that a sound noetic structure is ordered like a building. In fact, the more important image for apologetics would not be an image for the relatively static structure of *knowledge* in itself, but a more dynamic image of our *getting to know*, of our *learning* and *unlearning*. What most interests the apologist is how human beings add new ideas to their existing noetic structure and how they exchange what they thought to be true for new beliefs which they discover to be truer to reality. Here all foundationalist models imply that the wise development of human knowledge should follow the model of construction, slowly adding to the foundation, demolishing what is defective, and adding brick by brick to the quantity of their knowledge. This construction-type of learning might be valid for some formalized methods of learning or adequate for certain areas of life, such as learning mathematics in school. Yet most of our knowledge and learning do not fit this pattern. We do not start from scratch by laying a foundation and constructing thereon. When we arrive at the stage in life where learning becomes a conscious activity, we already carry with us many ideas and interpretation-schemes, which we acquired through our personal history and through our socialization within a specific historically grown culture. When changes in our beliefs take place, some will just be an addition of new information. Yet, the more radical changes, such as the ones involved in religious conversion, are different. They are much more like encompassing changes of perspective and like a reordering of all the beliefs at hand. To do justice to this fundamental characteristic of the development of human knowledge, later we will propose another model of human knowledge that uses the metaphor of the reading of a book as the root metaphor for human learning (see §5.2). For this we can draw on the ancient Christian metaphor of the "book of creation".

Let us just give a hint of what this new model would entail. Learning about reality is like reading a book in that we never start out without a set of preconceptions about what to expect, a set of preconceptions, that will necessarily influence what we pay attention to and what we discover. Yet these preconceptions are, in an important way, radically different from the foundations of a building: foundations you can never reconstruct unless you tear down the whole superstructure. Human knowledge is not like that, for there are moments in life when people exchange their most basic conceptions involving a reordering, but not a demolishing, of the superstructure. In that sense, knowing is also much more like reading a book: we start with a good number of preconceptions, and from that perspective we discover a lot about the book and the reality we read. Yet in reading a book and in reality our preconceptions may prove to be inadequate, provoking a change – maybe even a change of worldview – to reorder our ideas to be more in line with the book we read and with reality itself. So in the hermeneutical process of reading reality, also called the "hermeneutical circle", our understanding of reality becomes increasingly adequate and in line with reality. In terms of this model, the basic task of the apologist is no longer to provide a supposedly universal and cultural-independent foundation of knowledge. His task is to compare different ways of reading reality and to defend the adequacy and relevance of the Christian reading in relation to the specific alternative readings offered.

2.2 Criticism of modern conceptions of language

Modern and postmodern theories of language

Closely related to the postmodern criticism of foundationalism is the development of a new basic conception of language. Crucial to modern or Enlightenment understanding of language is the idea of *representation*. Words and phrases are more or less adequate and true in so far as they refer to objective entities and the relationship that exists between them. Because there are many types of language and discourse that don't seem to refer to any objective entity – such as, for example, moral language – the theory of representation was complemented with an *expressivist* or emotivist understanding of language. This theory explains language that doesn't seem to refer to objective entities yet is experienced as making sense. The solution is found in seeing them as expressions of personal attitudes or emotions of the speaker (Murphy & McClendon 1989: 193–196, 201–203; MacIntyre 1985: 11ff, 76).

If these two theories should account for the entire field of human language, all language belongs somewhere on a scale between the subjective and objective pole. A great deal of the linguistic debate revolves around the question which fields of discourse refer to an objective reality and which areas of discourse are mere expressions of subjective and individual experiences, emotions and attitudes. Within such an arrangement the main concern of theologians and apologists will automatically be the debate about whether religious and theological language refers to an objective reality or is an expression of subjective religious experiences. When religious language is considered to be expressing religious experience, the apologetic question to ask is whether this experience is universal, valuable and beneficial, as the liberal defenders of religion would claim, or rather if it is parochial, misleading and repressive, as claimed by Marxist and Freudian atheist theorists.

Sensitivity to the different functions of language has been one of the major characteristics of postmodernism (Lyotard 1979: 20–24; trans. 1984: 9–11). Postmodern thinking has drawn extensively from developments in the philosophy of language as related to such thinkers as J.L. Austin and the later Ludwig Wittgenstein (Grenz 1996: 112). These thinkers have stated that words and phrases don't become meaningful first of all by referring to objective realities or by expressing personal emotions, but by the "language-games" (Wittgenstein 1953: 23) or the "discourse" to which they belong. An obvious example of Wittgenstein's concept of language games comes from the area of sports. When the umpire shouts "corner", the meaning of the expression is neither a subjective experience nor an objective reference; rather, the meaning is determined by the rules of the game. This is not just true in sports, for when I refer to the eleven o'clock train, likewise the meaning is not just private, nor is there any specific objective entity that I refer to. The same vehicle is not the eleven o'clock train one hour later, nor is it necessary that tomorrow's eleven o'clock train be the same vehicle. The meaning of the expression "the eleven o'clock train" is determined by a combination of social conventions expressed in the railway timetable as its own rules of the game or code of law. The typical postmodern thesis now is not simply that we should add another theory of language to the referential and the expressive. According to postmodernists, all human language should be understood first and foremost, and according to some even exclusively, as gaining its meaning within the language game and form of life to which it belongs (Lindbeck 1984: 114). Thus the distinction between objective language as representing and subjective language as expressive effectively loses its force and significance.

A cultural–linguistic understanding of religious language: George Lindbeck

An important, and I would say paradigmatic, example of the implications of the linguistic turn from modernism to postmodernism for our understanding of religion and apologetics can be found in the "postliberal" theology of George A. Lindbeck and other thinkers related to Yale such as Hans W. Frei (1974), Ronald F. Thiemann (1985), George Hunsinger (1996) and William C. Placher (1989).[13] The term "postliberal" was given to this school through the publication of Lindbeck's *The Nature of Doctrine: Religion and Theology in a Postliberal Age* (1984). This study can be seen as "a programmatic statement" of this school of thought (Tracy 1985; cf. Placher 1985: 393; Wallace 1987: 154; Tilley 1995: 89). They call themselves *postliberal* theologians because, like the earlier theological school with the same name, these theologians do not, in the first instance, criticize modern philosophy; rather, they criticize the liberal modern theology that grew on the same soil.[14] Yet, the Yale school can also be called "postmodern", because its criticism of liberal theology draws significantly on postmodern ideas concerning knowledge and language.[15]

13 See on the school as a whole Placher (1997) and Wallace (1987).

14 The name "postliberal theology" was already used for a long time for a group of Anglo-Saxon theologians like the brothers John and Donald Baillie in Britain and Reinhold and Richard Niebuhr in the United States, who were all inspired by the theology of Karl Barth (Macquarrie 1988: 339–350). The theologians of the Yale school share the influence of Barth, particularly through the work of Frei. Lindbeck names Frei as the decisive thinker "by a very large margin" in the growth of this school of thought (Lindbeck, Hunsinger, McGrath & Fackre 1996: 247). For the influence of Barth on Lindbeck: Lindbeck 1984: 135; 1986: 361–376.

15 Lindbeck equally applies the label "postmodern" to himself (1984: 135).

There are two main reasons for concentrating our analysis on the implications of the turn towards postmodernism for apologetics on the work of Lindbeck and the other Yale theologians. First of all, the changes Lindbeck and his colleagues proposed with regard to the understanding of religion and theology and apologetics reflect the major change towards postmodernity in our culture particularly well. We find in their work a departure from Enlightenment foundationalism and individualism. Lindbeck himself gives particular attention to the need to leave the modern understanding of language behind (Murphy & McClendon 1984: 205–207). This is one reason why Lindbeck and his colleagues provoked a wide and rapid response equally among the more "traditional" liberal theologians, evangelicals and different streams of Roman Catholic theology.[16] Some conclude therefore that this school might well represent "the most influential postmodern experiment in the United States" (Mohler 1995: 76). A second reason is that as theologians, they reflect widely on the consequences the move to postmodernism should have for our understanding of apologetics (Placher 1989).

In order to understand the basic structure of Lindbeck's criticism of modern theology and apologetics, we need first of all to understand his cultural–linguistic model of religion, doctrine and theology. A fundamental thesis of *The Nature of Doctrine* is that we should distinguish between three fundamental ways of conceiving religion and theology.[17] In these models we will recognize three basic ways of conceiving religion which we can see around us.

The first, so-called "cognitive-propositional" model conceives doctrines as "informative propositions or truth-claims about objective realities" (Lindbeck 1984: 16). Religious and theological statements are thus conceived as a description of the way the world is, including God and His works. In this model, our understanding of the phrase "Christ is risen from the dead" is basically the same as our understanding of the phrase "Napoleon lost the Battle of Waterloo" – though the statement about Christ is, of course, infinitely more important. Lindbeck sees this as the basic model of pre-Enlightenment orthodox Christianity and although he does not state it explicitly, this model covers most modern evangelical and conservative Roman Catholic theology (McGrath 1996a: 29). Lindbeck considers this concept unacceptable because of its intellectualism and because it supposes an exact correspondence between language and reality. However, many evangelicals and other "cognitivists" will rightly want to criticize this description for being negligent of the sensitivity for the limitations of human language developed in the cognitivist tradition (McGrath 1990: 15ff; 1996a: 29–33; 1996b: 136–146; see further §5.2 & §5.3).

Lindbeck's main concern, though, is directed towards the modern-liberal

16 See for an overview of the early responses Gordon E. Michaelson Jr. (1988: 107–120). See for evangelical responses Phillips & Okholm (1996).

17 Although the concept of "doctrine" is central to Lindbeck's project, our interest in apologetics makes us concentrate on his understanding of "religion" and "theology".

approach to doctrine, theology and religion, which he calls the "experiential-expressive" model. Here the basic access to the world of religion and the basic element of religious life is religious experience. According to this understanding, true doctrine, true theology and true religion are symbolic expressions of universal religious experience (pp. 16, 31f). Lindbeck notes psychological pressures towards this approach to religion in contemporary culture such as the individualization of religious experience and the search for reconciliation between different religions (pp. 19–25). Yet, for several reasons Lindbeck also considers this model to be unsatisfactory as an approach to religion and doctrine. First and foremost, there is no universal religious core experience from which all particular religions originate. All religious experiences spring within the context of a historically grown tradition and are inseparably bound to the conceptual framework, which made them possible and influenced them to the core (pp. 32ff). An Islamic and a Hindu experience of the divine are different from the start because of the different ways these religions open up religious experience. Thus religious experiences in various traditions differ to such an extent that the supposition of a common core experience becomes wholly vacuous (p. 32). Furthermore, this experiential-expressivist understanding of religion can in no way explain why religious communities tend to stick to their doctrines with an incredible force and why they put such a high value on doctrinal continuity. Why is this, if doctrines are no more than interchangeable symbolic expressions of universal experiences (p. 78)?[18]

Because of the shortcomings of the propositional and expressivist models, Lindbeck chooses a third and radically new approach to religion, doctrine and theology, which he labels "cultural–linguistic". Both the cognitive-propositional and the experiential-expressive approach to religious phenomena share the presupposition that they look for the truth of theological and religious statements in a primary reality exterior to the social linguistic world of texts, institutions and the life of the religious community. This is equally true for those who locate their truth in their correspondence with a metaphysical reality as for those who see them as symbolic expressions of religious experience. According to Lindbeck, the value of doctrinal and theological statements should not be located in such an "extratextual" reality, but is utterly "intratextual". These propositions only make sense *within* the "textual", linguistic and social context of the texts and institutions of the religious tradition and community. Religion is thus neither referring to an objective reality nor an expression of an individual religious experience. It is an inter-subjective reality, which can only be understood as it is received from

18 Lindbeck develops this criticism particularly with reference to ecumenical dialogue, a process close to his heart, the explanation of which was actually one of the main reasons to write his study (1984: 7). With regard to ecumenical dialogue, his reproach to experiential-expressivism is exactly opposite his criticism of the cognitive-propositional model. If the latter, according to Lindbeck, cannot explain doctrinal *development*, because it understands doctrines to be either eternally true or eternally false (p. 47), then in no way can the experiential-expressivism explain why the different parties in ecumenical dialogue consider *continuity* and stability of doctrine to be so important.

and lived by the religious community (pp. 113ff). With the cultural anthropologist Clifford Geertz, Lindbeck wants to analyse *religion* analogously to culture as a "semiotic system" in which each part receives its meaning through the whole universe of meaning that a specific culture creates (p. 115; cf. Geertz 1993: 5). Borrowing from the later Wittgenstein, he defends the thesis that religions can be described as "language games", correlated with a specific form of life (Lindbeck 1984: 33).

Seeing the great variety of religions, the vacuity of the idea of a general religious experience and the ability of language to create a world of its own, the idea of religious worlds as human creations seems an obvious conclusion. Lindbeck does not deny all objective extratextual reference to the Christian faith (pp. 35, 51, 66, cf. Marshall 2009, xviif), yet he recognizes the creative character of human speech and of religions as "construing" and "creating" reality (pp. 47, 117). In this he draws from J.L. Austin's notion of the "performatory" use of language (Lindbeck 1984: 65). Austin spoke of language not only being referential or expressing feelings and attitudes, but also being "performative" and creating something that did not exist before. Marriage vows provide us with an example, for once given, they inaugurate a new state of affairs. In the Christian religion, the performative character of language has an important place, for someone's public confession of Christ changes their relationship to God and Christ and to the Christian community (cf. Rm 10:9). Yet Lindbeck seems to go much further when he states:

> A religious utterance, one might say, acquires the propositional truth of ontological correspondence *only* insofar as it is performance, an act or deed, which helps create that correspondence (p. 65).

Lindbeck's stress on the creative character of religious language reflects a major trait of the wider postmodern understanding of religion. Postmodernity stresses the creative activity of the human mind in the *modelling* of the world. This is generally called "conceptual antirealism" or "conceptual relativism" to indicate that the concepts people use to approach and understand the world are human creations. These concepts can only be understood in terms of their function within human-made conceptual schemes or as ways in which a community organizes its experience.[19]

The idea of religion as a human construct is of course not new but was also part of the Enlightenment criticism of religion in the line of Feuerbach, Marx and Freud. Yet, postmodernism brings a major change: for the modern critics the idea that religion in general and Christianity in particular was a human construct implied that they neither referred to an objective reality, nor reflected a valuable

19 For this understanding of "conceptual antirealism", see Jeffrey Hensley (1996: 72–74); for antirealism as a persistent trait of postmodernism in general see Grenz (1996: 40–44).

human experience. This automatically disqualified this religious language, for language was thought to have no other meaningful function. For postmodernists, however, the recognition that our religious conceptions are largely or even utterly human constructs does not in any way diminish their value. All human worldviews and religions, all human knowledge even, function this way: it is simply part of being human to belong to different traditions of conceptual structuring of the world.

In line with this change, many can nowadays respect the Christian faith because of its creative power and yet not feel in any way inclined to join this community. They have modelled their own world. This is also why many Christians feel less threatened from the outside and less motivated from the inside to give a justification of their religious convictions. Some may want to formulate this theologically in talking about the Christian faith as *their* "story", the "narrative" that gives meaning to their lives or as *their* dream they received and that gives them hope. Lindbeck joins this wider movement of narrative theology[20] and the recognition by cultural anthropologists of the importance of stories to understand cultures (Grenz 1996: 44) in his assessment of narrative as the most important and characteristic biblical genre (Lindbeck 1984: 120f).

If Christian conviction and Christian action only make sense within the context of the Christian story, we should question what the relationship could be with other "stories", worldviews or religions. According to Lindbeck, "[religions] may, [...], be incommensurable in such a way that no equivalents can be found in one language of religion for the crucial terms of the other" (1984: 48). The notion of "incommensurability" is derived from the philosophy of science of Thomas S. Kuhn who had a considerable influence on postmodern thought. According to Kuhn different physical "paradigms" like Aristotelian physics, Newtonian physics, and Einsteinian physics are incommensurable. This is to say that there does not exist one overarching conceptual scheme from which two or all three of these physical perspectives on reality can be compared and judged. One finds oneself always within one specific conceptual scheme or rationality, one of these three or a fourth, and can only operate from within such a perspective. A neutral standpoint does not exist. And as different opinions in physics only make sense within a specific paradigm, they do not make sense in terms of another (1996: 148–150; cf. Tilley 1988: 89ff).[21]

Implications for Christian apologetics

If religion, doctrine and theology are no longer seen as referring to an extra-linguistic reality, this has important consequences for Christian apologetic witness.

20 For an overview, see Gary L. Comstock (1987: 687–717).

21 See for the further debate among philosophers of science Del Ratzsch (2000: 61).

Lindbeck considers his major theological dialogue partners, the liberal experiential-expressivists, apologists *par excellence*: they try to defend and acclaim the Gospel by founding it solidly in universal human experience (1984: 12, 129). Considering Enlightenment theology as essentially "apologetic" is one of the common traits in many representatives of postliberal theology (cf. Thiemann 1985: 74; Hunsinger 1992: 104; Placher 1985: 407f; 1989: 11ff; Lindbeck 1996: 239). It is automatically, for these postmodern theologians, a reason to defame it. This search for a universally acceptable foundation for Christian theology is thought in vain and destructive for the particularity and thus proper force of the Christian faith.

This criticism of apologetics is precisely related to a point at which the revised postliberal understanding of religion is most closely reflecting the wider change towards postmodernity. For postmodern thinkers, religion is, after all, no longer seen as based in an understanding of God and His world existing objectively beyond us, nor as based on a religious experience common to all human beings. It is rather the construct of a particular historical community. It is not a way you recognize reality to be, but rather a way to organize your reality, community and culture. An apologetic defence of some religious truth in relation to a perceived "objective reality" or universal religious experience thus turns out to be both impossible and redundant.

However, many postliberal theologians do consider the Christian faith as being, in some way, related to an extratextual reality (f. ex. Lindbeck 1984: 35, 51, 66; Thiemann 1985; Placher 1989), and believe the life and faith of the Christian community worthwhile to be recommended to others. They also want to leave some place for apologetics. Yet, when the Christian faith can only be properly understood in terms of its own "language game", its own tradition-dependent rationality, this has major consequences for apologetics.[22] Postliberal theologians note several of them that are worth pondering. Later on, we will need to draw our own conclusions.

First, this understanding of the Christian faith as a particular language game has major consequences for the way in which we try to make the Christian faith

22 To indicate that human reflection and perception can never be understood apart from the social environment, the historical setting and the encompassing way of seeing things from which it forms a part, postmodern and related thinkers use different expressions. With different stresses, they all point to roughly the same reality: "plausibility structures" (Berger), "conceptual scheme" (Donald Davidson), "language game" (Wittgenstein), "language, culture" (Lindbeck), "rationality, tradition" (MacIntyre), "worldview". I will often use the expression "tradition" or "tradition-dependent rationality", or "tradition-dependent conceptual structure", for it expresses most clearly the theological notion of tradition, which is so important for the way we see reality (cf. 1Co 15:1). It is important to note that the expression "rationality" is thus used in a *descriptive* rather than a *normative* way. There can be a plurality of "rationalities" that developed within different traditions, but that all need to be judged to what extent they are truly rational, just as different theologies need to be tested to what extent they are really *theo*-logy and convey true knowledge of God.

understandable for our hearers. Understanding what the Christian faith entails is, after all, a prerequisite for the justification of our faith. If in terms of modern linguistics language is, first of all, thought to refer to an objective reality; it is natural to consider the dominant language as objective and universal. Thus the Enlightenment theologians and apologists shared the tendency to see a major cultural or philosophical trend as reflecting the objective and universal, be it rationalist philosophy, empirical science, romantic experience, Marxist ideology or modern psychology. Frei could thus describe the history of biblical hermeneutics since the Enlightenment as a matter of "fitting the biblical story into another world with another story" (1974: 130). He saw a continuous apologetic effort to make the biblical story understandable and believable by incorporating it into the dominant language and culture, which was understood to reflect the objective and universal.

In line with postmodern linguistics, however, Frei and Lindbeck think that there is no objective and universal language, which should be accepted as a norm over the Christian tradition or which should be shovelled under it as its foundation. Barth showed them that in this way modern theologians undermined the *sola Scriptura* of the Reformation. That is why Frei and Lindbeck propose a radical reversal of the direction of interpretation. Scripture should not be read and explained in terms of a "language", culture or conceptual scheme foreign to it. This should be exactly reversed: starting from Scripture and in terms of the Scriptural framework, the world, other traditions and other cultures should be read and interpreted. "Intratextual theology redescribes reality within the scriptural framework rather than translating Scripture in extratextual categories" (Lindbeck 1984: 118; cf. 1996: 226f). So explaining the Gospel to non-Christians does not entail making them look to Scripture with their own modern, postmodern or pagan eyes. From these perspectives the Christians faith does not really make sense. We should rather invite others to look to their own world and lives with new eyes, through the eyes of Scripture. The Christian world should not become part of the world they are already used to, but the audience should rather enter a new world. With reference to an early article by Karl Barth we could call this "The Strange New World within the Bible" (Barth 1924: 18–32; trans. 1957b: 28–50; cf. Lindbeck 1984: 226).

Like any other religion and worldview, the Christian faith is, therefore, a unified totality of an assessment of the central problems religion should attend to, and of the solutions that are offered. Thus its crucial convictions can only be justified and accounted for as a single whole. That is why we find among those sympathizing with the idea of a postliberal theology the Barthian idea that a good systematic theology is the best apologetics (f. ex. Ford 1985: 232–254). A reformulation of the faith in terms of the modern or of any other non-Christian worldview can only diminish its force. Christian systematic theology rather aims to show the inner coherence of the Christian faith with its own particular force and validity.

The apologist, though, is not only interested in the internal justification of the Christian faith, because he would like to build bridges to those who do not share this worldview. Lindbeck is right that a prolonged period of learning may be necessary for those from the outside, before they can fully understand this new Christian world from the inside. Thus Lindbeck pleads for something like the long period of *catechesis* that pagan converts in the Early Church were required to go through (1984: 132). The apologist wants to go one step further, and explain and justify the validity of the Christian faith to those outside, and maybe give them reasons to enter such a period of prolonged catechesis. The main criticism the postliberals constantly receive is that they seem to imprison adherents of different religions and non-religions within their particular language and rationality, thus blocking a public apologetic witness (Tracy 1985; McGrath 1996a: 39–43; David Clark 1996).[23] Yet drawing from hints in Frei and Lindbeck, postliberal theologians have been exploring two major paths towards a renewed apologetic dialogue with those who do not share the Christian tradition. The first path is the possibility of "Christianity absorbing the world" (Lindbeck 1984: 118; cf. 1996: 226f; Marshall 1990: 69–102); the second is the possibility of "*ad hoc* apologetics".

The first possibility is a direct consequence of the reversal of the direction of hermeneutics proposed by Lindbeck and Frei. Instead of the modern rewriting of Scripture, we should "redescribe reality within the Scriptural framework" (Lindbeck 1984: 118, cf. 123), by which the surrounding world with all its events and opinions is understood from the perspective of biblical rationality. This redescription has apologetic import. In this respect religions could be evaluated as scientific paradigms or as readings literary critics propose for a literary work. A scientific paradigm proves its superiority in being able to account for a wider variety of phenomena than alternative paradigms. A particular reading and interpretation of a book proves superior if it can give a convincing explanation of more elements of the book's content than alternative interpretations. According to Lindbeck, religions function likewise:

> The reasonableness of a religion is largely a function of its assimilative powers, of its ability to provide an intelligible interpretation in its own terms of the varied situations and realities its adherents encounter (1984: 131; cf. 1986: 375f).

If there are no conceptual schemes that are, in advance, universally recognized or directly recognizable as such, it means that there is no common starting-point for apologetic dialogue that a Christian shares with all non-Christians.

23 It is exactly at this point that some of Lindbeck's critics see a link with Barth, who they apparently likewise dismissed, reproaching Lindbeck "Barthian confessionalism" (Tracy 1985: 465; cf. Corner 1986: 112).

Therefore, postliberals state that apologetics should always be "*ad hoc*".[24] Christian apologetic defence is *ad hoc* because the points of contact to start a dialogue will vary from one particular partner to another. There is no longer a universally valid or universally applicable apologetics. This is also recognized by those apologists related to the so-called "Reformed epistemology" like Alvin Plantinga (1983: 73; cf. Mavrodes 1970: 31ff; 1983: 192–218). As Kelly James Clark notes: "The notion of proof is *person-relative*; since one is presumably attempting *to prove something to someone*, a successful proof will depend on what that person already believes" (1990: 42; cf. David Clark 1993a).

We need to go one step further and say not only that proof is person-relative, but also that it is *culture-relative*. This is implied in the postmodern discovery that we will analyse more deeply in the next section: what we believe depends on our community, our communal culture and our plausibility structures. The major implication will retain our attention for many pages to come: how to develop an apologetic that is culture-relative and therefore *contextual*.

This conclusion – that effective apologetics is person- and culture-relative and contextual – is far from new for those involved in practical apologetic dialogue and witness. Yet although this may be known by experience, the apologists in the Enlightenment tradition work with an understanding of apologetics that does not concur with it. One of the aims of this book is to develop an alternative framework for apologetics, so that theoretical apologetics will no longer be alienated from real life, but will rather be invigorating and enriching real-life apologetics.

2.3 Criticism of modern individualism and collectivism

The isolation of the modern subject

Because of the centrality of the Christian understanding of the human being for apologetics, we extend the analysis of the postmodern understanding of knowledge and language to the postmodern conception of the human being. Again, as a "post-"position, the modern conception of what it means to be human is its point of reference. The modern quest for a universal foundation of knowledge and for a universal rationality is closely related to the modern *individualist* conception of man, with the rise of the modern autonomous subject and its goodbye to traditions and authorities, be it religious or other (Newbigin 1996: 61). On the one hand it is the modern desire for autonomy, for

24 The references to such an "ad hoc" apologetics are scattered through the works of postliberal theologians, persistent enough to speak of a theme, yet not much developed because of their lack of interest in apologetics as a theological enterprise (Lindbeck 1984: 129, 131; Frei 1975: xii; 1992: 161; Thiemann 1985: 75; Werpehowski 1986).

emancipation from these authorities of tradition and religion that provoked the quest for a universally equally accessible foundation for human knowledge and rationality. On the other hand it is the supposition that human knowledge can be founded on a universally accessible foundation that opens up the possibility that modern man functions autonomously, individually and independently from the history and tradition he used to belong to. After all, without a universally and individually accessible knowledge, the departure from tradition will lead to scepticism. Such scepticism remains the perennial counterpart and threat of modern foundationalism.

The postmodern: the rebirth of tradition or the fragmentation of the subject?

We noted how postliberal theology strongly criticizes the possibility of a tradition-independent rationality and of a foundation of knowledge, which is neutral in regards to different traditions of thought. Human convictions can only be understood in relationship to the history of the community, in which the characteristic conceptual structures were formed through which its members inhabit the world. This criticism of modernity thereby frees the human being both from his individual isolation and the danger of his dissolution in some universal collective.

When human individuals regain their place within the wider structures to which they belong, this has important consequences. In the radical deconstructionist stream of postmodernism this even resulted in the idea of the "death of the subject" or the "disappearance of the self", which was placed over and against the Enlightenment belief in the autonomous individual (Taylor 1984: 34ff; cf. Middleton & Walsh 1995b: 50f). The idea is that the human subject is completely determined by the language he speaks and the conceptual schemes he receives from his tradition and environment. Yet when the human subject is thus pronounced dead, one needs to ask if this understanding of individuality, subjectivity and human reflection is not itself closely tied to modern ideas. From the death of the specifically modern subject, one concludes the pronouncement of the death of the subject in general.[25] However, when the particular modern self has disappeared, this need not force us to give up the idea of human individuality and selfhood. We should rather look for a more truthful comprehension of individuality and selfhood than the modern. In postliberal theology, for example, we cannot speak of a disappearance of the self, but rather of the human subject who regains himself within the particular religious tradition to which he belongs. Language and culture are characteristic of the human being, and Lindbeck has

25 For this critical analysis see: Murphy & McClendon 1989: 212; Griffin 1989: XI–XIV.

learned from Wittgenstein that private languages do not exist and from Geertz that culture is always tied to community (Lindbeck 1984: 37f).

We need to note that Lindbeck stands apart in his understanding of religion from a major trait of the wider postmodern ethos. An often-mentioned characteristic of postmodernity is the *fragmentation* of the self, the self losing its centre as both the world around him and his inner world lose a centre from which all its parts can be integrated (Grenz 1996: 19–22; 2001: 1f; Middleton & Walsh 1995b: 46–62; Iyer 2000). This fragmentation is itself a consequence from the understanding that the individual does not pose his or her identity over against the world, but rather receives an identity from the world to which he belongs or, stronger, is posed by this world. The reality of the postmodern society is that we belong to many different communities all at once. The postmodern person works for his boss til it wrecks his health; he is part of a nuclear family where he feels loved; he searches for religious experience in some cult or in church; he is a fan of baroque music; he supports Greenpeace hoping for a better world. All these worlds make some sense in themselves, but not in relation to each other. The media, particularly television and the World Wide Web, reflect this carnival of different unrelated universes. The postmodern consumer does not choose one of these worlds, but zaps and surfs from one world to another. In the process his inner self is likewise fragmented as he lacks a single perspective from which all these worlds and sectors of life could be valued and integrated.

The different modern worldviews already abandoned the Christian answer to the question opening both the Genevan and the Shorter Westminster Catechism: "What is the chief end of man?" Yet the different modern worldviews could all give their own answer to this question, be it in terms of the progress of science, the development of the self or the Marxist Utopia. Because postmodernity is characterized by the end of the "metanarratives", the end of the encompassing histories covering all aspects of life, it no longer has an alternative answer with regard to the chief end of the human life. Or it should be that today we choose for ourselves a chief end and tomorrow we are free to choose another or maybe choose different "chief" ends all at once. Here the self disappears in another way, not because it is not free to choose because of the way he is bound by his tradition and environment; the self is disappearing because it is *too* free to choose, so much so that real choices and real commitments become close to impossible. Who or what should make the commitment, if the self is so fragmented? (Middleton & Walsh 1995b: 55–58.)

Hence, what is the truly postmodern, the fast chaotic world of MTV or the plea to live a whole and integrated life in terms of one coherent religious tradition? The answer depends on the way the question is understood. If it is a question as to what type of culture or society will be the successor of modernity, the stronger case seems to be on the side of the un-centred self in a fragmented world. The perspective of cultural–linguistic approaches is not promising in a society with still huge pressures towards individualism, religious pluralism, and fragmentation of societal roles, where fewer and fewer people are so deeply embedded in particular religious communities as to be able to re-describe their whole world from that perspective (Lindbeck 1984: 21). The resurgence of particular traditions in no way precludes that both the young and old in the former Soviet Republics, in Africa, and in Asia simultaneously soak in Western television and Coca-Cola, thus contributing to the fragmentation of their own world (Samuel 1994: 314–320). This fragmented world is the future Christian apologetics has to deal with, both in the so-called modern world and elsewhere on the planet. The consequences are far-reaching and clearly detectable when we see how our dialogue partners can fluctuate from one moment to another, no longer being prepared to defend one specific position, but continuously changing their stance. If it were ever possible to hope to checkmate our "opponent" in apologetic debate, this is no longer the case, for she feels free to move all over the board forgetting all rules about which moves are logically acceptable and which are not.

At the same time we need to be critical of the fragmentation itself. It may be a social reality, but it cannot be our ideal. It leaves people adrift, without direction – moral or otherwise (Middleton & Walsh 1995b: 60f) – and in search for "home" (cf. Iyer 2000). This fragmentation cannot be the Christian ideal, for Christians believe that notwithstanding cultural variety and the multifaceted nature of reality, this reality has a unified basis. Reality has a unified basis as creation of the one God, whose aim it is to unify and reconcile everything by his Son (Eph. 1:10; Co 1:20; Grenz 1995: 96f). In this Christian metanarrative, all fragments find their due place. Therefore, for a real departure from the Enlightenment idols a positive revaluation of tradition and community may prove more promising for the development of an adequate and thoroughly Christian apologetics for our postmodern world than a surrender to a hypermodern or postmodern fragmentation of the self and its narratives.

Apologetics and the Christian community

The regaining of community and tradition against modern individualism has again important consequences for the changes needed with regard to modern apologetics, which treats both the apologist and those he dialogues with essentially as individuals, each having his most individual relationship with truth. This change does not only concern the way we treat our dialogue partners, but also the way the Christian apologist understands herself. An individual believer can only adequately learn to speak her religious language and continue to speak this language within a community that perceives the whole reality from that particular perspective. But the fact is that the dominant secular culture in the West no longer reflects the Christian tradition and rationality, and that the dominant cultures in most other parts of the world have never been

Christianized. That is why Lindbeck pleads for what he calls a "sociological sectarianism".[26] Only by developing strong alternative social bonds, as in a sect, can Christians form a counterculture, different and coherent enough to constitute an alternative "plausibility structure" and thus to be plausible to its adherents.[27]

The need of close-knit Christian communities who live their lives according to their faith is not important just for Christians themselves; rather, it is equally important to attract those outside. We noted that the value of Christian convictions cannot be fully recognized when they are considered in an atomized way and abstracted from the entire vision and the form of life to which they belong. If that is true, the form of life expressed in the Christian community is essential to its attraction. It is the life of the community that should witness to the healing force and wholesomeness of the Christian faith, to the possibility that it be lived and thought out in an integrated manner in all areas of life as well as in response to different challenges. Thus the life of the Christian community testifies to the reality and truth of Him, in whom they put their faith. We will elaborate later on this crucial role of the Christian community in apologetic witness (§7.5).

2.4 Concluding observations and prospects

Relativist dissolution of apologetics?

The analysis of modern Western apologetics in this chapter has shown that a new type of apologetics is needed. This form of apologetics has not only become out of date, but also it was never as sound and universal as it was thought to be. Because modern apologetics was largely unconscious concerning the specifically modern structure of its defence, it could easily compromise its Christian stance. Because of its modern character, it was likewise unable to adequately address those who did not share the Enlightenment culture, both those belonging to white and ethnic subcultures in Europe and North America and those hundreds of millions on other continents. The question as to how far the postmodern criticism of modern rationality will help us to formulate a truly Christian apologetic, which is at the same time adequate in a postmodern and multicultural world, will continue to guide us in the rest of this book. The first hurdle to an adequate answer is the recurring question of whether or not postmodern criticism will inevitably lead to a relativist epistemology and the entire abandonment of the question of truth.

---

26 Lindbeck carefully distinguishes this idea from the theological notion of a sect, for he does not plead for a community, which deviates from the mainstream of Christian doctrine. He wants to indicate that even an ecumenical Christian community can only survive and retain its particular identity if it takes within our wider society the stand and the sociological position of a sect (1984: 78, cf. 127; 1971: 226–243; Kelsey 1990: 7–33).

27 Here, Lindbeck (1984: 78) uses a concept of the sociology knowledge (f. ex. Berger 1969: 50).

Can Christian apologetics avoid the dangers of relativism on the one hand and fideism on the other if it uses an non-foundationalist epistemology, accepts the tradition-dependent character of all human language and rationality, and takes leave of modern individualism? If this is not possible, the idea of Christian apologetics would need to be adapted and emptied to such an extent that it would be more honest to stop speaking about apologetics at all. It would indeed no longer make sense to talk about "the intellectual justification of the truth and the relevance of the Christian faith" (§1.3).

The first remark to be made here is equally simple as it is far reaching. There is nothing that *a priori* inhibits the possibility that objective and universal truth can be found, when universalist foundationalism and the existence of tradition- and community-independent rationality are rejected. Often the reproach of fideism or relativism rests on the unspoken modern presupposition that universal starting points are essential if one wants to avoid relativism. A typical example is Netland's defence of context-independent criteria for judging worldviews:

> If we reject a thoroughgoing relativism, it seems undeniable that there are at least some criteria or principles which are context-independent and can legitimately be used in appraising various ideological and religious perspectives (1994: 104; cf. 1991: 180).

But why is it *a priori* impossible that some experiences of a particular community cannot yield objectively true and universally valid knowledge? And why is it that a process of rational reflection starting from one particular perspective cannot lead to a universally valid knowledge? Netland's and similar arguments presuppose the central trait of universalist foundationalism, that truth can never be found unless the starting point of our argument is already known to be true. Yet unless a solid argument is produced with this intent, there is no reason to limit the possibility of true knowledge that radically.

However, while the possibility that a tradition-dependent rationality yields objective and universally valid knowledge cannot be *excluded* from the start, it can neither be positively justified *a priori*. Therefore, we will need an elaborate argument to defend this thesis that tradition-dependent rationality and reasoning starting from particular historically located experiences, understood in terms of a specific worldview, can yield true and universally valid knowledge. To avoid fideism, we will even need to show that the validity of such knowledge can be substantiated even for those who do not from the start participate in the same tradition of rational reflection. Chapter 5 outlines such an argument. Yet, for the moment, the fact that a positive conclusion is not precluded from the start makes the exercise of trying to develop a Christian apologetics that takes seriously the postmodern criticism of Enlightenment epistemology a worthwhile enterprise.

A second remark relating to the relativism-charge against the postmodern criticism of universalist foundationalism is one fairly technical but crucial terminological clarification. In epistemologies and apologetics in the Enlightenment tradition, one not always clearly distinguishes between on the one hand those beliefs, which are *directly and from the start* universally accepted or universally accessible, and on the other hand simply universally accessible or acceptable beliefs.[28] In the first instance, these thinkers refer to what I will call *universal validity as given from the start*. One talks about what can be the universally shared premise of an argument of which the conclusions will be equally shared if the validity of the argument can be shown. In the second instance one talks about what I will call *universal validity as accessible in principle*, the fact that some universally valuable rationality exists, reflecting the objective rational structure of the universe itself and that some beliefs are objectively true because they represent some objective state of affairs.

Within a universalist foundationalist framework it is not surprising that these two aspects, universality as given from the start and universality as accessible in principle, are not clearly distinguished, for in this epistemological framework both are related. After all, within a foundationalist framework the only way to access any universally valid knowledge is to build on knowledge which from the start is considered universally valid.

Yet, though understandable, this lack of clarity as regards to distinguishing universal acceptability from the start on the one hand and universal acceptability in principle on the other hand completely undermines the modernist criticism of tradition-dependent rationalities as necessarily leading to relativism. For as far as "universal validity in principle" is concerned, a tradition-dependent rationality and ideas handed on through tradition could also claim, in principle, to be universally valid. That is at least true for the Christian faith, which originates in Israel and with Jesus of Nazareth, but claims to be the universal truth of the universe for all humanity (Newbigin 1991; cf. §1.3) On the other hand, as far as "universally valid and acceptable knowledge from the start" is concerned, not even Enlightenment thinkers and apologists answer to the standards of their own criteria. They never start with something universally accepted as valid from the start, but always need to start arguing why it is universally valid, thus showing that it is not universally accepted from the start. Thus Netland needs an elaborate argumentation to show that his context-independent criteria are context-independent, for not everyone accepts them from the start. One of the strongest

28 In the same manner one does not clearly distinguish between two ways of speaking about "universal rationality". On the one hand there is the idea that there exists a universally accepted or directly accessible rationality as a conceptual structure that all sane human beings share as a given reality. This idea, however, should be distinguished from the idea of the possibility that there is one normative rationality that is in principle accessible and acceptable to all human beings and which corresponds with the structure of reality itself, but which is not given, but more a reality to be explored. In a third sense one can speak of "universal rationality" not as a common structure of human thought, but rather as an indication an ability that equips humanity to explore the rational structure of reality (see also §4.2 & §5.1).

candidates for a context-independent criterion is the principle of non-contradiction (Netland 1991: 183ff). Yet, as Newbigin, a former missionary to India, notes: "Indian philosophy denies the principle of non-contradiction and regards it as one of the weaknesses of the Western tradition" (1994: 86).[29]

My problem with Netland and the like is therefore not that his criteria are not universally valid and thus finally universally accessible and justifiable, but that they are not universally recognized *from the start*. And if they are not recognized from the start, why not apologetically exploit all those other Christian convictions that are indeed tradition dependent, but in most cases much more attractive to dialogue about than such abstract ideas as criteria to judge different worldviews? To me an apologetic dialogue starting from the attractiveness of the Person of Jesus of Nazareth or from the precariousness of the human condition is much more engaging than one concerning the validity of the principle of non-contradiction. We may not share convictions about the uniqueness of Jesus or about the human condition from the start, but that does not mean that we cannot argue for their universal validity. This is what apologetics is all about. Moreover, there may be many strong convictions I share with a particular dialogue partner that may not be context-independent but that we both recognize as true. These can be important beacons for further dialogue. The examples change from one situation to another, but could include the inalienable value of each individual human being, the existence of a Creator God, or the frailness of our life in this world (see further §7.3).

The fierceness of argumentation and the force of the modern epistemological position is, of course, related to the fact that its adherents want to hold on to an in-principle universally accessible and justifiable knowledge. Yet, when the universalist foundationalist epistemology is left aside, there is no longer any need to hold on to this myth of a *from the start* universally acceptable knowledge. Other ways to arrive at true and justifiable beliefs can be freely explored. The blind alleys of both relativist pluralism and of modern universalist foundationalism positively invite us to explore this third way.

Characteristics of Christian apologetics after modernity

We will end this chapter with some preliminary observations of the contribution of the postmodern criticism on modern epistemology, linguistics and anthropology for the development for a renewed Christian apologetic. The question is how far this postmodern criticism will help us to develop an apologetic that is no longer tributary to the Enlightenment culture and that is more truly Christian. The question is furthermore how these insights may help us in formulating an apologetic witness to audiences that do not share the modern outlook on reality, be it

29 Newbigin refers to Christopher Kaiser's analysis showing that "this Western conviction about the ultimate coherence of the cosmos is the fruit of biblical faith" (1994: 86; cf. Kaiser 1991).

postmodern audiences or audiences in our multicultural and multireligious world who have never signed up to either modernism or postmodernism.

Notwithstanding some major problems with postmodern developments in theology, particularly relating to the recurring charge of relativism, the analysis of the shortcomings of Enlightenment philosophy and apologetics helps us to take four major steps forward towards a renewed apologetics.

First of all, the postmodern criticism of Enlightenment epistemology has shown that the Christian faith can be only adequately acclaimed as a whole. It is impossible to dissolve single threads of this whole web of belief and justify them apart from the conceptual structure to which they belong. What counts is the "illuminating power of the whole" (Lindbeck 1984: 11).

Second, the apologist and her dialogue partner are no longer isolated individuals who meet without a corporate and without an individual history, always starting anew from a neutral foundation. Both belong to specific communities, to one community or to a whole plethora of communities at once, in which specific rationalities have been formed and are related to particular forms of life. Both equally feel the pressures of the dominant plausibility structure of the wider society to which they belong. Christian apologetics should address these social realities, for Os Guinness' perception is still true today (1983: 35):

> Even that diminishing band of Christians still concerned to defend the faith are almost totally preoccupied with credibility (an intellectual problem) and have little concern for plausibility (a problem with social dimensions as well).

Third, if there are no universal starting points for apologetic argumentation, the possibilities for apologetic witness and dialogue with a particular audience will always need to be discovered "ad hoc". Thus apologetics should inevitably be *contextual* and *person-related.*

Fourth, new perspectives for such apologetics are definitely opened by the postliberal concept of the "assimilative power" of a religious or worldview perspective. Which perspective provides the most convincing reading of the reality we encounter, of the stories of our lives and of the traditions and the stories with which we were raised and those which we live by?

The need for a properly Christian and theological analysis

In developing an apologetics non-tributary to the Enlightenment, truly Christian, and adequate to our pluralist world, we cannot and should not wish to resist these new insights. Yet, the relativism implied in much postmodern epistemology and linguistics shows that we cannot consider this position as the final word on the issue. We cannot even accept the central place given to the cultural–linguistic understanding of religion and theology. According to this approach any propositional-cognitive content of Christian faith and theology is secondary to the cultural–linguistic understanding of religion as "the medium in which one moves, a set of skills that one employs in living one's life" (Lindbeck 1984: 35). This new, yet widespread, conception of religion thrives in our postmodern and pluralist world. The Christian story indeed opens up a new universe and a new set of skills to employ in living one's life. Yet, basic to the Christian's self-understanding is the claim that this faith is an answer to Gods invitation to a new existence and Christ opening new possibilities through his resurrection and the gift of his Spirit (cf. §1.3). Therefore, as far as the Christian is concerned, a cultural linguistic analysis of out faith depends on and is subsidiary to a cognitive-propositional understanding of its central confessional affirmations.

This lack of seeing the proper character of the Christian faith as dependent on a primary action of God shows a central inconsistency in a cultural–linguistic approach to the Christian faith.[30] Lindbeck and other postmodern thinkers use tools from postmodern linguistics and cultural anthropology to defend the right to respect the particularity of any religion and worldview, and thus of the Christian religion. Yet, in the process, he forces Christian faith and theology in the *general* conception and pre-theological harness of his cultural–linguistic model,[31] failing to respect the *particularity* of the Christian faith. Sue Patterson notes perceptively: "While aiming to be particular, the postliberal model becomes a general theory which then swallows up the specific Christian instance" (1999: 44). *If we want to truly respect the particularity of the Christian faith, we should understand the nature of the Christian truth-claims, the assessment of the truth in other religions, and the possibility of a Christian apologetics in a postmodern world from a properly Christian and from a theological perspective.* "Ad hoc" we may be able to profit from postmodern linguistic and epistemological analysis, but only in a way determined by a Christian understanding of religion, the many religions, and reality. The postliberal criticism of apologetics has shown some crucial faults in modern apologetics. Yet the postliberal approach, at least in its Lindbeckian form of subsuming the Christian faith to a general theory of language and culture, is in this respect more modern than postmodern.[32]

30 Cf. for a parallel criticism Phillips & Okholm (1995: 15): "The postmodernist use of language is not a morally neutral tool that Christians can employ for their own ends, for it focuses on psychological effectiveness over against the truth." Cf. Lundin 1995: 27f.

31 Cf. Lindbeck's intention stated aim "to give a *nontheological* account of the relations of religion and religious experience" (1984: 30; italics mine); see for this observation also Patterson 1999: 34.

32 Maybe because he understood this criticism, ventured earlier by his colleague Thiemann (1986: 378), Lindbeck himself later notes the proper order when he states with regards to the change to a postliberal understanding of religion and theology: "The nontheological warrants [...] are auxiliary, rather than foundational, to the theological ones" (1996: 225). Yet, it did not bring him to the basic changes in the cultural–linguistic model, which are needed, if the proper theological content and the particular character of the Christian message are taken serious (see further §3.3).

This analysis however opens the way for a properly and particularly Christian understanding of apologetics, which is neither modern, nor postmodern. Until now most discussions of the possibility of apologetics in a postmodern and multicultural world tended to be limited to more philosophical and sociological questions, yet even postmodern epistemology itself points to the need of a properly theological analysis. To this end we will, in the next chapter, give a Christian theological evaluation of modernity, modern apologetics, and of the possibility of a truly Christian apology in a postmodern world. In the fourth chapter, we will consequently show how a theological understanding of the human being as created in the image of God provides a basis for an alternative understanding of the place of the human being in the world. This will throw an unexpected light on the questions as to how human knowledge is possible and in what ways cultural embedded-ness is essential to human nature, yet does not foreclose neither a true knowledge of God nor a richly textured cross-cultural apologetic witness and dialogue.

Chapter 3

THEOLOGICAL APPRECIATION OF MODERN WESTERN APOLOGETICS

3.1 The need for and legitimacy of a Christian theological criticism of modernity

We concluded the last chapter with the observation that postmodern criticism of modern Christian apologetics is deficient if it does not start from a properly Christian and theological understanding of what Christian apologetics should look like, but rather from a general understanding of religion, religious knowledge and religious language. Let us elaborate on this need for a properly Christian and theological understanding of apologetics.

If Christians want to commend the Gospel, their recommendation should be in accordance with its *message*. Jesus' authority was as much shown in the way he spoke as in what He said about Himself (Mt 7:29). According to Paul, the cross of Christ as the centre of his message was reflected both in the feebleness of his words and in the constitution of the Christian community (1Co 1:26-31; 2:4f). If in apologetic dialogue, someone says that Christ sets people free, but uses manipulative rhetoric to convey this message, this person is inconsistent or does not really believe his own message (cf. §1.3). If Christians believe that God is not a human projection, but a real person, who makes Himself known, they cannot talk about this religious language as if it is simply the way they prefer to organize their lives. If they believe that God revealed Himself most clearly in the history of Israel and Jesus of Nazareth, their apologetic reasoning should reflect this.[1] For example, it should contain a testimony to what has happened in history. As we will see more profoundly later, the method or way into knowledge and the method of persuasion chosen should be adequate and aligned to the reality in question (§5.2 and §5.3).

The problem of the incompatibility between the method we choose and the reality we deal with is not just relevant to apologetics and preaching, but equally to other areas of Christian life and ministry. Thus an uncritical use of management

1 This is reflected in the abundance of historical reasoning in Scripture concerning the trustworthiness of its testimony as for example in 1 Corinthians 15:1-8 (see further §5.4).

methods in the organization of the life and growth of the Church can cloud and hinder the particular character of this community. An uncritical use of counselling methods in pastoral work can cloud the view of the particular calling of a spiritual counsellor and hinder his fruitfulness.[2]

The need for a theological criticism of methods of apologetic testimony or in fact of all Christian practice does not just follow from the content of its message concerning God and salvation, but equally from its *understanding of the human being*. The God who revealed Himself to Abraham and in Jesus of Nazareth is the Creator of the universe and of all humanity. This confession is crucial to the Christian faith, yet it has some implications that are considered offensive in our pluralist society. This confession implies that Christians believe they know something about their non-Christian neighbours that they do not know themselves. They believe that it is as true for others, as it is for themselves, that all are created by this God, whether one recognizes Him or not. They believe that the deepest truth about their neighbours' lives is revealed in the Christian Scriptures.

This claim may sound most intrusive or even imperialistic in our privatized and pluralistic society: "Who are you that you claim to know me?" "Who are you that you can know the truth?" "Who are you that you think that you can judge me?" The resistance to this kind of claims, which are considered most intolerant, reveals two central inconsistencies in mainline pluralistic postmodernism. The first inconsistency is that one proposes, on the one hand, that everyone should be coherent in his views and actions to the principles of one's particular worldview. At the same time, one considers intolerant and intolerable those who believe that their particular worldview implies that they know the truth about others.

The second inconsistency in mainline postmodern pluralism is that most people continue in practice to believe explicitly or implicitly to know something about other people. Many secular people have strong opinions on the origin of illnesses. When they hear that Africans traditionally ascribe many illnesses to the influence of malcontent ancestor-spirits, they consider such beliefs superstitious.[3] Some believe for example that our illnesses (mine also and not only theirs!) have their origin "between our ears", in our mental condition. Others believe that my Christian convictions have their origin in a narrow-minded education and thus claim to know better why I believe what I believe than I do myself. Others may be more open-minded and tell me that my Christian faith may be as worthwhile as their convictions, but at the same time, they may tell me that if I really understood my convictions and myself well enough, I would hold my convictions in a

---

2 See for a study concerning the proper role of a pastor: Peterson 1989.

3 The position of so-called "Witgensteinian fideists" implies that traditional African explanations of illnesses and other phenomena are as rational as any other as long as they find there place in a coherent worldview or language game. Yet, as Placher remarks (1989: 61), "Wittgenstienian fideism is one of those odd positions which sometimes seem not to have any adherents" – or at least very few outside the artificial environment of the philosopher's study.

non-exclusive way. They believe that it is good for me to be a pluralist. Here we find one of the inner paradoxes of ideological pluralism, which can be exploited apologetically (cf. Plantinga 1995). In the same way, the limits of belief in the absolute value of tolerance can be shown from the fact that in their defence of a certain conception of cultural tolerance, people themselves end up being intolerant. Even if only on the basis of fair play, Christians should be able to explain what they believe – according to their view of God and the nature of the human being – about the origin of pluralism and unbelief.

It is true, as postmoderns like to stress, that people behave mostly in accordance with what they believe themselves to be true. Yet our actions, reactions and beliefs are also influenced by some reality underlying our beliefs about ourselves, which may be completely hidden to us. The whole psychotherapeutic practice of helping people understand themselves is based on the idea that there is more to our identity than we are conscious of. Doctors, psychologists and sociologists all suppose that people who do not share their diagnostic ability, and maybe not even their convictions about the nature of the human condition and constitution, act in ways driven by unconscious psychological and social factors. They believe that these factors can be used, reoriented or made ineffective when made conscious. As a Christian and theologian, I would like to claim the same for the Christian perspective on the human being. I can place this perspective alongside others, sometimes as a complementary perspective, sometimes as a contradictory and alternative one.

This also implies that the way Christians testify and acclaim the Gospel in the world should be in accordance with what we believe to be the truth about the people we meet. This demands a Christian theological criticism of the method of apologetic testimony to the truth of the Gospel. If Christians believe that all human beings are sinners and therefore have clouded perceptions and minds, they should take this seriously in their apologetic approach. If they believe that they are at the same time reasonable and responsible as created in the image of their Creator, they cannot treat them as if they are only driven by irrational forces.

In the following chapters, we will develop an understanding of apologetics which coheres with both the nature of the human being (Chapter 4) and with the nature of its message (Chapter 5). In order to clear the ground for such a positive development of a truly Christian apologetics, we will, in this chapter, attempt a critical evaluation of modern Western culture and modern Christian apologetics from a properly Christian standpoint. In the process new light will also be shed on the force and limitations of postmodernism and the postmodern appreciation of modern Christian apologetics.

As our main guide towards this theological appreciation of modernity and modern apologetics, we will use the work of Karl Barth. Beginning in the 1920s this Reformed Swiss launched a criticism of the liberal theology and apologetics of his day that provoked a major shift in the theological scene. As the postmoderns would do later, Barth stressed the particularity of the Christian faith, which should start from the revelation of God in Jesus of Nazareth and not from general moral, religious or rational principles that human beings as such could share. In many of his remarks he sounds like a postmodernist before his time. Yet, unlike the general epistemological and linguistic considerations of the postmodern theologians that we considered in the last chapter, Barth's criticism of the Enlightenment-type apologetics is fundamentally theological in nature. His criticism springs from his understanding of Jesus Christ, of God and of human nature as seen from a Christian perspective.

We will first turn to a theological analysis of modernism at large. We will see how the epistemological shift to modernism and the corresponding challenge to the Christian faith flow from a changing self-understanding of the freedom and autonomy of the human being. When we look from that perspective to postmodernity, we discover that postmodernity, in most of its expressions, is not a sufficiently radical departure from the fundamental starting point of modernity (§3.2). Next, we will turn to modern apologetics and discover that the problems of modernist Christian apologetics are not only epistemological and linguistic in nature, but also and more fundamentally theological in that they do not do justice to the character of God's revelation in Christ (§3.3). In a separate section we will turn to the modern schism between the knowing subject and the object-world, from which most forms of postmodernism also do not liberate themselves. This will also give occasion for a few more critical remarks concerning Barth's criticism of modern apologetics (§3.4).

3.2 The anthropological root of the modern and postmodern mindsets

Epistemology and anthropology and the origin of modernity

In formulating an apologetic answer to the Enlightenment challenge, often all attention is drawn to epistemological questions. Both its defenders and its critics consider the Enlightenment essentially as a departure from pre-modern thought in terms of its epistemology and they see all changes as flowing from there. The Enlightenment is seen as a victory of reason over faith and as a movement closely related to the development of modern science. It is from this point that a worldview is developed in which there is less and less room for God, until He becomes a "superfluous hypothesis". Reason becomes the highest authority and will only make room for faith as long as faith submits to her sovereign reign.

Through trial and error, apologists have realized that the place which science concedes to God and the room that reason leaves for faith is not acceptable. They have discovered the hard way that accepting this rationalist and scientist starting-point leads to a gradual retreat of God, until He almost disappears. The process ends with an adaptation of faith to the whims of a non-Christianized reason. It is a better apologetic strategy to show the limitations of scientific reasoning and to show that reason itself cannot do without faith as its starting-point, companion and fulfilment.[4]

This analysis is valid and this apologetic response is necessary, yet it remains weak and superficial if it does not lay bare the fact that modernity is not in the first place an epistemological movement. From a theological perspective, Karl Barth saw an anthropological change as the origin and as the underlying force of the epistemological changes characteristic of modernity. Using postmodern language, we can say that as a Christian, he re-reads the history of modernity in the light of the master- or metanarrative in Scripture. This masternarrative from Genesis through Jesus to Revelations shows that humanity's deepest problem is not his epistemological predicament. It is rather his will, his sinful resistance against God. Barth interprets the inner drive of modernity accordingly (*KD* IV/1: 532; trans. *CD* IV/1: 479):

> The theology of the Enlightenment did not begin, as it is often shown to begin, with a criticism of trinitarian and christological teaching, or of the miracles of the Bible, or of the biblical picture of the world, or of the supernaturalism of the redeeming event attested in the Bible. Its starting-point was [...] a readoption of the humanist [...] rejection of what were supposed to be the too stringent assertions of the Reformers concerning the fall of man [...]. Originally and properly enlightenment means the enlightenment that things are not quite so bad with man himself. But if we cannot, and will not, see and understand in this respect, we will necessarily be blind in other respects.[5]

If this analysis of modernity is true, a concentration on the modern epistemological challenges to the faith will therefore, according to Barth, miss the real issue and be neither adequate nor convincing. The sinful rejection of God, rising from the human will, covers itself in the more respectable garment of philosophical and scientific criticism of belief in God (Barth 1947: 87; trans. 1972: 108). Rather than taking this criticism seriously and thus leaving the defence intact, an appropriate and effective response demands that the disguise rather be exposed for what it is: a way to hide a much less respectful opposition. This means that we need to be suspicious of too great a stress on epistemological

4 Stephen Williams (1995: 1–23) traces how this version of the story of modernity has been told by Lesslie Newbigin and Colin Gunton. For my retelling of the story of modernity from an anthropological perspective this study of Williams has, next to the theology of Barth, been an important source. For a shorter version of the argument, see: Williams 1994.

5 Barth considers the theology of Schleiermacher as a main exponent of this tendency (*KD* IV/1: 415–517; trans. *CD* IV/1: 376f).

questions in apologetic dialogue. Elaborate discussions about the epistemological problems in knowing God can be a way of avoiding another issue, the need to recognize our unwillingness to accept this God (Barth *KD* IV/1: 315–323; trans. *CD* IV/1: 286–294).

Barth's analysis of the driving force behind modernity springs from his theological understanding of the human being. However, both studies in cultural anthropology and in the history of ideas have confirmed the fact that self-perception and ideas concerning the way people form their beliefs mutually influence each other. A change at one end will sooner or later have consequences at the other. With respect to modernity, Charles Taylor shows that we can only understand modern *epistemology* if we understand the specific character of modern *identity*, which feels so natural to us that it mostly remains unconscious (Taylor 1989: ix, 111f).

Developments in the history of ideas are, however, incredibly complex and multilayered. Judging the inner motivations of great thinkers easily becomes an academic variety of calling names, particularly when one starts reading into a text what the author does not express himself. We can do no more here than point to some significant aspects of the historical development of modernity that show that the changing perception of human identity has been at least a major force behind the growth of modern epistemology. This interpretation of history is also confirmed by other "stories" like the way psychology has uncovered the relation between human willing and human reasoning and supremely by the way the human condition is revealed by the way humans reacted to Jesus.

The historical background of the development of the modern subject

The roots of modernity can be traced back to classical Greek philosophy and the origin of Christianity. Without these twin roots both modern anthropology and the modern understanding of reason are inexplicable. Yet, in the early Church and in the Middle Ages, the classical philosophical texts and ideas were transmitted and reinterpreted in the context of a Christian worldview. This tradition was classically formulated by Augustine of Hippo (354–430) and developed in the Western Church, in which this synthesis remained dominant until the end of the Middle Ages.

Accepting the risk of simplification, we can summarize the anthropological and epistemological core ideas of this "Augustinian synthesis" as follows. Human nature and all creation are seen as utterly dependent on God and created to find their fulfilment in God, by who and unto whom they were created (Augustine, *Confessiones*: I, I, 1):

> Thou hast prompted him, that he should delight to praise thee, for thou hast made us for [or "unto", BvdT] thyself and restless is our heart until it comes to rest in thee.

In a parallel way, reason is considered to be dependent on faith and to find its fulfilment in faith. This is expressed in the Augustinian adage: *credo, ut intelligam* – I believe in order that I may understand – as classically formulated by Augustine's famous eleventh-century disciple, Anselm of Canterbury (1033–1109) (*Proslogion*: X, 7).

A major alternative for this synthesis developed from the Italian Renaissance onwards. The Renaissance is generally described as a cultural movement, which puts the human being at the centre of attention (Barth *KD* I/2: 367; trans. *CD* I/2: 335; 1947: 56; trans. 1972: 76). Most Renaissance thinkers were Christians, and when they adapted the traditional Christian faith to make it fit more easily with their new worldview the adaptations were more anthropologically, than epistemologically, motivated. This is particularly clear from the new interpretation of the creation of Adam as we find it in Genesis 2 by Pico della Mirandola (1463–1494), which does not centre on the problems historical science would ask later, but gives a reinterpretation more suitable to the new image of what it means to be human. According to Pico the human being was created with the following admonition by his Creator (1946 [1486]: 3, 224f):

> Neither a fixed abode nor a form that is thine alone not any function peculiar to thyself have we given thee, Adam, to the end that according to thy longing and according to thy judgement thou mayest have and possess what abode, what form and what functions thyself shalt desire. The nature of all other beings is limited and constrained within the bounds of law prescribed by Us. Thou, constrained by no limits, in accordance with thine own free will, in whose hand We have placed thee, shalt ordain for thyself the limits of thy nature.

In the Scholastic Theology of the same period one finds parallel developments, which again are also predominantly anthropological in character. Neo-Thomism is seeing the day in the writings of Francis Suárez (1548–1617) and Thomas de Vio Cajetan (1468–1534). Instead of considering the human being as entirely dependent on and oriented towards the Creator, the neo-thomists start distinguishing between a natural part and a supernatural part of the human constitution. The natural part finds its fulfilment in what lies within the reach of the natural capacities of the human being. The supernatural supplement finds its fulfilment in relation to God who reveals Himself graciously in Christ. Sin is considered to have destroyed the supernatural segment of human nature, but is thought not to touch profoundly the natural capacities of humankind, like natural reason. In that area, the human being could start to take care of himself and does not depend on special grace. Parallel to these new anthropological formulations, an epistemological distinction is made between a natural knowledge of the world and of God that lies within the scope of reason alone and a supernatural knowledge of God that is known through faith in the supernatural revelation of God in the Scriptures.[6]

This new neo-thomist conception of the human being seems to be fruitful for a long time, because it leaves room for the development of secular life, while continuing to give a place for faith. The Christian faith can have some value, particularly because it helps in our relationship with God as an extra added to the natural life, and it opens the way to heaven as an extra after the natural life. Yet, the history of the following centuries can be described as a constant retreat of the faith and the Church, during which the natural order took more and more domains of life and society under its jurisdiction. The Christian faith is increasingly pushed towards the margins of life in birth and death until it becomes an optional extra, which many people feel that they can just as well do without.

Against the background of the modernization of Roman Catholic theology in the wake of the Renaissance, an unexpected light is thrown on the Protestant Reformation of the sixteenth century. With respect to its anthropology, it is not a renewal movement, but a return to the classical Augustinian conception of the human being from the Church Fathers and the Scholastics of the High Middle Ages.[7] Thus the *Shorter Westminster Catechism* opens by asking, "What is the chief end of man" and answers, "To glorify God and to enjoy him forever" (Schaff 1919: 676). In centring all on God, they deny implicitly that there is a natural goal of the human being that could be conceived of apart from the knowledge of God in Christ.

The flight from authority and the desire to master nature

The changing conception of human nature at the basis of the epistemological changes relating to modernity is equally visible in some of the main voices of modernity. From its conception onwards modernity can be characterized as "the turn to the subject", as "emancipation" ("*Mündigkeit*", Kant 1783) as a "flight from authority" (Stout 1981) and as "the will to master nature" (Blumenberg 1966; trans. 1983). Of course, people have always looked at nature and perceived its regularities. Why is it that empirical and technical knowledge became so dominant in modernity? Both in antiquity and in the Middle Ages knowing the truth was considered something valuable in itself. From the early stages of

---

6 These theological developments have been traced particularly by Henri de Lubac and other representatives of the Roman Catholic "nouvelle théologie". See particularly: de Lubac 1991.

7 It is interesting that this has been noted by the Roman Catholic theologian J.H. Walgrave from Louvain (n.d. [1966]: 148–158).

modernity onwards the wish to master nature became dominant and therefore the empirical and technical knowledge that would "make ourselves, as it were, the masters and possessors of nature" (Descartes, *Le Discours de la Méthode*: VI) became increasingly important. As we will see later (§4.2), the idea that the human being was created to dominate over nature certainly had its Christian roots. It became, however, radicalized and corrupted, when it was not sufficiently recognized that humankind was at the same time part of the created order and when furthermore the idea of caring stewardship, under the Creator, was denied or emptied of its original meaning.

It was René Descartes who made a very significant step in the so-called "turn to the subject". Looking for absolutely certain knowledge, Descartes set out to doubt everything that he thought could be doubted. After doubting all knowledge received by tradition, all convictions obtained through perception of the external world also fell under the verdict of doubt. As it is always possible that our senses deceive us, Descartes felt it is safer and compulsory to doubt them. Finally, the thinking subject withdraws into itself, because according to Descartes it can be certain at least about its own doubt and thus about its own existence. This is where the famous "*cogito, ergo sum*" – I think and therefore I am – is found. From there, Descartes gives an argument for the existence of a good God. It is because of this God, who cannot deceive, that the senses, if properly used, are to be trusted. God is the guarantor of the relationship between the thinking subject and the external world, as object of its knowledge. From here on all knowledge had to be re-constructed, but now starting from the self-conscious subject, who would accept no knowledge he himself[8] could not master (*Meditationes de prima philosophia*: I–II).[9] Charles Taylor notes that this turn to the subject was significantly different from the turn to the interior that Augustine made more than a millennium earlier. On Augustine's way inward he discovered his own insufficiency and his need for God. Descartes' way inward is a way to a self-sufficient certainty, after which God is only needed as the guarantee that we are not tricked by some bad spirit and can trust all that comes "clear and distinct" to the human mind (Taylor 1989: 156f).

The same anthropological root emerges in Kant's famous essay on the question "What is Enlightenment", in which the central trust of the Enlightenment is not seen as an epistemological programme but as the "emancipation of man from his tutelage which he owed to himself" (1783: 516). It is because the modern subject wants to be free from all these authorities that are his resented masters that he

8 In this text the masculine form of the personal pronoun is often used in an inclusive way for both the masculine and the feminine human being. Here it is properly masculine as feminist thinkers have noted that the Enlightenment subject that stands over against the world that it tries to master has particularly male characteristics.

9 See concerning the influence of the development of "ontological cleft" between the soul and the material world according to Descartes on "the making of modern identity": Taylor 1989: 145.

needs to enlighten his mind in order that he himself can distinguish truth from falsity without any recourse to the traditional authorities.

Systematic reflection shows *why* the desire for freedom and emancipation needed in the end produce a new epistemology. If you want to be independent from any external authorities, you need to be able to gain knowledge and develop your understanding of the world, independent from such authorities. This means that you need to arrive at knowledge independent from any primary confidence in the authority of the particular community in which you have been born. You can no longer start from the premises of the Catholic, Lutheran, Reformed, Anabaptist, Jewish or any other particular tradition or community. You therefore need to be able to access truth as an individual, and for truth to be so accessible it needs to be accessible universally to all sane human beings. Here we see how the universalist foundationalist epistemology of the Enlightenment follows naturally from the desire for autonomy, emancipation and taking leave of traditional authorities. Note again how individualism and universalism are closely related (cf. §2.3).

The modern attack on God

The anthropological root of the Enlightenment's problems with Christian faith also shows itself in its strongest anti-Christian expressions. Although there has been a constant attack on the Christian faith in the name of science and reason, the most violent and passionate criticisms have been formulated in the name of human autonomy and freedom. This is clear in the work of the three greatest critics of the Christian faith of modernity: Nietzsche, Marx and Freud.[10]

In this respect a closer look to Nietzsche's atheism is particularly revealing. Nietzsche has rightly been called "the patron saint of postmodern philosophy" for his attack on the Enlightenment conceptions of truth, language and knowledge (Grenz 1996: 88). Yet, interestingly enough he does not consider himself a critic of the Renaissance quest for freedom, in which so many see important roots of modernity. His atheism, again, is not primarily fuelled by his epistemology, but by his ideal for the human being, most clearly formulated as "the will for power" ("*Der Wille zur Macht*"). In the purposely blasphemous formulations of his "Antichrist" he scolds Christianity for its "slave morality". It suppresses the human will for power, protects the weak and teaches the strong docility and self-restraint (Nietzsche 1894). It is precisely in the name of freedom, autonomy, and the flight from all alien authorities, that Nietzsche's attack does not stop at Christianity, the authority of tradition, and the idea of a God, but goes on to the modern concepts of truth and knowledge and modern

10 See for a general overview of the criticism of Christianity by these three thinkers: Avis 1995; Küng 1978; trans. 1981.

metaphysics. If there is one universal truth, discovered by a universal reason that all human beings share and if there is one universal moral standard of good and bad, we are not really free. After the liberation from religion and other traditional authorities through reason, reason itself becomes the new master dictating what we should do. It is therefore the desire for a still more radical freedom and autonomy, for a more radical self-mastery and mastery of the world that makes Nietzsche take leave of the Enlightenment concepts of truth, knowledge and the good.[11]

Postmodernism and the modern strife for freedom and autonomy

Not only is uncovering the anthropological root of the Enlightenment epistemology revealing for understanding modernity, but also it is equally revealing for understanding postmodernity. The same radicalization of the Enlightenment ideal of autonomic self-determination can be seen in Michel Foucault, who has been called the main follower and interpreter of Nietzsche among the postmodern philosophers. Foucault has rightly shown how many claims to truth form a disguised exercise of power and how the powers that be always try to legitimize themselves by a claim to truth (see p. 14, n. 19). A central motivation for his rejection of all claims to truth as disguised instruments of power is his concern for all those that are oppressed by these truths. Reading his work taught me that in our theological and ethical reasoning, we should always double-check the question "Who might be the silent victims of the position I defend?" His attack on truth and morality seems, however, equally fuelled by a revolt against *all* set order. In the end, this destroys the structures that are needed for life to flourish. This generalized revolt became visible in his description of the history of sexuality and in his own sexual life, where he lived his homosexuality to the brink of the possible and experimented in the Californian SM-scene. In 1984, this made him one of the first well-known AIDS victims (Grenz 1996: 123, 125f).

Some of the clearest expressions of postmodernity as a radicalized search for autonomy and freedom are not found in philosophical writings but rather in popular postmodern culture. In many circles – inside and outside the Church[12] – strong resistance against any claims to universal truth and universally binding

---

11 See particularly Nietzsche 1886, and the wider analysis in Williams (1995: 83–112); Barth saw already that Nietzsche was not so much a departure from the Enlightenment, but more its consequence and radicalization (Barth *KD* III/2: 286ff; trans. *CD* III/2: 240ff).

12 A Christian theological expression of this mood can be found in Cupitt (1982: 10). See for an analysis of this position which balances between modernism and postmodernism: Williams 1995: 113–142.

moral standards is also driven by the fact that they are considered restrictive. People feel that this type of claims is an insult or an attack on their own sphere, on their freedom, on their right to decide themselves what they want to be good, and how they want to organize their lives. A return to tradition is a return to authority and a self-limitation of freedom. Even if there is a return to tradition, it is therefore mostly a return to traditions in the plural, from which people eclectically collect and tinker their own worldview according to their own liking. The postmodern belief that the world is not something that people find out there, but something that they create, is of course an expression of human autonomy to the utmost (cf. MacIntyre 1985: 259; Storkey 1994: 144; Edgar 1995: 378). It is developed in the extreme when it is suggested that each individual should create his own life and life-world, and that it can even be collected from many incoherent fragments. The loneliness in a world that I share only with myself is the inevitable consequence.

It is possible to respond that this is too radical a picture of our world. People still tend to reckon with the world out there, still keep to some general moral principles and still are not so individualized that they do not share the mass of their ideas and ideals with the majority of the people that surround them. However, this can also be understood as an indication that postmodern individualism, postmodern creationism and postmodern eclecticism are unrealistic creations of the mind. Yet, when postmodern people argue for their positions, their choices and their attitude towards Christianity and other worldviews, they often employ this language of radicalized freedom. This language needs be exposed and responded to, if a Christian apology is going to have any chance in a postmodern context.

3.3 Enlightenment apologetics and Gods revelation in Jesus Christ

The particularity and sovereignty of God's revelation in Christ

Just as modernity at large, the modern apologetic method should be critically appreciated from a theological angle. We indicated already that theological arguments were central in Karl Barth's criticism of apologetics, particularly the apologetics of nineteenth century liberal theology, to which he directed most of his attention. This theology wanted to be acceptable to a culture shaped by Enlightenment ideals, ideals that felt so natural and true to these theologians that most of the time they did not see either the need or the possibility to question them. Their theology was fundamentally apologetic theology in the sense that they tried to justify their Christian theology on the basis of a general conception of knowledge and science (Barth 1957a: 9ff).[13] Barth discovers that basic Christian convictions imply that this apologetic method is deeply compromised. From the 1920s onwards, Barth's theological arguments have decisively influenced theological reflection on apologetics, mostly in continental Europe. These theological reflections are still crucial for us if we want to arrive at a properly Christian evaluation of modern apologetics.

Barth consciously starts his theological reflection on the method and the possibility of human knowledge of God, with the revelation of God in Christ and the Scriptures. If we want to know *how* God makes Himself known, we should start from the recognition of the *fact* that He makes Himself known.[14] The Christian Scriptures are ordered around the discovery that God, the Creator of the universe, revealed Himself supremely in Jesus Christ (Heb 1:1f). And according to Scripture, the Church is called to witness to what God has done in Christ, particularly in his death and resurrection, so that the entire world might know the love of God (Mt 28:18–29; Jn 20:21). It is therefore starting from the witness of the Church to the person and history of Christ that we should reflect about the way God is known. Christians confess God to be free and sovereign, and it is therefore He who decides how He wants to be known. A direct consequence is that a Christian reflection on the knowledge of God cannot start from general principles and general observations concerning the human being, the universe and divine nature. This would be the procedure a universalist foundationalist epistemology would consider the only possible starting point for apologetics. Yet, the logic of the Scriptures is that the methodological reflection on the knowledge of God and concerning the possibility and character of Christian apologetics can only be done *after* hearing what God has to say and reveals Himself to be.[15]

Modern critics of the Christian faith would say, that starting from what we as Christians know about God through Christ and the Scriptures is circular reasoning and starts from a theological prejudice for Christianity. It renders an open evaluation of the Christian truth-claims impossible. The criticism runs like this: if in determining the way or method God is known we already start from the knowledge of God in Christ, we already presuppose what we apologetically hope to conclude and this first presupposition remains without basis and unjustified.

13 On Schleiermacher as the primary example of this procedure, see: Barth 1947: 392ff; trans. 1972: 392ff.

14 This becomes clear from the flow of his argument starting from the *reality* of the knowledge of God in Christ and from there analysing its *possibility* (*KD* II/1: 1–200, particularly 67–70; trans. *CD* II/1: 3–178, 63–65).

15 The question of the right order is crucial in Barth's methodological reflections, what comes first and what "nachträglich" or "subsequently". See, for example, his reflections on apologetics in: *KD* II/1: 6, 184; trans. *CD* II/1: 8, cf. 164; and on the knowledge of sin: *KD* IV/1: 395f; trans. *CD* IV/1: 358f, 390f. However, the importance of the methodological order is sometimes lost in the English translation of the German original.

Though this criticism has a strong initial ring of truth, it is not valid for the following reasons. First of all, to ask *how* God is known, *if* the claim is true that He makes Himself known foremost in Jesus Christ, does not presuppose that this claim is in fact justified. Let us consider an analogy. If a group of physicists claims that they have discovered a new sub-atomic particle, we need to ask how they came to discover this particle and what makes them believe that such a particle exists. Taking the particular way of discovery into account in our evaluation of the case for its existence does not presuppose that their conclusions are right. Second, as we shall see later, recent reflection on scientific method and discovery has shown that it is not so much *a priori* methodological reflection, apart from actual empirical research, that leads to new discoveries. It is, rather, new (and sometimes even unexpected and unintended) discoveries that lead to fresh methodological insights in the way we discover what reality is like (§5.3). In the same way, the actual encounter with God in Christ leads to a wholly knew understanding of how God makes Himself known and how He can be known.

It is in fact the alternative approach, starting from general methodological principles about the way to knowledge, that is the prejudiced and biased one.[16] How can we know beforehand how God can be known and thus how God-talk should be judged and justified? Epistemologically, this means that we use the limits of our human minds (or worse, the limitations of the presuppositions of our own culture) to put limits on reality. Theologically, it counts as pride or even megalomania to suppose that, from our own resources, we can decide how God can make Himself known and how He can be known. Claiming that because of being God, God cannot act to reveal Himself, or can at least not reveal Himself in a particular place in history, presupposes a quite detailed and firm knowledge of God. How can one be so sure about what God can do to justify not being open to the possibility of surprises?

Barth is thus one of the many theologians in the Christian tradition who dealt with the problem of "reason and belief" or "faith and reason". In accordance with a common and valid line of apologetic argumentation, he explains that human reason has its limits and should leave a place for faith and revelation. Yet, Barth digs deeper than most apologists in not limiting himself to an epistemological analysis of the nature and possibility of reason and reasoning, but in relating this question to the nature of God and the existence of the human being for God. Against the Enlightenment fight for the freedom of the human being, he biblically

16 This approach is characteristic for the epistemology of Immanuel Kant, with his transcendental analysis of the possibilities and limitations of the knowing human subject (1781), which has dominated most modern epistemology. In line with this approach liberal German theologians made an effort to incorporate theology in a general theory of the sciences. See for Barth's theological criticism of this characteristic of Schleiermacher's theology: Barth 1947: 392ff; trans. 1972: 439ff; cf. *KD* I/1: 8f, 35f; trans. *CD* I/1:10, 36f.

stresses the freedom and sovereignty of God,[17] which is revealed to be the only solid and valid basis for real human freedom (Jn 8:36). If we believe in the freedom and sovereignty of God, we should respect that He Himself determines how He makes Himself known. "Revelation is Gods sovereign action upon man or it is not revelation" (*KD* I/2: 322; trans. *CD* I/2: 295).[18] If God chose to reveal Himself in the history of Israel, in the Scriptures, and in Christ who is the centre of everything, our understanding of the possibility of knowing God and of how we know God should start from there. If this revelation of God is witnessed to by the Church, all theology, all scientifically justified knowledge of God, should start from the way God is known there (*KD* 1/1: 1–3; trans. *CD* I/1, 3–5).[19] Therefore, dogmatics as "Church dogmatics" is not in any way provincial or biased, but the only proper way of doing theology and apologetics. It is the way that God Himself invites us to follow. Barth does, to the contrary, criticize modern apologetics for not respecting God's freedom and sovereignty.

Sinful resistance

Barth resisted the modern idea of looking for a universally accessible starting point for human reasoning and apologetic argumentation not only because of the biblical understanding of revelation in Christ, but equally because of his understanding of the human being. Human beings are sinners and as sinners they are enemies of God. Therefore, they are never neutral towards the Gospel, but biased against its message.[20]

The role of this sinful bias in Barth's criticism of modern apologetics is particularly clear in his discussion of "natural theology". For Enlightenment theology this was an important concept and an expression of its search for a universal foundation for theology. "Natural theology" referred to that knowledge of God that the human being could acquire with the aid of his natural capacities alone and with what nature reveals. Natural theology can thus be formulated without the aid of special grace and special revelation. Barth's stress on the sovereignty and particularity of God's revelation implies that he considers it impossible to arrive through such a procedure at a valid knowledge of the God of the Scriptures.

17 See the concentration of Barth's doctrine of God starting from "The Being of God as the One Who Loves in Freedom": *KD* II/1, 288ff; trans. *CD* II/1: 268ff. Barth transposes in fact the modern stress on the freedom and autonomy of the human subject to the freedom and sovereignty of God (cf. Macken 1990; Rendtorff 1986).

18 Cf. also the idea that "natural theology" is an attack on the "unique sovereignty of Jesus Christ" (*KD* II/1: 183; trans. *CD* II/1: 163).

19 This structural moment in Barth's theology has been called his "particularism", as the knowledge of God does not start from what is universally known, but from the particular (Hunsinger 1991: 32–35).

20 Hunsinger names this "personalism" as a structural motif of Barth's theology (1991: 40–42).

Natural theology is therefore apologetically useless. What is more, the quest for a natural theology itself is an expression of a sinful desire to master God and a way to avoid submitting to His sovereignty and His revelation in Christ, for natural theology according to Barth (*KD* II/1: 93; trans. *CD* II/1: 85) is:

> a theology which makes a great show of guaranteeing the knowability of God apart from grace and therefore from faith, or which thinks and promises that it is able to give such a guarantee.[21]

With this attention for the sinful human bias against the message of the Gospel, Barth points to what is elsewhere known as "the noetic influence of sin", the influence of sin on our minds. The prophet Jeremiah was warned by God that the people of Israel would not be prepared to hear his message because of the stubbornness of their hearts (Jer 9:26; 16:12; Eze 36:26). In the Gospels, we see how people were willing to accept Jesus as long as He fit their own expectations, but rejected Him when they considered his words too hard (Jn 6:60).[22] The "evidence" for his being sent by God did not diminish, but his message and personality became less attractive or even repulsive with respect to their interests and perceived needs. In a crucial passage Paul states that what humans might know about God from creation is suppressed "by their wickedness" (Ro 1:18; cf. Col 1:21). Human beings as sinners just do not want to know God.

Suppressing truth is, of course, a human phenomenon with which we are all familiar. It is much easier to convince someone that he has won a prize than that he should pay a fine. The truth that smoking is bad is harder for smokers or for those who have a huge interest in the tobacco industry to accept. The debate about climate changes due to the extravagant use of fossil fuels is seriously clouded because of the enormous economic stakes. An alcoholic may at a clear moment understand the nature of his addiction, but his perception on this point is clouded as soon as he has taken a first drink – even before alcohol obscures the rest of his mind.

It is important to note that in pointing out sinful biases against the Gospel, Barth is not talking about a "mere" psychological reality but about the characteristics of human nature fallen to sin. These characteristics may show themselves openly, but they also hide themselves under a more respectable cover. We can distinguish four different origins of such sinful biases against acceptance of the Gospel.

First of all, the Gospel exposes perversion, guilt and wrong-headedness. This is a message people would like to avoid, or at least to soften as much as they can. Even more, this message tells us that on the most fundamental level human beings cannot help themselves. We must depend on God to save us from our ignorance, from our sinful bias and from our depravity. Most of us are more into self-help

---

21 This is related to what Hunsinger (1991) calls the "personalism" of Barth's theology.

22 Cf. 1Co 1:23; 1Pe 2:7f; McCracken 1994.

programmes than grace. Grace clashes with our self-image and our pride. The idea that someone needed to die for us on a cross is particularly repulsive, not so much the idea of the need for someone to die in that way for some ideal, but that he needed to die for us.[23] Barth perceptively notes that not only is our pride an obstacle in accepting the content of this message of grace, but also it is equally an obstacle to accepting the way in which this message is given. We would prefer to glory in discovering a truth by using our rational ability or deep religious insight, so that we could boast about the discovery. This is why apologists who appeal to these faculties receive an easier hearing. In line with this observation, Barth calls natural theology, the idea that human beings can know God through their own capacities, "intellectual work-righteousness" as it is the rejection of living by grace and through faith alone in the epistemological domain (1934: 38; trans. 1946: 102).[24]

Second, the human wish for autonomy to determine one's own life is in conflict with the biblical conception that God is our lawgiver and that He knows what is good for us – as becomes explicit in the work of maybe the most ardent modern critic of Christianity, Nietzsche (f. ex.: Nietzsche 1883–1884; cf. Williams 1995: 83–112). Particularly, the idea that we will be judged by God during our lives on earth and at the end of time does not automatically sound attractive to modern human beings, who glory in their emancipation from all traditional authorities. From a biblical perspective, this is not just a problem of modern times; it is also an expression of the more common quest for misconceived autonomy that Genesis 3 shows to be at the origin of human beings taking leave of God.[25]

To arrive at a balanced view, we should notice, third, that a bias against the Gospel comes not only from pride, but also from self-abasement. Liberation theologians have noted that the slavish acceptance of both the social and spiritual situation in which people find themselves can come from a sinful lack of courage to change their situation. Before the development of Liberation Theology, Karl Barth saw pride as the form of sin exposed by Christ's humility, but he also saw resignation as a basic sin exposed by Christ's kingship (*KD* IV/1: 395; IV/2: 423; trans. *CD* IV/1: 358; IV/2: 378). Sometimes remaining in sin and depravity can seem more comfortable than the challenge and insecurity of opening oneself to entirely new possibilities. This made the people of Israel regularly long to go back to Egypt. They were slaves there, but at least they knew what they had and their confidence in a God constantly leading them forwards was not yet stretched to the utmost (Ex 14:11; 16:3; 17:3). Paul equally needs to challenge the Roman

23 Thus in 1Co1:18ff the cross of Christ is considered foolishness particularly because of human pride. Cf. Barth, *KD* II/1: 158; trans. *CD* II/1, 142.

24 See also Barth's appreciation of religion as "human efforts at justification and sanctification" or "Werkgerechtigkeit" (*KD* I/2: 335–343; trans *CD* I/2: 307–314).

25 See for a careful theological exegesis: Blocher 1984: 121–133. Blocher also quotes Calvin, Barth, Roland de Vaux and Paul Ricoeur as in favour of this interpretation.

Christians not to accept slavery to sin as an unavoidable reality, but to live in their freedom from sin received through the death and resurrection of Christ (Ro 6:1–14).

Fourth, the claims of Jesus and the Gospel will always meet the resistance of the powerful in the society whose authority is questioned by the message. Jesus' new interpretation of the Judaic heritage met with resistance from the religious authorities. The authority, power and status of the Pharisees was based on their claim to be the legitimate interpreters of the law, while the authority of the Sadducees and the priestly establishment was based on their claim to be the legitimate cultic mediators between God and his people. Jesus of course went even further in that He resisted all human attempts to enlarge one's own status by striving to exercise power over others (Mk 10:45; Jn 13:14).

Some clarifications are needed in order to understand the nature and scope of these sinful biases against the Gospel. It is *not only* non-Christians who are influenced by them. They are even clearer within the Church itself where they remain influential in spite of the proclamation of the Gospel. Barth has rightly shown this in his analysis of the history of theology and particularly of its modern history. This history can be described as a continuing tension between the radical message of the Gospel and a tendency to soften its message concerning the depravity of the human being and the utter dependence on grace.[26] He calls this the "assimilation" and "domestication" of the Gospel (*KD* II/1: 155–158, 183; trans. *CD* II/1: 140–142, 163f) and nowadays we might compare it with the pressure for "political correctness" in the proclamation of the Gospel. In reality, however, the Gospel simply isn't "bourgeois"[27] or politically correct according to the biased standards of our society. Such a "politically correct" or "bourgeois" understanding of the Gospel actually greatly weakens its power, for the power of the Gospel is the foolishness of Christ crucified (1Co 1:23).

In this process of "domestication" and of formulating a politically correct Gospel, there is not only a constant seduction to adapt the content of the Gospel, but equally to adapt our conception of the way it is known. In the Age of Reason, there was a constant pressure to water the Gospel down to make it look favourable according to the demands of modern rationality. In the New Age, Christians are tempted to say that the deepest truths of the Gospel can be known through mystical introspection. In a pluralistic world, they feel the pressure to conform to the general conviction that Christians believe the Gospel only because their particular tradition tells them so, while others should keep to their particular cultural and religious traditions. However, because conceptions of what we know

26 This is not only clear from his historical works as his *Protestant Thought*, but also from the many historical overviews in small print in the *Dogmatics*.

27 Barth speaks about the "Verbürgerlichung" or "becoming bourgeois" of the Gospel, which is closer to the idea of political correctness, but vaguely translated as "making the Gospel respectable" (*KD* II/1: 155–158; trans. *CD* II/1: 140–142).

and how we know are always intricately related, submitting to the epistemology of the surrounding culture always leads to compromising what Christians believe.

A further clarification of particular interest to the apologist is that both the Christian and the non-Christian are *not only* driven by these sinful biases. All human beings are also driven by other desires and needs that positively predispose them towards the Gospel – such as their basic need for meaning, for direction, for God, for freedom, for truth and for salvation. Because of personal, cultural and inherited sinful biases these needs may be suppressed or misdirected in search of surrogates, but they show a need for God and the Gospel that is even more fundamental than the sinful resistance. This tension in the human being shows that the apologist is not without allies when confronting the sinful biases against the Gospel. There are also forces drawing people to God, and the tension between opposing forces shows the need that some of these forces be redirected (see further §8.1). Apologists are not powerless against these biases, strong as they may be, not only because human beings are created with a need for God, but also, and even more so, because of the Holy Spirit. The Spirit convicts the world of its rejection of Christ by overcoming the powerful sinful biases against the crucified Messiah (Jn 16:8f; cf. Barth, *KD* I/2: 264–304; trans. *CD* I/2: 242–279).

Creation of idols

Barth's theological reservations with apologetics based on "natural theology" are not only because of their lack of recognition of the obstacle of sinful human will, but equally with the ideas, which are the *result* of efforts to arrive at a natural knowledge of God. John Calvin had already stated that the human mind separate from God is "a perpetual forge of idols" (*Institutio Christianae Religionis* [1559]: I, XI, §8; cf. I, IV, §§1–3). Barth claims that the ideas concerning God that spring from human attempts to know Him are not, in fact, saying anything about the real God, but only concern idols. These imaginary gods are only human constructs and should therefore be rejected (*KD* I/2: 329ff; trans. *CD* I/2: 302ff). For many postmodern theologians, the idea that certain ideas about God are no more than human constructs is not particularly dismissive and disconcerting. For them religious convictions are all human or cultural constructs, but as such valuable to organize our lives (§2.2). Barth, however, is much more in line not only with Calvin but also with the Scriptures when he points to the futility, the destructiveness and the immorality of creating our own gods.

In the First Testament, the polemic against idolatry stresses the inability of our creations to save us: people carve out images of gods with ears and eyes, yet they do not see or hear (Ps 115:4-7). These gods do not have any power and need to be carried around by their worshippers (Isa 46:1f, 7). Satirically Isaiah relates how people cut trees, warm themselves with one end and bow themselves before the other end out of which they have carved a god. When they cry out "save me" to such a piece of wood, the satirical implication is that they will cry in vain (Isa 44:9–20). Unlike the non-realist postmodern theologians, the prophets do not believe that Israel is in the same boat: where the idols Bel and Nebo need to be carried around by their worshipers, the God of Israel carries and saves his people (Isa 46:3f). Here, again, we are confronted with the inner necessity that Christian theology should be either realist or invalid: a god people carry around can be their own construct, be it a linguistic construct or material creation. A god in whom people trust to carry them needs to be real in order to be able to carry!

Idolatry would be less of a problem if it were futile, harmless and unobjectionable. Yet, in the central passage on idolatry in Romans 1, Paul tells us that idolatry is objectionable because it is a rejection of the true God who deserves to be glorified. In Isaiah, we find a warning that idolatry leaves us unsatisfied (Isa 55:2). Paul himself also notes the destructiveness of idolatry because when the glory of God is transferred to idols and when creatures are deified, the order of creation is subverted and this reflects itself in distorted human relationships (Ro 1:22-31).[28] Jesus Himself points out that when people deify money, so that it becomes their god Mammon, then they will necessarily have a life full of worries, for a life not concentrated on the Kingdom of God will be a life centred on what is uncertain (Mt 6:19–34).

In line with this biblical view, Barth forcefully rejects as "natural theology" all ideas of god that sprout from human ideas and perceptions: these conceptions of the divine have nothing to do with the God of the Scriptures, but are human creations and therefore idols (Barth, *KD* II/1: 94–96, 98–100; *CD* II/1: 86–88, 89–91). Even atheism or other pseudo-religions fall under the same verdict (Barth, KD I/2, 330; trans. *CD* I/2: 302). This also helps us to understand why Barth so strongly rejects all efforts to integrate general philosophical and religious ideas of god into Christian theology in order to facilitate an apologetic contact with these ideas of the divine. According to Barth, such religious ideas found outside God's self-revelation in Scripture refer after all to a different reality. The use of natural theology within the Church for apologetic reasons, in order to function as a point of contact ("*Anknüpfungspunkt*"), should be considered "an attempt to unite Jahweh with Baal, the triune God of Holy Scripture with the concept of being of Aristotelian and Stoic philosophy" (Barth, *KD* II/1: 92; trans. *CD* II/1: 84). The many theological conceptions of Thomist and Enlightenment theology, which are found in the Church, that try to incorporate these general philosophical and religious ideas, thus try to reconcile what is necessarily opposed. According to Barth, this has major consequences for the understanding of apologetics. If we use such religious ideas as points of contact, we can only fail, for we will either give people a confused idea of the God of the Bible, or strengthen them in their

28 Cf. also §4.4, where it is shown how an adequate relation to God is necessarily to put the importance of the community to which we belong in proper perspective.

own religious conceptions which legitimize their rejection of the God of the Bible who is "wholly other" (Barth, *KD* II/1: 96ff; trans. *CD* II/1: 88ff).

On this point, however, we need to refine Barth's criticism of the apologetic use of general religious ideas in order to remain closer to the use of "points of contact" in Scripture itself, to do more justice to the doctrine of creation (see §4.2) and the actual partial correspondence between Christian and non-Christian religious ideas. Barth seems to have overstated his case because he distanced himself insufficiently from the subject–object dualism that characterized modernity. We will return to this point in the next section (§3.4). For the moment, it is sufficient to note that Barth had a tendency to answer the question whence people's ideas of God or god come in an either/or fashion: they arise either from the sinful subject and are therefore idolatrous projections, or they arise from God's revelation, which makes them a truthful reflection of the supreme truth.

Beyond the postmodern appreciation of modern apologetics

We end this section with a comparison of the Barthian and postliberal criticism of Christian apologetics. It is now all the more clear why we need the theological criticism of Barth as a supplement, a deepening and a correction to the postliberal criticism of modern Christian apologetics. The postliberals criticized modernity in three respects: for its universalist foundationalist epistemology; its representational and expressivist understanding of language; and its individualism. It is significant that two of these criticisms are prefigured in the theology of Karl Barth, thus showing the vitality of theology and underlining the relevance of a theological appreciation of modernity. As a postmodernist *avant la lettre*, Barth had already stressed the particularity of the Christian worldview and rationality because it started from the particular revelation of God in Christ. In line with this, he also broke off with modern individualism by stressing the fact that the Christian faith was entrusted to the community of the Church and that theology should be done in that context, as *Church Dogmatics*. However, Barth does not, in the same way, prefigure the third postmodern departure from modernism. Contrary to the postmodern trend towards a performative understanding of language, he remains strongly realist.

That said, it would not do to declare Barth's realism a simple relic of the modern age, which he would or should have left behind, had he fully understood the implications of his departure from modern epistemology.[29] Barth's realism can never be separated from his theology, not only because of the continuity

29 This seems to be the implicit assumption of those theologians and those numerous pastors – particularly in continental Europe – who in their own development learnt a lot from Karl Barth, yet ended in a more radical type of narrative theology.

of this element in his theology throughout its development (McCormack 1995; 2008; cf. Barth, *KD* II/1: 342; trans. *CD* II/1: 304; Dalferth 1986; White 1984; Hunsinger 1991: 165–173, 225ff), but primarily because of his most central Christian and theological convictions. Barth is the theologian of the sovereignty, freedom, and love of God, of the initiative of God and of grace. The fact that we can know God and can speak about Him has no other source than the love of God Himself by which He decided to make Himself known. Even Barth's particularism and communalism have their basis in his theological convictions about God's gracious and free acts. God could have chosen to reveal Himself in nature or equally in the heart of each human being. He has not done so but in His freedom has chosen to reveal Himself in Christ and make Himself known through the proclamation of the Church in the world. Therefore, we need to underline again: Barth's communalism and particularism are not based on general philosophical convictions but on the theological reality he has discovered in Christ, the same reality that made him a theological realist.

Barth is certainly aware of the possibility that human beings create their own worlds and postmodern ideas about the performative capacity of language would fit well into his understanding. However, the world human beings create out of their own capacity is a "phantom world" in which a "phantom man" lives who in creating this phantom world flees reality and the true God![30]

3.4 Modern and postmodern estrangement from reality

The possibility that human beings create their own "phantom worlds" as a surrogate for a reality to which they cannot properly relate or which they do not want to accept, shows that the human being is estranged from the reality to which he belongs. He is estranged from his Creator, but also from the creation of which he is a part. This estrangement is part of life under the effects of sin, but this general estrangement has taken a particular form in the Enlightenment, where it became visible in the dualism or schism between the knowing subject and the world in which it finds itself. The effects of this dualism on modern thought in general, but also on modern theology and apologetics, have been profound. In this section, we will trace some of them with the help of the Scottish theologian

30 I use the expression "phantom world", in the same way as Karl Barth speaks about the "phantom man" ("der Schattenmensch") as the image the sinful human being creates of himself (*KD* III/2, 87; trans. *CD* III/2: 75f). More in general he sees the creation of a shadow world, of "a reality of the second degree" as a consequence of a sinful refusal to accept reality as God has given it to us (*KD* IV/2: 462; trans. *CD* IV/2: 411; cf. *KD* II/1: 185–188; trans. *CD* II/1: 165–168). Thus "creative antirealism", which extreme postmodernism considers to be the normal and normative understanding of language and culture (cf. §2.3) is by Barth considered a consequence of sin.

Thomas F. Torrance, one of Barth's most important and creative disciples.[31] Like the anthropological roots of the modernity, understanding this subject-object dualism is important because mainline postmodernism is in this respect profoundly indebted to the Enlightenment, rather than being a radical departure of it. It is also because of this debt that this postmodernism – in theology and in general thought – cannot provide a viable alternative to modernism.

From modern to postmodern dualism

Classical Greek culture and philosophy was profoundly dualistic. The main dualism was between the eternal, immutable and spiritual world of the divine and of the soul and the transient world of matter and history. In the early centuries of the Church, this dualism was overcome by the Judeo-Christian belief in the Creator. Yet, Greek dualism remained influential and often disturbed the coherence of Christian thinking through the ongoing role of Neo-Platonist and Aristotelian philosophy in mediaeval Christian thought (Torrance 2001: 44–65).

This Greek dualism was revived in the early modern era. Again, René Descartes gave it a specifically modern form. Now the principal dualism was not so much between the divine world of the eternal and spiritual and the created world of matter and history, but between the knowing subject and the object world in which it found itself. After doubting all knowledge coming from tradition and sense-experience (§3.2), the human subject found itself entirely thrown back on itself. However, Descartes thought that he could re-establish the link between the thinking subject and the object world on the basis of an *a priori* argument for the existence of the thinking subject and of a good God who cannot deceive us if we properly use our reason and senses.

Even if many Enlightenment thinkers have refused Descartes' *solution*, they have accepted his *problem* as valid. A cleft between the thinking and knowing subject and the external world as its object is presupposed, and the philosophical problem is thus how this cleft can be bridged and how the world can be known. Descartes' solution soon seemed rather shaky, for he needed to trust an argument for the existence of a non-cheating god even before he had established the trustworthiness of such a use of his reason. The sceptics seem to have a solid case, when they claim, as exemplified by David Hume, that there is no way to bridge the cleft between the world as it appears to us and the world as it really is.

In the development of modern epistemology Immanuel Kant plays a pivotal role, also because of the way in which he, as a solidly modern thinker, prepared for the rise of postmodernism. Kant claims to have overcome Hume's scepticism.

31 See Torrance 1969: 110–306; 1985: 72ff; 2001: 1–74; Colyer 2001: 322–344; McGrath 1999: 214ff. For the criticism of dualism in theology and for the development of an alternative understanding of theology, see particularly: Torrance 1999.

He states that the organizational principles and structures we perceive in reality (such as causality, space and time) do not reflect reality as it is in itself yet are valuable as the *a priori* categories by which the thinking subject organizes its experience. They do not originate in the object world, but in the thinking subject. The net-result is that the object-world as it is in itself remains unknowable. We only know the world as it appears to us through our senses.[32]

The idea that the human subject organizes its experience of the world around in terms of the categories and structures through which the mind perceives it, is equally characteristic of postmodernism. The crucial difference with Kant is that the latter saw the subject as an isolated individual and at the same time as an expression of a "common human reason" ("*die gemeine Menschenvernunft*"; 1781: p. VII). Typically modern, for Kant the human subjectivity was universally shared by all sane human beings and his *a priori* analysis of how he himself perceived the world was therefore sure, necessary, and universally valid. For postmodernists, the isolated individual that exemplifies some universal subjectivity no longer exists. Kant's understanding of the human subject wasn't universal as he thought, but a particular modern Northern European expression of it. The way people perceive the world is profoundly determined by the particular community or by the plethora of communities to which they belong. Yet, both the Kantian modern subject and the equally Western postmodern subject – particularly in its relativist and pluralist form – are thoroughly separated from the external world. Neither believes it possible to bridge the gap and have any knowledge of reality as it is in itself. Both impose their own universal, private, or communal categories on the reality, which they only know as it appears to them in these personal or cultural–linguistic categories (Torrance 2001: 34).

Excursus: the contribution and limits of Barth's theological criticism of apologetics

In formulating a truly Christian apologetics, which takes leave of modernism, we should fully take into account Barth's profound theological insights concerning the anthropological root of modernist opposition to the Christian faith, the particularity of the starting point of our knowledge of God in Christ, the role of sinful resistance in the rejection of the Gospel, and the appreciation of false religion as man-made religion. Yet, in certain respects we need to go beyond Barth's criticism of modernist apologetics. Now that the study of the characteristics and limitations of Western modernity and modern epistemology have gone much further than in his time, we can see with hindsight that in some areas his analysis needs to be clarified and brought forward.

---

32 See particularly the preface of the second edition of his *Kritik der reinen Vernunft* (1781: pp. VII–XLIV).

In the first place, we need to note that Barth remains in certain respects indebted to the subject-object dualism of the Enlightenment. Barth moved in a decisive way beyond this dualism, when he starts his theology from the recognition that the human being cannot determine *a priori* and on a universal and neutral ground if and how God can be known. The possibility and nature of the knowledge of God is determined by the reality of God and by his free and sovereign decision to reveal Himself in Christ. Our subjective knowledge has to trace and follow the reality of the object (see f. ex. *KD* II/1: 342; trans. *CD* II/1: 304f).[33]

Nevertheless, in another way Barth remains indebted to the modern formulation of the epistemological problem, particularly in its Kantian form.[34] The modern dualism between subject and object implied that all knowledge had to be split in two parts: it originated either in the object world or in the knowing subject. Thus in Kant, knowledge was a mixture of the *a priori* categories of the mind and the appearances of the outside world. In the same way, Barth divides religious ideas in those that originate in the objective reality of the true God and on the other hand the thoughts about God that spring entirely from the human subject. The latter originating from the human subject will never touch the real God, as we discussed earlier. They are mere human creations and therefore idols, and there can be no apologetic bridge between "natural" religious or philosophical concepts of the divine and the God of the Bible. We equally noted that the Bible itself is much more nuanced and sees such images of the divine as a mixture of truth, error and deceit. They can therefore be critically used as a bridge towards the fuller truth of the Gospel, just as Paul did on Mars Hill (Ac 17:22-31). Such a mixture of truth and falsehood can be more easily understood when we consider the knowing subject and the object world as intrinsically related in the knowledge process. Such an understanding of knowledge is more in accordance with a biblical understanding of the human being as regent, yet part of creation, which we will develop in the following chapters.

The second limitation of Barth's criticism of modern apologetics originates from what is called the *actualism* of his concept of divine revelation. This actualism strengthens the strict separation between ideas about God originating with God Himself and those originating in the human subject. Barth's concept of divine revelation is *actualist* in the sense that God's self-revelation is always an act and never a given (*KD* II/1: 21–26; trans. *CD* II/1: 21–25; cf. Hunsinger 1991: 30–32, 67–70). This actualism has two sources. On the one hand, it originates from Barth's understanding of God. Over and against the idea of an immutable and static God, Barth rediscovers the biblical faith in a God who lives and acts (see particularly *KD* II/1: 288ff; trans. *CD* II/1: 257ff). On the other hand, it is a consequence of his stress on the sovereignty of God in his revelation. According

33 On his relation to Kant in this respect, see: Torrance 1984: 289, 292.

34 See for Barth's use of and partial dependence on Kant: Barth 1947: 237–278; trans. 1972: 266–312; McCormack 1995: 254f, 465f; Rehnman 1998: 280–284, 293f.

to Barth, a revelation that is not dependent on God's continuous acts is a revelation "at our disposal", a revelation we can master. It therefore cannot be the revelation of the true and sovereign God, who can never be at our disposal.[35] This implies that, according to Barth, God cannot be known from creation or nature and he thus denies the existence of what theologians call "general revelation". To know God we are always dependent on specific acts of God, who chooses to reveal Himself in Israel, in Christ and in the Scriptures. Even the Scriptures cannot be said to *be* God's revelation. They constantly need to *become* the revelation of God in that God constantly acts to reveal Himself anew through the Scriptures.

At this point, we need to ask if Barth is right in saying that we can only guard the sovereignty of God by denying the continuing presence of God's revelation in creation and in the Scriptures. This denial seems to be motivated by the Enlightenment understanding of knowledge that equalled knowledge and mastery, for it was in order to be masters of nature that knowledge was sought for (cf. §3.2). Such knowledge that envisages control is indeed impossible with respect to God. Yet, there is also a knowledge of other realities, we can never entirely master, such as intimate knowledge of other persons as persons. Even physical reality is not in our mastery if we want to know it as it reveals itself to us (cf. §4.2 and §4.3). In the same way we need to consider the revelation of God as something that is available, yet which we can never master and can only know if we submit ourselves to its sovereignty.[36] In this way, we can with the Scriptures and the mainline Christian tradition speak of a continuous general revelation, the understanding of which can be distorted but which we cannot master (see f. ex. Calvin, *Institutio Christianae Religionis* [1559]: I, III–V). So we can also speak of a special revelation "entrusted" to us in the Scriptures,[37] as a deposit of the living God, whose living and acting does not mean that He can be unfaithful to what He has been and given in the past.

If, as Barth believes, God's revelation is nowhere a given, concepts of God which do not spring from a special act of divine self-revelation, necessarily have their only source in the human subject. They therefore have no relation at all to the reality of God Himself. In that case, there is no bridge between conceptions springing from God's self-revelation in Christ and images of the divine found in the wider world. The latter should always, and entirely, be considered as idols with no relation whatsoever to the true God. If, however, God's revelation, though always based in God's continuous gracious acting towards us in creation and redemption,

35 The idea that we cannot and should not try to "master" revelation or consider it "at our disposal" is a recurrent theme in Barth's theology (f. ex. *KD* II/1: 21ff, 74ff; II/2: 580; III/4: 10; IV/3: 971; trans. *CD* II/1: 21ff, 69ff; II/2: 523; III/4: 11; IV/3: 847; 1970: 59ff; trans. 1963: 50ff); cf. also n. 17 in this chapter.

36 Cf. Rehnman's criticism of Barth and Torrance: "Knowledge can at the best be a necessary condition to exercise control of some object, but never a sufficient condition." (1998: 289)

37 This is implied in the logic of the encouragement to "guard the good deposit that was entrusted to you" (2Ti 1:14). Cf. concerning this criticism also: Torrance 1990: 155–159.

also becomes part of history in the process, human images of God will, in many cases, relate to these traces of God's presence and be a mixture of truth and distortion. They can therefore be used apologetically as a point of contact for the proclamation of the Gospel.

A third problem with Barth's criticism of apologetics is that, in some of his most radical passages, Barth suggests that all apologetics is a reprehensible activity (f. ex. *KD* I/1: 25ff, 360f; II/1: 96ff; trans. *CD* I/1: 27ff, 341f; II/1: 88f). It is these texts among other things that have led his numerous critics, such as Norman Geisler and David Tracy, to accuse him of being a fideist who no longer wants to justify his Christian convictions to those who do not share them beforehand (Tracy 1975: 162; Geisler 1976: 53–56). Yet a more precise analysis shows that his objections against apologetics are valid particularly against the modernist type of apologetics and against pre-modern apologetics often only because Barth conceives of them through modern spectacles (f. ex. *KD* II/1: 140f; trans. *CD* II/1: 127f). Other types of apologetics might be possible to which these objections would not apply. Barth himself recognizes this when in some lesser known passages he proposes a renewed form of apologetics, sometimes called "polemics", which no longer suffers from the draw-backs of modern epistemology (f. ex. *KD* I/1: 361; IV/3: 121; trans. *CD* I/1: 341/ IV/3: 109). The fact that Barth's critics did not note these proposals shows in fact a universalist foundationalist bias on their side. Because of their own stance, they cannot appreciate Barth's important contribution towards an apologetic, which takes the particular character of the Christian faith seriously!

Fourth, Barth believes that the epistemological status of theological knowledge is a specific case among the sciences because of its proper object. He believes that other sciences rightly follow the modern conception of science (f. ex. *KD* 1/1: 22; II/1: 47; trans. *CD* I/1: 22f; II/1: 44). Living too early to profit from the later twentieth-century developments in the philosophies of science and language, he unduly isolated the Christian faith and theology from the wider domain of human knowledge. Torrance, who developed an extensive and profound knowledge of the philosophy of science, explored and apologetically exploited the parallel between Barth's theological methodological reflection and twentieth-century developments in the philosophy of science which took leave from the universalist foundationalist scientism of modernity (Torrance 1962: 9, 31f, 205; 2001: 87–95). In 1968, some weeks before Barth's death, Torrance proposed this interpretation of Barth's method to him. "Karl Barth expressed full agreement with my interpretation of his thought, and said, rather characteristically, of the relation of geometry to physics: 'I must have been a blind hen not to have seen that analogy before'" (Torrance 1976: x). Now we can apologetically exploit many of the developments in those fields to show that the particularism and communalism characteristic of Christian theology in no way discredits it. It is not only justified by its particular subject matter, but also by the general way the human cognitive faculties work. We will come back to this promising parallel in Chapter 5.

Chapter 4

CHRISTIAN ANTHROPOLOGY FOR UNDERSTANDING APOLOGETICS

A key factor in Christian growth and Christian living is the "renewing of the mind" (Ro 12:2). Christians need to look at the world, at history and their fellow human beings with Christian eyes, as God sees them, for God knows our most profound being. He sees us for what we really are. We need to discover what it means to be created by God, to find our fulfilment in communion with Him, as part of a human community and as stewards of his creation. If we as Christians were more consistent in looking at human beings from a biblical perspective, we would distance ourselves more easily from what the world says we are. We would therefore also more consistently and more radically distance ourselves from modernity and its epistemology and apologetics. We would realize that modernity is grossly overestimating the human capacity to know and organize the world. If we understand ourselves, what it means to be human, from a Christian perspective, the crumbling of modern convictions and ideals under postmodern deconstructive analysis would not surprise us; neither would we be seduced by unsatisfactory postmodern alternatives. Humanity cannot look at the world from some divine and absolute perspective, for as creature he is part of it. Nor can we view the human being as a performer without limits, creating a linguistic universe, as if he did not first find himself in a given structure. It will remain equally unsatisfactory for a human being to consider himself as only the passive product of a culturally determined discourse, in which his individuality and subjectivity evaporate as mere linguistic constructs.

In this chapter, we will further elaborate a properly Christian understanding of the human being and condition as a basis for understanding the character of Christian apologetics. We do this so that our apologetics might respect what the Scriptures reveal to us as the most profound truth concerning human existence. Such an elaboration of a Christian understanding of the human being is urgently needed, because we have seen how mainline apologetics under the influence of the Enlightenment is flawed in forgetting the proper place of the human being in relationship to the rest of creation and to his Creator. We also saw that precisely in this respect the most influential strands of postmodernism remain generally in line with its predecessor culture. A truly Christian alternative should be developed in accordance with a profoundly Christian understanding of the human being. It is for this reason that we move on from a critical analysis of modern and postmodern attitudes to apologetics towards a positive and systematic elaboration of a Christian understanding of what it means to be human and of the implications of this understanding for Christian apologetics. Drawing from the treasures of the history of Christian thought, we want to see what the biblical understanding of the human being implies in the face of contemporary challenges, which go far beyond what the biblical authors could imagine.

As a key to understanding the human being we use the classical theological concept of the creation of the human being in the image of God. We will show how this theological understanding of the human being indicates the purpose for which God created humankind (§4.1). We will then analyse the three different relationships that are constitutive of being human: our relationship with the non-human creation (§4.2); with our fellow human beings (§4.3); and with God (§4.4). In this analysis we will see what a proper understanding of these three relationships implies for the way in which we are part of creation and social networks, and how at the same time we cannot be reduced to these relationships. We will finally address the question whether this analysis of human nature and the human condition may be considered valid for those who do not consider themselves created in the image of God, considering both theological and philosophical objections. We will explain why Christians can claim that this understanding of the human condition is universally valid and therefore an understanding that should be reflected in the way they conduct apologetic dialogue and witness (§4.5).

4.1 God's purpose for humanity

When Christians talk about human nature, they often say that the human being is created in the image of God. Though the number of biblical passages using this expression is very limited,[1] it is nevertheless justified to use it as a central concept in developing a Christian understanding of the human being. First of all the few passages using the term are found in crucial places in the biblical testimony. We find the expression in the first account of creation (Ge 1:26f), which is placed in both the Hebrew and Christian canon as an introduction to the Scriptures in their entirety. It is also used as an indication of the goal of our redemption in Christ, who is Himself the "image of the invisible God" (Col1:15; cf. 2 Co 4:4) and in whom we are "renewed in the image of our Creator" (Col 3:10). Second, what we find in these crucial passages serves well as a starting point to draw the rest

1 The passages are Ge 1:26s; 5:1; 9:6; 1Co 11:7; Col 3:10; Jas 3:9. For a discussion of these and related passages, see: Hoekema 1994: 11–32.

of the biblical understanding of the human being into one integrated whole (cf. Hoekema 1994; Berkouwer 1957; trans. 1962).

When we consider the basic passage in Genesis 1:27, which says that God "created humankind in his image", it is striking that little is said about what it is that makes the human being the image of God. This is one of the causes of the extensive and exegetically inconclusive debate about the sense of the expression.[2] We can start, however, from surer ground, when we do not ask what is the main characteristic that makes the human being image God, but when we ask what this *entails*. What is the place of the human being as the image of God in creation and within the wider purpose of God? (Sherlock 1996: 33.) Thus, starting from the creation accounts and reading them in the light of the unfolding of God's purpose for humanity and its accomplishment and restoration in the renewal of the image in Christ, we can see how our creation in the image of God entails three constitutive relationships – the relationship with the non-human creation, the fellowship of humanity and the relationship with God himself.[3] Biblically speaking, our attention is not drawn to some abstract entity called "human nature". The human being can never be "abstracted" from the relationships, which are constitutive of his being. Abstracting the human being in this way would mean *sub*tracting from what is essential to being human. Human nature is a thoroughly relational or personal reality. Our constitution as individuals is not an independent reality, but a constitution determined by and in view of a relational existence.[4] Without these relationships properly developed, this constitution may even turn against itself, against our very being, and become self-destructive. "If personal relationship is essentially ontological, then relational brokenness effects our very being" (Deddo 1997: 63).

Before we enter into these three separate relationships that are constitutive of human nature, we should note that they should not be considered as three independent aspects of our being. If so, they might provide a basis for a certain postmodern understanding of the human being that says that what we call human nature is a lose conglomeration of fragmentary phenomena. These fragments may not necessarily be reconcilable and may not go back to one centre of existence, which could be considered a unified subject (so f. ex. Taylor 1984:

---

2 Thus Gordon Wenham concludes his discussion of the several interpretations (1987: 31): "The above survey indicates the difficulty of the determining what Genesis understands by the image of God. None of the suggestions seem entirely satisfactory, though there may be elements of truth in all of them." Cf. Childs 1993: 568.

3 We find these three relationships for example in H.W. Wolff, which treats "The Destiny of Man" and gives a fourfold answer: to live in the world, to love his fellow men, to rule over creation and to praise God (1974: 223–229).

4 In order to express this essentially relational character of being human, T.F. Torrance – developing Barthian concepts – talks about "onto-relations", relations that are constitutive of our being itself, just as the triune God exists in the "onto-relations" of the three persons of the Trinity. See f. ex.: Torrance 1999: 42ff; Colyer 2001: 55f, 308–312; Deddo 1999: 57f.

46). To suppose such an underlying unity is – according to such a postmodern understanding – an unwarranted and illegitimate metaphysical presupposition (cf. Middleton & Walsh 1995b: 52–54).

From a Christian perspective, we can indeed affirm that human existence often shows itself in a fragmented form. Yet, as we shall see later, this is not characteristic of human existence as such, but rather for human existence as separated from God, who is meant to be the unifying centre of his existence. When the relationship with Him is distorted, the unifying centre is lacking and what remains is indeed a number of fragmentary elements. These fragments show traces of what being human is meant to be, yet become antagonistic for lack of their true unity (see further §6.2). If we want to understand the true nature of these three relationships (with nature, fellow human beings and God) that together constitute human nature, they are therefore not to be considered separately, and especially not as mutually exclusive or even antagonistic. They are meant to be one harmonious whole in which all the different relationships can only fully flourish in connection and interdependence with each other.

4.2 The image of God as authority over creation

The image of God as the created regent over creation

Of the three relationships that are constitutive of being human, the first creation account elaborates most of all the relationship of humanity with the rest of creation (Ge 1:1-2:4). It is understandable that the creation account concentrates on this relationship, for it is automatically in view when the creation of humanity is set against the background of the creation of "the heavens and the earth" (Ge 1:1).

When the human being is said to have been created in the image of God, this draws out his *special status* within creation, yet from the beginning we should not forget that it is a special status *within* creation. Human beings are created in line with the rest of creation, on the sixth day, a day which they share with animals living on the earth, with which they also share their habitat (Ge 1:24f). This conviction that human beings are not from another realm but belong to the earth and are created from "the dust of the ground", is a consistent line in Scripture as a whole (Ge 2:7; 3:19; Ps 115:16; cf. Sherlock 1996: 10–31). It is as part of creation that humanity is given a special place within creation.

Even if it is not entirely clear in what sense the human being is the image of God, its most direct and visible consequence in the first creation account is that humanity is given the authority and the task to subdue the earth and rule over the rest of creation (Ge 1:28; so Wenham 1987: 32; Wolff 1974: 159ff). Many exegetes have pointed out that this understanding of the image of God reflects the way in which images of rulers were used in the surrounding cultures. A great king, who could not be physically present in all parts of his kingdom, could place statues of himself in different parts of his realm representing his authority (von Rad, 1964: 44f; trans. 1972: 57f). In a similar vein a king could be called the image of a particular god, implying that he would be the representation of divine authority and order among his people and the guarantee of cosmic order in his land (Middleton & Walsh 1995b: 118). In the surrounding cultures, this honour and authority that belongs to the image of God was the prerogative of the king. The Hebrew Scriptures, however, accord this high place to the human being in general and to each human being without distinction (Blocher 1984: 86f).

From this perspective the desire to become "master and possessor of nature" so characteristic of modern identity seems at first sight in line with the Christian conception of humanity created as the image of God. It is only on Christian soil where nature was desacralized and considered as being under the authority of humanity that modern identity could germinate and flourish (Kaiser 1991: 1–52; Allen 1989: 23–34). However, a proper understanding of the image of God shows that modern identity is, in crucial respects, a secularized deformation of its Christian root.

First of all, little by little the modern concept of human authority over nature has been absolutized and become an authority without limits. By contrast, in the biblical understanding human authority over creation was always limited by the authority of God and by the inherent value of creation. The authority was derived from God and to Him accountability was due. It should be exercised *respect*fully and *care*fully in accordance with the will of the One who had given it (Ge 2:15).

Second, modern universalist foundationalist epistemologies, which we saw to be an outflow of the modern conception of human autonomy, presuppose a God's-eye view of reality. It supposes that we can have the absolute and neutral knowledge of a detached onlooker, provided with the neutral, universal, and indubitable basis, which the foundationalist construction of knowledge needs (§2.1). We saw how the development of modern epistemology was profoundly influenced by the separation of the knowing subject and the object-world (§3.4). To be objective and detached in his knowing, the knowing subject was removed from the world to which it belonged. Yet, this move bought the absolute certainty of the self at the expense of separating the self from the rest of the world. However, the Christian understanding of the world shows that this cannot be done. Though he is regent over creation, the human being is an inextricable part of creation. His dominion over the rest of creation presupposes that the rest of creation will open itself for his probing in its nature and functioning. It even presupposes that the structure of creation in some way corresponds with the rationality given to humanity. Yet it is from within creation that this should be done.

In this respect, the epistemological concept of "indwelling" as developed by the philosopher of science Michael Polanyi seems more promising to understand human knowing than the modern concept of the detached onlooker. It is in being part of the world that we know it – in "indwelling" our bodies, our instruments and our conceptual tools, of which we constantly presuppose the validity (Polanyi 1962: 58f; see further §5.1) The God's-eye view of knowledge thus greatly overestimated the human subject, and the separation of subject and object was disrespectful of the real place of the human being in creation. We need not wonder that these promises of modern foundationalism could not be fulfilled and ended in scepticism. It severs the subject from the objective world and thereby from the only access to this world a finite and material being can have. The logical consequence is a profound doubt whether we can ever know anything at the other side of this cleft between the self and the world, as we saw in our discussion of Kant (§3.2).

We have already noted in postmodernism a wavering between two opposite, yet related, understandings of the human subject. On the one hand, we saw the postmodern subject creating its own world by the "performative" use of language and culture and by creating it constantly anew. This can be labelled *hypermodernity*, for it extrapolates the autonomy of the modern subject to the extreme (§2.2). On the other hand, we encounter a deconstruction of the subject, which revealed how the subject is far from autonomous in relation to its world but rather formed completely by the language and culture that produced it (§2.3). From a Christian perspective, we can now see why neither of these understandings respects the reality of the way in which God created humanity in the image of God. Because both of these positions deny that the human being can only be understood in relation to God, they end up either overestimating or underestimating the human being. Neither of them therefore can be a final conclusion or a stable position. The underestimation and overestimation of the human being will constantly call for one another and flip over into their counter image unless a more realistic and satisfactory position will be found.

The cultural mandate and cultural variety

We should note that the creation story contains the germ of a conception of the human being as a creator of cultures and thereby perceives a truth, which is so central in postmodernism. In the Christian tradition, particularly in its Reformed expressions, the commandment to fill and subdue the earth has been properly called the "cultural mandate" (cf. Walsh & Middleton 1984: 53–56). Human beings should not just keep the earth as they find it; they should make it a liveable home and erect all the structures they need for this to happen. The formation of culture therefore is a divine command, for culture can precisely be defined as "all the things that we learn after we are born into the world that enable us to function effectively as biological beings in the environment" (Kraft 1996: 6).

The first chapters of Genesis already show that these "structures" needed to make the world liveable are much wider than physical structures alone and include different aspects of what we ordinarily call "culture".[5] In Genesis 2, Adam as the representative of all humanity is given the task to "cultivate" the earth – one of the basic elements of human culture. He is given the authority to name the animals and thus to organize his world through language. Furthermore, man and woman are given to each other in marriage as the primal social structure and as the beginning of all social structures that need to follow when humanity will multiply and spread out over the earth. The herding of cattle, the making of tools and musical instruments, and the building of cities follow shortly afterwards. Though these activities are placed after the fall, they seem to fit well in the pattern set out for Adam (Ge 4:2, 17, 21, 22).

This authority and creativity of the human being in creating culture implicitly entails the possibility of cultural *variation*. If Adam is given real authority to name the animals, he also has been given a certain freedom in doing so. There is after all no single way animals can be named as the incredible variety of existing languages shows. In the same way, there is not one single way to spread out over the earth, to cultivate, to organize our communities, to make tools and music, and to build cities.

The place of the human being as the image of God within creation thus leaves room and – as we shall see in the next section – even encourages cultural variety. It thus supports postmodernism in its criticism of the modern ideal of one universal culture, which turns out to be the imposition of one specific culture, the modern one, on the rest of the world. Yet, this biblical understanding corrects at the same time the two contrasting versions of the postmodern understanding of our relationship to culture.

First of all, Genesis 1 denies that humans can and are allowed to create our own world without limits. Our languages and cultures cannot create the world by themselves, but are limited by the reality in which we find ourselves and to which we are called to respond. Adam was given the authority to give names, but not to create a world of his own. He was to describe the world God had created and the animals God brought to him. So we *cannot* just create worlds of our own. This is the limitation postmodernists are forced to recognize, for the world does not let us organize and interpret at random. If we do not respect its structures it will show itself to resist our interpretations. These are the sorts of considerations that a Christian epistemology should respect and which our later epistemological

---

5 I am not suggesting here that mere exegesis of the first chapters of Genesis by itself would be an adequate basis to develop a Christian understanding of language and culture. The language of Scripture has another aim than providing us with a philosophical epistemology and theory of language and culture. It is rather the case that when looking to these chapters from the perspective of the current debate about language and culture, these chapters reveal aspects of human being, which are full of implications for a Christian evaluation of the current debate and a Christian understanding of culture. Furthermore, the way Adam is given the authority to name the animals appears to be a hint to such an understanding of culture and with hindsight entirely consistent with this understanding.

considerations will demonstrate to be more realistic and fruitful than modern and postmodern alternatives (see further §5.2).

To a certain degree our ability to create culture implies the possibility of creating our own world through language. Yet when our linguistic world does not correspond to extralinguistic reality, we are creating surrogate worlds or "phantom worlds" that are intrinsically unstable.[6] We are rather called to form our images of and cultural projects for creation in accordance with the given character of creation and the will of our Creator for it. As his image and representative we remain subject to the supreme authority of the One we are called to resemble. When Adam and Eve disregarded the place given to them by preferring the proposals of the serpent, the consequences were disastrous. In the same way, we are not free to create our technical and social projects at random, but we are called to respect the given structures of creation. In Genesis 2 marriage stands out as the prime example of such structures that we need to respect. This does leave room for variety, for there is not necessarily one single way to organize our marriages and other social relationships (Van den Toren 2002: 223–226). Yet if we create our social structures without respect for the parameters that are given in creation and by the Creator, the resulting structures will be inherently unstable and more prone to become oppressive and abusive.

The understanding of culture flowing from the first chapters of Genesis also critiques the postmodern idea that we are just *products* of our cultures, which determine how we think and act. The human being as created in the image of God is given authority over creation and also the *author* of culture (Grenz & Franke 2001: 137f). Here, though, a difficult question arises, for even if culture is a human product, we as individuals find ourselves part of existing cultures that definitely exercise an enormous power over us. It is to the relationship between the individual and his or her community that we now turn.

4.3 The image of God as being related to our fellow human beings

As the image of God we are social beings

When we ask what the creation of the human being in the image of God entails, the Genesis-account of creation not only points to a particular relationship between the human being and the earth. The story also draws attention to the fact that to be fully human entails being part of a wider human community. For this reason, many exegetes have considered the essence of the image of God to consist in our being created for fellowship. Karl Barth was the first theologian to point

6 For the expression "phantom world", see §3.3, p. 87.

out that the primary indication of what it means to be the image of God is "male and female he created them" (Ge 1: 27; *KD* III/1: 219; trans. *CD* III/1: 195). As such one can never be "human" as a single individual. Everyone human being is open to, and needs, fellowship with other human beings to become fully human. The fact that we are all created either male or female is not only the basis of marriage, but also points to a more general openness to our fellow human beings and to God (Grenz 2001: 276–282). It may also find fulfilment in a celibate lifestyle, when not lived lonely or solitarily, but within the wider community of the Kingdom (Grenz 1997: 181–196).

It may be too much to say with Barth that this is "an almost definition-like explanation" of the meaning of the image (*KD* III/2: 219; trans. *CD* III/1: 195).[7] Yet, there are more indications in the creation-narratives that the nature and place of the human being in creation cannot be understood without reference to his being created to have fellowship with other human beings and that this fellowship is wider than the marriage-bond alone. Thus, being human in the image of God entails the formation of families, of larger communities, and of peoples. This is particularly clear from the fact that the cultural mandate is not an individual affair. It is directly related to the benediction that humanity will be fruitful and multiply in order to fill the earth, for that is considered the proper way to subdue, develop, and take care of it (Ge 1:28; Wolff 1974: 161f). So it is not as individuals, but only together, as male and female, and as human community that we are created in the image of God.

This presentation of the beginning of history in the opening chapters of Genesis is unfolded in the rest of Scripture. The will of God expressed in creation – that we be fully human in relationship with others – is reflected in the continuous stress in the Scriptures on the second commandment that we love our neighbour as ourselves (Lev 19:18; Mt 22:39; Jn 15:12; Ro 13:9).[8] This commandment is repeated, refracted and reflected in a spectrum of moral rules and virtues governing the community so that this love can be practically lived. The fact that human beings are "created for community" (Grenz 1998: 80) is finally confirmed by the eschatological visions in both Testaments. In these visions it becomes clear that the openness of our existence towards each other is not a temporary and accidental reality and only characteristic of the particular phase of the history between God and humanity in which we find ourselves. The eschatological vision is always one of a fellowship of those who are united in Christ. In Him we find a new family in the eschatological community that He established (Mt 12:50; 19:29). The love we learn and experience in this community will have eternal

---

7 This is my own translation, for the given translation "the definitive explanation" is too strong for the German: "*eine fast definitionsmäßige Erklärung*".

8 I presuppose here a teleological interpretation of Christian ethics, according to which Christian ethics make sense in relationship to the structure and purpose of creation. See for a coherent development and strong defence of this approach: O. O'Donovan 1986.

value and eternal continuity in what has classically been called "the city [or society] of the blessed" (cf. Ap 21:2).[9]

This vision of the human being created in the image of God, which extends from Genesis to the Apocalypse, runs contrary to the individualism of modernism and the modern Western world. As Christians we should not be astonished or disconcerted when both the universalism and the individualism of Enlightenment anthropology and epistemology appear to be unattainable ideals and unrealistic with respect to our human nature and knowledge. We were never meant to function like that. The Christian understanding of human nature as personal entails that, abstracted from personal relations, the human being cannot be understood and human life cannot be properly lived. Being a person means that life cannot be lived humanly as an isolated individual. Even more, personality is not something that is received ready-made. Our personal identity is gradually developed in the community in which we are born and socialized. In the language of the Jewish philosopher Martin Buber: it is only in meeting a "thou", that I become an "I" (Buber 1958). A child only develops its own sense of being a person when it comes to know those most close to it as personalities who are genuinely other, yet personally related to the child.

If we can only become persons in relationship with others, this also implies that we can never become a person without being socialized in a *particular* culture. We learn our language and our cultural framework – the means by which we approach reality and in which we "indwell" reality – from our parents and the wider community that nourish and socialize us into adulthood. Of course, this has the downside that we will normally appropriate the distorted elements and even the morally reprehensible ones equally unconsciously as we inherit the riches and the strengths of a particular cultural framework. At least some concept of "original sin" or the sin we inherit from our parents is therefore the natural corollary of our personal and social nature. The fact that we are necessarily cultured and social beings can work for the good and for the bad, and usually it works both ways.

This characteristic of being human itself as a social and cultural reality is to be appreciated as a gift of God both for the joy of fellowship itself and because it is part of what has been called the human "openness to the world".[10] Animals do not need their parents for long in order to adapt to the world because the way they will relate to the world is instinctive and not appropriated by socialization. Yet

9 In the era before and after the New Testament, the city was not conceived primarily as just a conglomeration of people and services but as the most essential form of the human society, as shown for example in the political philosophy of Plato and Aristotle and in the title of Augustine's *De civitate Dei* or *The City of God*.

10 This concept of the biologist Arnold Gehlen, *Der Mensch: Seine Natur und seine Stellung in der Welt* (Frankfurt am Main: Athenäum, 1966) has had a fertile reception in different disciplines: in the sociology of knowledge (Berger & Luckmann 1967: 65ff), in cultural anthropology (Geertz 1993: 49f) and in theology (Pannenberg 1983: 33ff; trans. 1985: 34ff; Grenz 1994: 169ff).

this equally means that they will all live, act and react in a way similar to their kin. Animals lack the degree of openness and freedom to adapt to new situations, to develop new patterns of life and to always creatively reach beyond the given, that is so characteristic for the human being. Because human behaviour is not a given as for animals, we can only learn to live by being socialized in a community, for better or for worse (cf. Grenz 2001: 304ff).

The multitude of peoples and cultural variety

Scripture not only appreciates the cultural and social aspect of being human, it even lays the basis for celebrating cultural *diversity*, at least up to a certain level, as a gift of God. One may argue that God himself laid down the seeds of cultural diversity in creation in view of His purpose for creation. As a starting point for this thesis, we should recall that the authority of humanity over creation includes the authority to organize it by language, social structures and technical means. If this authority is real, it implies a certain freedom to do so in different ways.

The command of God to fill the earth does not just imply the freedom to diversify culturally, but even the need to do so. This command implies, first of all, an adaptation to ever-new situations. Cultural anthropologists have shown that different living conditions demand different cultural responses. The world over we can see that sedentary peoples tilling the ground need different techniques (as a part of culture) from nomadic groups living with and from their flocks. They also need other types of social organization (another part of culture). Living from fishing and hunting or living in cities again asks for cultural adaptation.

Second the command of God to fill the earth implies cultural variation because this spreading out explicitly is thought of as the formation of a diversity of peoples and thereby of languages and cultures. This becomes clear when one reads the so-called "table of the nations" in Genesis 10 as a sequence to Genesis 1. This table gives an overview of the nations of the earth divided among three major groups all descending from one of Noah's three sons. The chapter explains how these different nations "each with its own language" (Ge 10:4) "spread out over the earth" after the flood (Ge 10:32) in obedience to the creation-commandment. The spreading out was thus meant to be a spreading out not of individuals, but of peoples, all of whom God assigned their own place (cf. Dt 32:8). This would normally entail a diversification of cultures as the different peoples adapt to different situations and develop and hand on their own style of life. Among other things this becomes visible in the diversification of languages as a major aspect and reflection of the variety of cultural identities. Today socio-historical linguistics can trace how languages, which have one common origin, developed and diversified as people groups spread out and developed culturally. One does not need to read Genesis 10 as a precise description of the origin of the peoples of the earth to appreciate how this table of the nations provides us with a theological understanding of the multiplicity of the nations. The God of Israel and Jesus Christ is their Creator and the Lord of the nations (cf. Ac 17:26). All these nations and their variety fit into His plan even before He started His particular history with Abraham (Ge 12:1) in order to bless all these nations through Him (Ge 12:3).

A closer look at the story of the Tower of Babel story provides an even better grasp of the place of the variety of peoples, languages and cultures within the plan of God. Commentators often suggest that the diversification of languages in this story (a major aspect of cultural diversity) is entirely negative, a punishment of God, which, in principle, was overcome when the Spirit broke through the barriers of language on the Day of Pentecost. A closer reading of both Babel and Pentecost shows that the meaning of both stories is more complex. In Genesis 11 the primary sin is the desire to stay together as one mighty nation and not to "be scattered abroad upon the face of the whole earth" (Ge 11:4). The story shows this to be a refusal to accept their place as creatures, as is expressed in their wish to build a "tower with its top in the heavens" (Ge 11:4). It is, furthermore, disobedience to the command of the Creator to fill the earth. It is, in fact, through the confusion of languages that God punishes their pride yet at the same time gives a blessing in disguise. It runs counter to their wish to be as God, a wish that for a mere creature can only have destructive consequences. It also by force "scattered them abroad over the face of all the earth" (Ge 11:9), so that they end up following the original commandment and blessing of their Creator (cf. Anderson 1977: 63–70; Brueggemann 1982: 99).

This interpretation of the scattering and the resulting cultural diversity as something positive is confirmed by the Spirit's moving on the Day of Pentecost. The Spirit allowed all those present to hear the message of the apostles in their "own native language" (Ac 2:8). This was indeed a reversal of the misunderstanding, estrangement and enmity that is a part of life because of the variety of languages and cultures in a sinful world. It is, however, far from a reversal of Babel, for the miracle is not that, from now on, all people again speak one language; rather, all of them hear the Gospel in their own language.

This ethnic, cultural and linguistic diversity is equally reflected in the visions of the Apocalypse, which do not look for a future when there will be simply "one people", but rather see "a great multitude … from every nation, from all tribes and peoples and languages" (Ap 7:9; cf. 5:9), who will be "his peoples" (Ap 21:3).[11] Thus the final vision on which the Scripture ends reveals the same celebration of diversity as was already present in the larger context of the creation story and in the creation we see around us. Our Creator is a God who revels in variety. He did

11 Many translations read "his people", yet the reading "his peoples" has a slightly stronger textual basis and the singular should therefore probably be considered a later adaptation of the text to make it conform better to the more common Old Testament expressions in the singular (cf. Metzger 1975: 763).

not create just one type of tree, fish, bird or land animals – not even ten varieties of each of them. Rather, He enjoyed creating thousands of species with their own characteristics and a world with so many different habitats that can host all of them. The convergence of what we perceive in the variety both in nature and in human cultures might well point to this characteristic of the creativity of God. He invites humanity as His image to participate in this creativity by developing a rich variety of cultures. In this way they mirror the creativity of God.

This positive value of cultural variety has been recognized in the history of Christian missions from the earliest time onwards. The earliest Church never considered one language more holy than another. It did not widely use the Aramaic language of Jesus himself, for the Christian Scriptures were already a translation in Greek. From the start, Christian mission has been a translation movement and these translations were not only linguistic events, but also represented the translation of the Gospel in ever-new cultural idiom and clothing. Thus, the Gospel entered the Hellenistic world, the Latin world, the Celtic world, the Slavonic world, the Germanic world, etc., each time in new linguistic outfits and new cultural forms (Sanneh 1989; Bediako 1995: 109–125; Walls 1996: 26–42).

Implications for a properly Christian apologetics

According to the Scriptures, the human being should thus be understood as a social and cultural being who never exists in the abstract, but always as member of one or more communities and cultures. The epistemological and apologetic consequences are, of course, vast and will need to be spelled out in detail later. Again, we can conclude that Christians need not be astonished or disconcerted that postmodernism has shown the Enlightenment ideal and the modern apologetic quest for a universal and tradition-independent foundation for human knowledge to be a chimera. A properly Christian apologetics need not necessarily be based on a universal foundation equally accessible for each human individual. When the apologist relates to people, she relates to social and cultured beings. We should not consider that as a fateful consequence of sin[12] that we need to overcome as soon as possible in order to start all over again from a presupposedly tradition- and culture-independent point (so f. ex. Netland 1988). It is as cultural beings that we were created and as such that we should relate to each other. We may profit from the best of what our tradition has given to us and others, and we should fight against those strands of our traditions and cultures that have been sources of delusion.

12 Contrary to the suggestion of Os Guinness, who in this respect seems to be unduly indebted to an Enlightenment ideal, which is just pushed back to Paradise: "In an ideal world, untouched by the effects of the Fall, the credibility of any belief would be determined simply by whether it were true or false" (1994: 344).

From a Christian theological perspective, cultural variety always has two sides. On the one hand, cultural variety is, to a certain extent, legitimate. Its possibility is, after all, given with the authority of humanity over creation. It is given with the possibility that humanity names and orders reality and orders his life and community, in different ways and in relation to the great variety of challenges with which life confronts it. With respect to this type of cultural variety we need to say that the Gospel can be translated, understood and lived in different cultural contexts and different cultural clothing – as Christ has already entered many different contexts in the course of the history of the Church.

On the other hand, there is a kind of cultural variety related to the fact that human society may misinterpret the world and its own existence because of human finitude and because of sin. Human beings can even create their phantom worlds in rejection of the world as it is, in negation and alienation of their own being and in forcing what they perceive of God's creation and revelation in their own mould according to their own interests. In relationship to this type of cultural variety Christianity should stand over against other cultures as a counter-culture responding to God as He showed himself in Christ and respecting both the world and human beings for what they really are. In practice, all human cultures in the current age show both aspects of cultural variety. The Gospel can be incarnated in their structures and forms, but remains as such always a critical factor and is always pushing for the renewal of that culture or even for the formation of counter-cultural communities (Walls 1996: 3–15). Yet even counter-cultures or cultures in the process of renewal may retain important characteristics of the culture countered or in need of renewal.

4.4 The image of God as being created for community with God

The priority of the relationship with God

In our quest to understand what it means to be human, we have seen that our being created in the image of God entails specific relationships. It entails a relationship to creation and to our fellow human beings. The attention which these two relationships receive in the creation stories and in the rest of the Scriptures should not make us forget the obvious. As the image of *God* the human being is first of all related to God, of whom he is called to be the image (Blocher 1984: 85; Westermann 1994: 158). It is as the image of God, because of this special relationship with God, that he relates to the earth and it is because he himself and his fellow human beings are God's image that they are created for community. The relationship with God is therefore both foundational for the other relationships and has priority over them. Conversely, this relationship with God should not be understood in some ascetic or mystical way as if opening ourselves to God would demand a withdrawal from all other relationships. The relationship is qualitatively prior to the other relationships, yet does not exclude – rather, it encompasses – the other relationships. But because of this priority, the other relationships with the earth and with our fellow human beings can only flourish to the full if our relationship to our Creator is good.

According to the Scriptures this relationship with God should take precedence over our relationship with the rest of creation and with our fellow human beings. We should value Him and our relationship with Him infinitely more than all other relationships. This is reflected in the great commandment that calls us to love God with all our being and thus above everything and everyone else and even above our own lives (Dt 6:5; Mc 12:30; cf. Mc 8:34-38). This one great commandment, in turn, is refracted in the many exhortations to count all other relationships of secondary importance in comparison to the one with God, and to seek and value His kingdom and reign beyond anything else (Mt 6:33). This is what is rightly called the radical theocentrism of the Scriptures, as becomes tangible in a closer consideration of all the main themes of the Scriptures such as love, faith, hope, obedience and humility. As Richard Niebuhr has noted, each of these virtues, lived in an exemplary manner by Christ, "is intelligible in its apparent radicalism only as a relation to God" (1951: 27; cf. pp. 15–27).

In the historical sections of Scripture we constantly see how the relationship with God needs to take precedence over all other relationships and how it may even provoke a separation from those who are most near and dear to us. Abram's calling by God implied that he should leave "[his] country and [his] kindred and [his] father's house" (Ge 12:1). Moses is not only forced to leave the court of the Pharaoh in order to save his people; the need to side with God, who is the Liberator, also obliges him repeatedly to stand alone among and even oppose his own people. This pattern repeats itself time and again in the lives of the prophets who stand apart to call their people back to God. The lives of Elijah and Jeremiah show how lonely they could become in the process. This need to decide which relationship should have precedence becomes particularly sharp when people meet Jesus. As representative of God and even more as his Son, Jesus calls for a decision. "Whoever loves father or mother more than me is not worthy of me; and whoever loves son or daughter more than me is not worthy of me" (Mt 10:37; cf. Lc 14:26; Mt 8:21f).

This prioritization of the relationship with God over the human community to which we belong is not arbitrary. It is consistent with the nature of reality that Scripture reveals us and of which we are a part. It is consistent with the nature of God: God Himself infinitely surpasses the value of everything in the universe. If He offers Himself to us, as we know from the Scriptures, He offers the greatest and a necessarily unsurpassable gift, which we should value above anything else. Moreover, this relationship is God's goal for human life for which creation was intended from the beginning. As Paul explicitly said, sometimes with regards to

God the Father (Ro 11:36; 1Co 8:6) and sometimes with regards to the Son (Col 1:16): "to him are all things". This becomes even clearer when we consider the eschatological visions in the Scriptures in which God will be "all in all" (1Co 15:28). Then "the home of God is among mortals. He will dwell with them; they will be his peoples, and God himself will be with them." (Rev 21:3).

In interpreting the notion of the image of God, we need finally to take into account that it is Jesus Christ who is later called "the image of the invisible God" par excellence (Col 1:15) and that it is in view of Him that we are created (Col 1:16). Here we touch the much-debated question, if human beings are created for fellowship with God in a more general sense or more specifically for fellowship with God in Jesus Christ. If the latter is true, the incarnation of Christ is not only necessary to save humanity from sin, but it is the goal of creation even apart from the reality of sin. This question has major implications for the way in which we present Christ in evangelism and apologetic witness: as only the solution to our problems or also as the goal of our lives. Following Eastern Orthodox theology (Ware 1964: 230; Nellas 1997) and an important theological minority in the West, which comprises among others Duns Scotus (Cross 1999: 127–129), James Orr (2002) and Barth (*KD* III/1: 53f; trans. *CD* III/1: 50f), I want to claim that the biblical evidence for this position is much stronger than the single proof-text in Colossians 1:16. It is indirectly attested by Christ's role in creation (Jn 1:1-4; 1Co 8:6; Heb 1:1-3; Wilkinson 1996: 248ff), by his role as the goal of salvation (Jn 14:6; Rev 19:7; 21:17), by his gift of incorruptible life, which even Adam did not possess (1Co 15:45-49), by the unending nature of the incarnation (1Co 15:49f; Rev 21:22f; 22:1) and in the Christocentric nature of New Testament spirituality (Php 1:23). This question does, however, lead us beyond the confines of this study, and because the principal thesis does not depend on it, I will leave it (rather reluctantly) at this.

Putting the human community into perspective

Later in this study we will dig deeper into the question of what the Christian understanding of the human being and his relation to God implies for a Christian understanding of apologetics. We will explore the opportunities for dialogue and argumentation it presents and uncover the proper approach to our non-Christian co-images of God that it implies. Here we will explore some of its most direct implications, particularly as they relate to the crisis of modern apologetics, which we analysed earlier. We will consider first what it means for the relationship of the individual to the community. Second, we will ask what our creation for communion with God means for our evaluation of the modern ideal of autonomy and neutrality in knowledge. Third, we will begin to explore what this understanding of the human being implies for the possibility of using the human "need for God" as a so-called "point of contact" in approaching non-Christians.

The priority of our relationship with God over all other relationships is, in the first place, a crucial element in dealing with an important dilemma in the modernism–postmodernism debate. On one side, we find the individualist understanding of the human being that is characteristic of modernism and the hypermodern variety of postmodernism. This individualism is fed continually by the experience that there is something in an individual that makes it impossible to reduce him entirely to what the community makes of him. This individualism is opposed by the communalist type of postmodernism. It draws its strength from the fact that an individualist understanding of the human being is undercut by the profundity of the way in which individuals are influenced by their cultures and social contexts. Again, this dilemma in the debate between modernism and postmodernism (like the other dilemmas of this debate) reflects a polarity in the human being itself and a profound tension in the present human condition.[13]

When we consider this dilemma from a biblical perspective, it is crucial to note how the priority of the love for God and for Jesus as His representative makes all our human bonds of secondary importance. The counter-cultural character of this priority can easily escape the attention of individualist Westerners, yet becomes fully clear when contrasted with worldviews in which a human community becomes the prime reference for determining what is good or evil. We see modern examples in totalitarian societies, where the State becomes the primary value.[14] A more traditional form is seen in many primal religions as in African Traditional Religion, where the determining factor for distinguishing between good and evil is the harmony and flourishing of the family and the clan (Mulago 1969: 139–158; Turaki 1997: 49–53, 60–71). In both cases, this absolutist attitude towards the community is related to a conception of the primary goal of the human being. In Marxist totalitarianism, for example, the good of the individual is inextricably wound up with the good of the State as the vehicle through which utopia or the state of wellbeing will be established. In African Traditional Religion the goal of the human being is bound up with the harmony and flourishing of the clan. To be separated from the clan is to be cut off from life, even when one is physically still functioning. Even if many African Traditional Religions conceive of a High God, who is also the Creator, this High God is not the goal of life, but rather the guarantee for the flourishing of the clan (Manaranche 1985: 58). It is therefore that African Traditional Religion is often called "anthropocentric" (Mbiti 1991: 43f; Magesa 1997: 69). "Clano-centric", however, would be a more precise term, for it is not the flourishing of the human individual, and not even of

13 See for this dilemma as one of the continual tensions of the human condition: Macquarrie 1982: 83–95.

14 Thus truth becomes subservient to the state, as becomes visible in Aldous Huxley's *Brave New World* (1969), which though imaginary came all too close to the reality of the totalitarian states of the twentieth century.

the individual within the clan, that is the ultimate goal. The ultimate goal is the flourishing of the clan itself, and to that goal the flourishing of the individual is secondary.[15]

From such a perspective of life that knows the great value of being part of a family and a community, the prioritization of Jesus is even more stunning than for readers from the individualistic West.[16] Jesus' call to love Him more than one's own family is not an isolated idea, but is reflected in a series of seemingly harsh texts that show how Jesus will be a cause of division in communities. He proclaims that He has not come to bring peace, but the sword (Mt 10:34). He says that He will cause division between father and son, between mother and daughter and between mother-in-law and daughter-in-law (Lk 12:53), and when his own mother and brothers come to Him He does not take care to receive them (Mk 3:31-35). It is not that He does not care about human communities and brotherly love; it's more that He recognizes that our relationship with God counts for more than these things. Breaking these human bonds is not a goal in itself, but rather serves to form a new family on a better footing with those who live according to the word of God. "Whoever does the will of God is my brother and sister and mother" (Mk 3:35; cf. Mt 19:29).

This perspective on human bonds in the light of the all-surpassing relationship with God shows how modern individualism is ambiguously related to the biblical tradition. It parallels what we noted earlier concerning the ambiguous way in which the modern conception of human autonomy is related to the Biblical idea of the authority of humanity over creation. Modern autonomy is made possible by the recognition of this authority given to the human being, yet only after it is separated from its original qualification by the supreme authority of the Creator (§4.2). Similarly, modern individualism has taken off from the message of the Gospel. The Gospel places each individual before God and thereby it gives the individual both the freedom and the obligation to stand alone over against his community and culture when God demands this. Modern individualism radicalizes this biblical freedom of the individual and in the process it forgets the degree in which our communities form us and how a sound individuality is impossible without reference to the Lord of each

15 See on this relationship Alexis Kagamé (1976: 287f, 303f), who himself continues to use the term "anthropocentric". The repercussions on the relationship with truth are equally far-reaching. Human language in general serves two purposes: the uncovering and sharing of truth and the developing and maintaining of relationships. In our sinful world both purposes are often in tension: speaking the truth can hurt relationships and vice-versa. Traditional Africans will often bend the truth to save relationships, where modern Europeans will maybe too easily hurt relationships in name of the truth.

16 This contrasts strongly with traditional sub-Saharan Africa, of which Efoé-Julien Pénoukou, a Roman Catholic priest from Benin, says: "The belief in a godhead has for us always been a 'family business', an ancestral heritage, which served to the formation of the conscience of solidarity with and belonging to the whole of a group; it was thus perceived as a factor of social coherence" (Pénoukou 1984: 110, my translation).

individual. Hypermodern individualism forgets that the human being cannot live without a community, which is based on values other than ever-fluctuating alliances between individuals who happen to have the same self-chosen values and interests.

Human autonomy and our need for God

In our exploration of the implications of the biblical understanding of the human being for apologetics we turn now to the question of human autonomy, which according to our analysis in the last chapter played a crucial role in the development of "modern" apologetics. In our discussion of the relationship of the human being with creation, we already saw that it would be ill conceived to talk about human autonomy with regards to creation in an absolute way, for it is always an authority derived from and under God and needs to respect the structures of creation entrusted to humankind. With regards to our relationship with God, we can now conclude that the biblical understanding of the image of God is fully in line with the Patristic and Reformed theology that "the chief end of man is to glorify God and enjoy him forever" (§3.2). As in his relationship with creation, the human being is also not autonomous and self-sufficient with regards to attaining his destiny and the flourishing of his being in this relationship with God. The human being depends on God's grace for his salvation from sin and death. Yet, even if we would not consider sin and death, he can never claim that he has a right on God or arrive at communion with God by his own abilities and power. One of the greatest difficulties that the modern subject has in relating the God is the recognition that this dependence on God's grace is not diminishing his value but actually establishes and confirms it.

If we are created "to know God and to enjoy Him", it is to be expected that we can find traces of this orientation in the human condition, even as the human being tries to live otherwise. We already noted the famous phrase of Augustine: "You made us unto you and therefore our heart is restless until it finds rest in you."[17] In the Scriptures this restlessness is particularly visible in the Psalms, in which the believers express their deep desire for the presence of God (Ps 42:1ff; 63:1; 73:25f; 84:3ff).[18] Yet, when Augustine spoke about his restlessness, he did not speak about a deep desire for God, which he had come to know as a Christian. He used the expression in the introductory chapter of his spiritual autobiography. With hindsight he discovered this restlessness in his life before becoming a Christian, when he was looking for fulfilment through enjoying all sorts of earthly pleasures, through excelling in rhetoric, and through exploring truth and goodness

17 See for Barth's analysis of this important idea: *KD* II/2: 294ff; trans. *CD* III/2: 412ff.

18 Childs considers this one of the most central lines of canonical Biblical anthropology (1993: 590).

in Manicheism and Platonism. With hindsight he discovered that this restlessness was there all the time because all these things could never give him what the true God gave him in Christ, who alone fulfilled his deepest longing. In the same way, his seventeenth-century spiritual heir, Blaise Pascal, noted so perceptively that humanity is constantly pushed to fill or flee the emptiness in human existence. Yet, however much we try, by our own efforts we will never manage, "since this infinite abyss can be filled only with an infinite and immutable object, in other words by God himself" (Pascal, *Pensées*: no. 148).

This abyss may show itself in different manners: people may flee from acknowledging it, they may try to extinguish this deep desire or they may try to fill it with what is not God. Part of the great variety in human cultures is precisely caused by this divergence of efforts to deal with this fundamental enigma of the human condition (see further §6.2). This shows how the image of God continues to exercise an influence even when we try to live without God, yet in an "inverted" manner, in a twisted and perverted way (Sherlock 1996: 43). It shows itself in the inability to be fully satisfied with what is not God (cf. Ecc 5:10). Despite this inversion, the traces of our being created to know God remain visible. So the Christian apologist will claim that only the living God can be an answer to our unrest and that He is an effective answer, for in Him we find "eternal life", which is life in abundance, in its fullness. Some may want to go one step further in affirming the indispensability of Christ in this respect: "This is the eternal life that we know the Father, *in* Christ, whom He has sent" (Cf. Jn 17:3).

In order to understand the full apologetic importance of our need for God, we need to note that God's self-revelation in Christ should not, in scriptural terms, just be considered a solution to our depravity and despair because of sin. If God is only important for us as a solution to our problems, our sins and our depravity, His importance is not essential to our nature and is therefore transitory. Yet, if the love of God shown in Christ is essential to our fulfilment, the relationship with Him is the goal of our existence. When, at the end of time, sin will definitively be dealt with, this relationship is still the accomplishment of our being and we will still find our fulfilment in Him.

It is possible that one of the factors that provoked the development in the West of a type of humanism without Christ is precisely the fact that Christ was considered a solution only for our sins and weakness. After all, for a humanity that feels sound and strong such a Christ has nothing to offer, as Dietrich Bonhoeffer stressed (1951: 158–163; trans. 1956: 145–149). This conception therefore also leads to the type of evangelism and apologetics that needs to make its audience feel its sin and weakness before it can talk about God and Christ. It is easily understandable why this type of preaching encounters strong resistance, particularly in a culture that values a positive view of oneself. If we are created to know and love God, to be taken into the circle of love that God is in Himself – and even more if we are created to know God in Christ – the Gospel can also be presented in a different way. Then the human being by nature needs the Triune God to find its accomplishment, an accomplishment that by far surpasses our wildest imaginations of what life can hold for us. The reality of sin and evil radically enforces the need for this God, but even setting aside death and sin, human life remains incomplete and truncated without Him.

The way God answers our deepest need confirms another aspect of what we discovered in our analysis of Barth's evaluation of modern epistemology and apologetics (§3.3). Even if the modern ideal of a neutral and disinterested approach to knowledge would be applicable somewhere else, it would not be in our knowing of God. This is not because God is less real and our knowledge of Him in that sense less "objective". It is simply because the question of whether God exists and of who He is for us is the most important question of our lives. We can love God. We can hate Him. We can try to keep Him at a distance. But we can never seriously consider Him and his claims on our lives neutrally, unbiased, as if it is of no real interest to us (see further §8.1).

4.5 The image of God in those who live without Christ

Until now we have been drawing out the apologetic implications of the creation of the human being in the image of God, supposing that each human being, Christian or not, religious or irreligious, can be characterized as such. This supposition, however, can be criticized from two different angles – one more of a philosophical; and one of a more theological kind. From a postmodern *philosophical* perspective one might well object that this is a Christian understanding of the human being, which is only true for those who share the Christian "cultural–linguistic" outlook. People with another basic outlook on life and on themselves will not consider themselves as the image of God, and the apologetic value of the concept is therefore limited. The concept of the creation of each human being in the image of God may be helpful for Christians to determine their attitude to others, and even to non-Christians, yet it cannot be understood in a realistic way as a description of what the nature of all human beings is in themselves. From a *theological* angle the Lutheran confession *Formula of Concord* identified the image of God in the human being with the original righteousness in which he was created and to which he needs to be recreated through Christ, who makes us bear his image (Berkouwer 1962: 46, n. 16). This conception reflected Luther's proper understanding, who considers the image of God to be radically destroyed in the sinner (*Genesis-Vorlesungen*: vv. 1:26; 2:16, 17; 3:1; cf. Grenz 2001: 162–166).

The question of the extent in which those who do not consider themselves the image of God can still be considered to reflect this image is of course of major importance for apologetics. The theological question has traditionally been linked with the possibility of addressing non-Christians as rational and responsible beings who can in some way assess the legitimacy of the truth and claims of the Gospel (f. ex. Barth, *KD* I/1: 251f; trans. *CD* I/1: 238f). It has also been linked with the possibility of finding in them a desire for God, an emptiness that alone God can fulfil, to which the apologist can appeal (f. ex. Craig 1994). The postmodern version of the criticism confronts us with the question whether or not Christ can in any significant way be considered to have a relationship with their "true nature", or whether He remains essentially strange to them as long as they continue to be outsiders to this "cultural–linguistic" world.

In how far is the image of God marred by sin?

Regarding the theological question, the answers have mostly tried to avoid two extremes. An understanding of these extremes helps us understand what is at stake. On the one hand, there is the Lutheran position already mentioned that the image of God is entirely lost by the Fall.[19] Its biblical basis is found in the New Testament expressions that state that Christ has come so that we may *become* the image of God through Him (Ro 8:29; 2Co 3:18; Col 3:10; cf. Eph 4:24). This understanding of the image as entirely lost is, however, difficult to maintain in view of the other biblical texts, which consider that the human being in its fallen state is still the image of God and urge us to treat him accordingly (Ge 9:6, Jas 3:9; cf. Hoekema 1994: 16–20). It seems furthermore to be contradicted by the everyday experience (which we should of course interpret with care) that human beings not withstanding their often "bestial" behaviour are still radically different from the rest of creation (Pannenberg 1983: 25–39; trans. 1985: 27–42; Brunner 1941: 3–14; trans. 1939: 17–28).[20] Therefore, we have a tendency to classify certain behaviour as "inhuman"; this would make no sense if we did not have reason to expect better.

Many theological traditions do therefore distinguish between two aspects of the image, one aspect, which characterizes each human being, and another aspect, which is lost with the Fall and found anew in Christ. The twentieth-century

19 This is Barth's understanding in the thirties (see again *KD* I/1: 251f; trans. *CD* I/1: 238f). Barth's later development of the question is, however, slightly different and more nuanced (*KD* III/2: 206f, 387, 391, 474; trans. *CD*: III/2: 172f, 321, 324, 395).

20 This difference is not diminished by the fact that among certain species of animals some rudimentary forms of language, technique and culture can be found. They are rightly called rudimentary compared with the elaboration and centrality of those elements in human history. The calling of the human being as the image of God does not even in itself depend on the distinction between humanity and the rest of creation. Theoretically it is conceivable that we will one time encounter a sentient species from another planet, which may or may not be invited to a loving relationship with God as we are. This depends on God's plan for that species. Yet, if God calls human beings to be his image, it is to be expected that humanity distinguishes itself from the rest of creation and animal world around, even though it also belongs to that world.

Swiss theologian Emil Brunner, for example, made a distinction between the formal and material image of God. The "formal image" is the human constitution as a being endowed with reason and will and thus able to respond to God's call to live according to his image revealed in Christ. The "material image" is visible in the human being, who actually lives in accordance with this vocation, primarily in Christ and consequently in those who live in Him (Brunner 1941: 530f; trans. 1939: 512–515; 1946: 22–24; cf. J. O'Donovan 1986). Yet Brunner's partition suffers from the problem that it considers the formal image as some sort of "neutral" structure that characterizes the human being – as a structure that can be used either in accordance with God's calling or in rejection of it. In an extensive debate with Brunner, Barth rightly noted that there can be no *neutral* substratum common to both those living in Christ and to those living without Christ (J. O'Donovan 1986: 451f). His reason, will and deep desire for a fulfilment beyond himself are, as Brunner notes, indeed the necessary conditions for his being able to respond to God's call.[21] Yet these are not neutral faculties that can be equally used in different ways, but they are faculties meant to be used and to flourish in relationship with God. When used in incompatible relationships, these faculties go bad and are in continual danger of destroying themselves and their environment. This is better expressed by indicating the *dynamic* character of the image as a whole instead of dividing it into an aspect that cannot be lost and another "moral" aspect which can be.[22] There is then not some part of the image that remains in the sinner in some sort of intact form; what remains only exists in an *inverted* or twisted form, contrary to its original intention. Let me elaborate on both the dynamic character of the image and the possibility of its inversion.

The dynamic biblical language about humanity being the image of God and yet needing to become the image is not as strange, complex, and vague as it might seem at first. It is common to a whole range of expressions that indicate a status and at the same time a calling. A father has a special biological, social and legal relationship to his children, yet it may be required that he be asked to "become" a real father to his children, even if the biological, social and legal relationship is already there. A son has special status in the family, yet not all sons behave appropriately to this position, as both the younger and the elder son in the parable of the prodigal son show (Lc 15:12, 28ff). A spouse has a special status in relation to her husband, yet does not automatically behave as a spouse should do.

The examples already note the importance of precisely this type of dynamic concepts to describe our relationship to God. The creation of the human being in

21 This third decisive element of the human constitution, "this deep desire for a fulfilment beyond himself", is not central in Brunner, but needs to be added, if we want to avoid the somewhat rationalistic and Kantian slant of Brunner's anthropology (J. O'Donovan 1986: 457f).

22 The most elaborate statement of such a dynamic understanding to date can probably be found in Grenz (2001: 177–264); see for the limitations of a purely dynamic understanding of the "image of God": Kelsey 2009: 904.

his image confers on the human being a special calling. This calling is not a static gift. As a calling it invites us to the highest honour, joy, and the most exciting life we can imagine – to share the love of God in communion with Him, with the people around us and in the caring for and development of the wider creation. We are called to *become* the image of God in Christ, who is the perfect Image. Yet, as a calling it is not something that can be lost simply by rejecting this call. The prodigal son who left his father remained his son and this, for him, is an indication both of his worth and of his shame. If he had been born a pig-herder, it would not have brought such shame to find himself herding pigs, yet at the same time he would not have had the same importance in the eyes of his father. In the same way human beings who are not living according to the image still *are* the image and still are called to image God and this special status and calling constitutes both their worth and their shame.

So even in a fallen human being the special status and calling are still present, yet not as a neutral deposit, which can be used and activated when called upon, but in an *inverted* way. When God created the human being as the crown of creation to be his image, He endowed him with all he needed, both in his own constitution and in the world around. Yet, these are not neutral gifts that we can use for whatever we want. This is clear in our capacity to love God, to love the One who infinitely transcends all created reality. If we reject this gift to love Him, we continue to have this capacity for infinite love. In our rejection of God, this capacity is left without its intended focus, is left empty and is consequently inverted in an insatiable desire to fill our lives with what is not God. It therefore places us in a relationship to nature and to our fellow human beings which constantly vacillates between an excessive dependence and an unhealthy greed and possessiveness (Pascal, *Pensées*). Our will, therefore, which is meant to direct us freely to God, to others and to nature, becomes inverted and enslaved. Our reason, which was meant to discover truth and to know God and to serve Him and others accordingly, becomes irrational. It becomes inverted and an instrument, which we use to flee from the truth – although it still may know some truth – and to handle and mould the world around our own interests. Furthermore, our very being as the image of God becomes fragmented and at war with itself, for it rejects God who was meant to be its centre. It is this fragmentation of our nature and the resulting fragmentation of the human world and of human cultures, which gives postmodernism its force, as we shall see later (§6.2).

There is no aspect of the image, no formal remnant that is not inverted. Yet even while inverted, the human being still remains created in the image of God. This is not only a truth that is proclaimed to him from the outside as God continues to call him to be His image and to be His child. It characterizes his most inner being, for even the inverted desire is a desire which only God can fulfil – thus he is never at rest without God. Even the enslaved will is a will and can be freed by grace. Even our irrational reason is still a reason and therefore can never be at ease with its self-chosen irrationality. The Holy Spirit can still speak to this reason in a transforming way so that it can recognize the truth in Christ. These few sentences are packed with implications for the way in which we should address concrete people in apologetic dialogue. The eighth chapter will deal with the way the apologist should relate to concrete human beings as sinners. How shall we dialogue with them as with people that are created to love and be loved by God, as people endowed with will and reason? How shall we dialogue with them as people who at the same time are all too often far from rational as they are being pushed by all sorts of needs and interests that impinge on their rationality, bind their will and hide their deepest needs?

The dynamic understanding of the image of God also provides us with an important insight with regards to a question that needs to be raised in respect of an argument developed in the first chapter. There we argued that the proclamation of the Gospel should always address people as rational and responsible beings (§1.3). Would not this stress on the need for a responsible choice for the truth exclude small children from hearing the Gospel from the outset, when Jesus himself treated children with such respect? Does it not in the same stroke disqualify the mentally handicapped for entering the Kingdom of God, while this Kingdom is particularly open to the weak and those in low esteem? (cf. Barth 1934: 25f; trans. 1946: 88f; J. O'Donovan 1986: 440f, 452ff)

In this respect we need to consider the wider perception that we regard certain qualities characteristic of a human being, while accepting at the same time that some individuals for some reason do not (yet) have them. We consider that human beings are responsible for their deeds and therefore we judge them for their crimes, which we do not with animals, yet we accept that young children cannot be summoned and that minors are under a special legal dispensation. We are born as human beings and yet need to grow into humanity.

Those children whose development towards maturity is blocked because of certain mental handicaps may in this life never move beyond this passive participation in the community of love, and their responsibility may range from fairly limited to indiscernible. They may reveal the image of God more in certain respects than others – for example, in a deep desire for God. Yet other aspects of the image of God remain undeveloped in this life and we do not know what God holds for them in the life to come. The fact that some aspects of their being are blocked from further development confronts us with the broken state of creation. The fact that all of us are created for a fullness of life, which we will not reach in this life, gives us our value and reminds us of the dynamic character of our beings as created in the image of God. As God's image all our lives are open to the future and to God.

Does being the image of God depend on sharing the Christian cultural–linguistic outlook?

For many postmodernists these theological discussions about the way in which the sinner still is the image of God will at first sight be utterly missing the point. For them the idea that the human being is created in the image of God is a cultural–linguistic construct, which may at best be relevant only for those who share this outlook. For the deconstructive postmodernist it is even worse: it is an oppressive way to impose our unifying views on a fragmentary reality and on other people, who should remain radically "other".

At its most basic level this question leads us straight into the next chapter. There we will deal with the following question: is there, in our multicultural world beyond modernism, still a valid way in which we can claim to know something about a reality beyond our language and culture? We will argue there for a form of critical realism which imposes itself even after the demise of universalist foundationalism, after the linguistic turn, and after the recognition of the impact of culture on all we are, think and see. This critical realism is a constitutive element of a Christian apology. This critical realism is presupposed in any apologetic argument that God in Christ revealed the goal, the nature and the condition of all humanity and all human beings.

We will argue that an understanding of reality that makes better sense of the rich variety of what we perceive than alternative understandings can rightly claim a closer verisimilitude to reality itself. We therefore need to go one more time over our analysis of the Christian understanding of the image of God in this chapter while asking whether it makes better sense of the reality we live and encounter than alternative understandings of human nature and the human condition. It is true that our goal and condition are most clearly shown in Jesus of Nazareth. Yet, if what Christ reveals is the truth of all human beings, Christians or not, this understanding should be in some way reflected in what we perceive of the human condition. When we review the analysis of what it means to be created in the image of God, it shows indeed on many points, how it makes better sense of the way in which we perceive reality than the alternatives we have been discussing.

First, the Christian understanding of the human being and condition proves more respectful of reality and more coherent in its consideration of our relationship to the world around us. From a Christian perspective it becomes clear that the human being is not a detached, neutral, and infinite onlooker (modernism), nor completely subjected to what impacts on him from his culture and environment (postmodernism). It is more realistic to see the human being as part of creation, yet at the same time its regent, both as formed by culture and as a former of culture. In the next chapter we will dig deeper into the realism of this understanding of human knowing and we will further explore its implications for Christian apologetic dialogue in our relativistic age.

Second, the realism of the Christian understanding of the human being shows true with regards to the relation of the individual to the community. Anthropological and sociological studies show that the human individual is deeply formed by his particular cultural background, that he cannot dig to some neutral foundation beyond all cultural influence (modernism). At the same time, he is not simply the prisoner of his culture and community (as in traditional, totalitarian or postmodern forms of communalism). In the sixth and seventh chapter we will see more of the way in which the Gospel addresses us as cultural beings and opens a way to meet the Creator of the universe in our particular culture. It explores the more practical implications of our cultural nature for Christian apologetic dialogue in a multicultural world.

Third, the Christian analysis of the relationship of the human being to God is pertinent in comparison to its alternatives. It is not only Christians who note the unsatisfactory nature of all those things with which we try to feel the deep desire that haunts us. The desire in itself could of course both be openness for what is most worthwhile or the clearest sign of the misfit that the human being is as for now the latest stage in an arbitrary evolution. If the latter is the case, we have reason to ask for a plausible evolutionary explanation as to why this misfit has survived in the battle for the survival of the fittest. Yet, if he really has a Creator who offers Himself to fill this emptiness and openness of his being, this explains why the human being can never rest in this world as naturalistic modernism had hoped. It equally shows why the postmodern playful promenade from one stand to another in the carnival of life (Middleton & Walsh 1995b: 58ff) does seem shallow at crucial moments in life and it fortunately shows that this shallowness is not something to which we are inevitably condemned.

In this respect the *theological* reflection on the question in what sense even those we do not want to image God still are the image of God is also of major importance to answer the more *philosophical* question which we are discussing now. In what sense are those who do not share the Christian cultural–linguistic outlook the image of God? If they are, the image will be inverted and we need to look in them for traces of this inverted image. One important sign of the inverted character is that being created in the image of God is a reality from which sinners tend to flee. Therefore even its non-recognition need not surprise us. Yet, at the same time it means that nothing can be more healthy and liberating than meeting God who sheds new light on our being and condition. In the eighth and final chapter we will dig deeper into this very real tension in the human condition that we both flee from and desire for God. We will explore further how this helps to develop a Christian apologetics for concrete human beings that helps them deal truthfully and responsibly with the muddle of both healthy and unhealthy motivations, and of good and destructive desires that drive us all in our emotion-driven society.

Chapter 5

SURPRISED BY REALITY

The Christian faith is profoundly realist in character, for it lives by the conviction that God was there before we existed and could call upon Him. As Christians we live by God's grace and reality, because He came to save us, before we even knew Him. A realist – or more precisely, a critically realist – understanding of the knowledge of God is therefore a crucial component of the Christian faith. It rests on the joyful recognition that God is indeed who He is and that He acted indeed on our behalf, thereby showing who He is and breaking through our self chosen conceptions of the divine (see §1.3).

However, since biblical times, this joyful recognition has not been without questioning, because the reality in which we live often seems to contradict the existence of God. Postmodernity has given this questioning a new acuity, because of its pervading tendency to deconstruct all beliefs in God as culturally relative human constructs. The multicultural nature of the contemporary world gives this thesis a strong initial plausibility. The Christian joy about God's grace and action towards us can be profoundly marred under this pressure. It has even brought many Christians to the acceptance that their faith is indeed nothing more than their subjective construct to make life liveable and meaningful. This may have been caused by a misunderstanding of what the Christian faith is all about, or by the despair that postmodernity's challenge can ever be met. It may also result from the sin of sloth preventing a real engagement with these challenges.

The question addressed in this chapter is whether the Christian apologist has good reasons for believing that we can be in touch with reality itself, with the reality of God. We have already argued that the postmodern stress on the historic and cultural character of all our knowing does not *a priori* exclude the possibility of a realist understanding of this knowledge (§2.4). Yet when we look to the extent of cultural and historical influence on human thinking, the practical possibilities of being in touch with a reality beyond cultural and historical conditioning can still seem rather bleak. We therefore need to go one step further and show *how* in practice a historically and culturally conditioned human being can have confidence to be in touch with this reality. This task is not only of interest to us to answer the charges of relativist postmodernism; if we can show how we are brought in touch we reality, even while being historically and culturally conditioned, this will also provide crucial insights for developing Christian apologetics in a multicultural world. If our audiences are all culturally conditioned, as we ourselves are, and all in different ways, how can we build bridges between these cultures and the reality of God?

In the first main section of this chapter we will explore how discussions and discoveries in the philosophy of science help us to elucidate the way in which historically embedded traditions can be in touch with reality (§5.1). From that point, and from the Christian understanding of the human being developed in the previous chapter, we will give a more general picture of a Christian understanding of how human beings come to know reality, which is more like the reading of a book than constructing an edifice, as modern foundationalism would have it (§5.2). One central element of the argument will be that the nature of the reality we want to know, determines the way we can relate to it and know it and should determine our approach to it. We therefore need to look more specifically into the way knowledge is possible from the God, who reveals Himself in Christ. (§5.3) Although our quest for the nature of Christian apologetics will be with us all the time, we will use the last section to draw out some specific implications of this understanding of knowledge for apologetic witness. We will give special attention to the role of sound dogmatics and of testimony, which are both shown to be crucial for a properly Christian apologetic. In an excursus at the end, we will look back to the modern enterprise of evidentialist apologetics in order to evaluate both its strengths and weaknesses (§5.4).

All in all, we will discover how the classical Augustinian adage that "we believe in order to understand" remains crucial to a sound understanding of apologetics. It also gains fresh meanings. Faith is necessary as openness to and trusting acceptance of reality in general and particularly as a trusting openness and acceptance of what God has done in Christ for us and a trust in the faithfulness of those who testify to what God has done in Jesus on our behalf. Such a trust need not be afraid of critical reflection, for it puts us in touch with the reality that is seen to have an integrity of its own, which breaks through all our human frameworks. It shows that in some way understanding also precedes faith, for the thrust of the argument will be that trusting the testimony concerning Jesus and opening ourselves to this reality is a reasonable step to take (cf. Augustine, *Epistula* CXX, 3, 4).

5.1 In touch with reality

The proper use of the philosophy of science

In order to answer postmodernism and its use of multiculturalism, we will need to deepen our understanding of how knowledge can, at the same time, be culturally embedded and in touch with objective reality. We have already hinted on several occasions that in this respect we can be greatly helped by twentieth-century discoveries concerning the nature of scientific research and progress. The philosophy of science has moved away from a conception of science as based on neutral and value-free perceptions. Rather, it recognizes that all scientific research starts with prior faith-commitments, and is done within traditions of shared convictions about the world and the nature of scientific research. Yet for most scientists, this does not exclude the possibility of scientific theories aiming at truth and having an objective reference (f. ex. Polkinghorne 1991: 14f).

We should be on our guard when using the philosophy of science for the development of an apologetic argument for the possibility of an objective referent for tradition-dependent knowledge. Because science still has such a high standing in our society, it is very easy to fall into the modernist trap of considering the method of natural science as the norm, to which all our knowledge, including our religious convictions, should measure up. However, this would deliver Christian faith to the judgement of the scientific tradition that is far from neutral to it. Besides, it does not respect the proper nature of the object of the Christian faith as the final criterion for deciding how we can properly know it. We saw that not only was this the mistake of modern apologetics, but also, in a modified way, of the cultural linguistic approach of Lindbeck, who subsumed the Christian faith under a general postmodern understanding of the function of language games, cultures and traditions (§2.4). If generally accepted cultural assumptions concerning justified opinions and science are negative towards the Christian faith, we need to seriously consider these assumptions, but if necessary live without our wider culture's approval. We should resist the temptation of adapting theology to generally accepted standards of what a science should be (cf. Barth *KD* I/1: 6; trans. *CD* I/1: 8). We do not believe in Christ because of the cultural approval He receives, but because we have discovered that He Himself really has the words of truth and life, even though the world has rejected Him (cf. Jn 6:86f). The use of philosophical insights from our surrounding culture should therefore, in principle, be eclectic and guided by the proper content of the Christian faith (cf. Barth *KD* I/2: 815–825; trans. *CD* I/2: 727–736).[1]

Science and reality

The fact that the majority of those involved in scientific research suppose that they aim at discovering some objective truth about the reality with which they are engaged (cf. Polkinghorne 1991: 5; 1989: 162; McGrath 1998a: 143, 154; Ratzsch 2000: 70, 81) does not in itself prove they are right. They might be collectively wrong. Yet there are a number of arguments that altogether build a strong case for

1 In this respect we can say that our use of the philosophy of science does not have a "foundational" role, but an "illuminative" role. This is also the way Torrance uses the philosophy of science of Polanyi (McGrath 1999: 229).

a critical realist understanding of science. In order to show this, I will first point to three general characteristics of our relationship to reality. Next, I will point to two more specific scientific phenomena, for which I think it will be very hard to find a valuable explanation when not holding to a realist understanding of science.

We should first consider the fact that most people live their lives in some "naive" realist fashion. They suppose that most of what they discover about the world and what they hear from others about the world in which they live should be taken as "hard facts" that they cannot change according to their own wish or interest (cf. Berger & Luckmann 1967: 35ff). When people warn me not to cross the street just in front of a car, I do not suppose that the risk of being hit by a car is a social construct or a certain person's perspective that might be true for her but not for me. The Spanish-American realist philosopher George Santayana (1863–1952) makes a perceptive remark concerning absolute relativism, when he says: "I would be ashamed to countenance opinions which, when not arguing, I did not believe."[2]

This everyday realism may not directly bother someone tending towards relativism, for most tend to be relativistic in certain areas of life only. Yet the point about naive realism is still an important one, for it shows the absurdity of absolute relativism. If we respect our naive realism in at least certain areas of life, the problem is no longer whether realism is an option, for it is. The question is, rather, in which areas of life is realism an option and where isn't it? Do we have reasons to exclude in principal scientific language about unobservables, like electrons and photons, from the area where realism applies? Do we have reason to exclude in principal language about God and our relationship to God?

An astonishing fact about the universe that points to the validity of realism is the enormous effectiveness of science in dealing with reality. A main contestant for critical realism with regards scientific theories is the idea that scientific theories just point to regularities in human perceptions of reality and that they should be conceived as no more than helpful instruments in our coping with the world around us. For most scientists this will not suffice as a description of what they aim at in formulating scientific theory: they do not just hope to discover regularities; rather, they aim for an *explanation* of these regularities in getting a firmer grasp of the nature of the phenomena they are investigating (Ratzsch 2000: 30f, 81; Polkinghorne 1989: 172f). More importantly, saying that scientific theories only describe regularities and are merely helpful for our instrumental mastery of nature begs the question. It is obvious that they do so, but the question remains: how can it be the case that such theories are so impressively successful in describing and predicting regularities and in instrumentally mastering nature?

---

2 George Santayana, *Scepticism and Animal Faith*, p. 305, quoted in: Macquarrie 1988: 237. Torrance notes: "[I]n our regular communication with one another we use and interpret signs in the light of objective reference. Thus the natural operation of the mind would appear to be realist" (Torrance 1999: 58).

(Polkinghorne 1986: 22; 1991: 5; 1989: 172f.) How do you want to explain that a theory in physics about splitting atoms through breaking down the nucleus is so "successful" if it is not because these theories do, in some way, reflect the nature of the atom? How do you explain the enormous effectiveness of the manipulation of solids, liquids and gases in chemistry if the understanding of the chemical processes on which it is based do not in one way or another correspond with reality? Supposing that scientific theories do tell us something about reality in itself seems to be the best explanation of the instrumental effectiveness of the use of scientific theories.

Next to the validity of naive realism in many areas of life and the enormous effectiveness of scientific theory, we can refer to the intelligibility of the universe as a third general pointer to the fact that scientific theories refer to reality as it is in itself. This intelligibility shows itself in the fact that the universe yields to inquisitive probing and shows itself to be organized by a great number of intricately interrelated laws. From one perspective, belief in the intelligibility of the universe is, together with the belief in its uniformity, a presupposition of science (Ratzsch 2000: 14–16; Torrance 2001: 52f). According to the Judeo-Christian understanding of the cosmos this presupposition is justified, for it is the creation of an infinite intelligent mind. Yet, the impressive results of scientific probing in their turn confirm this intelligibility and uniformity. Science is able to uncover many intelligible patterns and shows scientific laws to fit large areas of reality, for which they were not even conceived. The main point here is that this intelligibility of the universe is itself also a signpost to a realist understanding scientific knowledge. If there was no reality out there, accept for what we project ourselves, there would be nothing to discover. Yet there is so much discovered and yet to discover (Polanyi 1946: 10, 13; 1962: 16; Polkinghorne 1989: 161, 166).

> If scientific realism, and the theories it draws on, were not correct, there would be no explanation of why the observed world is as if they were correct; that fact would be brute, if not miraculous (Devitt 1984: 108).

In an article entitled "Science and Reality", the philosopher of science Michael Polanyi (1891–1976) uses the distinction made in communication theory between a random noise and a message to show the way in which intelligibility is a pointer to reality. Although there are a number of cases in which we are not entirely sure that something we hear is just a noise or a message, in many cases we can clearly distinguish between the two. In contrast to a random noise, we discover in a message an order that is independent from us, an order that surprises us. Because it is an order that is there independently of our perceiving it, we can expect it to manifest itself in the future and be recognizable by everyone else. We can therefore hold it with "universal intent", claiming that everyone else will be able to recognize it for him- or herself. It is precisely this characteristic of being able to manifest itself ever anew that is intrinsic to any belief to something being real (1967: 191ff).

Those who oppose a realist understanding of scientific theories will not be impressed by the fact that science discovers all sorts of intelligible patterns in nature. For them, the language of "discovery" is not appropriate, for according to their understanding this intelligibility does not result from the nature of things but is a product of the human mind. It is more like the patterns we recognize in the stellar constellations. There is nothing inherent in these stars that is reflected in our pointing to them as "Orion" or "Hercules". The patterns we see there are products of our imagination, which we use to bring some order in the great quantity of stars and lights surrounding us. Both moderns and postmoderns share this belief in the enormous powers of the human mind to mould the universe according to either universal categories of perception or in line with a culturally determined intersubjective perspective. However, this way of understanding science simply does not fit the reality of scientific research and progress. First of all, it cannot account for the fact that good scientific theories have explanatory and predictive power far beyond the areas for which they were originally conceived and, second, it cannot give an adequate account of "the structure of scientific revolutions". Let us consider these two characteristics of scientific progress in turn.

A famous example of the predictive power of scientific theory is the confirmation of the wave-theory of light through an experiment proposed in the early nineteenth-century by Siméon Poisson. He noted that if light consisted of waves, the breaking of the waves would lead to the effect that when a point source of light would be directed to a tiny circular object, somewhere behind, there should be a round shadow with a bright spot in the centre. For Poisson this was inconceivable and meant to be a refutation of the wave theory, yet later on, when an experiment by Fresnel showed the bright spot, this was a major confirmation of the wave theory (Ratzsch 2000: 81; Kuhn 1996: 155). The theologian-scientist John Polkinghorne gives similar examples in his historical overview of quantum research from the 1950s to the 1980s, in which he himself participated as a theoretical physicist (1989: 166). It is important to know that the discovery of entirely new phenomena with the help of existing theories can be observationally entirely unrelated to the phenomena from which the original theory was drawn. This seriously undermines a non-realist understanding of scientific theories as only describing regularities in the phenomena as we perceive them (Ratzsch 2000: 81). How could these theories predict such phenomena, if it were not because it relates some unified reality underlying such diverse phenomena? It is only "[b]y bearing on reality, [that] scientific theories [...] have the power convincingly to surprise us" (Polanyi 1967: 190; cf. 1946: 9; 1962: 5, 37; Polkinghorne 1986: 23ff; Torrance 2001: 96f).

The radical Kuhnians have taken Kuhn's description of the social factors involved in scientific revolutions to imply that scientific theories are *mere* social constructions. Kuhn's analysis has definitely shown the power of social factors, but indirectly these factors provide a powerful argument for a realist understanding of science. Kuhn has, after all, shown that scientific communities are conservative. They undertake all their research from a certain perspective, interpret all the data in light of the given paradigms, and tend to be blind for contrary evidence or explain it away. It is only when the number of anomalies (experimental results that do not fit the paradigm) and the inner tensions within the paradigm grow too large and inescapable that some will start to propose alternatives. Furthermore, when such new theories are proposed, they are strongly resisted by the established scientific community, who will continue either to ignore the anomalies and tensions or to bend the existing paradigm as far as possible in order to integrate the new results (Kuhn 1996: 23–34, 77–91). If we could just bend reality according to social constructs, there would never have been such inescapable anomalies that would have forced such a change. The fact that the Aristotalian paradigm in physics was ever replaced by the Newtonian paradigm and the latter in its turn by relativity theory and quantum mechanics thus proves that reality resists our interpretations. Reality proves too hard and we cannot "beat nature into line"[3] without restrictions by our theories.[4]

In concluding this section, we may note that it could indeed be possible to think of scientific paradigm changes that are wholly induced by social forces. In some areas of life and in some social constellations, cultural pressures, social biases, personal interests and political correctness may be so strong that they overrule the way reality impinges on the scientific community. Yet, the intelligibility of reality encountered in scientific research, the effectiveness of the use of the results of scientific research, and the history of scientific research show that in science we are in fact confronted with an independent reality, which resists being forced in the grid of our preconceived ideas (cf. Torrance 1985: 54f, 74, 75; McGrath 1998a: 147, 156). One reason that relativist postmodernist nonetheless conclude from the impossibility of having a direct and culturally immune access to reality to the impossibility of a realist understanding of knowledge has its origin in a dualist and foundationalist conception of knowledge. This shows that their departure from modernism was not radical enough, because it is with the moderns that they share the understanding of the human epistemological predicament as created by the cleft between the knowing subject and the objective world (§3.4). The Christian understanding of the human being and his place in creation shows this understanding of the human epistemological predicament to be misconceived from the start. This Christian understanding thereby proves to give better insight

---

3 This expression of Kuhn himself is revealing, for it shows how nature can resist our interpretations (1996: 135, cf. pp. 52f, 96f, 206).

4 "Scientists find it hard to see what they are not expecting. […] Yet one must acknowledge that the stubborn facticity of nature imposes ineluctable constraint, whatever one might have anticipated would be the case. Discoveries such as *CP* non-conservation and the J/ψ were totally contrary to prior expectation" (Polkinghorne 1989: 167f, cf. about this "stubbornness" of nature also pp. 169f, 173).

into and a better explanation of the nature of human knowledge and the history of scientific progress.

Beyond dualism

In the previous chapter we saw that the Christian understanding of the world as creation and of the human being as the image of God suggests a radically different understanding of the human epistemological predicament. Human beings are not originally posited over against creation. We do not know the world around us nor ourselves as onlookers, but by way of "indwelling", to use this Polanyian vocabulary. We are part of it. We cannot separate ourselves from or put ourselves over against the world to which we belong. We indwell the world in our bodies and although we can reflect on our bodily existence, we ordinarily take it for granted and cannot separate ourselves from it. We relate to the world through our physical tools, but also through our language, our culture and our conceptual systems, which we indwell and through which we indwell the world (Polanyi 1962: 59f, 64, 173). We can critically attend to these ways of understanding the world, but we can never distance ourselves from all of them at the same time, for this is our life and the way we live and reflect, and without it there would be no place to stand on or to reflect from. When we indwell our bodies, our languages, our cultures and our tools, we also indwell the world around us, for as bodily beings we belong to it and our cultures and languages are as much impressed on by reality as we impress through them on reality. Though we are called to take care of and subdue creation, we can therefore never completely master it, for we are part of it and depend on it.

This understanding of the particular place of the human being in the world has far-reaching consequences for the way we know and discover. First of all, if this is how the human being is created it suggests the possibility of his having a valid understanding of reality. In order to exercise his authority over creation and in order to relate to other people and to God, such an understanding is a prerequisite. Second, it implies that his knowledge will not be the knowledge of a disinterested onlooker, for it always engages him in some way, in dealing with creation, in relating to people and to God. Third, this implies that we cannot detach ourselves from reality in the sense that we can look at it from a distance. Our knowledge is not like the knowledge of God. We know in being part of creation, in indwelling it. It implies, fourth, that either our relationship to reality should start with a basic trust or that our efforts to know reality will be aborted from the start. We do not come as outside onlookers who have some independent knowledge to compare if our knowledge of this universe is trustworthy and who can withdraw if this universe would not please us. Our mind is the only one that we have to reflect with. Our senses are the only ones to relate to the reality around us and the reality that we perceive as such is the only reality to which we have direct access. We therefore need either to entrust ourselves to it or to withdraw in relativism or nihilism. We need to trust creation and our own created being. We need to trust our Creator for it. The trust need not be a blind trust, for it may be confirmed in the process, yet we cannot do without such an initial and ongoing trust if we want to engage with reality.

When we turn back from this Christian theological understanding of the human being to the development of science, we see how it is compatible with an understanding of science that combines an understanding of the historical bedding of scientific research with the recognition of its objective referent. This is why theologians like Torrance (1980) and Newbigin (1989: x) were able to profit so much from the philosophy of science of Polanyi. His approach stressed on the one hand the personal involvement and judgement of the researcher, the need of basic trust, the role of the scientific tradition and community (Polanyi 1946; 1962). Yet he showed how science is, at the same time, undertaken "with universal intent", aimed at convincing the scientific community at large, because of the researcher's justified belief that through all this he is engaging with reality itself (1962: 65, 379). Though Polanyi wasn't a professing Christian, and maybe *precisely* because he wasn't, his analysis of the nature of science provides a confirmation for the Christian understanding of mankind's place within creation. Christian anthropology effectively provides an explanation for the combination of the historical and realist character of our knowledge, which on a dualist understanding remains an insoluble enigma, a crucial anomaly that shows the need for a postdualist paradigm for understanding knowledge. Christian anthropology also provides us with a model for such an understanding human knowledge in general and for the development of a postmodern, postfoundationalist, and postdualist understanding of Christian apologetics.

Comparing conceptual frameworks and reality

At this stage, we are able to address what is probably the main objection to critically realist interpretations of science and of human knowledge in general. I refer here to the postmodern argument, which we encountered already that the idea of a reality beyond our cultural and linguistic image of it does not make sense, simply because if such a reality would be there, it would in principle be inaccessible to neutral observation. As Thomas Kuhn argued (1996: 206; cf. Rorty 1991: 12; Kenneson 1995: 156):

> There is, I think, no theory-independent way to reconstruct phrases like 'really there'; the notion of a match between the ontology of a theory and its "real" counterpart in nature now seems to me elusive in principle.

In a non-dualist understanding of human knowledge, however, according to which we know reality by indwelling it, the idea of an extra-linguistic reality certainly makes sense even though it may not be directly accessible. In a dualist conception, conceptual structures, cultural frameworks, and language all find themselves on the side of the knowing subject on one side of the abyss dividing the subject from the objective reality. The subject would in some way need to be able to cross the abyss independently from this cultural framework in order to check the validity of this framework against reality. He cannot. Yet in terms of a non-dualist understanding of knowledge, our bodies as well as our cultural framework, worldview, language etc. are not simply at the subject-side of the divide. They are the clothing in which people indwell this world; the lenses through which they see the world; the instruments with which they handle the world. Rather than being at the subject side of the divide, they are actually both the screen and the lens between the knowing subject and his world.

Let me illustrate how all these tools can be both a screen and a lens between us and the world around us in elaborating on an often-used example with regard to the cultural relativity of conceptual instruments. My African friends generally have only one concept for snow. They therefore have a hard time distinguishing the two concepts of snow that I have inherited from my upbringing in the Netherlands, where people distinguish "wet snow" and "dry snow". Apparently some of the Canadian Inuit have eight concepts for snow. It is not, as some postmoderns suggest, that my African friends are unable to distinguish the two or eight types of snow; it is just that it is harder for them. Language provides a tool for understanding and for handling reality. It is a lens through which we see reality and not necessarily an impermeable screen between us and reality. If an African from the equator were to live in the Netherlands, she would easily discover that there are two types of snow, to which one relates differently. When the snow is dry and crispy, you protect yourself with particularly warm clothing that does not necessarily need to be watertight. When the snow is "wet" and melts easily, it is more important that your clothing is watertight, yet it does not need to be especially warm. Even if they did not learn Dutch, my African friend would probably, in time, learn to distinguish the two types of snow. Yet I may help her and speed up the process by handing her the concepts, the value of which she might otherwise discover by herself.

The simple conceptual tools we have to deal with snow show, in a rudimentary form, the way scientific theories function. They are lenses through which we see reality and tools that may be exchanged for others that give us a clearer view, or that help us to handle reality more delicately or more effectively. We can never do without *any* tool or lens. Yet we can compare them, just as someone who has never been able to see clearly without glasses can compare different glasses that the optician suggest for her – that is, compare them with respect to the clarity of view they provide. It is thereby that with hindsight glasses of a better quality can prove that the glasses she used to wear were of a lesser quality. We can even imagine a world in which nearsighted-ness is a universal ailment and where the first person trying a new type of glasses has no one with whom to discuss their clarity. The clarity may be undreamed of. Now it might be objected that in such a case there is no way to compare the quality of the old and the new glasses: how do you know if the real world is in fact blurred or clear? When stated this way, we know that this question is not difficult to answer. The first one in the world of the nearsighted to try these new glasses would generally not feel that she needs some knowledge of the world independent of these glasses to check if reality in itself is vague or clear. She would know that this clarity does not just come from her glasses, but from the reality she sees. As we just saw in Polanyi's distinction between a noise and a message, the new patterns that she discovers testify in themselves to their inherent reality, which impresses itself on her sight. Good theories work the same way: "Theories are certainly to be modified, or refined, like lenses, in the light of what is disclosed, but they are essentially disclosure models which claim recognition for what they serve to reveal" (Torrance 1985: 54f).

This example shows what happens when one scientific paradigm is exchanged for another one. According to Kuhn, there is no way to prove which paradigm is better, for neither do we have an access to reality which is independent of such paradigms, nor do we have an overarching scientific framework against which both paradigms could be assessed. Therefore, "the competition between paradigms is not the sort of battle that can be resolved by proof" (1996: 148, cf. p. 152). This conclusion is then used by the more radical Kuhnians and the popular brokers of the Kuhnian legacy to argue that scientific paradigms are mere social constructs. There is therefore no way we could ever say that one of two mutually exclusive paradigms is more true to reality than the other (Ratzsch 2000: 51–53).[5] However, this conclusion does not follow from the premise that we can never step outside the world of one paradigm or another. The fact is that paradigms are not utterly unrelated. If newer scientific paradigms are really successful, they allow from their perspective to understand both the relative truth and the relative falsity of the paradigm(s) they are replacing.

A clear example of such a newer paradigm is relativity theory, which shows why Newtonian physics was so powerfully able to explain the world. According to relativity theory the physics developed in the Newtonian tradition is indeed describing what reality is approximately like, but only within a certain range, in the world of low velocities and of entities of sizes that fill the world of our ordinary experience. Thus, Alasdair MacIntyre has shown how the relativism that

5 Kuhn himself does not want to be called a relativist. The fact that there is no *proof* for the superiority of one paradigm over another does not mean that there are no good reasons to prefer one over another (1996: 152). He states: "Later scientific theories are better than earlier ones for solving puzzles in the often quite different environments to which they are applied", he denies that this is "because it is somehow a better representation of nature" (1996: 206). I take this to mean that Kuhn does not consider scientific theories as mere social constructs, yet that he understands the relationship of these theories with reality in an instrumentalist way. This brings us back to the criticism of instrumentalism in the first section of §5.1.

seems to follow from the Kuhnian description of scientific progress dissipates if we realize that a valid new paradigm always includes an understanding of history that is able to show the relative truthfulness of its predecessors (1980: 56):

> When an epistemological crisis is resolved, it is by the construction of a new narrative which enables the agent to understand *both* how he or she could intelligibly have held his or her original beliefs *and* how he or she could have been so drastically misled by them. The narrative in terms of which he or she at first understood and ordered experiences is itself made into the subject of an enlarged narrative.

This is precisely what we would expect if human knowing should be understood in a non-dualist manner.

5.2 Some basics of a Christian theory of knowledge

We have just offered a defence of realism and an account of how human knowledge can be both historically embedded and refer to an extra-linguistic reality. We have yet to see how this applies to our knowledge of God, who for Christians is the Reality *par excellence*. Before we get to the specifics of our knowledge of God, though, we will need to sketch some of the central principles of a Christian epistemology, a Christian understanding of what it means to know and to get to know. This, in turn, will help us to understand better the nature of apologetics. For this our reflections on science prove an appropriate introduction, for there is a growing recognition in the philosophy of science that science cannot be set apart as a special type of knowledge distinct from the rest of life. It should rather be seen as one exemplification of how our human understanding and probing of the world functions in general. “Science is […] organized common sense” (Ratzsch 2000: 69, cf. p. 71; cf. Quine 1961: 45; Polanyi 1962: 161).

The primacy of the nature of the object over methodological questions

The first general principle of a postdualist Christian epistemology is that it subordinates the methodological questions about *how* we know to the question of *what* we actually know about the nature of the object with which we are concerned. In other words, it is not the method that determines where we will actually arrive in our search for knowledge; it is the actual knowledge we have on which we critically reflect in asking how such knowledge is possible. Karl Barth said with respect to God: it is only when we know God by His own grace and revelation that we can say something about the way in which this knowledge is possible. How could we from our end determine if and how knowledge of God is possible? (See §3.3.) The reflections on the nature of scientific research, particularly as appropriated by Torrance, have shown that the same is true for the natural sciences. It is only as we probe further into nature that we can sharpen our tools and our understanding of the way of probing that is appropriate to the nature of the world that we are probing into (1969: 10, 37, 130f; 1985: 82).

When we understand the human epistemological predicament in a dualist fashion and when we image proper human knowledge in a foundationalist way, the primacy of methodological questions automatically follows. If we, as thinking subjects, find ourselves at the subject side of the subject–object divide, we need to deal with methodological problems of how this divide can be crossed before we will confidently start out. When we are working with a foundationalist account of knowledge, the methodological issue about what counts as a proper foundation and the proper way to construct on it needs to be solved before you can validly start building. And yet it appears to be impossible to solve the methodological questions in this fashion.

By contract, in the Judeo-Christian tradition the human being is seen as created in the image of God and is part of the creation he indwells. This suggests that from the very start he has some knowledge of reality and we can critically and progressively inquire into the grounds of how this knowledge is possible and how to sift trustworthy ideas from those that are less so. In our further probing into reality, we will discover new ways of opening reality that all need to be critically tested. Yet, our methodological insights always depend on what we know or what we suppose we know (Torrance 1969: 10; Polanyi 1962: 161). In more technical terms: our methodological reflections and our epistemology cannot validly be developed in an *a priori* manner, as if we could tell how we can know before we actually find ourselves in an actual epistemological relationship in which we know something. Sound epistemology will be *a posteriori*: we critically reflect on what we have discovered, asking how we know what we know and if knowing in this way is warranted and appropriate. This is the way we will proceed when we ask what way of knowing is appropriate to our knowledge of God in Christ (§5.3).

The building, the raft and the web

The point we have arrived in our reflections reveals two pervasive and closely related characteristics of modern epistemology wanting: the dualist understanding of the human epistemological predicament; and the universalist foundationalist model for understanding knowledge. Now that we have replaced modern dualism with a more biblical and realistic understanding of the place of the human being within creation we are in a place where we can consider alternative models for understanding how human beings grow in knowledge and comprehension – and for what this means for understanding the nature of apologetic persuasion.

A first suggestion to solve the problems attached to modern universalist foundationalism is to continue to use the master model of the building, but to greatly enlarge its foundation. We already saw how Plantinga followed the Scottish philosopher Reid in criticizing modern foundationalism for having unacceptable criteria for limiting what we can accept as "properly basic", as a proper foundation for knowledge (§2.1). The foundation is so enlarged that it can no longer be called "universalist" foundationalism, for according to Plantinga beliefs do not need to be universally acceptable or accessible to be properly basic. Plantinga, after all, considers memory, belief in testimony (1993b: 57–64, 77–88, 3–20), the *sensus divinitatis* (2000: 167–198) and even the internal testimony of the Holy Spirit (pp. 241–323) as valid belief-producing mechanisms. These belief-producing mechanisms are aimed at truth, which when they function properly produce true and warranted beliefs.

Yet, in offering this solution, Plantinga still considers the basic foundationalist image appropriate for describing human knowledge. This, though, cannot be the last word, even on the basis of his proper account of knowledge. The elements of the enlarged foundation may be properly basic, but because they are not evident in themselves, the evaluation of these beliefs as properly basic depends on many considerations that are placed higher up in our noetic structure and are not themselves properly basic. When we consider, for example, the *sensus divinitatis*, its capacity to bring us in touch with reality is evaluated entirely differently by Calvin, Schleiermacher, Freud or Barth, and their evaluation depends on considerations relating to their understanding of the human being and of God that are themselves not properly basic. When we consider the different evaluations of sense perception by Parmenides, Descartes and Locke, to which we could add Hinduism and African Traditional Religion, they all tend to give different evaluations of its value in the light of convictions that are themselves not properly basic. The same is true for the evaluation of the value of testimony as a source of properly basic beliefs. All these considerations themselves are not properly basic. The crucial point here is that there is a certain circularity (which does not need to be a vicious circularity) between the beliefs we accept in a "properly basic" way and the rest of our convictions. This undermines what is crucial to the foundationalist model: the fact that that epistemological support in a proper noetic structure should always be uni-directional (Plantinga 1993a: 73, cf. §2.1).

Plantinga has contributed immensely towards the right understanding of the apologetic predicament of the Christian faith in relation to modernism and postmodernism. Yet, for understanding apologetic dialogue, we need to look for another model for the understanding of human knowledge and for the way we get to know as human beings, which does take leave of the uni-directional relationship between basic and non-basic beliefs, which is a defining feature of all foundationalist epistemologies.[6]

A first alternative root metaphor that has been proposed is the *raft* (cf. Sosa 1980). Our noetic structure is like a raft in that it can be held tightly together by its internal relations, yet it does not have any fixed relations with some objective or extra-linguistic reality. Like a raft it flows freely within the sea of reality. This understanding of knowledge and truth joins itself most naturally with relativist forms of postmodernism and with a cultural–linguistic understanding of religion. However, and for reasons we have already considered, this also cannot be seen as an adequate model for knowledge. This model cannot explain how, through our linguistic constructions, we happen to be in touch with an extra-linguistic world (§5.1). Moreover, from a Christian point of view this model is not acceptable for it denies that the basic Christian convictions can have an objective referent (§1.3). We need to notice, though, that this understanding of knowledge according to the root metaphor of a raft is, from a certain angle, merely the corollary of the building metaphor. Only when we first conceive of knowledge as of a building, the lack of an adequate foundation makes the construction run adrift without any adequate anchoring in reality.

A more promising model proposed by the philosopher Willard Quine is the *web* (Quine & Ullian 1978; Quine 1961: 42–46; Murphy 1996). The idea is that our noetic structure is "a man-made fabric, which impinges on experience only along the edges" (Quine 1961: 42). This image reflects some important characteristics of human belief structures. It is valid to distinguish between the core values of someone's worldview on the one hand, the beliefs that have a much more direct relationship with reality on the other, and a number of intermediate beliefs that mediate between them. In science, for example, we have the central paradigm, a number of related theories and the more direct perceptions of reality. The large-scale scientific theories that form the core of a certain scientific theory (and which are thus located more towards the centre of the web) are relatively immune to changes in the empirical data and need a major crisis provoked by persistent, important and irresolvable anomalies before they are changed. Around this central paradigm we find a number of related theories that explain how this master paradigm bears on reality. These theories are much more vulnerable to changing perceptions of the world and more easily changed, also because the scientific community has generally invested less in these minor theories (Ratzsch 2000: 65). Completely on the outer fringe are the most direct perceptions of reality, which are relatively clear, because for all the influence of our paradigms on the way we see and interpret the world, they do not make different scientists see different things when reading a number on a meter

6 Plantinga himself does not limit his apologetic arguments to those which are based on beliefs that from both sides are believed to be properly foundational, yet this shows that in order to understand the nature of apologetics we need to go beyond the foundationalist metaphor.

(Ratzsch 2000: 60).[7] We can see the same difference between the core convictions of a worldview or a religion and the intermediate ones that link these with our everyday life. The core beliefs (that our God is almighty and that He is love) can be related to whole different sets of experiences, by different theories about how God's love and almightiness touch our lives and world.

A number of Christian thinkers have serious objections to this image of the web, because to them it would result in relativism. The example of the love and almightiness of God suggests that you can, in this way, combine almost every conceivable coherent set of core convictions with almost every conceivable set of experiences. This is the way Quine himself applies the image, because according to him: "Total science, mathematical and natural and human, is […] extremely undetermined by experience" (Quine 1961: 45). However, this, does not necessarily follow from the image and depends on what the relationship is thought to be between the web and its outer support. Are the inner beliefs thought of as practically immune from outer changes, as indeed some of those using this model suggest? Or is there some significant relationship, even if it is indirect? Do changes in the outer sphere seriously impinge on our core beliefs? The image of a web itself leaves the latter use of it open. Think of a spider web as a more fragile example of a structure only outwardly related to a reality outside itself. In the Netherlands, the autumn is the time in which you could most clearly see the cobwebs covered with the dew of the early morning. When I would see them on my way to primary school, they were an open invitation to experiment. I soon discovered that you do not need to break many outward links to force the spider to serious reconstruction or even to make the web inhabitable and to be abandoned. Or worse, it could even collapse in a way as to trap the spider in his own construction.

In the natural sciences the limitations experience put to the formation of theories are much more restrictive than some philosophers of science make it look like when they reflect on it from a distance. According to Polkinghorne, "Philosophers of science seldom exhibit any understanding of how difficult it is to produce even a passable shot at a credible explanation of a wide range of phenomena" (1989: 169). My suggestion is that when if we attend well to the totality of experience, including creation, the human condition and what we perceive of Jesus of Nazareth through Scripture, the number of explanations that fit them well is fairly limited, and perhaps on the crucial points even limited to one. The problem is not that there are many possible explanations that are all equally valid; the problem is that our culture – and perhaps every culture touched by sin – promotes a negligence of the aspects of reality that according to the Christian are the most important clues to the nature of reality and life. The problem is that people can too easily get away with explanations that do not really fit and that there are too

7 Kuhn himself notes that the fact that "the proponents of different paradigms practice their trade in different worlds […] is not to say that they can see anything they please." (1996: 150)

many cultural and social pressures and personal biases that make people want to get away with these implausible explanations.

Turning back to another image, we may say that some worlds exist, but only as phantom worlds, as productions of our own imagination (§3.3). This already points us towards the importance of our personal and collective attitude to reality. There are moments when reality is hard on us and forces us to change some of our core convictions. Most of the time, however, much depends on our personal attitude: are we open to reality, earnestly seeking truth? And do we have the courage to take it for what it is? Or are we enclosing ourselves, bend in on ourselves and defending ourselves against what might make us change our comfortable and safe world, maybe because of egoism or anxiety? This shows that epistemology and apologetics can never be separated from issues of morality and psychological maturity. Neither can it be separated from the issue of expectancy. Is it worth taking the risk of opening ourselves to a reality beyond ourselves? Will it carry us or crush us? To discover what faith means we therefore also need to discover the meanings of hope and love.

Hermeneutical epistemology

The image of the web, though basically valid, will not suffice as an all-purpose metaphor for knowledge. It is a metaphor for the structure of the beliefs of a person or of a community, and it suggests how it can be well- or ill-structured. However, it has its limitations for explaining how we adequately *come to believe* or get to know something, how we change our beliefs and how we do so on the basis of adequate warrant.

The three images we just described correspond to three understandings of how belief structure may grow and change. The foundationalist image is not only an image for a final structure, but also for the proper construction of our knowledge. One later expands the body of existing knowledge by either adding beliefs that are justly considered foundational or by elaborating the superstructure using adequate procedures of induction or deduction from what is already known. If knowledge is like a building one can start from scratch, and that is precisely one of the presuppositions of the foundationalist model that is not adequate to real life.

When belief structures are like rafts, you can never start from scratch, for you would not be floating if you weren't already on a raft. The only thing you can do is look for driftwood (other beliefs) and tie them to the structure you already have. Its sailors (or are those on a raft more properly called castaways?) may even look for other rafts and join them together to a bigger one, getting rid of those parts that sit in the way of making a solid joint. So the raft may grow bigger and maybe more solidly intertwined, yet it remains without anchor as before.

When the web is used as an image for our belief system, we always find ourselves within one web or another, just as we find ourselves on one raft or another. We never build our belief system from scratch, but at the moment we start thinking consciously and critically we already find ourselves with a host of background beliefs received by our upbringing and culture, which we just take for granted. It is only because of the stability of these background beliefs that we can start questioning beliefs in the foreground (Polanyi 1962: 272ff). The image is not ideal to explain how we may come to abandon one web for another. For this, the image of reading a book is much more appropriate and helpful – and it is to this that we turn now in order to see what it shows about how we come to know, how we learn and how we unlearn.

Though the image of reading a book is not prominent in the authors that guided us thus far, it is very helpful to draw together what they and others have been noting about scientific discovery and about knowledge in general. In the Christian tradition the understanding of the world as a book has deep roots. Church Fathers and medieval theologians used to say that God speaks to us in two books – the book of nature and the book of Scripture – which are given to humanity (Augustinus, *Ennarationes in Psalmos* XLV, 7; Rothacker 1979). This metaphor helps us to understand and explain precisely what the foundationalist epistemology denied and what the metaphor of the web leaves open. It explains how we never arrive at reality without presuppositions, without a prior framework of beliefs, yet how reality in being read impresses itself on us and can make us change our beliefs so that they become increasingly congruent with reality itself. In hermeneutics this is called "the hermeneutical circle": we come to a text with our pre-understanding concerning its content, yet in reading our pre-understanding is challenged so that we change it in order that it becomes more appropriate to the book we read. When we return again to the book with our reformed understanding, we will grasp even more and this will, in turn, help us to tune our pre-understanding even better and so on. Because of its progressive character, we could better call the process a "hermeneutical spiral" (Osborne 1991), for in going back and forth from our limited understanding to the text, we enter into an ongoing movement of "progressive understanding" (Thiselton 1980: 104).[8]

This runs closely parallel to what happens in scientific discovery and progress: a scientist always stands in a tradition of research with a certain way of viewing reality and probing reality.[9] In the process she will find reality resistant to her understanding. If this will actually lead to a change in her central beliefs will depend on several factors. One of them will be the general bend of the researcher to conservatism or progress; another will be the social pressures under which she works; another will be the power of her imagination to conceive of other ways

8 Cf. the use of the same type of language for the description of scientific inquiry: Torrance 1985: 26f.

9 Vern S. Poythress (1988) elaborates insightfully on some of the parallels between method in science and hermeneutics.

of understanding reality; and yet another the availability of viable alternative understandings (cf. §7.2).

This image of reading equally helps us to understand what happens when we encounter and get to know other persons, other cultures and other historical epochs, when we encounter reality in general and also when we encounter God in the Scriptures and in everyday life. It shows how our initial readings can be corrected, even if our starting point wasn't right. In terms of the foundationalist metaphor this is impossible: you can never build a valid construction on a bad foundation. The hermeneutical metaphor also suggests how we can abandon previous readings of the world, of others, of our lives, and of the book of which Christians say it reveals God, if more adequate ways of reading are offered. As Torrance notes (1995: 1):

> in theological inquiry as in natural scientific inquiry our concern is essentially hermeneutic, in which we seek to penetrate into the intrinsic intelligibility of the field in question in order to let it disclose and interpret itself to us.

The main strength of this hermeneutical epistemology, particularly for understanding the possibility of apologetics in our multicultural world, will be clear. This epistemology is appropriate precisely because it shows how learning and understanding is thoroughly located in tradition, in history, culture and community and how, on the other hand, it can be geared to the discovery of an extra-linguistic world. It helps to understand why people can continue to read the world as they used to do, even against many odds. It also shows how people can be validly brought to consider other readings of reality which might well make more sense of the book of creation, of history and of their own life. (cf. Vanhoozer 1999)

5.3 The character of our knowledge of God and salvation

The nature of God's self-revelation

With Polanyi and Torrance we have come to the conclusion that method in science should be determined by the nature of the reality under consideration. It is only when we actually are relating to a certain reality that we can reflect on the method of investigation that is appropriate to this reality. Barth has shown that this is most of all true in theology. Here we equally need to take account of the fact that the reality under consideration has a structure of its own that cannot be known in advance. In considering this particular reality, God in His relation to humanity, we need furthermore to consider that He is sovereign and personal, and therefore chooses Himself whether and how He makes Himself known.

This methodological revolution went so much against the general philosophical outlook of the time that it is hard to know whether Barth could have ever reached this conclusion if it were not based on the way in which God had actually made Himself known in our world. God's self-revelation in the history of Israel, in Jesus and in the Church is a continuous challenge to the culturally prevalent pre-understanding of what the divine is like and how it can be known. In a polytheist world He revealed Himself as the one and only living God and, over the centuries, the people of Israel were led into an ever-deepening understanding of how God wanted to relate to them. His presence was not mediated in the form of a golden calf, but through His covenant and commandments (Ex 32). He wasn't a god that people could manipulate and approach on their own terms, as they tried when carrying the Ark of the Covenant where they needed Him (1Sa 4:1ff).

When God became a human being in Jesus of Nazareth, his disciples had to radically change their conception of what it meant to be the Messiah of Israel (Mk 8:27-31). As this Messiah was proclaimed in the Hellenistic world as the wisdom and power of God, not only did it radically change how people thought of God but it also challenged their ideas of how God can be known. The privileged way to meet God was no longer philosophical reflection or ecstatic experience, but rather the proclamation of the cross and the resurrection of Christ (1Co 1:18-2:5). Jesus breaks through all cultural understandings with which we approach him. He is "the man who fits no formula" (Schweizer 1971: 13). As such He surprises us and that is, in fact, one of the ways He shows how real He is. He confronts us with Himself as a reality from beyond our preconceived ideas, and resists all our efforts to reduce Him to known categories. Furthermore, in encountering us, He has an integrity of his own, which after generations of reflection resulted in a whole new understanding of God and of the human being. The reality that we meet in Jesus proved to have a coherence, a structure, a wisdom and power of its own, which shows itself to be real just as Polanyi's message distinguishes itself from a mere noise.

We now need to examine the characteristics of the ways in which God makes Himself known in the history of Israel and particularly in Jesus Christ (cf. Torrance 1969: 41, 295–312). When we look more closely at the way God makes himself known we discover how marvellous a way God chose. We will indeed discover that this reality has an inner coherence and logic of its own, the logic that characterizes this sovereign and free self-revelation of God. We will concentrate ourselves on what is known as God's special revelation as distinct from His general revelation, for it is in the former that God reveals His plan for the world and humanity. The characteristics of the nature of this self-revelation will be decisive for how it can be known by human beings.

God's self-revelation is first of all *sovereign*. This means, as we already stressed with Barth (§3.3), that it is He Himself who decides how He makes Himself known, and not us. This is also a consequence of the fact that the possibility that we know God is a gift of *grace* and thus something beyond our power (Barth *KD* II/1: 74; trans. *CD* II/1: 69; cf. Torrance 1969: 37). We therefore cannot manipulate God. We cannot "put God to the test" (cf. Mt 4:5f) in the same way as we can manipulate the natural world in all sorts of experiments (Polkinghorne 1991: 15). If He makes Himself known it is because of His sovereign grace and not because He is in any way within our control or "grasp". This has major consequences for our appreciation of the modern trend to align knowledge with mastery, as in Francis Bacon and Descartes (cf. §3.2). We need to recognize that our knowledge of God will always have a mode in which it is God who masters us, rather than the other way around. Because of their being created in the image of God, human beings can up to a certain level have mastery over creation. Yet in relation to God, the search to master Him can only be counter-productive. The proper attitude is to open oneself to His grace.

God's self-revelation is, second, *particular*. Though He shows His majesty and divine power through His entire creation (Ro 1:20), He has decided to make Himself known most clearly in a particular time in history and to a particular community. He has made Himself known to Abraham, with whom He made a covenant (Ge 12; 15; 17), and He revealed His name to Moses and the people of Israel (Ex 3; 19–24). He revealed Himself most clearly in one person, Jesus of Nazareth, and through Jesus to the community of his disciples, the Church. This is in no way a limitation, for He Himself wants Israel to be a light for the nations (Ge 12:3; Ex 4:5-8; Es 42:6; 60:3) and the Gospel of Christ to be proclaimed to the ends of the earth (Mt 28:19; Ac 1:8).

With hindsight, we can understand some of the reasons why God revealed Himself in this particular way. He chose this way, because it reflects the type of relationship He envisages with humanity – a relationship of election and covenant (cf. Newbigin 1989: 80–88). Revealing Himself in this manner was, furthermore, needed in order to reconcile the fallen human race to Himself, before it could start listening to Him. How could we ever have seriously listened to Him when we were still His enemies? (cf. Ro 5:10.) Again, we would never have dreamt of it ourselves, but seeing God becoming a human being in Jesus, we realize that this is indeed the nearest God could come to humankind, the profoundest way in which He could give Himself to them. Yet, to become a real human being – and not just a Hindu *avatar* who only takes on the appearance of a human being – is necessarily to be limited to one place. The incarnation means that God became a human being with all its limitations and thus also with the limitation that so much determines our lives, that we can never redo our lives another time. This "scandal of particularity" is a major problem from a modern perspective and from the perspective of Eastern religions, which all look for religious knowledge that is equally universally accessible. Yet, if we succumb to this modern criterion for valid reasoning, we betray the way God chose to reveal Himself.

That God's self-revelation is particular implies in the third place that it is entrusted to a *community* (cf. Barth *KD* I/1: 1; trans. *CD* I/1: 3;[10] Torrance 1999: 87, 91ff; Newbigin 1989: 97ff). If God's revelation is given at a particular point in time, it means that it is entrusted to a community that is shaped by this revelation and that is called to let itself be shaped increasingly by this revelation and develop a rationality that corresponds to this reality (Torrance 1999: 46f, 86ff). The Gospel is entrusted to the people of God and it is this community that has the task to show within the world what it means to live by this Gospel and to invite everyone to join them in recognizing their Lord. The manner in which the Gospel message is embedded in a particular community is, in fact, concordant with the community- and tradition-based character of knowledge and science pointed out by Polanyi and Kuhn. It reflects a more realistic understanding of knowledge than the individualist and universalist epistemology of modernity (§2.3).

God's self-revelation is, fourth, *personal*. God wants to have a personal relationship with us, even if we need to recognize that this will be a different relationship from the personal relationships we have with fellow human beings. This means that we cannot relate to God in a neutral way, even less so than we can do in relationship to non-personal objects (Torrance 1969: 38f; cf. Hunsinger 1991: 40–42, 152–184). God's self-revelation is always an invitation to live with, and obey, Him; it calls for obedience and love (Barth *KD* II/1: 26ff, 38ff; trans. *CD* II/1: 25ff, 36ff). This becomes even clearer when we realize that God's self-revelation in Israel and in Jesus is in itself an offer to be reconciled with Him. If we are created to live as the people of God and if that relationship is broken by our sin, the renewal of the offer to know God is a *conciliatory* act on his part. As such it simultaneously exposes our sin and our deprived state. Such a message will evoke either a contrite heart or rejection, but does not allow for the attitude of a neutral observant (Torrance 1969: 48f.). "[W]e cannot know it without being drawn into its redeeming and reconciliatory activity" (Torrance 1969: 41).

Fifth, God's self-revelation has the character of *word*. He called Abraham, He gave his commandments to Israel and He sent his prophets. Jesus himself was called the "Word that was with God" (Jn 1:1) and it is through the words of the prophets and apostles collected in the Scriptures that all this comes to us. "This means that theological thinking is more like a listening than any other knowledge" (Torrance 1969: 30; cf. 39f). This means also that to understand these Scriptures in accordance with their divine aim and meaning we need hermeneutical categories. We need an appropriate hermeneutic, first of all to discover what the various human authors intended to convey, but more decisively in order to read them as the Word of God, as revelation pointing to a reality, a Person beyond all those human words (Torrance 1969: 327; 1999: 96).

10 It is for this reason that for Barth dogmatics is always done in the context of a specific community and therefore "Church Dogmatics".

God's self-revelation is, sixth, a revelation of the divine within the *created* order. God is Spirit (Jn 4:24), otherwise He would not be God. Created beings cannot know Him directly, but only if God makes Himself known in something that is not Himself, only if the Creator shows Himself through his creation.[11] God speaks through the words of the prophets and the Scriptures, but these are also human words. Even if God could speak with a directly heard voice, it would need to be a voice transmitted through the vibrations of the air or through our eardrums. When God became a human being in Jesus of Nazareth, what people saw from the outside was not God but a human being. That is precisely one of the reasons why we can so easily misunderstand or deny God's self-revelation by trying to reduce it to the form in which it appears to us: human words, a human person, a book. The fact that such reductionist interpretations are *possible*, however, does not make them *reasonable* any more than it is reasonable to say from a letter that it is nothing more than a piece of paper covered in traces of ink. As soon as you start to understand the message it conveys, the reality forces itself on us that there is a message and not mere traces of a chemical substance on a piece of paper.[12]

A seventh characteristic of God's self-revelation needs special attention, for its apologetic implications are most properly drawn out in this chapter dealing with the reality-reference of Christian apologetic witness. God's self-revelation is revelation *in history* and therefore mediated to us by the *testimony* of others. Because of their importance, we shall deal with the apologetic implications of these two characteristics of God's self-revelation under a separate heading in the following section.

5.4 Apologetics as testimony to Gods revelation in Christ

Good dogmatics as the starting point of all apologetics

This is the point where we need to draw out more elaborately the implications of the Christian understanding of the way we acquire knowledge for the way in which we can engage in apologetic dialogue and witness. We have concluded that the only basis for the Christian knowledge of God is his self-revelation, his initiative to make Himself known. This demands a constant effort on our part to

11 This is what in what Karl Barth called a "secondary objectivity", because Gods proper objectivity simply is not directly accessible to us (*CD* II/1: 16ff = *KD* II/1: 15ff).

12 See for a fuller discussion of the more general discussion whether "unobservables" can be known by science: McGrath 1998a: 145ff. See for the question whether God's nature excludes the possibility of knowing Him f. ex. Plantinga 1980.

align our ideas and our probing to the reality under consideration. This implies that the crucial basis for all apologetics is sound dogmatics.

Good dogmatics is the basis of all sound apologetics, for it is precisely the task of dogmatics to show the inner coherence and integrity of God's self-revelation in Christ and of the understanding of the human condition and the world that this implies. It is the task of dogmatics to critically attend to all language and conceptual structures we use to clarify this reality and to see to it that we do not cloud our understanding by describing it in categories that are strange to its proper integrity. It is the task of dogmatics to critically trace all our ideas concerning God and his relationship to the world to its proper basis in God's self-revelation and ultimately in God Himself. It is her task to give an account of why we believe that the way or method in which these beliefs were acquired is valid and trustworthy, and to show "the self-evidential force" of revelation (Barth *KD* I/1: 364; trans. *CD* I/1: 345). In this manner it gives an account of "the hope that is within us". This is the strength of the postliberal theology (Chapter 2) and of Barth's proper understanding of apologetics (*KD* IV/3: 121; trans. *CD* IV/3: 109):

> the apologetics which is a necessary function of dogmatics to the extent that this must prepare an exact account of the presupposition, limits, meaning and basis of the statements of the Christian confession and thus be able to give this account to any who may demand it.[13]

This understanding of dogmatics as the basis of sound apologetics reflects a particular understanding of dogmatics – or more generally of theology – as a scientific enterprise that seeks to probe into the proper reality of God and his relationship to humanity and the world (Torrance 1999). Although dogmatics has other functions, too (like guiding the teaching of the Church, defining heresies and critically guiding the contextualization of the Gospel), all these other functions depend for their validity on the fact that dogmatics is also a scientific probing for the truth of the Gospel. This understanding of dogmatics takes leave of models of dogmatics that consider the proper task of dogmatics to be the apologetic translation of the message of Scripture in terms of something that is not its proper subject matter – in terms of psychological or political categories or in terms of religious experience, for example.[14] Dogmatics has a lot to say about psychology, politics and religious experience, but it says this from its proper perspective: its understanding of God and his relationship to the world as revealed in Jesus Christ.

---

13 Cf. *KD* I/1: 361; transl. *CD* I/1: 341f, where it is called "polemics".

14 These theologies aim at translating of biblical categories in terms of another conceptual structure and are all varieties of what Lindbeck called "experiential-expressivism" (§2.1); cf. Lindbeck 1984: 129.

This understanding of dogmatics as a proper basis of apologetics also goes against the grain of a distinction between dogmatics and apologetics, which is common in neo-thomistic and differently in certain forms of evangelical theology. It is sometimes said that dogmatics presupposes the authority of Scripture and systematizes its contents, while apologetics sets out to defend our belief in the authority of Scripture. However, apologetics should never try to justify our belief in the authority of Scripture apart from pointing to the trustworthiness of our belief in God's self-revelation in Christ, of which dogmatics should speak. It cannot find any other foundation as if its authority depends on something else. It may find pointers elsewhere to the validity of the Christian belief in the authority of Scripture, but it may never find a proper basis for this belief elsewhere than in the reality of the self-revelation of God in the Scriptures itself.

This priority of dogmatics over apologetics does not mean that in apologetic witness and dialogue we should always start with dogmatic expositions. In many cases it may be wiser to start dialogue on the basis of shared convictions, rather than to start with what is unique to the Christian faith. Yet, it means that we will always want to invite our dialogue partners to see the world from a Christian perspective and to invite them into "the strange new world of the Bible". It also means that we need to constantly challenge them to consider God and his revelation on its proper terms and not according to their cultural presuppositions, which often exclude such a revelation and such an understanding of the human condition from the start.[15] We need to explain that real openness to the world and to God also means that we approach Him with an "*open* epistemology" (Torrance 1969: 10). If our openness to the world is real, our methods should "carry in themselves self-correcting devices so that we may always be directed away from ourselves to the compulsive force of objective connection in the real world" (Torrance 1969: viii). In this way it becomes clear that the invitation to understand the world from a Christian perspective is, in no way, a flight from objectivity. It is given with the desire to approach the objective world on appropriate terms, on its proper terms. This privileged place of dogmatics in apologetic witness is therefore in no way a flight from "the free investigation of the truth". This freedom is, though, different from modern and postmodern understandings of autonomy and freedom. The search for truth is free in the appropriate manner, when it seeks to be "free to its own inexhaustible object" (Barth *KD* I/2: 317, 319; trans. *CD* I/2: 291, 293), God, whom we seek to know.

This reference to a misconceived search for autonomy that can function as a screen between us and reality points to the need for an openness to reality that is more profound and existential than a methodological openness, which is only one of its constituents. This shows again how profoundly epistemological questions are related to our basic attitude to ourselves, to others, to reality at large and to God to which we will return later (§8.1).

15 I have tried this myself in: Van den Toren 2009.

Apologetic testimony

If apologetics should bring us and our dialogue partners in touch with reality, the question automatically arises: "Which reality?" Religions and worldviews differ regarding the question of the most important aspects of reality and the most appropriate way to be in touch with them. Is it the world of natural laws that reveals itself in the laboratory? Is it the world of spiritual forces that visits us in dreams and trance? Is it our deepest divine self with which we can be unified when we empty ourselves from all perceptions and memories of the outer world and from all that is personal in our inner world?

Christians claim that the most decisive reality is the ground of everything – that is, the Creator Himself who invites us to know Him and live with Him. We can encounter and know Him in his revelatory acts in history, in Jesus Christ and in the Scriptures. Against the grain of all Gnostic tendencies in philosophies and religions that want to keep the divine far removed from the complexities of history, we believe that God's self-revelation is historical and enters creation. This is possible, because the world of creation itself is not far from God or anti-God, but created by God in view of being the medium of his self-revelation. It is possible because this creation, though it has drifted from God because of human sin, is the object of God's salvation (Cullmann 1951; Pannenberg 1991: 230ff; cf. Dulles 1992: 43–67). If this is how He makes Himself known, this automatically implies that the testimony to his salvific deeds is crucial to our knowledge of Him and our relation to Him. This is precisely how major parts of the Scriptures present themselves: as testimony. We need not fall into the temptation of trying to find one single model of understanding Scripture. Yet, we can confidently claim that the primary genre of Scripture is to be found in the narrative sections that testify to God's mighty deeds for our salvation in the history of Israel and in Jesus Christ (Goldingay 1994: 19ff).

If this is the way God makes Himself known, apologetics also should be testimony to God's mighty deeds. Christian apologetics should point to reality and to what we consider the most decisive reality, God entering our history. This is the reality that surprises us, which we can never mould as we would like, but which rather presses itself on us and presses us to change our ways of understanding the world. This shows that the opposition that is sometimes created between testimony and apologetic justification is false. It is sometimes said: "We cannot justify our beliefs, we can simply testify to what God has done." When we consider the way God has chosen to make Himself known, this is an unwarranted opposition. It is precisely by testifying to what God has done that we point to what gives us reason to believe what we believe. That is why I like to speak of "apologetic testimony" or "apologetic witness": properly Christian apologetics is, among other things, always also testimony to the salvific acts of God on our behalf, in which God has revealed Himself as our God.

The reason for the lack of attention for the role of testimony in Christian apologetics cannot be sought in Scripture. It is rather the tendency to align the Christian faith with a culture that used "seeing" – either with the mind or with the physical eyes – as the prime model for understanding knowledge. This automatically relegates testimony and what we hear as producing only second-degree beliefs (cf. Torrance 1980: 1ff). We also saw how the category of testimony was disregarded, because it was hard to reconcile with the universalist foundationalist epistemology of modernity (§2.1). Testimony is equally hard to reconcile with the individualism of modernity, for it makes us dependent on others who need to tell us what we cannot know by ourselves (Coady 1992: 13f, 80; Plantinga 1993b: 85f; Vanhoozer 1999: 142).

However, it is not so difficult to show that this demeaning attitude to testimony does hurt itself on real life and that the negation of the value of testimony will finally obstruct the whole scientific enterprise and lead to scepticism. We start life trusting the testimony of our parents and we would not even know our roots or name, let alone our identity, if we did not trust the testimony of our parents. All the practicalities of our lives heavily depend on testimony – for example, the fact that I trust what the food package testifies with respect to its contents or what the woman on the market testifies with regards to what she is selling. I could never be in Oxford working on this book if I did not trust the testimonies, both written and spoken, with respect to Wycliffe Hall and Oxford University, the ferry service and all other aspects of our life here (cf. Coady 1992: 6f).

Even in science we cannot function without testimony, because the introduction to the field of study is only possible when we start trusting the testimony of our teachers to what is considered established scientific truth. Scientific progress constantly depends on the acceptance of testimonies of colleagues in the field to what they have been doing and perceiving. No one can do all the relevant experiments himself and all would want others to trust their testimony to their findings (Coady 1992: 9ff).

It is indeed true that testimony can be unreliable and that we make some of the worst mistakes in life because we have wrongly put our trust in others. However, this is just a consequence of the more general fact that life is a risk, particularly in a world where we depend on the testimony of others who are finite people and who are sinners at that, just like us. Yet, we still need the testimony of others, for better or for worse.

Fortunately, recognizing the value of testimony does not mean that we need to urge ourselves and others to accept every testimony without distinction. It means that we have reason to accept testimony as a *prima facie* valid source of knowledge that we can trust unless we have positive reasons to distrust a particular testimony. All sources of our knowledge have this *prima facie* character (cf. Plantinga 1993b: 155f). We perceive something and we trust our senses unless we have positive reason to distrust them. We perceive a bend in a stick and we believe it is bent unless we have reason to distrust our perception – for example, because it is bent where it enters the water and we know that water can produce the illusion that something straight seems bent. We trust our memory, unless we have positive reason to distrust it. We accept a syllogism that appears to be self-evident, unless we have positive reason to doubt this *prima facie* impression. All these are examples of *prima facie* beliefs that we have reason to hold onto unless there are specific possible *defeaters*. Defeaters are reasons to doubt what we have come to believe in this way; they give us reason to critically consider whether they have the sufficient warrant we thought they had. They may either undercut or rebut the value of the testimony given. They can bring us to reject certain beliefs suggested to us by our senses, by the testimony we hear, or by other valid sources of *prima facie* belief. Yet, in reflecting on both these *prima facie* beliefs and these possible defeaters, we may also decide that the *prima facie* beliefs have better warrant and that we have more reason to reject the candidate defeaters on the basis of certain defeater-defeaters. And so we could go on (cf. Plantinga 1993b: 40–42).

If beliefs produced by testimony are *prima facie* acceptable yet open to being defeated, this means they cannot function as a basis of a foundationalist type of noetic structure. In such a structure the truth or degree of probability of truth of the foundational beliefs needs to be determined *before* you can start erecting the rest of the building. However, possible defeaters for accepting certain testimony can always come in later and from unexpected angles. In apologetic dialogue, both dialogue-partners will not engage in dialogue on the basis of an initial agreement about the value of the testimony that is given. Christians simply testify to the great events in salvation history about which they have heard in the Scriptures. It is only in the process that we can discover what type of possible defeaters will come up in the dialogue. The number of possible defeaters is infinite and we cannot answer them in advance, even if we might manage to keep up enough interest for dealing with such questions, many of which will be rather boring. Christians simply share the testimony of the Church and of what God has done in their own lives, explaining why it has been convincing to them and showing their openness to consider possible defeaters when they occur.

Such possible defeaters of testimony come in two types. First of all, people can question the *quality* of the testimony – for example, concerning the resurrection of Jesus Christ – in the sense that they believe we do not have sufficient warrant to accept the testimony concerned because of a lack of trustworthiness of the witnesses or the chain of witnesses. Part of the answer will be that we simply invite others to read with us the testimony of the apostles in the Scriptures to see if they come across as reliable people or not. Many people have no idea of the personal integrity of these writers that shows through in their writings. Much more elaborate exchanges may be needed.[16] In many cases it might be as profitable to ask what we ourselves consider in our daily dealings with people

16 For a debate between a Christian and a (at the time) atheist philosopher concerning the testimony of the resurrection in which many of the crucial questions come out, see: Habermas & Flew 1987.

indices of the trustworthiness of those on whose testimony we depend. In such cases, we will mainly want to discuss the integrity and honesty of the witnesses and whether that witness was well placed to have a good grasp of what he is testifying to in order to exclude the possibility of illusions and delusions. With respect to both criteria – integrity and being well placed – the testimony to the resurrection of Christ does very well.

There is a second type of defeaters to testimony. We often mistrust testimony not because of the quality of the witness, but because of the content. We do not accept the account because we believe the events testified to be impossible or very improbable. In most cases the question of the quality and the content maybe closely related. A possible objection to the apostolic testimony might be: "Of course we would trust the quality of the apostles as witnesses if they had for example testified to the death of Herod or of Jesus of Nazareth, but for such an improbable story as someone's resurrection, you need something more solid." According to David Hume:

> But as finite added to finite never approaches a hair's breath nearer to infinite; so a fact incredible in itself acquires not the smallest accession of probability by the accumulation of testimony.[17]

So Hume argues here that if something in itself incredible is witnessed to, we could never accumulate enough testimony to make it credible. Yet, is this true?

The main problem with discarding testimonies to the incredible out of hand is that what we consider incredible or not depends on the range of what we have experienced before and more profoundly on our worldview. Coady gives an interesting and revealing example of the influence of our range of experience on our appreciation of testimony. Before the existence of television and even photography there was a Dutch ambassador to Thailand, then Siam, who became a personal friend to the king. One day he explained to the king how during the wintertime in his own country the water could become so hard that even elephants could walk on it without sinking. Then the king exclaimed: "I have always considered you a trustworthy man and believed all what you said, but I now know that I have always been mistaken!" (Coady 1992: 180.)

In this respect postmodernism is an ally of the Christian apologist, for it has made us conscious of the fact how our worldview tends to filter those elements that do not fit out of our perception of reality (cf. Kuhn 1996: 64). For our day-to-day living this may be necessary, for otherwise our world becomes chaotic. Yet, if this is made an absolute principle, this may well block us from discovering something genuinely new.[18] The Christian faith tells us that reality is much richer

---

17 David Hume, "Of the Authenticity of Ossian's Poems", in: David Hume, *Essays: Moral, Political and Literary*, ii (London, 1875), p. 424, quoted by Coady (1992: 182).

18 Cf. on the need to balance openness and faithfulness to our existent framework of belief in judging astonishing reports Coady 1992: 196–198.

than we tend to expect and the Scriptures say that our God is known for doing things that are genuinely new (Isa 43:19). He surprises us with unexpected "Good *News*". In testifying to truth we therefore need to invite and encourage others and ourselves to be open to something really new and not to become enclosed in ourselves and in the world we create according to our own image and liking and within the limits of our own imagination.

There is one characteristic of testimony in general and of biblical testimony in particular that will help in bringing people to consider more seriously testimonies to the improbable. Testimonies ordinarily do not convey mere facts. There is no bare and isolated "evidence that demands a verdict". Testimonies refer to facts within and along an interpretative framework in which they make sense and have meaning. Otherwise the unexpected event testified to would simply be an oddity and we would have little interest in handing on the testimony. Oddities rarely make it beyond the first witness. Testimonies that are treasured and handed on are those that make sense and have meaning (Goldingay 1994: 49ff; Vanhoozer 1999: 145). This is clear from the testimony to the cross and the resurrection of Jesus of Nazareth (Torrance 1969: 326). Both were, for the disciples, equally unexpected events. They could not make sense of their Messiah being crucified and of his resurrection in the middle of history (cf. Pannenberg 1968: 66f). They needed an entire re-thinking in the light of the Scripture of what it meant to be a Messiah to make sense of it. In the process they discovered it to be genuinely Good News about God and his dealings with humankind. When they began testifying to the cross and the resurrection of Jesus, they didn't testify to odd facts, but to events together with a new understanding of God and the world, which was called for by these events and made at the same time sense of them. In the same way our contemporary testimony to the cross and the resurrection of Christ is also an invitation to a change to a radically different perspective on life, on the world, and on God (cf. Wright 2003). From this new perspective the events in the cross and the resurrection of Christ are no longer impossible or incredible, but even more astonishing.

Evidentialist apologetics: making up the balance

It is worthwhile drawing some of the epistemological considerations in this chapter together in asking what all this means for the project that is often called "evidentialist apologetics" (cf. §2.1). I use this term for the effort of arguing for the existence of God and the truth of the Gospel on the basis of the evidences of nature and history.[19] The evidentialist project is basically right in its search for contact with reality through the way reality enters the human mind through our

19 This is a broader use of the notion of "evidentialist apologetics" than in Habermas (2000), who says that "the chief interest of this method is the postulating of historical evidences" (p. 94).

different cognitive faculties. We meet God in the creation in which we live, in his revelation in and through the Scriptures, in our religious experiences. They all count as evidences of his existence, of who He is, and of what He envisages us to be. Evidentialist apologists are right in their criticism of the rationalist type of apologetics, which aims at giving an argument for God or for the Christian faith starting from a rational *a priori* or from some type of transcendental argument. Maybe we can say something about God in this way, but this should always be controlled by the way our God has chosen to make Himself known by letting his majesty shine through his creation, by his salvific acts in the history of Israel and by entering history Himself in Jesus Christ. If this is how God makes Himself known, that is what we should attend to.

However, both presuppositionalists (§8.1) of what I have called "worldview apologists" (§2.1, cf. §7.6) are right in their criticism of evidentialist apologetics when they point to the fact that there is no neutral and unambiguous evidence. They are right in pointing out that worldview, culture, conceptual structure, plausibility structure, cultural–linguistic framework, or whatever one calls it, determines the selection of evidence, the interpretation of what we perceive and, to a certain degree, even what we perceive. "[Value-free] facts, like telescopes and wigs for gentlemen, were a seventeenth-century invention" (MacIntyre 1988: 357; cf. 1985: 78–87). Consider the resurrection of Jesus, which is both crucial to New Testament and contemporary apologetic witness. From many worldview perspectives it does not make sense to give so much attention to consider the truth of one specific historic event in order to discover who God is and what life is all about. Furthermore, if the resurrection is shown to be the logical conclusion of a number of facts that many serious historical scholars, Christian or non-Christian, will concede,[20] one can still begin to doubt the formerly accepted premises, because the conclusion seems so wild. Even if the resurrection of Jesus of Nazareth could be undeniably established as fact, it could be interpreted as not being the resurrection of the Messiah, the Son of God. It could be "interpreted" as a meaningless historical oddity (cf. Van Til 1967: 240) or as the resurrection of another precursor of the Messiah by the God of Israel (as in Lapide 1983).

At the same time, and here the evidentialists can score their point, this does not mean that what we perceive is pliable *ad infinitum*. Sometimes the world just resists our interpretation and organization of it. In many cases we can only keep to our own way of seeing things if we withdraw consciously or unconsciously from paying careful attention to what the world is like. In this sense much of the work on natural and historical evidences in evidentialist apologetics remains – if re-interpreted – of great importance for apologetic dialogue.[21]

20 For an example of such an argument by Gary Habermas, see: Habermas & Flew 1987: 25–27.

21 Contemporary evidentialists like Habermas may agree with other apologists that "historical occurrences are not brute facts, that interpret themselves" (Habermas 2000: 94), which is part of a

We have already shown that a hermeneutic model is more appropriate for understanding knowledge than the foundationalist model, which is a corollary of evidentialism.[22] The hermeneutic model frees us from the need to find evidences as a basis of the Christian faith that are culturally neutral and universally equally accessible and acceptable. The impossibility of finding these is the main obstacle on which a modern-style evidentialist form of apologetics constantly hurts itself. Yet following this hermeneutic model, our perceptions of the world around us continue to have a crucial place in apologetic dialogue. The apologist will want to urge both herself and her dialogue partners to be attentive to the world in which we live. Yet, the way we use these perceptions apologetically will be different from their place in evidentialism.

First, Christian apologists will want to say that the Christian faith provides the perspective that helps make sense of reality in the most encompassing sense, considering all relevant aspects. This remains true, even if we recognize that what we consider its relevant aspects is itself a culturally relative notion. This recognition itself does not push the question of what we consider most relevant beyond what we can discuss and evaluate. Apologists will want to show both the inner coherence and beauty of the Christian faith and the way it makes sense of the world we encounter, thus showing its correspondence with the way the world is.

Second, Christian apologists will want to enlarge the field of what counts as evidence. Because of their implicit or explicit adherence to the idea of neutral evidence, evidentialist apologists tend to concentrate on the type of evidence that can be most easily mistaken for being culturally neutral, such as historical data or the order of the natural world. Among the historical data, evidentialists tend for the same reason to put much weight on archaeological evidence and on extra-biblical testimonies to the existence and life of Jesus. Preferring this type of evidence may have an *ad hoc* or *ad hominem*[23] value in dialogue with an audience who share the modern idea of neutral sources. An example is the sociologist Peter Berger, who explained in a personal exchange with Wolfhart Pannenberg that he could not accept Pannenberg's view that the resurrection of Jesus is as well documented as any other event in ancient history. He could not, because

more general movement of different apologetic theories to move towards each other. Yet, his statement that "evidentialists insist that there are a number of epistemological similarities in areas such as sensory data (perception), scientific theories, and the general rules and application of inference" (p. 97) betrays a lack of insight in the much more profound influence of worldview on perception, its organization and evaluation, unless the "similarities" become too vague to support an evidentialist apologetic argument.

22 According to Habermas (2000: 92ff) evidentialist apologetics can go with different epistemologies. It is hard to see though how you can make sense of it as the principal model of apologetic dialogue, if these epistemologies are not of a foundationalist variety

23 Ford points out that Lindbeck's proposal for *ad hoc* apologetics could best be read as a proposal for an apologetic *ad hos* or *ad has*, for it should be directed to specific persons with specific views and interests (Ford 1985: 251).

he considered the Christian sources biased. "I could believe it if there would be something like a first century police-report."[24] Yet, even if supposedly neutral data may have a certain persuasive force in a modern context, we would want to criticize the idea that historical reports are only trustworthy if they are handed down disinterestedly. Of course people were not disinterested; that precisely why such reports are written up and handed down and that goes as well for Julius Caesar's *On the Gaelic War* as for the Gospels. Moreover, would it be right not to be personally engaged either positively or negatively when confronted with reports concerning the resurrection of the one who is claimed to be Son of God and Messiah? Furthermore, there is no need to limit the apologist in principle to evidence from the two domains of nature and history, be it neutral or not. A wide variety of perceptions and experiences can function as valid pointers to the validity of the Christian understanding of the world: an experience of the divine, an experience of the utter reprehensibility of evil, an experience of anxiety, of morality, of guilt, of thankfulness or of beauty. None of these can constitute a neutral *datum* in itself, yet they can be valid pointers to truth (cf. McGrath 1992: 51–73).

Finally, we would want to point our dialogue partners particularly to those experiences and aspects of reality, that are not easily integrated in their worldview and fundamental approach to life. If these enigmas and anomalies are serious enough, these are the points that can bring people to reconsider their worldviews and ask whether the Christian faith might make more sense of their lives and the world in which they live. This is in fact what we have been doing throughout our analysis of both modernism and postmodernism. We have been pointing to the inconsistencies of both approaches to reality and the inability to deal with the way both moderns and postmoderns perceive themselves, their knowledge and the world around them. At the same time we have tried to show that where modernism and postmodernism were unable to deal with these anomalies, from a Christian perspective they made good sense – showing its better grasp of the place of the human being in the universe. We will return later to the use of anomalies in apologetic dialogue between radically different ways of understanding reality (§7.4).

It may be that this respect I believe Christian apologetics should to continue to have for the role of some sort of evidence makes me defend a renewed or reformed version of evidentialism as Don Carson contends.[25] So be it, if this means I believe that a Christian on this point should be opposed to those forms

24 Peter Berger himself shared this event in a meeting with the Regent College faculty on 7 November 2002 at Regent College, Vancouver. Berger himself believes in the resurrection of Jesus, but for the reasons mentioned above he does not think there is sufficient evidence for this belief, thereby qualifying it as a religious belief short of knowledge.

25 This is Carson's contention after his reading of an indeed not fully thought out article of mine (Carson 1996: 185f on Van den Toren 1993).

of postmodernism that state people can completely mould the world around them according to their own cultural–linguistic framework. This is not Christian and is simply not true. All readings of the world are not equal and one's web of belief is, in a significant manner, attached to the outer world. Yet evidentialism by itself and particularly in its modern form is not a valid basis for engaging in apologetic dialogue, for it does not sufficiently take into account the degree to which what we consider evidence is culturally relative. Furthermore, abstracting beliefs from the interests and the power structures that determine what people consider plausible amounts to presenting apologetics on a plate for either postmodern or Vantillian deconstruction. We will, rather, need to keep culture and reality, evidence and interest, truth and relevance, reason, will and emotions together in view of an apologetics that deals with real life.

Chapter 6

CONTEXTUAL APOLOGETICS

All human life is culturally embedded. We realize this with a shock when we come to live in another culture and discover how differently other people relate to the world, to life and to others. What is evident for us isn't always so for others. What is most valuable to us isn't always thus to others. In the mirror of discovery of the strangeness of others, we ourselves also change. We discover that all those things we took for granted with an "of course" and nothing more, may not have the same for-grantedness for others and therefore may no longer have it for ourselves.

That we are culturally, socially and historically embedded beings has received major attention in the social sciences and, in the twentieth century, even in biology.[1] What's more, we have seen how this is implied in the biblical understanding of the human being. Several times, we have indicated that this cultural embeddedness of human existence has profound implications for apologetic witness. Our cultural perspective plays into what we perceive to be true, in how we experience reality, in how we reason and in what we find worth pursuing. In a sense people with different cultures "live in different worlds" (cf. Polanyi 1962: 151). The history of apologetics and Scripture itself provides examples in the cultural sensitivity shown in apologetic dialogue and witness. Jesus himself proclaimed the one message of the presence of the Kingdom of God in his Person, yet addressed each audience differently. The same sensitivity can be found in the addresses in the book of Acts. We find here a number of speeches by Peter, Stephen and, particularly, Paul addressed at specific audiences: Jews, Greeks and Romans. In every case different bridges are built to the audience's grasp of the truth, different sensibilities are respected and different barriers are addressed, following patterns of reasoning adapted to the respective audiences (McGrath 1998b).

We therefore have a threefold reason to engage in the search for a culturally sensitive apologetic: the biblical and historical examples; biblical anthropology; and the need to witness effectively in a multicultural world. Yet, until today the implications of the cultural coefficient of being human for the nature of apologetic witness and dialogue have received little attention. A main reason for

1 See §4.3, p. 102, n. 10.

this neglect needs to be sought in the Enlightenment prejudice against cultural prejudice, which supposed that all valid reasoning – and therefore all valid apologetics – should start from a culturally neutral and universally acceptable point and follow universally acceptable patterns of reasoning.

On the basis of the biblical anthropology and the Christian epistemology developed, we will (in this and the following chapter) explore the possibility and character of apologetic dialogue across cultural boundaries. In the first major section, we will elaborate on the need for culturally sensitive or contextual apologetics. We will do this by drawing attention to the sociological processes of globalization and pluralization, by digging into the meaning of the crucial notions of "culture" and "worldview", and by showing the place of contextual apologetics in the overall apologetic programme (§6.1). In the following section, we will return to a proper biblical understanding of cultural diversity, digging one layer deeper in relating this diversity not only to creation (as in Chapter 4) but also to the reality of humanity's sinful alienation from its Creator. This helps us to understand how every culture in this world is a mixture of truth and falsity, of good and evil, thus opening up possibilities for fruitful apologetic dialogue (§6.2). When we come to cross-cultural dialogue itself, we need to distinguish between two different, even if inseparable, moments: cross-cultural understanding; and cross-cultural persuasion. We will start with the questions relating to cross-cultural understanding. We will consider the barriers to arriving at an adequate mutual understanding. Against this background we will see whether and how a sufficient understanding of other cultural perspectives is possible, and how the Gospel can be communicated cross-culturally (§6.3). Even more than with communication, cross-cultural apologetics is concerned with persuasion and therefore we will dedicate the whole next chapter to the different ways in which we can build bridges between worlds and how we can urge people to pursue Christ as a clue to the real world.

6.1 The need for culture-sensitive apologetics

Globalization and cultural diversity

Before we start dealing with the implications of cultural variety for Christian apologetics, it will be helpful to give some indication of how cultural diversity presents itself in our contemporary world characterized simultaneously by pluralization and globalization. A proper understanding of globalization is necessary first of all to understand what a proper respect for multiculturalism would entail. This respect needs to go beyond what I would call modern multiculturalism. It furthermore helps us to understand yet another apologetically important aspect of the impact of multiculturalism, the fact that the availability of multiple cultural outlooks tends to diminish the plausibility of each one of them and tends to create a widespread "awareness of relativity" (Berger 1963: 64).

Globalization is the social and cultural process by which an increasing number of regions in the world are progressively interrelated and integrated in a single global society and culture (cf. Tiplady 2003). This process began its course seriously at the beginning of the modern era and, on several occasions, has shifted to higher gears – decisively so in the latter decades of the twentieth century. Its main actors are the international political and business elite on the one hand, and the Western and Westernized international intelligentsia on the other. Its main vehicles are English as the new *lingua franca*, international commerce, the Internet, and international pop-culture expressed in films, music, etc. (Berger 2002: 1–16). We do not need to fully analyse this complex process, yet for this undertaking several characteristics of this new globalized culture are of special interest.

First, the new global culture is, in its global traits, Western in scope, predominantly modern; yet, particularly among the global intelligentsia these are important postmodern influences.

Second, this globalization does not seem to lead these days to one uniform culture, but is combined with the resurgence and even renaissance of cultural differences and religious identities both in the world at large and in the heartlands of modernity itself (Berger 1999: 1–18). Many players in this global network combine their participation in the new global society with a conscious choice for a well-defined particular cultural identity – such as "the computer professionals in Bangalore [who] succeed in combining such participation with personal lifestyles dominated by traditional Hindu values" (Berger 2002: 4). In fact, the globalization process itself has been one of the major factors leading to a deeper consciousness in the modern world of cultural and religious diversity. This consciousness has been brought about by a better acquaintance of those who live in other parts of the world and through contact with major cultural minorities who live on almost every continent and particularly in the West.

Third, those particular cultures can relate in different ways to the global culture. Perhaps the easiest way is when they accept the terms of the relationship set by the modern global culture, which allows for private cultural preferences, moral values and religious allegiances, as long as they do not impinge the "public values" of globalized modernity. This is the form taken by many of the cultural minorities (including a significant segment of the Christian minority) in the West and by important sectors of the business- and intelligentsia-elite in the rest of the world. It is also possible that a counter-cultural programme is formulated that functions as a wholesale alternative to the modern worldview – even while integrating some of its benefits. This may happen by isolating oneself from the world culture (as exemplified by the Taliban and North Korea) or by trying to live such an alternative while continuing to play a role in the local and global field. For an example of the latter, we can point to the Islamic renaissance, which sociologically is one of the most important alternatives to modernity. Between these two extremes of adaptation and rejection are many intermediate forms, inclining towards one or the other end of the spectrum.

This difference in attitude towards modernity points to two different understandings of multiculturalism. There is the understanding of multiculturalism as modern society allows for it, as private preferences within the overall perspective of modernity, which should govern public life. In this case modernism is not a particular cultural perspective as the others are, but the dominant understanding of culture that appoints all the others their proper place.[2] This reveals modernity's lack of self-understanding, for it is not able to see itself as a particular historically located cultural project, just as the others (MacIntyre 1988: 335; Newbigin 1986: 15f). Postmodernism often suffers from the same evil. It criticizes all cultural metanarratives, including modernity's claim to be the metanarrative and the modern understanding of cultural diversity. Yet, in the process postmodernism itself also becomes a metanarrative, which assigns all cultures their proper place (Edgar 1995: 380).

This points to the fact that modern and many postmodern conceptions of multiculturalism and cultural and religious pluralism do not go far enough in their respect of cultural differences. A more genuine respect of cultural difference requires that we accept that both modernism and postmodernism are themselves particular cultural projects. Respecting other cultures implies that one should take seriously the way they want to be understood according to their proper self-understanding as an all-encompassing approach to reality and culture. If we want to take multiculturalism seriously, in apologetics and in other facets of intercultural relationships, we should take each other's self-understandings seriously, rather than subsuming cultural differences under some grand modern or postmodern theory.

This does not mean that we do not need some metanarrative for understanding cultural difference. We do need one and in §6.2, I will elaborate further on a proposal to understand cultural differences, for which we set the stage in the fourth chapter. It is a consciously *Christian* proposal, yet I propose it with universal intent, believing that it is indeed the truth about these cultures and a truth that can in principle be recognized by others. Yet, I do not imperialistically force it on others as an allegedly neutral understanding of culture, for I know that their self-understanding may be radically different.

The fact that we are encountering cultural pluralism today in a global context in which most people are well aware of the existence of many religious and non-religious alternatives strongly influences the way people relate to their proper religions and cultural outlooks. Religious alternatives become realistic options in a way those we only know by hearsay can never be. For an average Christian in a homogenous context in the Middle Ages, stories about the Muslim "Saracens"

2 See for a critical analysis of this modern understanding of multiculturalism: Newbigin 1989: 14–26.

and "Turks", did not impinge on the plausibility of their own beliefs as it does for many people today. Globalization and pluralization easily lead to religious doubt and to a diminishing commitment to one's particular cultural values. These factors lead to an unprecedented "proneness to change one's entire *Weltanschauung*" (Berger 1963: 64; cf. 2006). In the last few decades more people than ever have begun to move and even commute between cultural environments, and have thus become closely acquainted with other religious perspectives.

Not only does acquaintance with the many cultural and religious options available lead to openness, but also it can easily degenerate into an inability to choose or commit oneself to any perspective at all. Theoretically, cultural and religious pluralism does not, in any way, exclude that one perspective may be truer and even radically truer than the others. Yet in practice the social reality of multiple choices in our pluralistic world leads to what Peter Berger calls the "vertigo of relativity" so characteristic of the postmodern era and to the inability to commit oneself to any perspective at all (Berger 1980: 9).[3] It also provokes profound doubts in the Christian community, leading to a less confident witness to non-Christians. Berger suggests that the difficulty to deal with the uncertainty produced by this pluralization may, as a reaction, also cause a search for new certainties, as in fundamentalist religious movements (Berger 1999: 7). If this is true, there may in these cases remain little openness to listen to any Christian apologetic witness, precisely because of the anxiety that the regained yet threatened certainty may be lost again.

Culture, worldview and conversion

To understand how culture impinges on the apologetic task, we also need a basic understanding of what culture is. In this section we will point to some facets of the concept of culture that are most crucial for the apologist's task and to its relationship with the narrower concept of worldview. This will, furthermore, help us to understand the extent to which conversion to the Christian faith implies a change of culture and worldview.

The concept of culture already had a long history before it was appropriated in the 1920s in the newly developing science of cultural anthropology. I would like to note three developments of the concept in cultural anthropology that reflect a progressively deeper understanding of this phenomenon of culture and are of particular importance for the elaboration of a contextually appropriate Christian apologetic witness.

The first important element in the development coincided with the birth of

---

3 For Berger this vertigo only concerns what falls outside the realm of science, thus classifying himself as a modernist. For the postmodernist this vertigo has a much wider range (cf. Middleton & Walsh 1995b: 55ff).

cultural anthropology itself. Previously, the concept of culture had been used in the singular as a qualification of the well-educated person – closely parallel to the idea of civilization. It was used to make a distinction between the cultured and the uncultured, between the barbaric and civilized. The development of cultural anthropology became possible when it was recognized that not only so-called civilized peoples and persons have culture, but that all people have a culture of their own. Culture thereby came to be used to refer to the particular conglomerate of beliefs and practices characteristic of different societies and groups. Now one begins referring to "cultures" in the plural. This also led to the understanding that other cultures are not just lacking something called civilization or are just steps on the road to civilization. They have an integrity of their own and a proper coherence and logic (Grenz & Franke 2001: 131–134). This also means that human "reason" and "rationality" never exists in a culturally disembodied way, but always as culturally embedded in the form of a specific rationality with a specific understanding of reason and its powers and specific practices of rational discourse (Wilson (ed.) 1971).

This proper integrity of different cultures also means that the traditional formulation of a central apologetic problem as the relationship between "faith and reason" is somewhat misleading. We could better formulate it as the problem of the relationship of "faith and *reasons*". Apologetic dialogue is dialogue between the proper Christian use of reason in accordance with the Christian understanding of the nature of faith and reason on the one hand and multiple alternative understandings of what is rational on the other.

A second important development in the understanding of culture was inaugurated by the anthropologist Clifford Geertz, whom we have already encountered as a major influence on the postliberal theology of George Lindbeck (§2.2). Geertz argued that:

> culture is best not seen as complexes of concrete behaviour patterns – customs, usages, traditions, habit clusters – as has, by and large, been the case up to now, but as a set of control mechanisms – plans, recipes, rules, instructions (what computer engineers call "programs") – for the governing of human behaviour (1993: 44; cf. p. 216).

As such, culture is "an historically transmitted pattern of meanings embodied in symbols" (p. 89), in which those who participate reality indwell the world, through which they give meaning to life and to the world. One implication of this is that the interpretation of culture is a semiotic procedure; it is like "penetrating in a literary text" (p. 448). Cultures should therefore be understood in terms of the meaning its participants themselves give to these cultural practices and not in terms of a foreign interpretative pattern (sociological, psychological, or other), under which the categories of culture are subsumed (pp. 452f) – we recognize Lindbeck's theory of religion here. Another implication of this understanding of culture as a symbolic system through which we relate to the world is, as far as I am aware, not developed by Geertz himself. The first generations of cultural anthropologists had a tendency to look to cultures *from the outside*, seeing it as closed systems. If we consider cultures as symbolic systems through which those who live with them look *to the outside*, to life and to the world, they are no longer closed systems but are constantly impinged upon by the realities of life and the outside world. The latter constantly provide new challenges, to which these symbolic systems need to adapt in order to continue to remain adequate.

This leads to a third change in the understanding of culture in cultural anthropology, away from its original understanding of culture as a coherent whole. In line with postmodern sensitivities for fragmentation and a multiplicity of perspectives, cultures are rather understood to be internally fissured, constantly changing, and constantly interacting with alternative currents within and outside the community (Tanner 1997: 38–56).[4] The older conception of cultures as stable and coherent wholes is probably influenced by the fact that the first anthropological studies concentrated on relatively stable and isolated cultures. However, such cultures are an exception in our globalizing and changing world. Most cultures show much more clearly the inner conflicts they embody and the constant change they go through because of evolving inner tensions, because of their dealing with the always-new challenges of life, and because of the interaction with other cultures. Indeed, cultures need a certain degree of coherence in order to function and survive (Geertz 1993: 17), yet they are as much characterized by inner tensions and dialogues that may be particular to these cultures. In this way the Western culture that is currently exported in the process of globalization is far from a monolithic unity:

> Western "culture wars" are exported as part and parcel of the globalization process. […] free market ideology versus environmentalism, freedom of speech versus "politically correct" speech codes, Hollywood machismo versus feminism, American junk food versus American health foods, and so on (Berger 2002: 15).

This attention for internal dialogue and tension has also "heightened sensitivity to the role of persons in culture formation" (Grenz & Franke 2001: 135). The phenomenon of cultural development itself confirms what we have already concluded on theological grounds (§4.2 and §4.3). Individuals receive their identity from the culture in which they are socialized, but are not mere passive receptors of culture. As players in a field, they find themselves confronted with

4 Tanner notes that postliberal theologians like Lindbeck do not sufficiently recognize that also the Christian cultural–linguistic world is not closed of from surrounding worldviews and that in that respect they are too much indebted to a modern rather than a postmodern concept of culture (1997: 104ff).

various options demanding a choice on their part and perhaps even opening up possibilities of as yet unforeseen renewal (Tanner 1997: 49f).

Central to a culture is a worldview, which, in a non-controversial way, can be defined as "a person's interpretation of reality and a basic view of life" (Naugle 2002: 260). Though it is easy to agree on a basic definition, a further development of the relationship between worldview and other aspects of culture, and between worldview and reality, steers us into areas of significant disagreement. As David Naugle has noted, the concept of worldview is differently interpreted in accordance with different worldviews. As a worldview-dependent concept, the idea of worldview itself needs to be christened in order to use it in accordance with a Christian understanding of the world (2002: 253–259).

One such disagreement concerns the relationship between particular worldviews and other aspects of culture. The options range from considering the worldview merely as a reflection of other aspects of culture – as a way to deal with psychological needs or to provide the legitimization needed by those in power – to seeing the basic worldview as the foundation on which the whole culture is built and the motor propelling all cultural activity. Christian theological anthropology suggests that the truth lies somewhere in the middle. People build their lives in accordance with their basic beliefs. Yet, because of the deceptiveness of their hearts they often also conceive their basic beliefs in a way as to flee from their real needs and to justify their sinful behaviour and their place in society (see further §3.3 and §8.1).

Another crucial area for a properly Christian understanding of the concept of worldview relates to the question of objectivity. In this the Christian understanding stands against the option of Romanticism, which, in its opposition to Enlightenment rationalism and empiricism, shows one of the internal fissures and oppositions that characterizes modernity. For Romanticism, worldviews are person- and culture-relative perspectives on reality with no anchor in objective reality. This was precisely the private area of values in which modernity could leave room for disagreement (Naugle 2002: 257). Christians want to maintain that worldviews do indeed spring from the heart as the subjective centre of human existence (p. 267ff), yet that they are responses to reality. Therefore they should be evaluated with respect to the question whether and in how far they are true to reality or on the contrary "phantom worlds". Worldviews may be distortions of reality springing from the sinful and deluded human heart (cf. §3.3, pp. 80ff).

This understanding of worldview is extremely valuable for the apologist, for it keeps together the fact that a worldview is subjectively reflecting someone's basic attitude to reality, yet should objectively reflect the basic nature of reality itself for it not to be a delusion. If the apologist hopes for the conversion of her dialogue partner, she needs to help him to change perspectives, to change worldview. One should, however, be careful here. Although conversion as *metanoia* definitely demands and implies a change of worldview (cf. Ro 12:2), conversion cannot simply be put on par with it (G. Clark 1996: 201–218). Conversion to the Christian faith means, first of all, a change of attitude to God as He encounters humanity in Jesus Christ (cf. §3.3). It means placing our confidence in Jesus Christ (Ac 16:31), changing allegiance to Him (Ro 10:9) and becoming his followers (Mt 4:19; 28:19).[5]

Such a change of allegiance to Christ is at the same time only possible if people have an initial openness to change their worldview, for within most worldviews such a step would not make sense. Some people may need to understand the basic worldview changes implied in and required by this change of allegiance to Jesus, before they can accept following Him; yet this is not necessarily true for all. One should be careful about placing everyone and every conversion under one single mould. In one sense conversion is a one-moment change from darkness to light and from death to life, in another sense conversion takes time and is a process that in this life is never finished, particularly regarding the conversion of our mind (Stackhouse 2002: 73–81).[6] "Paradigm shifts are rarely sudden or total" (Hiebert 1999: 91). The Christian apologist's task is therefore not necessarily to provide a wholesale alternative worldview, but first of all to point to Christ as the way, the truth and the life. She will need to deal with those aspects of the Christian worldview that would help her dialogue partner make sense of Christ or to help him further on his personal road with Christ. What those aspects are and how profoundly she needs to penetrate questions of worldview will therefore be highly person-relative.

If conversion demands and implies a change of worldview, does this mean that there is only one legitimately Christian worldview to which all Christians should adhere? Should a complete conversion in principle touch our entire worldview? The answer to this question hinges on our understanding of worldview and cannot be univocal because of the ambiguity of the concept when one goes beyond the basic definition as given above. When one uses the term in the limited sense as used by worldview theorists in philosophy (such as James Orr, Abraham Kuyper, Brian Walsh and Richard Middleton, etc.), there is indeed only one Christian worldview that encompasses certain basic ideas concerning God, creation, human nature, the meaning of history, etc. Cultural anthropologists, however, tend to use the idea of worldview in a wider sense – including, for example, the mental picture we have of the world (as flat or round?) or of time (as defined mechanically or by events). In that sense one can say that there is no single Christian worldview (Kraft 1996: 67), or we might better say: no one Christian "world-picture".[7] One can be as good and as rational a Christian within the three-layer

5 On worldview and allegiance, see further §7.1.

6 Cf. also the distinction Os Guinness makes between "to convince of the new belief" and "to construct the new world" (Guinness 1981: 284).

7 In a different sense some German thinkers have made a distinction between "*Weltanschauung*" (worldview) and "*Weltbild*" (worldpicture) (Naugle 2002: 121).

universe of much of classical antiquity as one can in a heliocentric universe, or in a universe started by the Big Bang.

Distinguishing two sides to the apologetic enterprise

We come now to the point of exploring further the question of the relationship between apologetics and culture, and the attentive reader may have detected that the argument so far leads in two different directions. One line of argument in this book has been that the Christian faith cannot be justified in terms of a foreign framework but only in terms of its own understanding of reality and of the specific inroad it proposes – the revelation of God in Christ. We have simultaneously underlined the need for contextual apologetics, pointing to the inappropriateness of Western apologetics in other contexts and to the biblical examples of contextualized apologetic dialogue and witness.[8] At first sight, both lines of argument point in contrary directions – the former to a single form of apologetic argumentation, uniquely appropriate to the Christian faith; the latter to a great variety of culture- and audience-specific apologies. They agree only in their criticism of modern apologetics with its presupposed universally available rationality underlying all valid argumentation. If all argumentation, though aimed at universal truth, is culturally embedded, this means we in fact need to distinguish between these two different sides of the one apologetic enterprise.

On the one hand, we have the apologetic argumentation that is closely related to dogmatics. It aims to show the inherent rationality of the Christian faith, tracing it back to its proper foundation in God's being in Himself and in his self-revelation in Christ testified to in the Scriptures and handed down by the Church (cf. §5.4). On the other hand, there is the need for apologetics witness relating to specific audiences, of building bridges to other culturally embedded ways of understanding reality and of finding ways of persuading their adherents to consider Christ as the clue to the truth and the way to life.[9] The first side of apologetics was explored in the previous chapter. Whether and how the second side can be taken into account will be addressed in the following chapters.

Both sides of the apologetic enterprise need to be distinguished because of their different aims and types of argumentation, yet both are closely related. Within a Christian community that is not seriously contested by alternative perspectives on reality, the first side will attract all the attention in internal apologetics – the

8 For the first line of thought, see particularly §§2.3, 3.2, 5.4, for the second line §§1.1, 1.4, 6.1.

9 This distinction between a first and second task parallels Emil Brunner's distinction between the first and "the other task of theology" ("die andere Aufgabe der Theologie"). Yet Brunner, as a child of his time, did not consider the second task audience- and culture-specific, but a task dealing with universal reason and it is precisely therefore that he all too easily gave it too much authority (Brunner 1929; cf. for Barth's criticism: *KD* I/1: 25ff; trans. *CD* I/1: 27ff).

apologetic witness directed to the Christian community. Yet, as soon as contestant worldviews present themselves as not entirely implausible, it becomes necessary to deal with the culturally specific alternatives that present themselves. This is not because the Christian worldview would not be sufficiently well founded in itself, but because the mental make-up of the human beings as created for community is such that they are prone to critically consider their own convictions when confronted with more or fewer plausible alternatives.[10] Conversely, the second apologetic task can never be fulfilled without reference to the first project. The Christian faith can never be shown to have warrant or to be justified in terms of foreign frameworks of understanding. In relation to other perspectives on reality and life, the apologist can only aim at building bridges that persuade people to take the Christian faith seriously on its own merits and precisely *not* on the merits it has according to other cultural perspectives. The distinction between this first and second task of apologetics cannot therefore be set on par with the distinction between internal and external apologetics that is used conventionally with respect to the different audiences of apologetics, be they Christian or non-Christian. In dealing with both audiences both tasks of apologetics need to be given proper attention. I propose distinguishing the two sides of apologetics as the "reality-oriented" side and the "audience-oriented" side. Both are different *aspects* of apologetics, yet belong to the one apologetic enterprise, which constantly moves between the two poles of the reality of God in Christ and a culture-specific audience.[11]

---

10 Netland rightly notes that the epistemic design of the human being, on which Plantinga majors, may imply that in a pluralistic world the *sensus deitatis* and the inner testimony of the Holy Spirit are no longer a sufficient basis for well-grounded belief. As social beings, it is after all natural for us to start doubting experiences that are not shared with those closest to us (Netland 2001: 272). Most of us are not in the epistemic situation of "the 14-year-old theist brought up to believe in the community where everyone believes", who Plantinga (1983: 33) uses to show that we can be in our epistemic rights without evidence for our belief in God. Even if we have these beliefs as *prima facie* properly basic, the pluralistic situation enhances the need for an internal apologetic to show the warrant of these particular beliefs. Plantinga's *Warrant*-trilogy itself deals with this question of the warrant of these beliefs, yet there is no reason to exclude the validity and even need of other apologetic procedures to prove this point.

11 The distinction, which Netland makes between "transcultural apologetics" and "culture-specific apologetics" (Netland 1988: 293), and later between "theoretical" and "applied apologetics" (2001: 249), resembles the distinction proposed here in its call for a culturally sensitive apologetics. Yet both terminological distinctions are somewhat misleading, for the first side is not transcultural if this is taken to mean that it argues from culturally universally available starting points. Netland's defence of the use of culturally neutral criteria for the comparison of worldviews, to which we will return later (§7.6), suggests that this is indeed how he envisages "trans-cultural apologetics". Furthermore, the second aspect also has an important theoretical component, which is not simply a reflection of the theoretical work that enters into the first aspect. Comparing Christian and Buddhist understandings of ultimate reality, for example, is a theoretically challenging enterprise and not just a question of application. The recognition of the need for a cultural sensitive apologetics lies equally at the basis of William A. Dyrness' *Christian Apologetics in a World Community* (1982: see particularly 13f), yet did not (in this book) lead to a serious reconsideration of the nature of apologetics.

6.2 The unity of human nature and contradicting cultural perspectives

The quest for a universal human nature

A century of research in cultural anthropology has brought to light an enormous variety of cultures and thus ways in which human communities understand themselves and the world. This enormous array constitutes the challenge that contextual apologetics needs to address. It is, at the same time, this wide-ranging cultural variety that gives a strong initial plausibility to relativist postmodernist understandings of truth and human nature as social constructs. If there is no such a common reality as "human nature" this would, of course, defy the whole description of Christian anthropology developed earlier and it would impinge upon that apologetic effort to search for a so-called "point of contact" in the beliefs and lives of our dialogue-partners. For a long time cultural anthropologists themselves like G.P. Murdock and Clyde Kluckhohn have searched for cultural universals which would provide a common ground across the board and which would provide a fixed human nature (Geertz 1993: 38). Yet, as Geertz has noted, in order for these cultural universals to retain their universality in spite of the great variety, they need to be emptied to such a degree of any specific content, that they become virtually empty designations. In order to say, for example, that all human beings are religious, or that all cultures have a concept of truth or of marriage, these concepts need to become extremely general and vague to be able to cover the great variety of cultural expressions. This procedure can thereby even unwillingly contribute to cultural relativism, when what is left does not go beyond "vague tautologies and forceless banalities" (Geertz 1993: 41).

But why would the most universal phenomena among humankind tell us what is most important about it? Geertz rightly notes that some specific cultures or particular ways of living might give us the deepest insight into what being human is about. The same is common in other sciences too. For example, one could look to a very limited phenomenon such as the proliferation of sickle-cell anaemia to understand human genetics in a way that has a much wider validity. In the same way, scientists look into the behaviour of uranium to understand the nature of the kernel of the atom, which is much harder to detect yet equally present in other instances (Geertz 1993: 44). As Christians, we want to argue that what is most important about the nature of being human becomes visible when we look to the kind of life to which God invites us. We perceive it most clearly in Jesus of Nazareth, who not only showed who God is, but who equally is the most "accomplished" human being. We explored this understanding of human nature in the fourth chapter and have already seen that the view clearly leaves room for cultural variety as a consequence of the cultural mandate and the creation of humanity to live in community.

In this section we will go one step beyond this explanation in showing that not only does the Christian understanding of human nature, in principle, allow for cultural variety, but also it explains the *type* of cultural variety we detect around and among us. In doing so, we find further confirmation of the truthfulness of this understanding. We noted how Polanyi argued that a scientific theory shows itself to be truthful when it appears to provide explanations for ranges of phenomena the explanation for which it was not originally designed (§5.1, p. 125). This is precisely what happens here with the Christian theological understanding of human nature. Originally designed to account for the wide variety of Scriptural data, it already helped us to understand and explain the nature of the opposition between modernism and postmodernism (§4.5). When it is also able to explain the nature of the cultural variety that we encounter, this will be a further important confirmation of the truthfulness of this account of human nature. Not every explanation will automatically fit the data! When we will be able to account for the wide variety of cultures flowing out of one common human nature, this will furthermore show us the way in which we can make apologetic use of "points of contact" in the nature of the human being and in specific cultural constellations.

The contrasts in human nature and contradicting cultural perspectives

When Scripture speaks about the unity of human nature, it ordinarily refers to it as to the heart (Naugle 2002: 267ff; Wolff 1973: 90; trans. 1974: 55). Every personal life has some sort of unity and therefore we can justifiably address people as identifiable persons. The existence of people with multiple personalities confronts us with serious questions about the unity of personal identity, yet the fact that we consider such cases pathological shows that we perceive persons as ordinarily having one personality centre.

At the same time the human being is characterized by many inner tensions and distinctions. In discussing the tension between modernism and postmodernism we have already noted the tension between our being part of creation and standing apart from creation, between individuality and community orientation, between being earthlings and having a God-ward orientation (§4.5). These three tensions in turn are consequences of the three constitutive relationships of being human. Such tensions are so characteristic of being human, that John Macquarrie has developed an analysis of human nature exploring a whole field of such tensions. After all: "Every property or quality or possibility that we discover in the human being seems to be accompanied by its opposite, so that humanity appears a contradiction" (Macquarrie 1982: 5). As Macquarrie rightly notes, these tensions often appear to us as contradictions. This "appearing", rightly understood, not only reflects a tension between outer appearance and inner unity. More profoundly, the human being appears as a contradiction because of sin, for because of sin its inner unity is not only hidden from sight, but it is lost. The heart as the unifying centre of the human being can only bring harmony among the different tensions in the human condition when this centre is oriented towards God. He only can bring unity to human existence. Before we see what this implies for our understanding of cultural diversity, we will need to explore this relationship between sin and the inner contradiction characterizing the current human condition. We will do it with the help of an example.

One of the most visible tensions in human existence noted by all major thinkers and religions is between our finitude on the one hand and our relationship with the infinite on the other. This was vividly expressed by Blaise Pascal when he called the human being a "thinking reed" (Pascal *Pensées*: no. 113, cf. no. 200). The human being is small and vulnerable as a reed, almost nothing in the vast universe, yet he is a *thinking* reed and can contain the whole universe in his mind. Following Søren Kierkegaard, Reinhold Niebuhr has shown that this tension causes anxiety when the human being is thrown back on himself. He is created for a relationship with the infinite God and therefore to find his fulfilment in something infinite, but is on all sides limited because of his finiteness and creatureliness. He therefore needs to either master the world and people around him and forget in his pride that he is part of this world, *or* he needs to suppress this orientation towards the infinite and choose a life that seeks fulfilment within the world of sensuality (1941: 190ff). Yet it is important to note that he does not necessarily live in this contradiction. He can live without anxiety when he heeds the call of Jesus to put his trust in God alone (Mt 6:25ff). His life forms a meaningful unity when it is lived in accordance with the plan of God, when he finds fulfilment in his relationship with the infinite God (pp. 195, 179). However, this is not something to be grasped and mastered; rather, it is a gift to be received by grace. The duality in the human condition of being, on the one hand, a finite creature and being, on the other, created for an infinite goal only becomes a contradiction when in sin he is no longer open to attain this fulfilment in accordance with God's will for his life.

We thus perceive a duality in the human life that becomes a contradiction when life is not lived according to God's plan with Him as its unifying centre. The same pattern can also be recognized with regard to other basic tensions in human life. We have already referred to the tensions between his individuality and community-orientation and between his having authority over creation and yet being part of creation. Both poles of these tensions find their proper place within an overarching Christian understanding of the human being, yet the tension between modernism and postmodernism and many ongoing debates in the history of ideas show that without such a Christian perspective these dualities are hard to reconcile.

How this pertains to the issue of cultural diversity becomes clear when we return to Pascal. Pascal drew a straight line between the greatness of humankind (his being a *thinking* reed) and the smallness and misery of the human being (his being a thinking *reed*) to two main philosophical positions in antiquity and in his own times. On the one hand, there were the sceptics who were very conscious of the limitations of the human being and the human mind. On the other hand, there were the rationalists who saw their great power.[12] Because the human being cannot live with the contradictions of his nature, he will tend to create his own syntheses ordinarily by neglecting one side or the other of a given tension, creating different personality types or different cultural options. Worldviews, cultures or streams within cultures will therefore represent different ways of dealing with the tensions in human nature, given that the true unity is no longer in view.

The opposition between a rationalist worldview and (sub)culture and a sceptic worldview and (sub)culture are just one sign of the inner tensions in the human condition. There are also individualist cultures and societies (such as the modern West) and communalist or collectivist ones (such as in traditional Africa or in communist societies) (Van der Walt 1997: 28–49). In the same way there are cultures that can be characterized as concentrating on life within creation (for example, Taoism) and those concentrating on life beyond creation (for example, Buddhism) (Brunner 1941: 181f, 186–190; trans. 1939: 183f, 187–191). From a Christian perspective we can see that contrasting understandings of human nature and the human condition and completely contrasting cultures can all be an outworking of the tensions that make up the human being as a sinner. It becomes understandable that the same human being can become an ascetic Buddhist monk and a lecherous boozer, and that both are, in their own way, "typically human".

Implications for apologetics

In what way does all this help us in apologetics? First of all, it gives us an entirely different perspective on the reality of cultural diversity. Ideological pluralists often claim that the simple fact of plurality implies we can no longer believe one such cultural perspective to be closer to the truth than others. We saw that the impact of cultural pluralism indeed creates a "vertigo of relativity", which gives ideological pluralism initial plausibility. Yet, we have seen now that the reality of cultural pluralism is perfectly coherent with the Christian understanding of the world and of the human condition. It not only leaves room for a degree of cultural variety as fruit of different outcomes of the cultural mandate (cf. §4.2); it also explains that the multifaceted human nature, because of sin, loses its unity and therefore stands at the origin of a great variety of mutually exclusive and contradicting understandings of human nature, of life and of the world.

This understanding of a single human nature underlying a variety of sometimes contradicting cultural expressions also helps us deal with a problem that has

12 See particularly his *Pensées* no. 131 and his "Entretien avec M. de Saci" (Pascal 1963: 291–297).

haunted theoretical reflection about the prospect of apologetics. It has been a recurrent question whether there are some features essential to human nature that the apologist can use as a point of contact – for example, his being essentially religious, moral or seeking after meaning. One problem in answering the question in the affirmative has been that there is no feature that is not virtually absent in some cultural constellation or personality type. That said, if the human being in his current condition tends to suppress aspects of his being that contradict others, we can understand why significant features of human nature can be essential, yet in some situations are suppressed to the point of becoming virtually undetectable.

Let me clarify this with the help of an example. As a first-year theology student I was doing evangelism on a campground on the coast in the Netherlands. We were organizing all sorts of recreational activities and getting to know the young people, hoping for opportunities for sharing the Gospel. On one occasion we found ourselves together with a group of teenagers who were open to hear us. When we tried to explain that Jesus Christ was the one who gave our lives meaning, to my utter shock these young people apparently had no receptors for this idea of "looking for a meaning in life". For them life did not need meaning. They simply lived and enjoyed it as it came, without asking further questions. This was a major upset in my understanding of what it means to be human, and of myself, for I simply considered such an attitude impossible, yet here I saw it sincerely held. By the way, this illustrates how my own understanding of reality was not immune from the reality I encountered. With hindsight, I think now that I approached these teenagers and the theological question they raised for me with an inadequate framework. I supposed that if the need for meaning is an essential feature of human nature, it should be universally detectable and they should have this quest, and if not, that it could not be essential. I think that it is better to explain this situation differently. The need for meaning is universal, but is in tension with other aspects of life – including the fact that we find ourselves in a world that, for many, seems meaningless. These young people had grown up with a fundamentally evolutionist and materialistic perspective on life in which the quest for meaning was meaningless. Therefore they did not recognize this quest within themselves.

Yet, how does this essential need for meaning help the apologist, when it is no longer detectable? To begin with, it encourages us to look for a variety of points of contact rather than just for one or a few. Each worldview always reflects some truth and represses other aspects of it, even if the truth we encounter may not be the truth we expect. It also encourages us to continue using this quest for meaning in those cases where it is present, and not disparage its apologetic value for not being universally detectable. Finally, it encourages us to wait and to be patient, for if the need for meaning is essential it is not absent but merely dormant and it can awake later on in life. In fact, this is what happens regularly. People who never thought about the meaning of life may start doing so when confronted with death or another major crisis or, on a more positive front, the birth of a first child. Sometimes a sensitive apologist just needs to keep the channels of communication open, hoping that there will come a time when there is more openness to the Gospel.

6.3 Cross-cultural communication

The difficulty and possibility of cross-cultural communication

Because of the profound way in which all our thinking and perception is influenced by the worldview we share and the cultural framework which we inhabit, communication across cultural barriers is a hazardous enterprise. When a child grows up in a certain culture, it internalizes its specific outlook on reality as simply "the world *tout court*" without any second thought (Berger & Luckmann 1967: 154; Kraft 1996: 55–57). Unless it is radically challenged from outside, we continue to perceive the world in that way. It has a certain naturalness to it, both in what we perceive it to be and in how we perceive it to be ordered. This sense of the naturalness is so strong, because most of the way we process our perceptions happens subconsciously. Most of the presuppositions with which we and others approach reality are out of our sight. When we note differences with the way others conceive of reality, we will first be struck by those differences that show themselves at the surface: by the fact that others, for example, wear amulets or that they spend part of their lives in a Buddhist monastery. Yet, we will only be able to make sense of these more superficial differences in practices and in beliefs in terms of the more basic framework of perception that is largely hidden from direct view. Therefore all too often the more superficial cultural differences that we perceive simply do not make sense and at best we conceive of them as interesting curiosities.

The largely unconscious natural character of our basic ordering and interpretation of reality becomes clear when we see that the language we use already reflects a certain classification and interpretation of the world. Yet, it is an ordering we take for granted for it is the only one we can speak about, as we already showed in talking about the various words different cultures have for "snow" (§5.1). As anthropologist Charles Kraft notes (1996: 248f; cf. Berger & Luckmann 1967: 53):

> Each language embodies a whole set of unconscious worldview assumptions about the world and life in it, so people see and hear largely what their language makes them sensitive to and trains them to look for.

With the use of English (or rather American-English) as the *lingua franca* of the globalization process, people also appropriate and propagate certain ways of understanding reflected in its vocabulary, its idiomatic expressions, phraseology, and ordering principles. Berger (2002: 3) points to revealing examples such as "religious preference" (which categorizes religion as a personal taste) and "sexual orientation" (which suggests the parity and exchangeability of different orientations).

This degree of the impact of culture on our understanding of the world, of ourselves and of others need not amaze Christians, for it reflects the Christian understanding of the cultural and communal character of human existence, for better or for worse (§4.3). This, in itself, does not help us to solve the problems of cross-cultural communication that are so profound we might wonder if different cultural perspectives are not incommensurable. Let us recall that worldviews cannot only be conceived of as incommensurable with regard to the possibility of giving a rational evaluation of different worldviews, but also with regard to the possibility of cross-cultural communication (§2.2). The incommensurability thesis with regards to communication states that our cultural perspectives influence our understanding not only of the world, but also of each other, so profoundly that real mutual understanding and communication across cultural borders is impossible. Convincing as such a thesis may seem when one is confronted for the first time with a radically different perspective on life, it must still be considered an overstatement of the case, both in principle and in practice, for the two following reasons.

First of all, if different cultural perspectives were incommensurable in the sense that the understanding of other worldviews is impossible, we would in principle not be able to know and express what is incommensurable. As Donald Davidson rightly noted (1984: 184):

> Examples like these [that are invoked to prove the incommensurability of different perspectives], impressive as they occasionally are, are not so extreme but that the changes and the contrasts can be explained and described using the equipment of a single language. Whorf, wanting to demonstrate that Hopi incorporates a metaphysic so alien that Hopi and English cannot, as he puts it, "be calibrated" uses English to convey the contents of sample Hopi sentences. Kuhn is brilliant at saying what things were like before the revolution using – what else? – our post-revolutionary idiom.

If some degree of incommensurability between two frameworks can be shown to be present, this demonstrates that these two frameworks are not wholly incommensurable; rather, they are incommensurable on some points and commensurable on others, while the degree of commensurability can vary (cf. Griffiths 1988: 27ff).

The thesis of the impossibility of communication hurts itself, second, on the simple fact of the experience of understanding across cultural boundaries and of the possibility of anthropological research leading to a certain degree of understanding (Netland 2001: 287–289). I have the experience of communicating with Sub, a Buddhist from South Korea, and experiencing mutual understanding. Notwithstanding the mutual recognition of how different we are and the recognition that this difference runs much deeper than we thought at first sight and often results in unexpected misunderstandings, there is the experience of mutual understanding. This experience of understanding is confirmed precisely by the fact that the other proves to be so much different from what I initially thought him to be.

A radical postmodernist might of course retort that this is only an illusion of understanding, while we remain imprisoned within our own framework. However, that this experience of understanding is provoked by something beyond our own framework of thought, which impinges on this framework, is confirmed in the same two ways that we saw present in the way extra-linguistic reality impinges on our thought (§5.1). First of all, we discover our own interpretation of the other person and culture time and again to be inadequate and leading to anomalies of interpretation, which forces us to change our perspective and hermeneutic framework to better fit the reality of the culture and person we meet. Second, we discover that the thoughts of others also have a coherence and structure of their own, which is foreign to us. We therefore cannot have projected this structure on in it. It can only be something that was already there which we simply dis-covered. Precisely when we are conscious about how our own frameworks influence and cloud our understanding of others, we can make a conscious effort to understand others on their own terms (McGrath 1990: 82). In revealing such hidden presuppositions, cultural anthropological and postmodernist analysis thus contributed significantly to a better understanding of others across cultural boundaries – and to a better understanding of ourselves in the same process.

The very possibility of cross-cultural communication is partly given with the fact that cultures are not watertight compartments, as earlier anthropological research in the most remote cultural groups suggested. Cultures are going through changes, sometimes revolutions, yet guard some degree of continuity over these changes. Cultures constantly interact and develop many shades and hybrid forms with all types of overlap between one culture and the next (Tanner 1997: 53–56; McGrath 1990: 87). At a deeper level the possibility of a degree of mutual understanding is not only given because of the reality of cultural overlap, but because of the human nature we share and because of the common world in which we live. Even if our common human nature presents itself in many different and often conflicting ways, it is still the same human nature, which underlies these different manifestations. Even if we can relate to the world and ourselves differently and often in mutually exclusive ways, it is still the same world to which we relate.

Understanding others

If different outlooks on the world hamper cross-cultural communication, the search for real understanding of our dialogue partners is a crucial element of all apologetic dialogue and a crucial prerequisite for all apologetic witness. Not only does this hold true for apologetic dialogue in distant countries or in strange subcultures, but also for dialogue with those who are close to us. The simple fact that the latter do not accept the Christian outlook means that they also live as it were in a different world.

How is such an understanding possible? Understanding is obviously a matter of degree and we should therefore ask more precisely: how can we arrive at a degree of understanding that will make a genuine dialogue concerning the Christian faith possible? Such an understanding of another person and of another culture is basically a hermeneutic process (Geertz 1993: 448, 453; Hiebert 1999: 75), as is the understanding of the extra-textual world itself (§5.2) and requires, as a basic rule, that we understand others on their own terms. This is a consequence of the need to understand cultures and worldviews as wholes, with a proper integrity in and of themselves. As in hermeneutics the best way to understand the other according to his own self-understanding is to keep the appropriate balance between respecting the strangeness of the other's views – often indicated to us by what seem at first sight anomalies in our interpretation – and becoming familiar with it by exploring its proper integrity and coherence.

This understanding of the other in terms of their *own* framework of beliefs is particularly important with respect to a quantitatively important domain of apologetic dialogue, the need to deal with objections. Dealing with objections occupies much of the attention of the apologist, so much so that some would even define the nature of apologetics as Christian "defence", directed against objections to the Christian faith. Too often we think we have understood an objection, because we have heard it before or because we have seriously pondered it ourselves. Yet, the same objection can have rather different backgrounds and needs to be dealt with accordingly. The objection that Christ can never be the only way to God can be brought to the fore by a traditional African, a Hindu, a modernist or a postmodernist, each time with different origins. The traditional African may come up with the objection, because he believes that all tribes have their proper religion and the Hindu, because he believes that there are many *avatars*. The modernist may object to the Christian claim of Christ having universal significance because he believes that religion belongs to the realm of personal preference, and the postmodernist, because he believes that religion is a human construct. A serious answer will try to deal with the specific background from which the objection arises. This shows again why attentive listening is so crucial in apologetic dialogue.

In another respect, however, the answers to these objections that spring from different roots will also be similar. Just as Christians should make an effort to understand others against the background of their framework of thought, they may and need to ask others to understand the Christian faith in terms of its proper understanding of God. The Christian apologist needs to invite others to step into the Christian world. Others need to understand why Christians believe the way Christ opens to God to be different from all the human-made religious roads to God. Outsiders need to understand why Christians believe that Christ can justifiably make this universal claim.

This is not the place to develop a full theory of communication. Yet, against the recurrent postmodern suspicion of purported understanding, some remarks are in place to show how a significant degree of understanding is possible in order to facilitate real apologetic dialogue. Just as in the hermeneutic process of reading a text, the most common way of entering into another person's or community's self-understanding will be that we take our departure from those areas where we share a number of beliefs about the world and ourselves. From there on we can probe progressively into the parts that are more foreign. In the process we can arrive at an understanding of the alternative perspective on its own terms. Thus we can learn the "language" of another culture as we would learn a second language. In this way we can even feel how it is to inhabit such a world, even if we do not really inhabit it by conviction, but as a world we visit, as a world in which move as a visitor.[13]

It is also possible to become acquainted with another culture not in the way we learn a second language, but in the way we learn our first language. In the West, we ordinarily learn a second language by first translating the concepts of the new language, say French, into the language that we already know, Dutch in my case. This inevitably means that at first we read and listen to French as a variation of Dutch and not according to its own structure. Our first language, though, we learn differently. We learn it by simply participating in a community, by entering its symbolic world and by appropriating it as our own. This is how my own children learned French. They simply went to the French school not knowing the language. They did not try to translate what they heard into Dutch, but tried to make sense of the language within the new context of the school – which was really different from the schools they were used to in the Netherlands. In this way they learnt what MacIntyre calls a "second first language" (1988: 374). In this way we can also learn about other cultures as a second first language by living there, by becoming part of that culture and being socialized in it on its own terms. Newbigin (1989: 55f, 65) and Lindbeck (1997: 428f) use this idea of a "second first language" to show how real mutual understanding is possible, when one moves from one world into another, understanding both worlds from the inside. This is the most profound understanding that we can have of a second culture.

In order to know a second language as you know a first language, however, it is not strictly necessary that we learn it as a first language – although this will

13 On the possibility of getting acquainted with a different understanding of reality without appropriating it for ourselves, see: Berger & Luckmann 1967: 192.

help greatly. Some people have the experience of learning a language as a second language that later becomes their first after immigrating to another country, for example. We can gradually become so comfortable with another language or with another culture that we can really understand it on its own terms without treating it as a variation of our first language or culture. Many Christians will have natural affinities with one or two sub-cultures and will be able to share their faith within a number of closely related communities. Some Christians may also be called to become acquainted with one or more cultures to which they are originally strangers for the sake of the proclamation of the Gospel, so that the Gospel may be heard and understood till the ends of the earth.

Communicating the Gospel

If different culturally embedded perspectives on the world have their own integrity and if the different elements of such an understanding receive their meaning in relationship to other elements within this structure, communicating cross-culturally is obviously a hazardous enterprise. This is particularly clear, when we consider that even the language of the receiving culture used to express ideas reflects and unconsciously supports its values and perspective. However, this does not make such communication impossible. Though language receives its initial meaning from the context in which it belongs, it can at the same time acquire new meanings and can be used to express contents hitherto unanticipated. In this way a language can point beyond the world, which it originally used to express. Communicating cross-culturally is essentially an exercise in translation, yet an exercise which not only touches the level of simple wording, but which touches the deeper levels structuring a thought-world. It means taking concepts of the receiving culture and using them to point to realities beyond their original field of reference (cf. Newbigin 1986: 4ff).

This process of translation also happened in the Scriptures itself. The Gospels referred to Jesus as the Messiah, but in talking about Him as the suffering Messiah, they gave “Messiah” a previously inconceivable meaning pointing beyond what was earlier considered to be real and possible (Mk 8:29–31).[14] John’s Gospel used the concept of *logos* to explain who Jesus was, which had many resonances with a Hellenistic audience. Yet, in the process this Gospel radically changed its range of meaning in witnessing to the fact that this *logos* became flesh, incarnate, in Jesus of Nazareth (Jn 1:1, 14; cf. Lausanne Committee 1980: 314f).

---

14 This tension between the reality of Jesus and the conceptual structures developed in Israel does not diminish the special place of Israel as the community that God chose so that a conceptual structure might develop as a subjective counterpart prepared to receive his revelation in Christ (Torrance 1999: 86ff).

The same procedure has been used, up to present times, in the history of the Church and in missions. The African theologian Kwame Bediako speaks about Jesus as the true and great Ancestor, who does everything that was rightly expected from the traditional ancestors – and more. This Great Ancestor is at the same time radically different from the former ancestors in not being from one's own tribe, but from the tribe of David, into whose people Christians are adopted or grafted (cf. Ro 11:17; Bediako 2000: 22ff; cf. Van den Toren 1997: 224f). When using modern English to express our Christian convictions, we may talk about our "religious preference", but using it in a way that shows the inadequacy of the term when describing the Christian faith. We only prefer Christ because we believe He first preferred us; we have chosen Him, because He has first chosen us (Jn 15:9).

These examples point to a general characteristic of language – that, on the one hand, it reflects a certain view of reality and in many hidden ways supports it, but that, at the same time, it does not simply imprison us in its perspective on reality; rather, it can acquire new meanings. This will not normally happen when a language remains isolated and closed in on itself, but becomes a very real possibility when two languages meet and when people start moving between two language-worlds. Christian theologians are familiar with this process because of the relationship between the Hebrew and Greek sections in the Scriptures. The New Testament theologian James Barr pointed to the importance of a right understanding of this relationship, when in his *The Semantics of Biblical Language* (1961) he criticized the theory of language underlying the so-called "Biblical Theology movement". Until then the Biblical Theology movement majored on developing the contrast between the "Greek mind" and the "Hebrew mind", which they saw reflected in these respective languages and which they analysed through a thorough study of the meaning of concepts in both languages. Barr brought a valid criticism and an important caution to this whole procedure by pointing out that a message is not given in words but in sentences. In sentences we can convey meanings that the words by themselves did not originally have, as in "the Messiah will need to suffer" or "the *logos* became flesh."

The same warning is needed in anthropological research. This is one of the many examples in which interdisciplinary exchange can protect us from oversimplification. In anthropological research the influence of what with regards to Africa is called "ethno-philosophy" is considerable (Tempels 1945; trans. 1969; cf. Masolo 1994: 46–102). A significant part of such "ethno-philosophy" consists of the analysis of language-structures to uncover the hidden philosophy (or, more appropriately, worldview) of a certain people. Although the relationship between language and worldview suggests that this may be *a* valid analytical instrument, it is an instrument that needs to be used with much caution. It cannot be assumed that current ideas of a certain community are the same as were reflected in the formative stages of their language. There is for example an extensive discussion of whether African languages reflect a particular concept of time because of their lack of linguistic tools to refer to the distant future.[15] Yet, the understanding of time of most Africans below the Sahara has greatly changed over the last century. Even if the concept of time reflected in these languages can be detected, it cannot be assumed that those who speak these languages still share it. The whole effort of Bible translation presupposes that this need not be so anymore, for it uses African languages to lead people into the world of Scripture and thus to introduce the speakers of these languages to a completely new understanding of time and history.

This capacity of languages to point beyond their original *Sitz im Leben* and to acquire new meanings points in itself to limitations in the usefulness of the understanding of language and culture in terms of a Wittgensteinian "language game" or in terms of a Lindbeckian "cultural–linguistic framework". Language, indeed, has a meaning with reference to the other parts of a given language structure. Yet language also points to an extra-linguistic reality, sometimes rather directly – for example, when we use the word "green" or "snow" to point to something beyond our language system. After some dialogue and clarification, people using other languages may understand this reference, even though their word "*vert*" or "*neige*" may have different connotations. Languages may also be used to point beyond themselves in more complex ways, for example when we use the expression "*kurios*" or "Lord" with reference to Jesus. For those using the expression "the Lord Jesus", the reality of Jesus Christ remains an independent reality. Our expressions point to and are given meaning by this reality, which always retains a measure of critical independence *vis-à-vis* our language (cf. Deddo 2001: 204f).

The hazards of cross-cultural communication show that cross-cultural apologetics will need to draw heavily on the more general enterprise of the contextualization of theology. One of the tasks of systematic theological reflection is to see how the Christian message can be understood within the thought-forms of other cultures. This is not only true with regards to cultures which we would traditionally consider of missiological interest, but as much with regards the late and post-modern Western culture, which is equally foreign to the Gospel (Bosch 1991a: 456; Newbigin 1986: 2f).

Contextual communication of the Gospel is, of course, only a halfway house. Of even more interest to the apologist is the question of whether there are possibilities to persuade her dialogue partners of the truth of this new perspective on life. It is to this question that we now turn.

15 The main defender of this thesis was John S. Mbiti (1969: 15–28; 1971: 24–32). For a criticism, see: Igenoza 1989: 36–47.

Chapter 7

CROSS-CULTURAL PERSUASION

The apologist does not only hope for effective communication. She hopes to persuade her conversation partner of the liberating truth and goodness of Jesus Christ (cf. Ac 18:4). Yet, if all arguments for whatever point of view are culturally embedded, as we have seen, such an effort at persuasion will encounter enormous barriers. Apologetic dialogue across cultural boundaries cannot and should not aim for formulating knock-down arguments for the Christian faith on the basis of premises that all reasonable participants to that dialogue should necessary share. Apologetic witness will have to be much more subtle than that.

The fact that apologetic argument across cultural and worldview boundaries can never be conclusive does, however, not mean that it cannot be rational. The proverbial madman who believes that he is dead can be given no conclusive argument that he is not. But the fact that he cannot be convinced does not make him any more rational.[1] Reasoning will need to be more complex and many-faceted. This is the reason why the term *persuasion* is preferable to *argument*, when talking about cross-cultural apologetics. This term not only shows that the forms of argumentation can be varied and complex, but also it respects the fact that it has an emotional and moral component. A rational evaluation of different worldviews is not possible when one's primary interest is to defend one's proper beliefs and interests. It is only possible when one has the appropriate openness to seriously consider alternatives on the basis of their inherent truthfulness and goodness. As Polanyi says: "Demonstration must be supplemented, therefore, by forms of persuasion which can induce a conversion" (Polanyi 1962: 151).[2]

Before we explore issues of emotional predispositions and morality in cross-cultural dialogue in the next chapter, here we will explore three major openings for apologetic persuasion: the role of the overall Christian worldview and *ethos* (§7.2); the possibility of building bridges (§7.3); and the proper use of anomalies (§7.4). We will also discuss role of the Christian community for the plausibility of the Christian message (§7.5); and conclude with observations on the finality of

1 Cf. the perceptive remark by G.K. Chesterton that the most rigid and irrefutable rational arguments can be found in Hanwell, the London lunatic asylum (1996 [1908]: 9ff).

2 The apologetic use of the concept is prominent in Guinness (1981: 327–372), Torrance (1971: 195ff) and Murphy (1996). Murphy defends, that "Holism understands justification as a process of rational persuasion" (1996: 108), referring to Thiemann (1985: 75f) and Quine & Ulian (1978: 125ff).

the Christian message and "worldview apologetics" (§7.6). Before we reach that point though, we will start with a further exploration of the different barriers that such cross-cultural apologetic witnessing will need to take into account (§7.1).

7.1 Barriers

Before we can explore the more positive aspects of cross-cultural persuasion, it is good to have a clearer picture of the different barriers that need to be overcome in the process. Although these barriers all interconnect, it is helpful to distinguish three types: some barriers are related to the nature of the human being; others are related to the nature of the impact of a worldview on our lives; and still others are related to the way possible anomalies or criticisms are addressed.

Barriers related to the nature of the human being

There are, first of all, barriers related to the nature of the human being. All human beings are profoundly bound up with their culture, and receive their basic outlook on reality from the community in which they are socialized and from which they receive their identity. Even the consideration that this outlook might not be in accordance with reality in itself is profoundly unsettling. Kraft notes: "Tradition is a powerful deterrent to change. It seems easier to continue with a tradition, even if it is widely acknowledged to be deficient, than to go to the effort of changing it" (Kraft 1996: 380; cf. Torrance 1971: 197). Our community gives us a sense of security, and the idea that I may need to disengage myself from this community is unsettling – even if I knew there is a new supportive community welcoming me. Christians from the individualistic Western world often do not realize how little supported their community generally provides in comparison with some of the communities to which their dialogue partners belong. A Muslim woman in the West considering conversion is not only considering a new religious allegiance and a new outlook of the world, but also converting to the community of the Church, which often seems rather shallow compared to the close-knit Muslim communities in the diaspora on which she depends.

A second aspect of human nature that forms a barrier is the twisting of our openness to God, which in the fallen human being manifests itself as a sinful allegiance and enslavement to what is not God (Torrance 1971: 205). The role of sin will receive more attention in the final chapter of this book.

Barriers related to the nature of worldviews

Next, there are barriers related to the nature of worldviews and the impact they have on our lives. Worldviews do not represent a loose collection of ideas that can be exchanged for others in a piecemeal manner. The different basic elements of a worldview do reinforce each other – such as, for example, the concept of *nirvana*, of *karma* and of reincarnation in Buddhism. A worldview also coheres with an *ethos* – a way of life. The following relationship that Geertz sees in religious communities also holds for non-religious ones (1993: 89f):

> In a religious belief and practice a group's ethos is rendered intellectually reasonable by being shown to represent a way of life ideally adapted to the actual state of affairs the worldview describes, while the worldview is rendered emotionally convincing by being presented as and image of an actual state of affairs particularly well-arranged to accommodate such a way of life.

In the same way a worldview also coheres with a certain allegiance to what we consider most worthwhile to pursue (Kraft 1996: 452f; Naugle 2002: 267ff) – be it individual happiness, the continuation and flourishing of the clan, entry in the Koranic Paradise, absorption in the *Nirvana*, loving communion with God or whatever. Again, the worldview gives this basic allegiance its most profound rationale and the fundamental allegiance provides the worldview with a strong attraction, for it renders it possible to pursue what we consider most worthy.

So far, most social scientists will be able to agree with this analysis. As Christians we should go one step further in our analysis and also see alternative worldviews as either vehicles of spiritual oppression or freedom. Worldviews represent spiritual forces, and a change of worldview, particularly from an oppressive worldview, to the liberating Christian faith therefore also implies liberation from spiritual bondage in the context of a power encounter (Newbigin 1989: 204–208; Naugle 2002: 274ff; Kraft 1996: 453).

These threads of allegiance, worldview, ethos and spiritual power weave together to an almost unbreakable bond(age) in which our mind, will and emotions are all pulled in one direction. If it were not for the many inner tensions between our basic allegiance, what we sometimes discover to be true and our emotional and other needs, this fourfold cord could indeed never be broken. We can only take courage and engage in apologetic dialogue because we can rely on the Holy Spirit, who sets people free from bondage and opens blinded eyes, and because the phantom-worlds that people create themselves are inherently unstable.

Barriers related to the way in which individuals and communities can deal with objections

Third, we have to consider barriers related to the way in which individuals and communities can deal with objections and experiences that do not fit their basic outlook. The way worldviews function makes them relatively immune from criticism. Polanyi has drawn attention to these barriers with the help of the example of the way in which the Azande deal with challenges to their understanding of magic. The Azande are an African tribe living in the area where Sudan, the Central African Republic and the Congo meet. The use of magic by the Azande has often been used as a paradigmatic example in discussing the inner coherence and stability of non-Western outlooks on life, though most of those contributing to this discussion probably never met any Azande.[3]

Polanyi shows that the stability of central Azande beliefs in the face of possible invalidation is first of all guarded by dealing with counter-experiences and objections one by one. When they were confronted with a poison oracle that did not give the expected result, they would handle such a single objection against a vast background of uncontested beliefs, with respect to which one objection does not put much weight in the balance. When a second objection to their belief-system as a whole was considered, the working of the poison oracle would be moved back to this stable background of uncontested beliefs (Polanyi 1962: 289ff). Defenders of a worldview or scientific theory can also set aside unexpected data as "anomalies", which will be explained later. This often proves to be a fruitful procedure, for otherwise scientific progress would be greatly hindered (p. 293; cf. Polanyi 1946: 15; Kuhn 1996: 81), yet it can contribute to the virtual immunity of a theory.

A second factor contributing to the stability of beliefs is the fact that the interpretative system can expand with new explanations that deal with possible objections (Polanyi 1962: 291). There are a number of explanations available why, at a given instance, a poison-oracle does not work as expected. Maybe the poison was not good (p. 288), or maybe one of those involved in the ritual had consciously or unconsciously transgressed some taboo. In the same way, defenders of contested worldviews or scientific theories can add additional theories to explain phenomena that at first sight seem to contradict the main theory (p. 291; cf. Kuhn 1996: 78; Berger & Luckmann 1967: 122ff, 133; Quine 1961: 42f).

A third factor contributing to the stability of theories and even more to the stability of worldviews is the fact that experiences that could refute the theory are denied any ground on which they can be aligned to gain the strength they

3 In the discussion people take recourse to the work of the anthropologist E.E. Evans-Pritchard (1950). For the discussion, see (among others): Polanyi 1962: 288–294; Placher 1989: 55–73.

need in order to count as instances supporting an alternative view. Polanyi calls this the "principle of suppressed nucleation" (1962: 291). From the perspective of an adherent of a certain worldview or theory, the provided counter-instances do not seem important enough to give them real attention (p. 294). This may be directly related to the fact that different worldviews, just like different scientific paradigms, have their own perception of the real problems that need our attention (Kuhn 1996: 148f).

To the factors contributing to the immunity of an outlook to objections and critical instances, we could finally add a number of social pressures within scientific communities, which lead to the isolation of thinkers and researchers working with alternative paradigms. This isolation hinders the development of extensive research on the basis of the alternative paradigm and of an alternative scientific community. The same is true of communities that share a common culture or worldview. They often exclude or isolate individuals that provide an alternative account of reality, thus hindering such an alternative movement from gaining a wider hearing (cf. Berger & Luckmann 1967: 103).

After considering these three types of barriers that hinder the change of one worldview and one basic allegiance to another, the prospects for apologetic dialogue seem rather bleak. We need to accept that apologetic argumentation addressing someone with a different basic outlook on life will never be absolutely conclusive. From her perspective our dialogue partner will give a different weight than we do to the arguments we use and the experiences to which we point. Even if we could give a logically tight argument starting from a belief that she shares and leading to the conclusion that God exists – we are not yet talking about Christ – she could always withdraw from the conclusion by rejecting one of the premises she formerly shared (Murray 1999: 10–15). Yet, when we change our approach and stop looking for watertight arguments aimed at checkmating our dialogue partners, but rather start looking for persuasive ways to invite them to consider a new perspective on reality, a whole new range of possibilities for apologetic dialogue opens up.

7.2 The illuminating power of the whole – and of Jesus

Christ as the clue to an alternative way of life

Because of the inner coherence of the Christian worldview and of alternatives, we will *in the final analysis* only be able to persuade our dialogue partner because of the persuasive power of the person and message of Jesus Christ, and the window He opens on our world and condition as a whole. We need to keep both elements in view and in balance: Jesus Christ, and the whole of our experience. Jesus

Christ is central, because we believe that, in Him, God and the nature and destiny of his creation are revealed. Because the new perspective we gain in Christ illuminates our world and lives, and the whole of our experience, we can subsequently present it confidently to those who point to other clues for the understanding of life – such as the Koran, modern science, the mystical enlightenment exemplified by the Buddha, or the tradition of the ancestors. Because the Christian alternative as a whole is able to "absorb the world" (Lindbeck 1984: 118) and give a better reading of all aspects of life as we encounter it, we consider it better than its alternatives (§5.2).

When we say that this is true "in the final analysis", we call attention to the fact that in actual apologetic dialogue we will not ordinarily point to the Christian faith as a whole; we will more often concentrate on particular areas of life and on particular bridges towards the Christian faith. Yet, for two reasons it is important that we draw attention to "the illuminating power of the whole" from the very beginning (Lindbeck 1984: 11; cf. §2.3). We need, in the first place, to keep this in mind in order to create openness to future dialogue with those whom we encounter. They need to understand that our initial explanations of the Gospel can only be considered *initial* introductions into a whole new world, which they will not be able to understand adequately at first glance. They especially have not understood the Christian faith if they dismiss it from the outset for not making sense *from their own perspective*.

The presentation of Christianity in its entirety as providing an alternative worldview and way of life is also crucial, because people will never seriously reconsider their own outlook and way of life when they see no alternative. This is also true in major debates in the scientific world: people will not let themselves be swayed by the limitations of their existing paradigm if they see no valid alternative (Kuhn 1996: 77, 145). This is all the more true when one considers the alternation between worldviews as a whole. We cannot live without such a basic outlook of life that gives our lives meaning, structure and at least a glimmer of hope. In an important sense our worldview provides us with the world in which we live. Even when we are confronted with serious limitations of this worldview, we will cling even harder to what we have and defend it even more vehemently. If we have no other place to go, we will defend the only place we have, whatever its limitations. Unless we wind up in utter despair, it is only when we consider another way of life and another outlook on the world to be at least initially plausible that we will have the courage and freedom to leave the place where we stand. Karl Barth identifies a deeper theological side of this general psychological truth when he points to the fact that the natural human being, living without Jesus Christ, simply has no place to go outside his self-made religion, ideology and natural theology (Barth *KD* II/1: 188–190; trans. *CD* II/1: 168–170). If human beings do not know about grace, they themselves will need to make sense of the world as it is and they will therefore do so in spite of or even because of the lingering despair that underlies all these efforts to make sense of it.

This need of knowing about a plausible alternative to be able to take seriously the limitations of one's present worldview may be one of the reasons why our pounding on non-Christian worldviews is often so futile. Take the in-itself valid argument of the self-defeating nature of relativism (as developed in Plantinga 1995: 191–215), the argument that relativism should itself be relativized (Berger 1980: 9), and the argument that few have the courage to live moral relativism to its logical conclusion (McGrath 1992: 227–229). These arguments – when used as a "battering ram"[4] – will only force people to barricade their doors more strongly, notwithstanding its cracks and even because of its cracks, as long as they feel that they have no valid escape. That is how you deal with battering rams. Such arguments only make sense intellectually and in our lives we present plausible alternative places to go. Even so, the door will be opened more easily when the battering stops and the arguments are used in an altogether different tenor.

I often try to show this graphically to my African students by chalking two separate circles on the classroom floor – which is much easier when the surface consists of concrete instead of carpet. Let us imagine our dialogue partner standing in a circle, which represents her own world. The best way to bring her so far that she leaves this circle is to invite her to explore the Christian way of life in a non-committal way with one foot already within the Christian circle, the Christian world, to see if it is tenable. It is only when she feels that this is a viable option and when she gradually moves her centre of gravity to the Christian circle, that she will feel comfortable leaving her former world behind and putting both her feet in the Christian world. It is of course quite possible that people just simply leap out of their own world in utter despair, but there is no reason to suppose that this is the paradigmatic case of conversion.

When some initial exploration of the Christian faith happens, it is still possible that conversion takes place with no real understanding of the Christian faith, but is undertaken on the basis of a simple trust. This trust can be awakened by the personality of Jesus, as encountered in the Gospel, or by Christians or a Christian community with whom one is acquainted. Yet in those cases the personality of Christ and the life of Christians provide precisely the initial rationale and plausibility one needs to be able to leave one's former worldview and allegiance. Without such an initial plausibility of the Christian faith we need to batter very hard to get someone moving.

The apologetic use of narrative

In order to introduce our dialogue partner into the Christian world many means of communication and literary genres can be used. This is not the place to explore

4 The image is McGrath's (1992: 227), who, fortunately, in his approach is generally much more sensitive to his audience than this image suggests.

all of these things; that said, one literary genre – narrative form – deserves special attention. The central role of narrative both in Scripture and in human life in general has been stressed by postmodern theologians and needs to be taken seriously by the apologist. Early modern apologetics considered narrative of little apologetic use, and majored instead on inductive and deductive forms of argumentation. However, the use of narrative in apologetics has some particular strengths.

A first advantage of narrative is that it appeals to other and more comprehensive sides of our humanity than the classical types of argument – particularly the imagination and the emotions. Second, it does not lead us step by step into another world; rather, it plunges us right in the middle. The world from the very beginning retains its strangeness in comparison to what the reader or hearer is used to. It becomes increasingly familiar – not by accommodating it to the world we know but by expanding our experience of its foreignness. When we plunge into J.R.R. Tolkien's *The Hobbit*, into C.S. Lewis' *Narnia* cycle, or into a nineteenth-century Russian novel we know that we are in a different world despite becoming increasingly familiar with that world's own logic. When we consider the need to become accustomed to a foreign world, we can see that use of the fantasy or fairy-tale genre is apologetically helpful to counterbalance the modern reduction of the world to what is visible and measurable. Lewis and his fellow-Inkling member J.R.R. Tolkien have done a great deal to rekindle the imagination as bridge to the world of the Gospel.[5]

This reference to fantasy confronts us directly with the main problem that a number of more conservative theologians have with narrative theology and therefore with narrative apologetics. It is the relativist connotation that many narrative theologians indeed consciously exploit or about which they seem to remain purposely vague (Sims 1995: 334; Clark 1993b: 508–511).[6] We need to note, however, that different narrative genres can be used for different apologetic purposes, all with their proper relationship to reality. There is parable, which takes a familiar aspect of the reality of ordinary experience to point to a reality beyond itself. There is fantasy, which creates an imaginary world and functions as a mirror of our own, and so helps us to look at ourselves and our familiar world with new eyes and from a critical distance. There is the encompassing true story of salvation history, in which many "small stories" find their place and meaning. The different ways in which our small individual stories find their meaning within the encompassing narrative of salvation history can be explored in realistic novels, biographies and personal testimony.[7] All these contribute in their own ways to making the Christian world familiar, inhabitable and, in that sense, plausible.

5 Cf. on the role of fantasy as a bridge to the Gospel: Tolkien 1966: 82–84.

6 Clark refers to a famous debate between Carl Henry and Hans Frei over these issues.

7 On the role of stories in apologetic witness, see: Sire 1995: 120–124.

A main reason for the neglect of narrative in modern apologetics is probably that within a modernist framework narrative and argumentation are mutually exclusive. Yet this need not be the case. Narrative rather embodies different types of argumentation. On several occasions in Africa I have experienced how narratives can be used in this way. When a debate entered into an impasse and when a conclusion needed to be reached, someone present told a parable, which either convincingly tipped the balance of the debate or, more often, pointed to a solution in which the legitimate interests of both sides could be respected. The parable – or a well-chosen proverb – often evoked a valid experience from a wholly different domain that unexpectedly shed light on the debated question.[8]

The apologetic relevance of different domains of worldviews

Within the Christian metanarrative and worldview, the story of Jesus of Nazareth is obviously crucial. Christian apologetic witnessing should therefore be unashamedly Christocentric, for it is here that the meaning of world history and personal history uniquely intersect. We believe Him to be the clue to reality, to our lives, to history and to God. There are so many things that can and sometimes need to be addressed in apologetic dialogue: the nature of the universe; the value of the Bible; the human condition; the power of religion; the existence of God; the scope of scientific reasoning and so on. Yet among these there is one theme, or rather person, that remains central. This prevents the apologist from needing to say everything at once and from creating information overload. Apologetic dialogue is essentially witness to this person and an invitation to further personal discovery of what life with this Jesus entails and what the world with Him at the centre looks like.[9]

When, in ever-widening circles around the person of Christ, we explore further domains of reality, some will require more attention than others. Some of these domains are given with the nature of the Christian faith itself. We will soon need to start talking about God, for it is to Him that Christ introduces us. In Christ we discover that God is not irrelevant or distant; it is only in relationship with Him that life in its fullness can be lived.

Themes related to the human condition are also found near this centre. Christians believe that the basic problem of the human condition is given with the disparity between the high calling of the human being and the way he actually

8 The need for narrative in apologetic witness in non-Western contexts is also noted by Clark (1993b: 513) and Sims (1995: 333).

9 This communicative method of pointing people to clues for personal exploration rather than presenting a complete case follows the example of Jesus himself (f. ex. Matt. 22:41-45; cf. Kraft 1999: 53f).

lives. All religions and worldviews that I know of provide some explanation of the human condition that is partly adequate and partly inadequate. These explanations need to prove their soundness precisely in the face of the enigma which we are to ourselves. As Blaise Pascal said (Pascal, *Pensées*: no. 149, cf. no. 208):

> Man's greatness and wretchedness are so evident that the true religion must necessarily teach there is in man some great principle of greatness and some great principle of wretchedness.
> It must also account for such amazing contradictions.[10]

For most human beings the question of who they are and what they want to be touches a central tension in their lives, thus creating a need and openness for dialogue. Questions concerning the human condition will be considered to be highly relevant and worth exploring not only by Christians but also by most non-Christians.

Other crucial areas of exploration in apologetic dialogue will be determined by the particular interest of our conversation partners or of the particular communities with which we are dealing. Dialogue with traditional Africans, for example, would look particularly at questions of illness, healing, curses and protection – questions that are generally less urgent in a modern Western context. In a Muslim context one would need to deal particularly with the question of the relationship between the different alleged prophets and Scriptures. In a Hindu context we cannot avoid questions of reincarnation and the afterlife. Dialogue with moderns will need to address the success of modern science.

This points to the need that the Christian community as a whole provides alternative Christian viewpoints on all areas of life and particularly on those that a given culture considers crucial. This is not only needed to provide plausibility for the Christian worldview for non-Christians but also for Christians, who otherwise live in a continual tension of what sociologists call "cognitive dissonance". This dissonance is produced when different areas of our lives are lived according to different incompatible overarching principles, which tend to mutually weaken the commitment we can give them (cf. Herbst 1987: 125f). As C.S. Lewis said (1987: 17f; cf. Plantinga 1992: 308–312; Lindbeck 1986: 375):

> We can make people (often) attend to the Christian point of view for half an hour or so; but the moment they have gone away from our lecture or laid down our article, they are plunged back into a world where the opposite position is taken for granted. [...] What we want is not more little books about Christianity, but more little books by Christians on other subjects – with their Christianity *latent*.

10 For twentieth-century versions of the same type of apologetic argument, one can point to Brunner (1941; trans. 1939) and Niebuhr (1941).

Absorbing other perspectives

The truth of the Christian understanding of the world is shown even more clearly, when it does not simply provide an alternative understanding of reality, but an alternative from which the relative truth and falsity of the other worldviews can be understood and evaluated. It needs to become clear that from a Christian perspective one can make sense of both the relative truth and goodness, and the limitations of alternative ways of living. As MacIntyre noted, it is because Einsteinian physics provides a new narrative in which the relative truth of Newtonian physics can be incorporated that it shows its greater verisimilitude (§5.1). If the Christian understanding of other religions (§3.3), of modernity and postmodernity (§4.5) and of other cultures (§6.2) makes sense, it shows its adequacy.

Integrating the relative truth of alternative worldviews is not simply a theoretical endeavour; rather, it is required in order to appropriate the Christian faith as whole people and to give one's past a proper place. Proper conversion presupposes an "I", a person who is converted and who, in important respects, remains the same person before and after conversion.[11] This does not necessarily mean that one's past and former beliefs are all positively integrated as a prior apprehension of truth. They may be integrated as errors of which one now understands why one erred (Berger & Luckmann 1967: 179f). Yet, positive or negative, such integration is necessary for a sound and firm conversion. A past that is not integrated in the Christian present will simply remain dormant till it presents – or avenges? – itself in unexpected ways. The influence of an unintegrated past is shown in the often unbalanced return to pre-Christian roots by many second-generation Christians whose parents were converted in a context where little consideration was shown for their cultural heritage (Newbigin 1986: 8f).

When we interpret others from a Christian perspective, others graciously return the ball. Muslims will provide their explanation of the Christian religion as a corruption of the *Injil* given to the prophet Issa. Traditional Africans will consider it the tribal religion of the Whites. Buddhists will interpret it as a reflection of a religious experience, which has not yet penetrated beyond the personal and dualist experience of God to a non-personal experience beyond all dichotomies. We have already encountered the modern Feuerbach-Marx-Freud explanations and the postmodern understanding of religion in terms of the performative function of language. All encompassing metanarratives need such explanations of alternative worldviews precisely in order to be able to function as metanarratives (Berger & Luckmann 1967: 122ff, 133, 179f). Yet the fact that all metanarratives

11 As missiologist Kenneth Cragg notes: "Given this integrity in Christ, there must also be integrity in conversion, a unity of the self in which one's past is genuinely integrated into present commitment. Thus, the crisis of repentance and faith truly integrates what we have been in what we become" (1980: 194; cf. from a philosophical point of view, also Bambrough 1990: 246f).

attempt to mutually explain one another does not in itself make each explanation equally invalid. Apologetically the search for the understanding of alternative points of view is both needed and legitimate. The exploration of the adequacy of different mutually excluding explanations of what different people and communities believe forms an important part of apologetic dialogue.

Though the validity of the Christian faith and the claims of Christ can "in the final analysis" only be appreciated in terms of itself and of the reality it opens for us, this does not mean that the Christian world is a closed world with no way in. Looking for further means of persuasion, in the next sections we explore the possibility of building cross-cultural bridges in order to prompt people to explore the Christian faith.

7.3 Exploiting bridgeheads

A variety of bridgeheads

In an important sense, Christians and non-Christians live in different worlds – and not just in two worlds, but in many. Nevertheless, in another significant sense Christians and non-Christians live in the same world, for they relate to the same extra-linguistic reality and their responses to this reality are influenced by their shared human nature. Thus we can expect some overlap between Christian and non-Christian conceptions of the world.

The same expectation of being able to detect overlap is also warranted on the basis of Christian anthropology. We have seen how, because of sin, the human being has become fragmented and internally divided. We have noted how this provokes a tendency to live with some aspects of his nature at the expense of others and with some characteristics of the nature of the world in which he finds himself at the expense of others (§6.2). This implies that his understanding of himself and the world around him is always a mixture of truth and error, and that a Christian can therefore expect to find common ground when meeting non-Christians. Yet this common ground may vary from one person to another because of the possibility of dealing in many different ways with the inner tensions and fragmentation that are part of our fallen state.

The fact that this common ground may vary from one situation to another does not make it less valid for apologetics. This would only be the case in a universalist foundationalist approach to apologetics, according to which a certain belief needs to be universally directly accessible in order to count as an appropriate foundation for an apologetic argument. We find all sorts of common ground when meeting non-Christians, yet the common ground we find may vary widely from one case to another. This becomes clear when we try to imagine meeting a Muslim, a Buddhist, an adherent of African Traditional Religion, a modern atheist and a postmodern pluralist. One can argue with a modern audience about the existence of God, starting from a particular area of common ground – such as in C.S. Lewis' argument starting from morality, or the argument from the fine-tuning of the universe, which recently became popular (1955a: 15–34; 15–34; Collins 1999: 47–75). Such arguments have often been treated as if universal in their scope. They are not, though, and are better treated as directed to a specific modern Western audience.

The problem of many classical modern apologies is not that they are *not* valid, but that they are *only* valid for a specific audience that shares a particular common ground and a particular approach to reality.[12] When such apologies do not recognize their limited validity, they overstate their case and fail to look for the possibility that in dialogue with others completely different points of contact may be detected. With a traditional African audience one might start from the shared recognition of a Creator God and with Muslims one might add the belief in prophets, in revelation and in Jesus of Nazareth. With Zen-Buddhists the apologist may not share any of the previously shared convictions, but there is other common ground such as the recognition that the highest vocation of the human being is not to be found in the visible world.

Relevance

When we look for bridgeheads in other religions and worldviews from which bridges can be built to the Gospel, we need to consider that some bridgeheads may be stronger and more important than others. We need to look for those that are closest to the centre of interest and of life. Many people may believe in the possibility of extra-terrestrial intelligence, which might function as a bridge for considering the possibility of being addressed from beyond. Yet my feeling is that, even for most people who are open to this possibility, it is rather marginal to their lives and will not so easily impact their more central convictions and allegiances. For many Westerners today the feeling that certain forms of evil are utterly reprehensible and should fill us with justifiable indignation is much more central to their experience of life. Though many have used the reality of evil as an argument against the existence of a good God, the experience of the indignation over evil is in fact a pointer to the existence of a personal and good God. Either in a naturalistic evolutionary universe or in a pantheist or monist universe, such an experience of the nature of evil should be dismissed as deceptive. The difficulty of dismissing such a strong, central and basic awareness opens up the possibility for an argument for the existence of God based on the experience of evil.

12 Cf. Netland's evaluation of the apologies of C.S. Lewis and Francis Schaeffer (1988: 296). The same narrowness of audience is oddly enough characteristic of the "postmodern" apologies proposed by Murphy (1996: 105, 108), Handspicker (1991–1992: 72–81) and Allen (1989). All three mainly address an audience impressed by science and the scientific method.

When considering the central or peripheral character of certain convictions or experiences in a worldview, we need to take into account that worldviews are structured in terms of relevance (Berger & Luckmann 1967: 59; cf. Guinness 1981: 322–325).[13] We need to address people in terms of what they consider to be relevant for their lives, for apologetics is not only about truth, but also about relevance (§1.4). If we want to gain a hearing, we need to address issues that are considered relevant to those whom we desire to hear the message. The Gospel invites us to take questions of relevance seriously, because not only does it talk about the truth of God, but also about the salvation of humanity, knowing that both are intrinsically linked in Jesus who is both the truth and the life (Jn 14:6). Jesus himself related his message of the Kingdom of God to the most pressing needs of his audience (cf. Kraft 1996: 395, 398; 1999: 53). We should be careful not to build our whole apologetic around the perception of needs, for many people may not feel an urgent need at a given moment (Guinness 1981: 371f). Yet we should be perceptive to listening to real needs, realizing that the message of Jesus and the apostles was also most welcomed by those who knew their need and could not hide it either for themselves or for others (Mk 2:17; 1Co 1:26-31).

However, we must be careful here. What we experience as relevant and our most important need do themselves reflect our worldview. The relationship between human needs and the divine answer cannot therefore be a simple relation of correlation, as Paul Tillich proposed. In this correlation the needs were considered to be given on the human side and to be discovered by appropriate existential analysis. As a second step the Gospel should then be correlated to these needs (Handspicker 1991–1992: 72f). This understanding of correlation in the first place neglects the influence of sin, which obscures an understanding of our real needs. It furthermore overlooks the fact that the proposed existential analysis is the analysis of a particular form of human life as developed in the modern West and with the help of a method that is philosophically far from neutral. Other cultures and worldviews will have their own understanding of the most fundamental human needs. If we want to be heard, we must address our audience in terms of the needs they experience. Yet in the process we may have to point out that their felt needs are in need of reinterpretation, and what they experience as most pressing may not be their most profound needs. Their deepest needs are revealed by the Gospel (Kraft 1999: 49ff).

Felt needs are a prime example of predispositions that can predispose us for or against acceptance of the Gospel. Because of there apologetic importance, we will later elaborate on these predispositions towards reality and truth and particularly towards God and the Gospel. We will then equally touch on the way we should deal with the fact that there is no direct relationship between our needs and

13 A valid example of what attention for relevance in some non-Western societies might mean can be found in: Kraft 1995.

their fulfilment in Christ, but that this fulfilment takes the detour of conversion and the cross. This will also help us to deal with two pitfalls, for which we should be on are guard when addressing such needs: the pitfalls of manipulation and paternalism (Chapter 8).

The theological value of these bridgeheads

At this moment in time we are able to give a better appreciation of Barth's criticism of the apologetic use of points of contact or "*Anknüpfungspunkte*" (§3.3).[14] Looking for points of contact is, or course, precisely what we have been doing when looking for bridgeheads from which we can build bridges to the Gospel. For Barth this was a theologically reprehensible project, for it would mean looking for a foundation for the faith outside the Scripture, Christ, and faith. However, this is only true when such points of contact are understood as an independent foundation for belief, as in modern foundationalism. Yet when we look for bridgeheads for the Gospel from a Christian perspective, they no longer count as a foundation in themselves. They cannot count as such, for they are, by themselves, not recognizable as "foundations". It is only from a Christian perspective that they are assigned this status (cf. *KD* II/1: 304–324; trans. *CD* I/2: 280–297). The faith is not based on these bridgeheads; rather, these bridgeheads are claimed for the Gospel in the belief that all truth that can be recognized elsewhere is God's truth.[15]

The same procedure was used by the Fathers of the Church (for example, Augustine) when they used truths discovered by Pagan philosophers in their defence of the faith. It was an expression of the belief that all things and therefore also all truths were to be "recapitulated", brought together under the one head of Christ, who is the Lord of creation (Eph. 1:10). It is an expression of our vocation of "taking captive every thought to make it obedient to Christ" (2Cor 10:4). Under this new headship of Christ, all foreign ideas are judged. Some will be unmasked as lies and errors, but others will be recognized as true and good in

---

14 For Barth's criticism for the search of apologetic "points of contact", see: *KD*, 25ff; 249ff; I/2, 196f; 289; II/1, 96ff, 134; trans. *CD* I/1, 27ff; 236ff; I/2, 180f; 265; II/1, 88ff, 121.

15 This is, as Barth himself says concerning the use of general and philosophical notions in Christian ethics, similar to what happened when the Israelites conquered Canaan: "The concern of the apologetic school of theological ethics in its recourse to a general moral inquiry and reply can, of course, be recognised as justifiable upon one condition: that is, if in its annexation of general ethical problems theological ethics behaves as the Israelites did or should have done on their entry of Canaan. They had to invade Canaan, not as a foreign country which did not belong to them, but as the land of their fathers. Had it not for a long time belonged to Yahweh? [...] Therefore, when it turns to this general moral inquiry and reply, it will do so with the understanding that it has the origin and meaning from the divine command which objectively applies to man, whatever attitude man may take to it" (*KD* II/2: 579; trans. *CD* II/1: 522f).

order that all that is true and good may find its accomplishment and true meaning under Christ as the true head of creation.[16]

Another staunch theological critic of the search for common ground or points of contact was Van Til. He likewise defended the idea that the Christian and non-Christian live in different worlds, determined by a different basic orientation in life (Van Til 1967: 201). Of course, he also saw the many examples of common ground to which we have referred. Yet, according to Van Til, this commonality was only appearance, for following neo-Hegelian logic he stated that the basic presuppositions of each worldview determine the smallest particular beliefs that form a part of the whole (pp. 115f).

This argument, however, seems to be flawed in at least two ways. First of all it supposes that all worldviews are ultimately coherent so that all parts are intrinsically related. Van Til himself knew that they are not (pp. 49, 200f; cf. §6.2), and if so this implies that many elements of non-Christian worldviews can find their most proper home within the Christian worldview under the headship of Christ. Second, this neo-Hegelian approach to truth does not make an appropriate distinction between basic truths expressed within a certain context and the further connotations they receive because of the larger context in which they are expressed. We can often separate the two in the way we have separated, for example, the basically valid notion of worldview from the relativist connotation that it often receives when used in cultural anthropology (§6.1). When such elements are incorporated in a new overall paradigm – under the headship of Christ – they take on new connotations. Hiebert says: "In critical realism elements of the old paradigm can be incorporated in the new, but because they are part of a new configuration, they take on new meanings" (1999: 79).[17]

Such incorporation of elements of an old paradigm within a new one is precisely what happened when Paul used Hellenistic ideas about the divine, yet rearranged them around the revelation of God in Jesus Christ, giving these Hellenistic ideas new meanings (Ac 17:22-31; cf. §3.3). All religious practices and beliefs reflect this mixture of truth and error. All human religion ranging from the crudest idolatry to the highest mysticism is a human distortion of truth, because of sin and ignorance, and precisely as a distortion of truth it still contains traces of truth. Take the practice of human sacrifice, so strongly condemned in the Old Testament (Lev 18:21; 20:1-5). Sacrificial practices in many religions reveal a certain understanding that there exists a rift between the human and the divine that needs to be crossed and which is not simply a matter of ignorance. The practice of human sacrifice, utterly reprehensible as it is, reflects the consciousness that in the final analysis not a rooster or not even a thousand bulls can stand in for us, but that only a human sacrifice can reconcile us to God. This accentuates again the wide variety of possible apologetic bridges (cf. Bediako 2000: 28f).

16 See on this apologetic procedure: Chang 2000: 144–156; cf. also Bavinck 1960: 179.

17 On Van Til, see further §8.1.

Religious experience

In this context it is appropriate to say something about the apologetic use of religious experience, which plays a crucial role in liberal apologetics and which in practice seems to function for many people as bridge to the Christian faith. Religious experience is, in our world, as widespread as it is hard to define. This may be partly due to the fact that perhaps there isn't a special type of experience, which in itself can be characterized as "religious". They may simply be experiences that we know from other domains of life (such as feeling reverence, thankfulness or guilt) directed to the divine (James 1960: 47). Part of the problem of religious experience is that it is so flexible it takes up a variety of forms in different religious contexts (Netland 2001: 263f). The flexibility itself gives plausibility to Lindbeck's evaluation that religious experience reflects a certain cultural–linguistic framework in which it is generated. It renders impossible the Schleiermacherian variety of universalist foundationalist apologetics that tries to found the whole Christian faith on some allegedly universal religious experience (see §2.2; cf. Griffiths 1988: 37f). Furthermore, it is not clear how religious experience could be specific enough to convey to us the most central elements of the Christian faith, such as belief in the incarnation, in the Trinity and in reconciliation in Christ (Plantinga 2000: 288).

The fluidity of religious experience substantiates the fundamental Christian conviction that sound theological knowledge cannot be based on general religious experience that is part of general revelation, and which is considered limited, vague and clouded by sin. A sound knowledge of God is only possible through the Scriptures and through Christ. Religious experience obviously plays a part in this, but as an experience evoked by, purified by and rearranged around the encounter with Christ.

This flexibility of religious experience, however, does not mean that religious experience has no apologetic value whatsoever. First of all, religious experience belongs to the world in which we live and any valid worldview that needs to account for all aspects of life needs to account for the phenomenon of religious experience. Second, religious experiences found in other religions that reflect the truth of the Gospel – for example, an experience of the holiness of God in Islam – can be used as bridgeheads and can be shown to find their true significance when rearranged around Christ.[18] Third, we need to reckon with the reality of religious experiences that do not fit into the existing cultural frameworks of people and that have a critical function towards these frameworks (cf. Tilley 1995: 97; Lindbeck 1984: 33f). People may, for example, be overcome with

18 Cf. the analysis of McGrath of the relationship between doctrine and experience, amounting to the conclusion (1996a: 33): "By being viewed in a particular light, experience is correlated with the scriptural narrative and the conceptual framework it engenders, and is allowed to assume a new significance. Doctrine thus opens the way to a new 'experience with experience.'"

rage against God, while professing no belief in Him. They may be overcome by a persistent feeling of guilt, yet have an image of a non-judgemental God or believe God to be beyond good and evil. These are examples of a particular type of apologetic bridge, a bridge that does not so much use relative truths as its starting point, but rather the tensions, anomalies or antinomies that appear within religious or non-religious cultural–linguistic outlooks on reality. To the consideration of these we turn in the next section. Some religious experiences point much more directly beyond the confines of the religion in the context of which they occur, such as the vision of the star that pointed the Magi to a Jewish king (Mt 2:2) and the dreams or visions of Christ that occur today among Muslims. Finally, considering that many postmoderns are particularly looking for "a personal and transforming experience of reality", we can invite them and others to participate in the life of the the Christian community as the appropriate context for having such experiences with Christ and the Holy Spirit (cf. Sims 1995: 331f).[19]

Apologists cannot neglect religious experience, given the thirst for religious experience in our world and given the place of religious experience in the Scriptures. However, we should not consider religious experience the only or even the principal inroad to the Christian world, for people enter this world from many different directions. Such high expectations from religious experience do not do justice to the simple fact that many people are "religiously unmusical", perhaps by nature or as a product of their secular culture (Dulles 1992: 79; cf. Plantinga 2000: 288).

7.4 Using antinomies

The role of tensions, anomalies and antinomies in inducing change

Those who have studied the development and interaction of different cultural linguistic frameworks have discovered that changes in worldview or a conversion from one worldview to another are most likely to occur when certain tensions arise within a given understanding of reality. Such tensions can occur either because of growing tensions between different major areas of a certain cultural–linguistic framework or because of the confrontation with an aspect of reality that impinges on this framework and reveals certain inadequacies. We have

19 The effectiveness of the popular *Alpha Course* developed at Holy Trinity Brompton Anglican Church in London and now used all over the world as an evangelistic tool can be ascribed for a significant part to the experiential component, both in the experience of community and of the work of the Holy Spirit.

already encountered this pattern when considering the development of scientific paradigms (Kuhn 1996: 6; cf. §5.1).[20]

It is also revealing in this respect to consider Alasdair MacIntyre's study of the development of different traditions of moral rationality. Like Kuhn, MacIntyre stresses the role of crises in this process. MacIntyre's examples point to the fact that these crises are not only provoked by incongruent findings of research, but also by growing inner tensions in the development of a community's paradigm and by the confrontation with alternative paradigms (1988: 164–182, 349–369). An "epistemological crisis" is a situation in which new discoveries and inner tensions provoked by social and cultural developments are accumulated to a degree that presses for change (1980). This change can either be brought by renewal within a certain tradition or by the abandonment of the given tradition for another available one that proves more adequate with respect to the given anomalies (1988: 362).

In the development of their sociology of knowledge, Berger and Luckmann also deal with "crisis situations" that involve "the risk of a breakdown of reality" – that is, reality as a social construction (1967: 175). They highlight the role of the pressures of life, particularly those related to "marginal situations". These situations are precisely marginal, because they fall outside the scope with which the accepted symbolic universe ordinarily deals (p. 114). In a society that lives in a permanent "denial of death" (cf. Becker 1973), the experience of death is a primary example of such a "marginal situation".[21] Such "marginal situations" both in the life of individuals and of societies put the given worldview under high pressure and create openness for change if other candidates are available. "The validity of my knowledge of everyday life is taken for granted by myself and by others until further notice, that is until a problem arises that cannot be solved in terms of it" (Berger & Luckmann 1967: 58).

These analyses of basic changes of perspective in science (Kuhn), in practical philosophy (MacIntyre) and in the symbolic system that we receive in primary socialization (Berger & Luckmann) help elucidate what happens in religious conversions. Many people experience moments of sudden or slowly mounting

---

20 One counter-instance (or even a number of counter-instances) in itself is not enough to entirely disprove a theory. This is where Popper's falsification theory was false (Polkinghorne 1989: 170ff). A number of anomalies can just be ignored, trusting that they will be solved in the future, or can be dealt with by additional theories. This is the proper procedure, for scientific progress would not be possible if a whole tradition of research were immediately abandoned at the occasion of one counter-instance (Kuhn 1996: 82). Yet, when too many anomalies present themselves, one needs to look for alternative frameworks or paradigms, even if the number of paradigms that should bring us to abandon a paradigm cannot be set beforehand. Much hangs on the availability of a valid alternative.

21 Berger & Luckmann call death "the marginal situation *par excellence*" as "the most terrifying to the taken-for-granted realities of everyday life" (1967: 119). I believe that this evaluation is typically modern and Western. In many societies in history and today life is very precarious and death far from marginal. Denying death is no option, and that is precisely why a worldview that lives in denial of death would have little plausibility in Central Africa for example.

crisis in their (a-)religious perspective on life, which opens them up to a serious consideration of the Christian faith. This can happen in individual lives, such as when someone is confronted with death or enters a new phase of life like parenthood. It can also happen for a community or culture as a whole, when it goes through rapid changes with which the old worldview cannot adequately deal. Then people start looking for other ways of understanding reality that are more suited to the way the world is and to the condition in which they find themselves. What does this mean for the apologist?

Tensions within worldviews and in people

The apologist needs to be alert for the tensions within worldviews or in the lives of the people living within certain communities that reveal the discrepancies between these worldviews and the way the world is. We have already noted some tensions within worldviews – such as the tension between the modern conviction that nature should be mastered and the anxiety this produces (§6.2). Such tensions can also be located in religions. Consider, in Zen-Buddhism, the relationship between the high moral awareness with the understanding of ultimate reality as surpassing the distinction between good and evil. This understanding of ultimate reality implies that "[w]hile in a human, moral dimension the Holocaust should be condemned as an unpardonable, absolute evil, from the religious point of view even it should not be taken as an absolute but as a relative evil".[22] This points to a serious tension or even inconsistency between the promotion of the moral life as a Buddhist ideal on the one hand and the concept of ultimate reality which undermines the validity of the very notion of good and evil, on the other.[23]

Sometimes the tensions are of a more personal nature, when an individual who inhabits a certain worldview has experiences or develops convictions at odds with this worldview. This is movingly shown in the haiku of the Japanese poet Issa (1762–1826), quoted by Os Guinness. This poet had a tragic life. First, his five children died and then his wife. This led him to question a Zen-master about why these things had happened to him. The Zen-master told him that this world is only evanescent dew. All our grief is only a sign that we are unable to overcome our egotistic bondage to this reality. As a response to that perspective, Issa wrote (Guinness 1973: 225):

---

22 According to the Zen-Buddhist Masao Abe ("Kenotic God and Dynamic Sunyata", in: John B. Cobb Jr. & Christopher Ives (eds.), *The Emptying God: A Buddhist-Jewish-Christian Conversation*, Maryknoll: Orbis, 1990, pp. 52f, cited in Netland 1991: 307).

23 See for other tensions between the Buddhist metaphysics and ethics of selfless love: Hackett 1979: 106, 117f.

The world is dew –
The world is dew –
And yet,
And yet …

This poem shows how Issa could not accept the answer, although it should make sense according to his worldview. This is one of those instances that demonstrates one is never entirely imprisoned by the symbolic universe one inhabits and that the world does not let itself knead *ad infinitum* within any given symbolic confines. The world was just too hard, and in Berger's terms Issa was suffering an acute "breakdown in reality" (Berger & Luckmann 1967: 175). The apologist can use such anomalies, tensions and needs in cultures and in individual lives as bridges for the Gospel, as a trigger to start exploring the new world inaugurated by Christ.

Jesus Christ as the capstone

This apologetic use of tensions and anomalies should, again, avoid the pitfalls of manipulation and paternalism. Yet, the existence of these pitfalls does not mean that these tensions cannot be used in another way, as an introduction to an honest presentation of the faith and of Christ. We do, after all, believe that Christ is the answer to the inner tensions of life, which we believe to be caused by the loss of the centring of our lives on God. The apologetic exploration of cultural and human tensions does not just reflect an epistemic phenomenon revealed by Kuhn, MacIntyre and Berger. It is such a worthwhile apologetic procedure, because it is based on the fact that the human being who lives far from God and without Christ, and who lives in perpetual crisis, inevitably ends up with much tension (§6.2).

Sometimes these crises mount in major cultural debates and tensions, and some of the best apologies have been those which exposed such tensions and showed their insurmountability without Christ, pointing to the Christian faith as the third way. Thus Blaise Pascal's *Pensées* exposed the tension between rationalists and sceptics, unveiling a mistaken understanding of the human nature and condition as their common fault and proposing a Christian understanding of the nature and destiny of the human being. *The Nature and the Destiny of Man* (1941–1943) was, equally, the theme of Reinhold Niebuhr's Gifford lectures in which he contrasted rationalism and Romanticism and showed how the Christian faith makes sense of the shortcomings of both. The same apologetic procedure reflects itself in the title of Os Guinness' analysis of the revolutions in the sixties of the twentieth century: *The Dust of Death: A Critique of the Establishment and Counter Culture – and a Proposal for a Third Way* (1973). Comparable apologies could exploit the tensions in the contemporary world: between modernism and postmodernism, individualism and collectivism, naturalism and creative antire-alism, between a sense of Western superiority and cultural relativism, secularism and the new quest for the sacred, between capitalism and environmentalism, the arts and the sciences, between the value of the family and pan-economism, and between sexuality and intimacy.

These examples mostly reflect those sectors of our globalized culture that are dominated by the West, yet similar tensions can be shown to exist in non-Western societies or societies on the edge of Western culture. We could, for example, single out the enormous tension between the search for protection against spiritual powers and the continued existence of fear characterizing traditional Africa or the opposing tendencies of growing individualism and mounting ethno-centrism in modern-day Africa. We could equally point to the tensions between legalism and mysticism in Islam.

From a modernist apologetic perspective the fragmentation produced by all these tensions seems a disaster: there is nothing solid on which to build. Yet, if one probes the world in which we live for traces of the fragmentation of the human being without God, the apologetic opportunities are multiple. Many of these tensions have been exposed in earlier apologetic work; yet analysing these tensions remains an ongoing project, not only for Christian writers but also for Christians ministering as teachers and preachers in the pulpit, in the classroom and in the media.

The apologist can of course not limit herself to uncovering and exposing the often hidden tensions that characterize cultures and ways of life. We need to bring people to begin doubting some of their old certainties, yet when we just expose the inconsistencies and anomalies, people might easily start to doubt what is most truthful in their belief-system. When we expose, for example, the tension between a respect for human rights and evolutionism, you could in principle conclude that human rights should be discredited – and some have done so. When you expose the tension in Buddhism between a strong sense of morality and the non-moral nature of the ultimate, any of both horns of the dilemma might come under pressure or one might – more likely – prefer to doubt the value of this type reasoning with regards to religious matters.

In order to avoid a mere impasse, we will need to point out that the most crucial antinomies can be solved when Christ is brought into the centre of our life and worldview. We will need to show that what is most valuable in life finds its fulfilment, coherence and meaning in Him. He is, in one of the Old Testament sayings that is more often quoted in the New, "the stone which the builders rejected" that has yet "become the capstone" (Ps 118:22f; Mt 21:42; 1Pe 2:7). Only with Christ as the capstone will the worldviews we construct become a coherent and solid whole. The apologist should aim for a sort of "*Gestalt*-switch" in which it becomes apparent that all crucial aspects of the former worldview suddenly fall in place and make much better sense when they are rearranged and perceived from a different angle with Christ at the centre.[24]

24 For the epistemological and apologetic value of the psychological concept of the "*Gestalt*-switch" see: Kuhn 1996: 204; Guinness 1981: 343.

As we noted, anomalies and tensions in worldviews and cultures are created by a lack of "fit" between these conceptual frameworks and the world in which we live. Because of the role of Jesus Christ as the capstone of our lives and of our worldview, we need to consider one group of anomalies or misfits in particular. I am thinking of the misfits between different understandings of Jesus and the reality of the person of Jesus Christ whom we encounter in the Gospels and whom we still meet today. The anomalies resulting from a deficient understanding of Jesus have a particular apologetic importance, because it is Jesus whom Christians present as the clue to understanding the world, ourselves and God. This clue is not automatically understood, for as with everything we encounter, most people will interpret Jesus in terms of their own framework, their own system of reference. The reading metaphor we looked at earlier proves helpful here. What we need to show is that all non-Christian – and all non-orthodox Christian – views of Christ break down on the reality of Jesus Christ Himself as He meets us in the Gospel. This is the apologetic strength of the classic dilemma that is often formulated as the dilemma whether Christ is "Lord, liar or lunatic" (Lewis 1955a: 51f; McDowell 1977: 25–35). Other possible explanations could be added: was He a religious genius, a mythological figure, a guru, or maybe a guerrilla-fighter? (Kreeft & Tacelli 1994: 161–171.) The apologist will need to show that all readings of Jesus that do not recognize Him as Son of God and Lord break down on the reading material. And in the process it should become clear that this reading material does not only consist of the text of the Gospels by themselves, but that the texts reflect a reality which just cannot be explained away.

7.5 The Church as counter-culture and alternative plausibility structure

Plausibility for the believer

Postmodern epistemological reflections and life in a multicultural world have shown that modern individualist epistemologies miss out on essential characteristics of the way human beings know and come to know new things. Beliefs are formed within a tradition; they are culturally and socially embedded. Beliefs are formed in correlation with the praxis and particularly the epistemic praxis of a community (Polanyi 1962: 203). It is therefore essential, and not just accidental, to conversion that there is a change not only of our beliefs and allegiance, but also with regard to the community to which we belong and in which we find our identity (cf. 1Pe 2:4-10). It is in that sense that the Church can be called "the pillar and foundation of the truth" (1Ti 3:15); it is "the social correlate of God's self-revelation" (Torrance 1985: 117).

The community of believers is first of all crucial for believers themselves. "Only a genius or a madman can believe by himself or herself" (Guinness 1994:

344). The need for a supportive community is part of human nature. We need a community in order to be socialized in a certain understanding of reality. We need a community to maintain the plausibility of this outlook for us, for as Berger and Luckmann have rightly stressed, if the community support is lacking, for most people the "realness" of our outlook diminishes in our experience. This does not mean that all around must share the same outlook, but ideally a number of people that are particularly significant to us (1967: 169ff). Our human epistemic make-up is complex and we can imagine that there are ways to make up for social isolation, as we see with some Christians and others who have very strong convictions in places where they are extremely isolated.[25] Yet, God Himself created us as relational beings who depend on the community to which we belong and who are meant to flourish within that community. It means that though we cannot reduce our Christian faith to the social constituents that play into it, faith cannot be formed, maintained, and developed without the appropriate social constituents.

The fact that Christians will often be in the minority underlines the need to belong to a strong community that can maintain a radically counter-cultural perspective on the world against opposition and unbelief. The role of sinful predispositions furthermore shows that we are in need of such a community not only for narrowly intellectual reasons. Believers need the Christian community to develop and maintain the virtues and type of personality that will help them fight and overcome their proper sinful biases against the recognition of the truth.[26]

The role of sinful dispositions also explains why, in our present world, the Christian understanding may never gain the status of what Kuhn calls "normal science", the uncontested norm that has decisively gained the upper hand in the community, or why the Christian faith may even lose this status after a certain period (Kuhn 1996: 77–91). A Christian view of human rationality as embedded in traditions cannot suppose that the more truthful perspective will always have the upper hand. This presupposition is one of the main limitations of MacIntyre's analysis of the tradition-embedded development of rationalities. MacIntyre does not sufficiently reckon with the power struggles and biases of communities and of individuals against certain paradigms, notwithstanding their truth. He is far too optimistic in his expectation that the best understanding of justice and ethics will prevail (Murphy 1999: 108–110). Regarding the Gospel, we will need to count with even more negative biases (§3.3). We might expect a thinker with such an outstanding reputation in the study of Marxism as MacIntyre to be more sensitive to these factors.

---

25 If the human being is also created to respond to the urge of the Holy Spirit in his life, God may have ways of supporting isolated Christian believers by his Spirit. Our openness to special directions and support by the Spirit can be part of a Christian understanding of warranted knowledge in terms of proper function (Plantinga 2000: 249ff).

26 For the role of the community in the appropriation of epistemic virtues, see: Zagzebski 1993: 215f.

Initial plausibility for non-Christians

For those outside, the Christian community also provides initial plausibility. The first problem most non-Christians have with the Christian faith is not that it is not *credible*, but rather that it is not even *plausible* (cf. Dockery 1995: 17). This need for the life of the Christian community to confer an initial plausibility on the Christian faith for those outside has recently been recognized by a number of writers dealing with apologetics in a postmodern world (Newbigin 1989: 228, 223; Guinness 1981: 295–298; Stackhouse 1995; Potter 1995; Hollinger 1995). When this is said, the idea of plausibility has a different meaning from its original meaning in the sociology of knowledge. There it is mainly used with reference to people who already share a particular perspective. For its inhabitants a cultural framework is plausible in a much stronger sense, often even in the sense of being entirely natural to the point that it becomes almost inconceivable to consider having another perspective on life. When it is said that the Christian community is necessary to confer an initial plausibility on the Christian faith for those outside, it means, in a much weaker sense, that the Christian faith becomes worth considering, that it becomes a valid option.

In our pluralist world, virtually all people are vaguely acquainted with many beliefs and worldviews, which they know to be held sometimes even by many people, but which for them remain entirely implausible. They seem to be so remote from reality as they experience it that they would never seriously consider them. Most Westerners would put Muslim fundamentalism in that category. They would therefore consider it a waste of time listening to a fundamentalist Muslim explaining his beliefs. Christianity seems equally outlandish to many people in this world. It is precisely the Christian community or the life of individual Christians that needs to confer on the Christian faith an initial plausibility before people can even begin to seriously consider its credibility. People need to see in the Christian community that Christians have a way of life that is appealing. They need to encounter Christians who are open to reality and sufficiently sensible to be taken seriously. They need to see a conviction that is deep, yet, that is not fanatical in the sense that it is not afraid of serious questioning. They need to discover that Christians have a faith that is worth living and in many countries the situation is such that people can also see that it is a faith worth dying for.[27]

In order to confer such an initial plausibility, the Christian community needs a double quality. It needs to be sufficiently different to provide a real *alternative* and sufficiently recognizable to provide a *plausible* alternative. It needs to be sufficiently different, sufficiently counter-cultural, to remain itself, and to be faithful to its Lord, in order to constitute a serious alternative to other cultural perspectives. The weakness of many modernist accommodations of the Christian

27 Cf. Vanhoozer (1999: 147–149) on the apologetic value of martyrdom.

faith to the values of the surrounding culture is not just its lack of faithfulness to the Lord and the Scriptures. Such accommodations also lack an ability to provide an alternative that is sufficiently different to challenge those belonging to the community and the tradition to which they accommodate (Berger 1980: 58, 107). This is the anti-thesis needed between the Church and the world. This is expressed in what Lindbeck calls the need for "sociological sectarianism" (§2.3) and what Berger calls "the heretical imperative" (1980: 23–29).

Yet, the need for the Christian community to be considered heretical needs to go further than Berger and Lindbeck acknowledge. As Newbigin has shown, Berger's proposal for a Christian community that distinguishes itself from the beliefs of the wider society as a particular "hairesis" or opinion is largely formulated in terms that modernity itself allows for. Berger formulates his religious convictions largely as an unverifiable personal opinion in contrast to the shared convictions that science can provide us with, yet as a personal opinion that itself springs from religious experience as a general anthropological phenomenon.[28] We saw that Lindbeck's understanding of religion aligns with postmodern analysis of cultural–linguistic frameworks, without sufficiently taking into account the specificity of the Christian faith over against postmodernist understandings of the nature of such frameworks (§2.4). The Christian community needs to set itself apart as a counter-cultural community that does not let itself fit in or be subsumed under a larger modern or postmodern umbrella, but challenges both modernism and postmodernism to their core as themselves culturally embedded options in a multicultural world.

In order to give the Christian faith initial plausibility, the Christian community needs to show that it values what many people crave for. It would do much for the initial plausibility of the Christian faith if the Christian community were first perceived as a community that teaches faithfulness through difficulties and as a place where those who are struggling in their marriages can find help, rather than indifference or reproach. It should be known as a place where those shattered by divorce can find compassion. Against that background the negative attitude of Christians to divorce can be properly heard. The Church should be a place where those who are anxious about spells and curses can find protection against the power of evil, before it also condemns taking recourse to diviners, because such recourse enslaves rather than liberates. It should be a community of hope and therefore a community that evokes questions for an apology, for an account of the hope that is in her (1Pe 3:15). In being such a liberating and healing community, the Church also plays a crucial role in reaching the reasons of the heart and in touching the deepest needs of those we encounter, a subject that will be more widely explored in the next chapter.

---

28 Berger explicitly places himself in the tradition of the modernist liberal Protestantism of the Schleiermacher variety (1980: 58–60, 114–142). See for Newbigin's criticism: 1986: 12–18.

7.6 Concluding observations

The finality of the Christian faith

Apologetic dialogue can thus be analysed as a dialogue concerning different tradition-embedded readings of reality – and of the particular reality of Jesus of Nazareth – with a view to answering the question which reading does most justice to the reality we encounter. This image of different interacting and developing traditions makes all our understanding relative to possible future correction. Within our tradition we may make radically new discoveries – or theologically speaking: we may have radically new experiences of God – which may force us to a major paradigm shift. Furthermore, within a rationality that develops in its interaction with other traditions we may encounter other traditions that are superior in dealing much better with the anomalies and antinomies that become insoluble and unbearable within our own tradition. Within the framework of a rationality embedded in traditions, an argument for a particular worldview is always provisional and should remain open to new insights.[29]

At first sight this seems hard to reconcile with the Judeo-Christian confession that in the Scriptures we meet with the true and living God, who is radically different from all idols. It seems hard to square with the Christian confession that in Christ we have met with God in Person, that He is the Way, the Truth and the Life in a manner that cannot be surpassed by any new perspective on the Divine. Does an understanding of a rationality embedded in traditions commit us to be open to the possibility that we may encounter some long-existing or radically new tradition of religious reflection that makes better sense of our lives and world than the Christian tradition does? This would furthermore undermine the possibility of radical faith and trust in God, for God might later be shown to be radically different than the way we conceive of Him – or Her, or It – now.

It is difficult to find the answer to this question on the side of the knowing subject – that is in the quality of our experience of God or of the type of argument that could lead to such knowledge. All our reasoning is the reasoning of finite and fallible people with a limited perspective, which could very well be erroneous. Neither can we appeal to some privileged experience. Some would appeal to a self-authenticating experience of the Holy Spirit (f. ex. Plantinga 2000: 242ff; Craig 2000: 29–38). The problem, though, is that adherents of other religions also claim such experiences. This does not mean that such an experience may not be

29 MacIntyre conceives of his rationality of traditions as an open-ended process (1988: 360f), though does not consider this a necessary consequence of such a tradition-embedded understanding of rationality (1988: 81). Werpehowski notes (1986: 81): "If we consider a religion to be a cultural–linguistic interpretative scheme [...] any argument for the scheme over religious and non-religious competitors must be cumulative in character; it must show the way in which the scheme makes better sense of features of reality, than do alternatives."

a valid ground for belief and even for certain knowledge. If God reveals Himself in Christ through the Spirit, such a testimony of the Spirit will be part of the way through which He communicates Himself to us. Yet, the experience may not be qualitatively different from an experience that a Buddhist would have and claim to be self-authenticating. Even if it were different, it would be very hard to know, for only my own experiences are directly accessible to myself. As soon as I start comparing my experiences with those of others, I enter into a type of argument that is characterized by the same finite perspective as all human argumentation.[30]

Such an effort to base religious certainty on some specific feature of the knowledge on the side of the knowing subject is, however, reminiscent of the subject–object divide characteristic of modernity, which does not do justice to the nature of the human being. As we have seen, human nature is such that we can only know when we accept our place within a wider network of relationships with God, the world and those around us. We therefore cannot understand the nature of our knowledge without considering *both* poles of the knowledge relationship. This is particularly important regarding the question of the finality of the Christian knowledge of God and the nature of the certainty of this faith. The finality of the knowledge of God in Christ is not guaranteed by any particular quality of the knowing subject in knowing Him. It is neither the quality of the confidence nor the nature of this knowledge that justifies its finality. Christians are not confident because of their confidence, but because of the Lord in whom they trust. This is the way Paul expresses the nature of his confidence: "I know the one in whom I have put my confidence, and am sure that he is able to guard until that day what I have entrusted to him." (2Ti 1:12).[31]

With regards the nature of the reality to which Christians entrust themselves, we need to note two characteristics that justify taking it as a trustworthy perspective, of which they have no reason to suspect that it will be defeated by some radically new perspective. The first is its being the self-revelation of God, and the second its being His eschatological self-revelation.

If we consider religious faith to be based on religious experience of the divine that is in some diffused manner everywhere present among humankind, Christians have no reason to presume that their experience of the divine is qualitatively different form the experience of others.[32] Such a presumption would indeed be arrogant and disrespectful. Yet, one cannot exclude beforehand that there is a personal god who can reveal himself in a particular manner in a specific place and to a specific community. If we believe that God has revealed Himself in some historically localized place, we cannot simply put such a revelation on

30 For a wider discussion of self-authenticating religious experiences, see: Feinberg 2000a: 69–72; Netland 2001: 260–265.

31 I was pointed to the epistemological implications of the text by Newbigin (1995: 66).

32 This is exemplified in the understanding of religious experience in Berger (1980: 114ff) and in Hick (1977).

a par with other religious experiences. We have either to dismiss it or entrust ourselves to it as a qualitatively different way of knowing God from whence we have to evaluate all other religious experiences anew. This is precisely what happens in the Scriptures (Newbigin 1995: 96f). That is why apologetic dialogue between religions who claim a special revelation – such as between Christians and Muslims – will always follow different lines than dialogue between those religions that accept a revelation in history on the one hand, and those who do not on the other.

A personal revelation of God does not by itself exclude the possibility of a progressively deepening understanding of God and his plan with the world. Muslims believe in a succession of prophets, and Jews and Christians believe in what is called a *historia revelationis*, a historical progression of God making Himself known to his people and to the world. In this history subsequent acts and revelations of God may reveal radically new aspects of God. Yet, as a historical fact, these three religions have all decided on a closed canon of Scriptures containing the principal revelations that their believers consider entrusted to their community and which they claim to be supremely authoritative. What reason could they have for such a limitation of authoritative revelation?

For Christians the limitation of the canon of authoritative Scriptures is a consequence of their understanding of Jesus Christ as the final revelation of God. It is central to the New Testament that the revelation of God in the sending of Christ, in his cross and resurrection and in his gift of the Spirit, is eschatological (f. ex. Heb 1:1-2). Therefore no decisively new revelations of God are to be expected before the final consummation of history. All later claims to revelation have to be tested against what God has already revealed at this time in history. The end of history has dawned in Jesus in whom the eschatological reign of God is present and in whose being and ministry humanity is reconciled to its Creator. This makes Jesus himself much more than an enlightened person, much more than a prophet even. In his Person and life, God Himself is decisively present and active. The fact that Jesus is the Son of God incarnate correlates with the uniqueness and unrepeatable nature of the Christ-event and intensifies it.[33] He is not just a prophet, but God Himself. That is the reason why Christians cannot accept a later prophet, such as Mohammed, who claims to bring a revelation that surpasses the encounter with God Himself in Jesus (Manaranche 1985: 17f, 166). Neither can they accept Jesus as one avatar among others, who are all revelations of the divine to different people and different places. Jesus is not simply the divine appearing in a human form. Jesus is God incarnate, taking on a real and therefore unique human existence.

If Jesus is indeed the Son of God incarnate and the inaugurator of the *eschaton*, the Christian community has a unique access to the source of the universe and

33 On the relationship between the eschatological character of the Christ-event and the unique nature of Christ, see Pannenberg (1968: 53ff).

to understand its aim. The finality of the knowledge of God in this tradition is not based on anything specific about this tradition in itself. It is given with the object of its faith, with Christ as the final revelation of God. If this faith is justified, then the reality encountered here draws humankind out of the relativity of all its thinking. It places humanity face to face with the source of the universe Himself. The Christian acknowledgement of Him is a human acknowledgement and therefore a finite and fallible human act, yet it is acknowledgement of *Him*, and therefore it draws Christians into a community and a reality with an eternal, universal and eschatological character. Christians may give all sorts of reasons why they believe that their trust in Him is justified and they should do so. However, their confidence does not rest in those reasons, but in the Person to whom they point and the finality of their convictions is therefore not bound up with anything in them, but with Him. "We know in whom we have believed."

If the finality of this faith is thus bound up with Jesus Christ, Christians cannot claim finality for *their* particular understanding of Christ or for their understanding of what a Christian worldview should look like. Their understanding of Christ and of what a Christian rationality and worldview entail is to be continually redirected to and purified by the reality from which they draw their meaning and validity. It is only as they continually subject them to this eschatological reality that they can hold on to the claim that the Church is indeed an eschatological community and that she has the clue to what opens up the final understanding of what life and the universe are all about.

The fact that the finality of Christian belief is not based on anything Christians possess, but only on the reality in which they trust, also has major consequences for understanding religious certainty. Such a certainty can never be based on the epistemic powers that human beings possess. The belief that humanity might obtain certainty by mastery of the world was one of the central misconceptions of modernity and such a certainty would, in all cases, never be attainable with respect to the Creator (cf. Newbigin 1995: 16ff, *passim*). It is only in entrusting oneself to the God who revealed Himself in Christ, that human beings can obtain proper confidence and discover that indeed this confidence is not deceived. Christian confidence rests on the belief that they are taken up in God's plan for the world in which He has a place for them as they are, with their finitude and failures. Christian confidence is based on God's faithfulness rather than on human mastery of reality and on the depth of human probing. As soon as we discover that we can answer his invitation and entrust ourselves to Him, the centre of our world is relocated and this relocation includes the centre of our epistemological world. Our faith is put elsewhere and justifiably so for this is what accords with what we are like and even more with what God is like for us. As Barth saw it (*KD* II/1: 81; trans. *CD* II/1: 75),

> The dialectic [between certainty and uncertainty] still remains on our part: yet not in such a way that we are still in the grip of that dialectic; rather in

such a way that the dialectic is directed and controlled from the side of the event which is God's part. For us the event of our knowledge of God shews itself to be a continual winning and losing, winning again and losing again. But through it all the will of God is there as the preponderant force, so that we are not lost in that ascending and descending movement, but held – held as by the mercy of God, but for that reason really held.

Excursus: comparing worldviews and the problem of the criteria

To elucidate the particularity of the apologetic method I have been proposing here, I would like to compare it with an alternative method – an approach that, in shorthand, could be labelled "worldview apologetics" (cf. §2.1). This apologetic approach envisages comparing different worldviews according to a number of criteria: logical coherence, consistency with knowledge in other fields, moral adequacy, etc. (f. ex. Netland 1991: 183–195).[34]

The main strength of such a worldview approach is that it takes seriously the profound influence of our worldview on the way we experience the world, without yielding to relativism. The main limitation is that it lends too much weight to the criteria proposed to evaluate the different worldviews. The problem is not that such criteria are not universally *valid* or that they are not valid independent of any particular worldview. They are. Yet, they are not universally *recognized* as valid. This is shown by the example of certain Buddhists who reject the criterion of logical consistency, particularly when one wants to apply it to ultimate reality,[35] or by the rejection of certain postmodernists of the criteria of logical consistency and of empirical fit.[36] This remains true even if one could make an argument that everyone *should* at least accept some logical principles (*contra* Geisler 1976: 141ff) or that everyone *implicitly* accepts an idea of correspondence even while openly rejecting it (*contra* Feinberg 2000b: 170f; Netland 2001: 296). All this only underscores that those criteria are not given *a priori*, but need in some cases to be themselves the object of discussion. Such criteria can only *a posteriori* be discovered to be indeed universally valid and adequate for comparing worldviews and knowledge claims.[37]

Though defenders of a worldview approach may recognize this *a posteriori*

34 The so-called two-stage apologetic that first tries to establish general theism on the basis of a comparison of worldviews and on that basis considers the historical data concerning Jesus of Nazareth, has, as far as the first stage is concerned, the same strengths and weaknesses (f. ex. Geisler 1976).

35 As conceded by Netland (2001: 293) within the context of a defence of context-independent criteria.

36 Cf. the criticism of Mark C. Taylor in Feinberg (2000b: 167–172).

37 Cf. for a more philosophical analysis of the *a posteriori* nature of the basic criteria that we use to distinguish truth and error: Polanyi 1962: 160–171; Chisholm 1989: 6f; Plantinga 1983: 74–78.

character of these criteria and may be willing to defend them, the apologetic implications of this concession are often missed. If these criteria for comparing worldviews are not *a priori* given, but to be discovered in the process, I can still use them apologetically, when my audience accepts them. Yet, then I may likewise use other truths that are universally true, though not universally recognized, but shared by my specific audience. So in that respect all truths are on a par with one another as far as their apologetic value is concerned. There is therefore no reason to give these allegedly context-independent criteria for judging worldviews an apologetic value over other points of contact we may find in specific audiences. As human beings we generally commit ourselves more strongly to other ideas or values that are more specific for our community than to some abstract criteria. Average Muslims are probably more strongly committed to the prophet Muhammad and to their belief in the oneness of God than to any abstract criterion. They might easily be brought to give up an abstract criterion if it implied that they should deny their prophet or their God.

I doubt if a consistent simultaneous commitment to the other major criteria is even possible, if we are not first committed to Christ. It seems to me that in a sinful world the principle of the viability of a worldview on the one hand does not cohere smoothly with openness to the world as it is on the other hand. If we recognize the world as it is without Christ, it is a hard place to live in. That means that we are left with a trilemma. Either we close ourselves off from reality to make life more liveable, or we give up on the liveability or viability of our worldview in order to respect reality as it is, or we give up on the consistency of our worldview to do both at the same time. My Christian commitment tells me that only Christ can save me from this trilemma. We should not be amazed, therefore, that non-Christian worldviews have a hard time giving equal respect to these three criteria. Something needs to yield.

What remains of worldview apologetics is a defence of the Christian worldview, valid for a very specific audience, which may be mostly found in limited Western intellectual milieus that consider it a valid procedure to evaluate worldviews in a disengaged manner according to an abstract procedure. In all the other cases other points of contact will be more viable. The evaluation of worldviews according to such criteria can also function as an important *confirmation* for Christians who are understandably troubled by the multiplicity of worldviews. Yet, also for Christians their commitment to the Christian worldview is not *based* on such an abstract comparison, but rather on an encounter with Christ. All human thinking, including the criteria we propose to evaluate worldviews, should be brought under his Lordship (2Co 10:4).

In looking back on this chapter we are able to see that the four insights discussed that allow for cross-cultural persuasion are not four isolated ways of showing the relevance and truth of the Christian faith. Showing the validity of the Christian perspective as a whole, building bridges and unveiling anomalies are but three aspects of the overall apologetic witness. The anomalies show the need to look elsewhere for alternative points of view. By building bridges the apologist shows that the Christian faith is coherent with and the fulfilment of what is best and what is most true in the former worldview. The rearrangement of all these elements around Christ reveals first and foremost the illuminating power of the whole picture. And all this is only possible against the background of a vibrant Church that gives the Christian faith an initial plausibility and attractiveness and that provides an environment in which it can be explored.

Conversion narratives and larger studies of the process of particularly interreligious conversions confirm the importance of all these four instigations to change (f. ex. Williams 2002; Maharaj 2004; Gaudeul 1991; trans. 1999). Further study of such conversion narratives might be revealing in indicating whether one may show specific relationships between these factors that facilitate and motivate a change of perspective and whether others might be added.

Chapter 8

REACHING THE REASONS OF THE HEART

In the last two chapters it became clear that Christian apologetic dialogue and witness should address people not as free-floating individuals but as members of a community and embedded in a tradition. Neither should the Christian apologist approach her interlocutor as a free-floating mind, but as persons driven by emotional needs and all sorts of biases of the will. It should not only address the mind, but also the "reasons of the heart", to use a famous expression of Pascal (*Pensées*: no. 423; Green 1992: 214–230; Edgar 1996). Throughout this book a number of considerations have pointed in this direction. We concluded that the opposition of both modernity and postmodernity against the Christian faith is not simply an intellectual opposition. Both antagonistic cultural constellations are fuelled by a desire for autonomy, which has its origin in a rejection of God (Chapter 3). We saw furthermore that human beings are created to be the people of God and that this goal engages their entire personality. They are driven by a deep need for a home in this created world, for fellowship with others and for God's love. Human reason never functions in a void; rather, it flourishes in this relational environment in which it belongs or it is driven by the need to fill the void for a home and for God with surrogate homes and gods (Chapter 4). We saw how, because of these biases, it is easy not to be open to reality as it presents itself to us, and how we tend to fashion reality and our image of it in order to deal with our own needs and fears. A genuine openness to reality therefore involves the will and emotional dispositions. Biases on these levels can put a screen between us and reality, against which the mind, left to itself, is powerless. Knowing reality as it is in itself and for itself demands that we let go of our desire to master it and approach it with the openness and respect due to a reality that exists independently from us (Torrance 1985: 104f, 109f). Knowing reality demands a certain moral posture (cf. Polanyi 1946: 25) and this is particularly true with regards the knowledge of God (Chapter 5; Torrance 1971: 198f; Plantinga 2000: 213–215). Finally, we saw that it is impossible to provide "airtight" and logically coercive argumentation across cultural boundaries. This is not to say that cross-cultural persuasion is irrational, but it does mean that a basic openness is needed in order to see this rationality, openness to genuinely engage with others and to question one's proper biases and felt needs (Chapters 6 and 7). This role of the emotions and the will in apologetic dialogue will be the subject of this final chapter. A properly Christian and effective apologetic should address the entire person.

Considering this role of emotional biases and the will in apologetics does not mean that we are now leaving the domain of reason to deal with the irrational aspects of human nature. Some apologists would allow for the consideration of the will and the emotions, but only as the pre-condition for proper rational dialogue or as a function of applied apologetics. The proper use of reason is considered to be devoid of such considerations. The intellect, however, only functions as an aspect of the human personality as a whole. Though apologetics as a theological discipline concentrates its attention on "the *intellectual* justification of the truth and relevance of the Christian faith" (§1.4), it cannot isolate the human intellect from other aspects of life. The proper use of the intellect does not simply require that the other factors be *neutralized*, but that we set our commitments straight and that our emotional life is opened up to God, to our fellow-human beings, to reality and to truth.

We cannot, therefore, distinguish between an irrational persuasion of the will and the emotions and a rational persuasion of the mind. This distinction in rhetoric is itself a fruit of the faculty-psychology, which was developed in the seventeenth century. This faculty-psychology separated the rational and irrational components of the human make-up (cf. Berlo 1960: 8), leading to rationalism on the one hand and a-rational romanticism on the other hand. Christian anthropology demands that we view the human being as a whole and this is confirmed by the understanding of Polanyi and others of knowing as an eminently personal enterprise. On the one hand, the intellect can only flourish together with the will and the affections. On the other, a responsible consideration of the will and of the affections demands that they be judged and guided by the intellect in accordance with the truth. We already argued that this is implied in the fact that God holds the human being responsible (§1.3) and in this closing chapter we will explore some further apologetically crucial aspects of the relationship between the intellect, the will and the affections. In the process we will also evaluate the presuppositionalist approach to apologetics, which makes the will the all-determining factor in apologetic dialogue (§8.1). In reaching the reasons of the heart of the dialogue partner, the character of the apologist is of central importance. We will elaborate on the main virtues of the apologist to which she is morally held because of her message and because of the aim of apologetic dialogue. In this context we will also be able to return to the recurrent criticism of postmodernists and students of culture that the defence of one cultural perspective over another falls under the indictment of cultural imperialism. A community that serves a Lord who became a servant needs to take this indictment with utter seriousness (§8.2).

8.1 Desires, will and reason

To gain a proper understanding of the role of the emotions, the will and reason in apologetic dialogue, a fully fledged sketch of the place and interrelation of these aspects of the human psychological make-up are not required. It is sufficient to explore their interrelation only in so far as they impinge upon apologetic dialogue. My contention is that the basic conclusions which we will draw will be warranted by a Christian theological understanding of the human being (cf. Chapter 4), by their coherence with the way in which Scripture itself addresses the human being, and by rather general perceptions about the behaviour of ourselves and others belonging to our species.

The noetic influence of sin

One of the principal elements of the theological criticism of modern epistemology in this study was directed against the modern idea of a neutral or disengaged attitude to knowledge. If humankind is created to find life in its fullness in relationship with God, with fellow-human beings and with creation, it is impossible to remain neutral towards these realities. The meaning of the entire human existence is bound up with them. Therefore, the search for knowledge of God, of other human beings and of the world is meant to be driven by a deep desire to know these as objects of love and care. If this desire for God is diverted to something else and if the relationship with fellow human beings and with creation is inverted, human beings are even less neutral. They start using God and others for their own projects and fear to truly know God, others, creation and themselves. Knowing them for what they are would constitute a threat for the project they have set for themselves or that their community has set for them (cf. §3.3).

According to Christian doctrine, all human beings by birth in the human community inherit this malfunction in their thinking. How this enslaves and imprisons humankind in a faulty view of reality becomes clear when we realize how the basic attitude inherited consists of a disorder in desires, will and mind. Desires are directed to what is not God and, as a result, human beings develop emotional barriers against God, whom they thus experience as a danger to either their pride or their sloth. The will affirms the desire to direct their lives without God and becomes bound to a desire to lead such a life. The mind inherits and contributes to an understanding of the world in which there is no place for a God who radically challenges this way of life, and this understanding, in turn, confirms the desire and choice for a life without this God. As such, individuals find themselves in a world in which they are not only wilfully participating in sin but also trapped in sin.

When sin is called "original", it means that human beings find themselves in a sinful constellation that is their fate before it is their choice, even though afterwards they may come to heartily affirm the sinful state in which they find themselves. Because of this affirmation by the will, the enslavement is deepened, and thus we need to keep in mind that "ordinarily there will be a complicated interplay between *guilt* and *damage*" (Plantinga 2000: 216). The postmodern stress on and analysis of the distorting role of the "will to power" on human knowledge of themselves, others and of reality, need not surprise Christians. According to Nancey Murphy, "it is strikingly what an Augustinian Christian would expect", (1999: 109) yet "apart from any concepts of grace, regeneration and revelation" (p. 108).

In order to understand the implications of the noetic influence of sin, we do not need to be able to distinguish the extent to which this situation is fate or personal responsibility. We also do not need to discuss the difficult question of whether this sin has its origin in a flaw of the mind, of the will or of the emotions, in all three of them or in none of them.[1] What *is* important for this inquiry is to understand how mind, emotional life and will interplay in the difficulty many people have in accepting the Christian message and in appreciating the reasons the apologist may give for its acceptance. Understanding the interrelation of these factors is equally important for knowing how the Christian apologetic witness should address persons as integrated beings with mind, will and emotions in order that they may indeed come to see the Jesus Christ for who he is.

Theologians in the Reformed tradition, such as Karl Barth (§3.2), the presuppositionalists along the lines of Van Til (1967: 46–50) and Reformed epistemologists along the lines of Plantinga (2000: 199–240), have been most sensitive to the noetic influence of sin. Their theological heritage with its stress on the so-called bondage of the will has made them sensitive to the role of this barrier for a proper knowledge of God and proper understanding of the Gospel. We can never develop a properly Christian apologetic if we do not take seriously their stress on the role of predispositions towards the Gospel – such as we encountered in our analysis of Barth's criticism of modern apologetics. Yet, in my opinion, the Barthians and Vantillians, particularly, went too far when they made the cognitive influence of sin a major factor in their rejection of the possibility of the apologetic quest for common ground between non-believers and the Gospel. I will argue that we must give due place to the cognitive influence of sin, yet recognize that this does not prevent all possibility of apologetic dialogue. We will only be able to see this after a more detailed analysis of the role of predispositions and the will on human reasoning.

1 For discussions of this question, see: Blocher 1984: 135–154; Plantinga 2000: 211–213.

Apologetics and predispositions

For lack of a better overall expression, we use the term "predispositions" for all those forces that push or pull people's thinking in a certain involuntary and pre-rational direction. These predispositions can present themselves in our consciousness as desires to fulfil certain physical needs – such as the need for sleep, for food, for shelter, or the craving for sexual fulfilment. These predispositions can also be related to more emotional needs – such as the need for respect, the need to feel loved, the need for power and so on. Quite often, such predispositions are related to anxieties resulting from scars people carry with them from past hurtful experiences. All these needs predispose people emotionally to search more fervently for knowledge and beliefs that help gratify such needs. They predispose them to accept more readily beliefs that contribute to the gratification of these needs than those which do not. As Guinness notes: "Both [the Christian faith and the sociology of knowledge] agree that, deeper even than presuppositions, predispositions pose the strongest challenge to translation" (1981: 328).

From a theological perspective some of these desires are perfectly natural in the sense that they belong to God's good creation – such as the desire to feel loved. Some may be the result of the distorting influence of sin on creation – such as the desire to live a life free from any accountability. Some predispositions are good in and of themselves, but may, in the context of a fallen world, become barriers between human beings and God. This is the case with, for example, the predisposition to trust what we learn from our parents and community, and the predisposition to remain faithful to this community, which can result in accepting a mistaken view of God and a mistaken attitude towards God.

In the face of these "irrational" or rather "pre-rational" factors, some conclude that in most situations the intellectual justification of the faith is of little use. This need not be the conclusion because even if the influence of such motifs goes unnoticed, it does not deterministically influence the manner in which people think and act. This is true because of three factors which show that, although strongly influenced by inner drives, human beings are nevertheless not entirely determined by them – as a deterministic psychology would have us believe.

The first factor is that such inner drives are not self-explanatory and do not drive us into a predetermined direction. The way we experience them and the way we deal with them depends on the worldview or wider interpretative scheme through which we interpret them and which guide their effect. During a study leave that I spent as scholar-in-residence in Vancouver (Canada), I frequently met with another visiting scholar – a Buddhist from South Korea – engaging in an intense dialogue about our respective religious convictions. We shared a love of academic work and teaching, and we shared a number of deep basic experiences, yet we interpreted them entirely differently because of our different religious frameworks. Both of us deeply loved our wives. For me, true love is part of what is most valuable in life and reflects the love of God, which is the origin and purpose of human existence. For my Buddhist friend such love may have some limited value in the world of shadows in which we now live, but when we are enlightened it will be considered a mere appearance in the light of ultimate reality beyond personal love.

The second factor is that our drives are not monolithic and are not all on a single track. I may, for example, feel the need for collegiality, leading me to take the opinions of my colleagues seriously and be honest with them. At the same time I may have such a strong desire to be promoted that I bring myself to accept a distorted view of both myself and my colleagues, in order to justify such a promotion. Most human beings form a fragmented ensemble of contradicting drives, of which they can only gratify some while wittingly or unwittingly stultifying others. Even if some inner drives or emotional barriers may predispose people against the Christian faith, other, perhaps even deeper, drives and needs may draw them towards Christ or the Christian faith.

Apologetics and the will

A third reason why our desires and emotional needs do not have a direct and deterministic impact on the mind is that we need to reckon with the will. The need to make this distinction shows itself on a number of accounts. Most obviously, we ordinarily deal with each other and with ourselves as if all these drives and needs, while strong, are not completely determining our lives but can be affirmed, contained or steered in another direction. I see no reason to suppose that this is merely a manner of speech. It points to a certain distance we may take with regards of the forces that drive us in our lives. We may say: "I know you are craving a cup of coffee right now, but I really think we need to continue with this work for some time yet!" or "I know that you feel hurt by this proposal from your boss, but I think you need to look beyond that for a moment, since it seems your boss has a really valid point." Such language presupposes that the will can affirm and enforce, deny or redirect and mitigate these pre-voluntary dispositions.

The biblical call to conversion also supposes that people can distance themselves in a certain way from their desires that they are not entirely subject to the powers that push and pull them, but that they are responsible for what they do with them. Even if "at one time we too were foolish, disobedient, deceived and enslaved by all kinds of passions and pleasures" (Tit 3:3), "the grace of God […] teaches us to say 'No' to ungodliness and worldly passions, and to live self-controlled, upright and godly lives in this present age" (Tit 2:11f).

There is another reason for distinguishing the role of the will and of pre-rational and involuntary motifs in our analysis of their role in apologetic dialogue. We need to counterbalance what we just noted concerning the fragmentation of the different predispositions that push and pull us in our lives in different and often contradictory directions. The Christian faith understands this fragmentation of our lives – so deeply experienced in the postmodern era – as a consequence of the loss of the centring of our lives on God (cf. §6.2). Yet, this fragmentation of our lives is not the only side of our experience of ourselves and in others. We also experience some sort of unity, for we do not experience the direction we take to be just the causal effect of the tipping over of the balance of our fragmented needs in one direction or another. We actually opt for some needs we feel over others and sometimes over pressures we immediately and urgently felt because of long-term goals we set for ourselves.[2] In the same way, the Scripture also considers sinners to be still governed by a basic unity originating from the heart that gives life a relative coherence (Mt 6:21; cf. Brunner 1941: 229f; trans. 1939: 228f.). It is true that many people waver between different desires and this may even be a phenomenon more characteristic of our postmodern time and culture than of any other (cf. §1.2 & §2.4). Yet the fragmentation of desires does not exclude the possibility that people, particularly those we call strong-willed, can be very focused, choosing a path in life that involves the control of many such forces. The biblical call to repentance presupposes such a basic unified centre in the midst of the fragments of our life, for such a call is directed to persons and not to a loose conglomerate of desires. Repentance is the prerogative of persons with a relatively unified will. Desires may be redirected, but desires do not repent.

The final reason why we need to distinguish between the role of the will and pre-voluntary dispositions is that we can sometimes meet people who would want to believe in Christ, but feel unable to because of all sorts of emotional bonds and scars. Their cry is: "If only I could believe" (cf. Rietkerk 1993; trans. 1997). Here the relationship seems to be the reverse of the way in which, ideally, our will guides the way we respond to and direct our desires. Yet it equally points to the need for distinguishing between the will and the different pre-voluntary forces that drive us. Even this cry implicitly recognizes the need for liberating the person from such inhibiting forces so that they can freely believe what they want to believe because of its truth and goodness.[3]

---

2 For a philosophical analysis of why an understanding of the human being needs to respect both its fragmentary nature and the existence of some unifying centre, see: Rorty 1988.

3 The need to distinguish between the role of involuntary predispositions and the role of the will in the formation of beliefs reveals a limitation of Plantinga's analysis of the cognitive influence of sin and, in the wake of this, points to a more general problem of his warrant-epistemology. Plantinga conflates both under the heading of the "affections", a term he borrows from Jonathan Edwards (f. ex. 2000: 292, 309.) The fact that he does not distinguish between the role of involuntary emotional predispositions and the will reflects his more general thesis that we have no significant control over the beliefs that are imprinted on our mind (1988: 37; cf. on the involuntary character of our beliefs as a general characteristic of the thought of those associated with Reformed epistemology: Zagzebski 1993: 201–205).

Plantinga rightly asserts that our knowledge is dependent on crucial factors, which are external to the mind and over which we have no control. We have only a very limited control over the proper functioning of our epistemological faculties and over qualities of the environment on which we depend, such as the trustworthiness of witnesses whose testimonies we accept. Knowledge is only

In terms of the theological anthropology developed earlier, this is a consequence of the fact that the human being is not simply passive towards the influences of creation and not just determined by his community. Unlike what we know of animals, he is not only perceiving but also thinking; he is not only desiring but also willing (Barth KD III/2: 487ff; trans. *CD* III/2: 406ff). Barth shows how this characteristic is grounded in the way God created us in order to respond to Him (*KD* III/2: 498; trans. *CD* III/2: 415):

> God elects man in order that he may elect him in return, and therefore on the presupposition that man is capable of this election, not only of desiring [...], but also of willing [...], in which he takes up a positive and negative position to his desiring, "pulling himself together".

He has his proper responsibility before God and before his fellow human beings.

Considering that the noetic influence of sin is a consequence of original sin, we should ask if we can really suppose that people have such latitude for distancing themselves from their desires – sinful and otherwise. Does the doctrine of the total corruption of fallen humanity mean that people have no such latitude unless the Spirit liberates their will, bends their desires and enlightens their minds – that is, unless the Spirit regenerates the whole person? For the purpose of this book, it is possible to leave open the larger theological question about the nature of the bondage of the will. We can restrict ourselves to a far more limited question: If Christians believe that the unregenerate person is utterly dependent on a supernatural work of the Spirit to regenerate his will, before he can hear the Gospel for what it is, does this imply that it does not make sense to appeal to his will and mind?

For in all we know of the examples in Scripture and in the contemporary life of the Church, God does not just instantly change people in order to open up their lives and hearts for the Gospel; He often changes them more gradually, and the latter may be the more common procedure. The fact that God addresses sinful people with the Gospel and calls them to conversion shows that He addresses

---

possible when we can trust the design of creation at large and the crucial testimonies on which we depend. Yet, Plantinga overstates his case when he says that we have no control whatsoever over our beliefs. This may be one of the factors behind the low expectations he has of the possibility to give a defence of the faith to those who are not already believers. We have significant influence, for example, with regards to the question where we look to form our beliefs and what we find is not worth looking into (Helm 1994: 28ff). Furthermore, we have a certain influence with regards to the question of whether we really want to be open to reality or to certain aspects of reality as it presents itself to us, or not. We have a certain choice of whether we really want to be open to certain voices that come to us, or whether we close ourselves off in irrational distrust or because we simply do not want to hear. We also have a certain influence with regards to the belief policies we choose, that is, the policies we use to order, evaluate and interpret the phenomena that present themselves to us and the convictions that are communicated to us by others (pp. 83f).

them as responsible people, and the apologetic character of this proclamation furthermore underscores the way He addresses them as such (cf. §1.3). We may therefore equally address our audience as responsible people asking them not to give themselves over wilfully to the forces that drive or block them but to repent and redirect their wills and minds to God. We address them as a responsible and attentive audience knowing that God may be at work in their lives by his Spirit to bend their will, mind and desires towards Himself and that He may be using our apologetic witness as part of his history with these people.

The role of the will in the way people form their beliefs in general and particularly their beliefs about God and about themselves has important consequences for the nature of apologetic dialogue. Apologetic witness cannot limit itself to the presentation of information and arguments, believing that the audience will automatically process this. Part of the dialogue will need to be a call to open oneself to God and to reality as it is – an openness the apologist will need to model herself. Apologetic dialogue will need to include a call to deal critically with the predispositions that pull us in certain directions. Being human implies we are called to opt for those desires that pull us in the direction of what is true and good instead of choosing – or simply letting oneself be carried along by – those desires that lead us away from truth and goodness. Part of apologetic dialogue will thus be a call to conversion and repentance (cf. Barr 1980; Hicks 1998: 171ff; Guinness 1981: 329). We need to be conscious of the fact that people may even resort to raising all sorts of intellectual problems as an escape route for avoiding the Gospel, its offer of salvation and its call to repentance.[4] The apologist will need to model herself that her gaining knowledge is an inherently moral affair and that acquiring knowledge requires a development of "the virtues of the mind" – and of fighting its vices.[5]

A critical consideration of presuppositionalist apologetics

In the context of our analysis, the role of the will in apologetic dialogue, a consideration of the role of the will according to presuppositional apologetics as developed by Cornelius Van Til and his followers, is definitely in place.[6] Drawing on a combination of Calvinist Christian anthropology and

4 As such Barth speaks about the raising of certain epistemological objections as a flight for the reality of Christ: *KD* IV/1: 321f; *CD* IV/1: 292.

5 Developing the virtues of the mind goes beyond the more common notion of "epistemic duty". We are not simply to avoid the violation of epistemic duties, but we positively need to search for truth (Zagzebski 1993: 214f). Cf. for an application of this idea with regards to the proclamation of the Gospel: Vanhoozer 1999: 131, 136f.

6 Most important is Cornelius Van Til, *The Defense of the Faith* (1967); for a sympathetic introduction in Van Til's presuppositionalism, see: Frame 1995.

neo-Hegelian epistemology, Van Til has majored on the role of presuppositions in all human thinking. The main presupposition to be considered originates from our relationship to God. Human beings either reason as a covenant-partners of God, accepting his sovereignty in creation and redemption or as a covenant-breakers, placing themselves in an autonomous position independent of God. One of these two basic presuppositions determines all human thinking. Drawing on an image from Calvin, he says that these presuppositions are like lenses that determine all that we see, for "these colored glasses are cemented to his face" (1967: 201).

> Reason is not the autonomous arbiter of truth, but the servant of the heart, believing or not. […] Reasoning is an activity of a religious orientated heart, whether undertaken as a covenant-keeper or as a covenant-breaker. (Van Til 1971: 366f)

The sinner can never lay this aside unless the Holy Spirit regenerates him supernaturally, placing him in a new relationship with God.

On the basis of this theological analysis he concluded that there is no common ground whatsoever between the believer and the unbeliever on which the apologist can build. What was supposed to be common ground was only apparently so, not realizing the impact of the basic presuppositions. When building on them, the apologist only reinforces unbelievers in their belief that they have a right and a reason to build their life on this foundation independent from God. According to Van Til, the only valid apologetic approach is to address directly the question of presuppositions, and developing a presuppositional argument that it is only on the basis of a Christian starting-point and understanding of reality that proper knowledge and a coherent worldview is possible (1967: 99–102, 114–122, *passim*).

Van Til has provided an important corrective of evidentialist and rationalist apologetics, pointing to the role of worldview and basic presuppositions and to the role of non-rational pre-dispositions and the will, showing the need for regeneration and conversion. Yet his position seems to be a typical example of one that draws on an important theological truth without balancing it adequately by placing it within a larger theological framework. Thereby he simultaneously estranges himself from the reality in which we live. The estrangement from reality becomes clear in the difficulty he had in working out its practical implications. In real life, we always suppose some common ground – or "common true belief" to avoid the foundationalist metaphor – with non-Christians. Even Van Til himself appeals to such truths recognized by his intended audience, when developing his presuppositional argument. After all, the argument that an adequate worldview and true knowledge are only possible on the basis of biblical presuppositions presupposes that non-Christians can: (1) follow this argument; and (2) share the desire for an adequate worldview and for true knowledge (Lewis 1976: 146f).

Van Til rightly defends this move on the basis of the doctrine of "common grace"[7] – although the doctrine of "common creation" would also suffice. Yet, in the process he becomes entangled in a second inconsistency. The doctrine of common grace plays a significant role in Van Til's theology of culture. It explains why non-Christian life and culture do not fall in complete disarray notwithstanding their basic attitude to God and their basic presupposition that should lead to irrationality. God's common grace, God's grace extended to all people, withholds sinners from living out their rejection of God with all its consequences. It helps them recognize the truths they know because of their metaphysical and psychological make-up as God's creatures, notwithstanding their sinful efforts to suppress these truths (1967: 169–175). However, we must ask why the many true beliefs that Christians and non-Christians share because of the influence of common grace cannot be used as a starting point for apologetic dialogue (Lewis 1976: 148).

The reason why Van Til could not do justice to the never fully suppressible truth in the life of the unbeliever was due to the second major influence in his thinking – that is, the pervasive idealism, which he inherited from Immanuel Kant and Georg Wilhelm Friedrich Hegel through the neo-Hegelians Francis Herbert Bradley (1846–1924) and Bernard Bosanquet (1848–1923) (Van Til 1967: 115ff). The main characteristic of idealist thought is the belief in the priority of mind over the reality we know, be it of the individual mind of the knowing subject (as in Kant) or of the absolute Spirit (as in Hegel). The idea that our basic presuppositions determine all our thinking reflects the Kantian idea that the world as it is in itself can only appear to us as it fits in the grids of our (sinful) minds through which we perceive it. Yet, from a theological perspective, this priority of the mind over reality maybe attributed to God – as did Hegel – but not to finite human beings. We simply cannot fit reality into the grid that we bring to it. We are part of creation and the rest of creation has a sturdy independence, which makes it impossible to model it entirely according to our own presuppositions (§4.2). We may try to do this and in our desire for autonomy and our self-aggrandizement we may think we can do so, but from a Christian understanding of the human being this effort should be considered presumptuous and a product of self-deceit. We saw that the reality of the way we gain knowledge actually reflects and confirms this anthropology (§5.1).

A more modest and Christian understanding of the human being can thereby explain what in Van Til's analysis remains insoluble. It explains that sinful beings will indeed try to mould reality in accordance with basic predisposition and presuppositions of reality. Yet it explains at the same time why they can never succeed in this project and why vestiges of truth and reality always shine through

7 The doctrine of common grace has been developed in neo-Calvinistic theology. By "saving grace" God's saves sinners from damnation; by "common grace" God upholds the creation, which left to itself would otherwise disintegrate entirely. This doctrine receives much attention in various writings of Van Til (f. ex. 1967: 165ff).

even in thought-systems and worldviews based on non-Christian or anti-Christian presuppositions. It is towards these vestiges of truth that the apologist can build bridges. The inner tensions in such necessarily incoherent approaches to reality furthermore underscore the invitation to consider how all these partial glimpses of reality find their true home and appear in a clearer light when reoriented around Christ (cf. §7.4). If the Christian apologist does extend such an invitation, she should always take into account the most significant contribution of Van Til. We can only fully see what these partial truths imply when we stop reasoning like covenant-breakers and let our wills and minds be redirected and reconciled by the Holy Spirit to our Creator.

Van Til saw an enormous divide between his position and the theology of Karl Barth, particularly with regarding their respective conceptions of revelation and Scripture (1946; 1962). Yet a close reading reveals that, notwithstanding the great differences between them in style and content, both criticize modern apologetics for similar reasons based on an understanding of sin, grace and the sovereignty of God. In their criticism of the possibility of finding common ground between believers and unbelievers, both demonstrate being strongly influenced by idealist epistemologies. Like Van Til, Barth could not see it as being unrealistic and unhelpful to divide knowledge neatly between that which originates from God, and from reality and beliefs that originate completely from the subjectivity of the knowing subject (§3.4). Yet, when we are finite creatures we are living in constant interaction with the rest of creation, and our beliefs will always be a mixture of the reality we encounter and the cultural grid through which we perceive this reality. Because each false construction of reality is parasitic on the reality that it misrepresents, the apologist will always find traces of truth and goodness both in the beliefs and in the dispositions he encounters in others. These can function validly as a starting point for dialogue.

Some later presuppositionalists have realized that our presuppositions do not tightly determine everything we believe. While stressing the importance of revealing the role of presuppositions, John M. Frame, for example, leaves more room than Van Til for the use of evidence (Frame 2000: 220f n. 18). This reflects a wider tendency in evangelical apologetics as noted by Don Carson for the different positions such as evidentialism, classical apologetics, worldview apologetics and presuppositionalism to move closer together (Carson 1996: 184–188).[8] This overture is definitively justified by the limitations of the extremes and the partial truths that all these positions express. It is my hope that this book provides us with the theological basis for understanding why these different positions are limited. As such it also supplies a theologically sound and culturally sensitive alternative that indeed integrates these partial truths within a larger perspective on and deeper understanding of the nature of apologetic dialogue and witness.

8 This mutual rapprochement of positions can also be seen in the different contributions to: Cowan (ed.) 2000.

8.2 THE CROSS OF CHRIST AND THE CHARACTER OF THE APOLOGIST

The character and attitude of the apologist

The possibility of taking them into account presupposes that we are not only aware that such predispositions exist but also that we seriously inquire into what they are. This again forces us to confront the need for careful listening as an essential element of all valid apologetic dialogue. We already underlined the need of careful listening in order to understand the *presuppositions* related to the worldview and wider cultural–linguistic framework of our dialogue partner. Now we must stress that we need to listen equally carefully to understand our dialogue partner's *predispositions*. The problem with understanding and getting to know the more basic worldview presuppositions is that they are often taken for granted to such a degree that they exert their influence on a partly or largely subconscious level. The main problem with the predispositions is not so much that they are subconscious – though they may be – but rather that they are very sensitive and therefore people may not readily share them. They may be related to our hurts, our dearest ideals or to our secret wishes – all areas in which we can be easily hurt by others and of which we tend to be protective. This points to the importance of the personality of the apologist, which may invite the type of dialogue in which such predispositions can be touched upon but which can equally be the principal hindrance.

The effectiveness of any communication depends a great deal on the personality of the communicator. As Aristotle noted in his *Rhetoric* (1356[a]):

> Persuasion is achieved by the speaker's personal character when the speech is so spoken as to make us think him credible. [...] his character may almost be called the most effective means of persuasion he possesses.

Aristotle's point has been confirmed by modern research in processes of communication (cf. Clark 1993a: 234). In the postmodern world the personality of the apologist is all the more important because of the widespread distrust of all attempts at persuasion as a simple pursuit of one's own agenda and as a reflection of some hidden power game. Only the personality and attitude of the apologist can reduce such mistrust. Her dialogue partners will also only be able to understand her witness and the reality to which it points if they are in an appropriate mindset, and they will need to have seen that mindset in others and, first of all, in those who share the Christian faith.[9]

---

9 Cf. the role of the virtue of *phronesis* in knowing, a virtue which according to Zagzebski (1993: 215f) can only be learned from others.

However, the interest here in the character of the apologist, is not primarily motivated out of a desire for effectiveness; rather it is the desire that the attitude of the apologist is worthy of the message and the God to whom she bears witness. If our attitude towards reality has a principal role in our understanding of reality in general and particularly in our understanding of God, the apologist should reflect the appropriate attitude to truth. An appropriate attitude therefore is not first of all called for because of the nature of communication, but because of the nature of knowledge and particularly knowledge of God. We are not primarily dealing with the effectiveness but with the ethics of apologetic dialogue, trusting that the appropriateness of our attitude will also contribute to effective communication. I propose to call the characteristics needed the virtues of the apologists, in line with the resurgent interest for virtues in Christian ethics.

First of all, the apologist will need to love God and the truth above anything else (cf. Lindsley 2008). This is not just a necessary corollary of a proper knowledge of God; it also reduces likely mistrust that she is only pushing her own agenda out of hidden self-interest. The methods of communication used should also reflect this love for God and the truth and the desire not to press our personal viewpoint on those who hear us. This is particularly important in our postmodern era in which, as Craig Loscalzo remarks, people "view the church's preaching as a marketing strategy to maintain the institution" (2000: 24). All persuasive power should be used to point to the truth; rhetoric means are abused when they actually cover up the truth (cf. Augustine, *De Doctrina Christiana*: II, 36, 54). The apologist should use rhetoric only insofar as it will not hinder but rather accentuate that her message does not rest on human persuasive power, but on God's (cf. 1Co 2:1-5). Her language should point beyond herself to a reality and a truth, which Christians master as little as others do. The need to show this love for God above anything else has a particular importance in a postmodern context, which is characterized by apathy and ironic indifference. In a time when many doubt if there can be anything worth committing one's life to, the Christian community needs to model God's love and commitment to her and the commitment she gladly gives Him in return. This commitment should not be fanatical or despairing; rather, it should be a grateful response to what God did for us, showing that this is not only worth staking a claim, but staking oneself on it.[10]

Second, the apologist should show a genuine love for those with whom she dialogues. This demand is laid on the apologist as part of the general ethical principle to love others as ourselves, but has a specific importance in apologetic dialogue. All too easily apologetic dialogues tend to revolve around the question of who is right. That automatically places dialogue partners in a win-lose situation. None of us wants to lose and such a scenario automatically forces both partners to become defensive. This is confirmed by a number of studies concerning

10 Vanhoozer argues that this is part of the epistemology of the cross and the testimony of the martyr characteristic of Christian proclamation (1999: 139).

negotiation processes in business, which show that negotiations are most likely to be effective when the issues can be formulated in a win-win formula in which both parties can gain (cf. Fisher & Chry 1984; Covey 1989: 204–234). This love for our dialogue partners also implies a genuine respect in accordance with the biblical command to give an account of our hope "with gentleness and respect" (1Pe 3:15) and "always full of grace" (Col 4:6). The possible effects of such an attitude become clear in a moving testimony of Klaus Klostermaier (1969: 98f. cited in Anderson 1984: 192):

> I wanted to see a famous man in Benares, a sagacious [Hindu] philosopher, feared by many as a merciless critic of Christian theology. I had my own reasons for paying him a visit. He was polite, invited me for tea and then mounted the attack. I let him talk his fill, without saying a word myself. Than I started to talk about the things I had begun to understand within the dialogue – quite positively Christian. We got into a sincere, good, deep discussion. He had intended to send me away after ten minutes. When I left after two hours he had tears in his eyes …

Such respect implies an unwillingness to exploit their needs and weaknesses along with a positive desire to build on their strengths (cf. Netland 2001: 282f). It implies an empathic listening that will encourage others to share both their deepest convictions and their doubts, what they believe to have found and what they are still seeking (Brent & Chismar 1984). Christians need to remain honest about the Christian conviction that people need to give up some of what is most dear to them when they embrace the Gospel. Yet they believe that, in doing so, their dialogue partners gain much more than they lose and find an answer to the much more fundamental quest of their lives. Christians can, therefore, confidently proclaim the Gospel as "Good News" hoping they will surrender what they need to "in their joy" over what they have found (cf. Mt 13:44).

Third, apologists should be persons of integrity. They owe this to God and the Gospel, but it is also a prerequisite if they want their hearers to seriously consider their apologetic witness. It is equally important because proper dialogue demands that the non-Christian dialogue partners be honest about their convictions and predispositions. This is only possible when the apologist herself models such an attitude. This reflects the attitude of the apostle Paul who says to the Thessalonians: "The appeal we make does not spring from impure motives, nor are we trying to trick you […] we never used flattery, nor did we put on a mask to cover up greed […]. We are not looking for praise from men, not from you or anyone else." (1Th 2:3-6). This requires that Christians begin by learning to be honest with themselves, about their own questions as well as about their own convictions. In a time when words and slogans are often so devoid of meaning, Christian apologists need to model an honest dialogue in which they share both their convictions and their doubts. Such a dialogue will be more powerful than joining in the game of putting on ever-changing roles and masks which mean so little that they are dropped as easily as they are put on.

Fourth, a Christian apologist needs to grow in humility. In the Christian tradition, humility has always been considered a major virtue and is particularly appropriate in apologetic dialogue and witness, for it is a direct consequence of the fact that the Gospel is as much a gift to us as it needs to be to others. In themselves, Christians are no less lost, no less sinners and no less unbelievers than those with whom they share the Gospel (cf. Barth *KD* II/1: 105; trans. *CD* II/1: 95f). When they point others to the Gospel, they do so – with a well-known image from Martin Luther – as beggars who tell other beggars where to find food. This humility will open up the way for their dialogue partners to respond in humility to the Gospel and to overcome the barrier of autonomous self-assertion, which we have shown to be a dominant force behind both the modern and the postmodern rejection of the faith. This humility is furthermore urgent as a rejoinder of the persistent postmodern criticism that in a multicultural world every claim to a universal truth, particularly to a universal religious truth, is sheer arrogance. For Christians this universal truth is not something they arrogantly claim to have discovered, but something they humbly accept as a gift of unmerited grace. Humility is also required because the Gospel remains beyond the grasp of the believers and many aspects greatly surpass their understanding. This is a consequence of the personal limitations of the apologist but unavoidably also of their necessarily limited grasp of the truth in this dispensation. "Now we see but a poor reflection as in a mirror; then we shall see face to face. Now I know in part; then I shall know fully, even as I am fully known" (1Co 13:12). Finally, humility is a prerequisite of a healthy and realistic apologetic witness, because we realize that it is not in our power to convert those we encounter. We simply have to present the Gospel as clearly as we can, realizing that the Gospel will sometimes be rejected, even if it is well understood (cf. Mt 19:22; Jn 6:66; cf. McGrath 1992: 76–91). Yet this impossibility in no way disqualifies the need for and possibility of apologetics; rather, it shows its proper place. As William Lane Craig rightly remarks (Craig 1984: 26f.; cf. Stackhouse 2002: 227–232):

> Many times a person will say, "That argument was not effective because the unbeliever I shared it with was not convinced." Here we have to be very careful. [...] effectiveness in apologetics is presenting cogent and persuasive arguments for the gospel in the power of the Holy Spirit, and leaving the results to God.

Yet, in our postmodern world humility can be easily mistaken, if it is not balanced by courage, or to use a more biblical expression "boldness" (Ac 4:31; 9:28, etc.). Christians should boldly testify to their belief in Christ as "public truth" (Vanhoozer 1999: 150; cf. Newbigin 1991). They know after all that it isn't for themselves they speak but out of the commission they have received from their

Lord. They know that within a world where many gospels are proclaimed, there is "no other name under heaven given to men by which we must be saved" (Ac 4:12). They know that they have not followed "cleverly devised myths" (2Pe 1:16), but that they have believed on the authority of trustworthy witnesses testifying to the acts of God in history on their behalf. Christian civility therefore needs to be a *convicted* civility (cf. Mouw 1992: 12, *passim*; Lamb 1997). Such conviction and boldness is particularly needed in the face of fierce anti-Christian apologetics, such as in the Muslim world or in the face of ridicule. In the same way, conviction is needed to speak about the Christian faith as God's message of salvation to all human beings when this happens in a world in which such language is considered arrogant and intolerant. Christian proclamation cannot only be distorted by the sin of pride, which needs to be corrected by developing the virtue of humility, but also by the sin of sloth, which demands that the apologist develops the virtue of courage and boldness (cf. Vanhoozer 1999: 149f).[11]

The importance of a combination of courage and humility for effective communication has also been recognized in secular circles.[12] Yet it is very hard to see how both can be effectively balanced, except in people of great maturity. If we try to grapple for courage, we had better forget those things that give us reason to be humble and, as we concentrate on what gives us reason to be humble, it becomes hard to take courage. The Christian apologist, however, should not seek reasons to be either humble or courageous in herself. Only if Christians concentrate on the message of the Gospel and the reality of God's revelation in Jesus Christ are they simultaneously humbled and empowered. They are humbled, because none of it rests on their strength or their cleverness. They are at the same time empowered precisely because they no longer depend on their own strength and cleverness. They step into a community and tradition of reflection initiated by God's gracious self-revelation and guided by His Spirit, who is the source of their boldness (cf. Ac 4:31).

The power of the cross

It should be clear by now that the apologetic challenge of proclaiming the Christian faith as public truth in a multicultural world can never be dealt with solely at the formal level by developing a new epistemology and new forms of argumentation. The answer to the challenge is bound up both with the *content* of the message and with the personal character of the witness. Of these two, the content of the message is prior and the attitude of the witness should reflect this message. This becomes particularly clear when we look to the cross of Christ

11 See on humility and courage in preaching in general: Stott 1982: 299–337.

12 Covey (1989: 217–219) talks about courage and "consideration", which is weaker than humility but in an important sense tends in the same direction.

at the centre of the Christian message that should reflect itself in a cruciform Christian witness. This aspect needs to be stressed as both a deepening and an underpinning of the argument that Christian apologetics needs to be done with both humility and courage. Stressing the cruciform character of the Christian faith is particularly important in response to the postmodern and postcolonial criticism that each claim to a universal truth and a metanarrative is necessarily totalitarian and oppressive (cf. §1.2). This criticism is based on a systematic and an historic observation. Systematically this conclusion is drawn on the basis that all particular perspectives originate from limited human beings representing particular interests. Therefore, they can never be genuinely universal in scope. Historically it is based on the discovery of how all communities guided by metanarratives have a tendency to refer to others as outsiders, heretics and infidels, and oppress them accordingly (cf. Middleton & Walsh 1995b: 70f). It is therefore claimed that in our global village and in our increasingly multicultural societies, Christians will need to abstain from every claim to the possession of such a metanarrative. This is claimed to be the only way of respecting real diversity and avoiding the oppression of minorities.

Though postmodernism has validly criticized a number of serious problems of modernity, Christians cannot accept this rejection of the possibility of a valid metanarrative. It is a central conviction that the Christian narrative is, in fact, a metanarrative that encompasses the whole of reality (Grenz 1996: 163ff; Middleton & Walsh 1995b: 75ff, 87ff; Bauckham 2003: 90–94). This conviction is given with the central confession that in the history of Israel and in Christ humankind meets the Creator of the whole universe and all people, and that Christ is equally sent to reconcile and renew the whole of creation (cf. Col 1:15-20). The apologetic response to the reproach that every metanarrative is necessarily totalitarian and oppressive consists of two elements: one negative and one positive.

Negatively, Christian apologetic witness needs to criticize the belief that we can do without a metanarrative. It needs to show that, finally, it will be impossible to fight oppression and coercion from faulty metanarratives when no alternative can be provided. Local narratives are equally prone to being taken hostage by the particular interests of those in power (Middleton & Walsh 1995b: 75). If there is no alternative, the strongest community will have its say and there will be no ground from whence to fight their destructive influence (cf. p. 77). The main reason why oppressive power systems try to manipulate the concept of truth may be an implicit recognition that it is only by truth that they can be undermined. In their own way postmodernism (pp. 76f) and the ideology of multiculturalism (Gunton 1997: 162ff) have also become metanarratives with their own overarching values and beliefs and with their own totalizing tendencies towards minorities that do not fit their framework. The question, therefore, is not whether we need a metanarrative; rather, it is whether there is one on offer that can validly claim to have a grasp of reality beyond our finite human perspectives and which has sufficient resources to fight the totalitarian tendencies that are inherent in all human efforts to formulate metanarratives.

Positively, Christian apologists need to explain why they believe that the Christian metanarrative provides such resources. The conviction that Christ draws us into a reality beyond limited human perspectives is implied in the belief that in Him we meet the Creator of the universe and the eschatological revelation of His universal salvific plans. It is precisely the belief that here we meet the Creator of the universe which opens up the possibility of an appeal for the marginalized, the weak and the oppressed beyond the powers that reign in our human society (Middleton & Walsh 1995a: 142, 145–151). Furthermore, Christians believe that the Lord of the universe was among us in the Christ who was crucified by the totalitarian powers that He defied. The Christian faith is not simply a message that claims to be of universal significance, it is also an inherently antitotalizing message, precisely because it recognizes these totalitarian forces and because it centres on Christ crucified, who defies all human powers (Middleton & Walsh 1995b: 102–107; Newbigin 1989: 159; Vanhoozer 1999: 138; Bauckham 2003: 103–109).[13]

The history of the relationships of Christians with minorities within Christian societies and with those from other cultures in missions has indeed often been oppressive. Even interreligious apologetics can easily deteriorate into a power struggle (Netland 2001: 282f). Christians themselves constantly need to remember that their witness to those who do not share the belief in Jesus should always be cruciform (cf. Bosch 1991b). Living out this antitotalizing force is greatly helped when they realize that this message centres first of all on a person, Jesus, and only secondarily engenders a worldview (cf. §6.1). Indeed, the way in which Christians formulate their worldview will always be limited by a finite historical perspective. This has often meant that in the history of missions a form of Christianity was forced on new Christians or minority Christian groups that hindered their flourishing as human beings in Christ. In dealing with Christians from other cultures and in proclaiming Christ to other cultures, Western Christians need to remember that from their particular cultural perspective they cannot know beforehand in detail, what following Christ will mean for those they meet. In the end they themselves have to discover what it means to them to reorder their whole lives and worldviews around Christ.

It is appropriate that we end this study on the character of a properly Christian apologetic witness with a reflection on the cross. It is the cross – or rather the crucified and risen Christ – that stands at the centre of the Christian story. The revelation of God in the crucified and risen Christ challenges the basic tenets of modernity and of a Christian apologetics modelled on a modern grid. It invites us to develop an apologetics that begins with a very particular event witnessed

---

13 This also needs to be worked out in specific practices for the pursuit of truth. For an example from an Anabaptist perspective, see: Murphy 1999: 116–118.

in a particular community instead of an apologetics that starts from an allegedly universal rationality and an allegedly universally accessible common ground. It defies the modern conception that the deepest truth about who we are and where we belong can be discovered from a neutral standpoint, for it exposes our enmity with God and our idols, it calls us to conversion and it engages us from the very start. This witness to the crucified and risen Christ should be at the centre of our Christian apologetic in our multicultural world.

If we want to counter the claim that all reasoning is relativized by its being imbedded in history and culture, and by its being driven by particular interests and biases, no purely formal answer will do. We examined the possibility that we are surprised by a reality that breaks through our preconceived conceptual frameworks and that shows possession of an integrity of its own. Yet how do we know if there really is such a reality, and that we are not simply confronted with a void and chaos that, according to so many worldviews, is the background in which our tiny island of structured reality floats? How do we know if there really is a unity underneath the fragmentation of our culturally constructed selves? Even if we know that cross-cultural communication is possible, how do we know that there is a message worth communicating that has a meaning for those whom we encounter? How do we know whether our sinful biases can really be challenged and overcome? These questions can only find their answers in reference to Jesus Christ.

On the basis of a general understanding of the nature of most religious beliefs it may be possible to argue for the moral obligation to set forth an interreligious and cross-cultural apologetic. How can you assert that you have privileged knowledge about the indictment and possible salvation of all human beings and not be urged to share this knowledge with those who remain ignorant (cf. §1.3)? Yet, by itself this does not show that there is such a message that is worth communicating cross-culturally. As a Christian I believe that it is the knowledge of the crucified and risen Christ that gives us knowledge of ourselves and of God that all should hear. He motivates us to look for a contextual apologetic witness that can cross cultural boundaries, and He gives us the hope that such a cross-cultural apologetic dialogue is indeed possible.

BIBLIOGRAPHY

Achtemeier, P. Mark, 1994. The Truth of a Tradition: Critical Realism in the Thought of Alasdair MacIntyre & T.F. Torrance. *Scottish Journal of Theology*, 47, pp. 355–374.

Adeney, Bernard T., 1995. *Strange Virtues: Ethics in a Multicultural World*. Downer's Grove: IVP.

Allen, Diogenes, 1989. *Christian Belief in a Postmodern World: The Full Wealth of Conviction*. Louisville: Westminster/John Knox.

Anderson, Bernhard, 1977. The Babel Story: Paradigm of Human Unity and Diversity. *Concilium* 121 (1), pp. 63–70.

Anderson, J.N.D., 1984. *Christianity and World Religions: The Challenge of Pluralism*. Leicester: IVP.

Anselm, 1962. *Proslogion*. In: Saint Anselm, *Basic Writings: Proslogion, Monologion, Gaulino's In Behalf of the Fool*. La Salle, IL: Open Court.

Aristotle, 1952. *Rhetoric*, translated by W. Rhys Roberts. In: Robert Maynard Hutchins ed., *Great Books of the Western World*, vol. 9: *Aristotle*. vol. II. Chicago, London, e.a.: Encyclopædia Britannica, pp. 593–675.

Augustine, 1912. *Confessiones*. Trans. *St. Augustine's Confessions*, with an English translation by William Watts, vol. 1, Loeb Classical Library. London: Heinemann.

Augustine, 1953. *Epistula* CXX. Trans. "Letter 120", in: Augustine, *Letters*, vol. II (83–130), translated by Wilfrid Parsons, Series: "The Fathers of the Church: A New Translation", vol. 18. Washington D.C.: The Catholic University of America Press, pp. 300–317.

Augustine, 1996. *De Doctrina Christiana*. Trans. *Teaching Christianity: De Doctrina Christiana* I/II, introduction, translation and notes Edmund Hill, series: The Works of Saint Augustine: A Translation for the 21st Century. New York: New York City Press.

Augustine, 1998. *De Civitate Dei*. Trans. *The City of God against the Pagans*, edited and translated by R.W. Dyson, Series: Cambridge Texts in the History of Political Thought. Cambridge: Cambridge University Press.

Augustinus, Aurelius, 1956. *Ennarationes in Psalmos I-L, Corpus Christianorum*, Series Latina XXXVIII. Turnhout: Brepols.

Austin, J.L., 1962. *How to Do Things with Words*. Cambridge. MA: Harvard University Press.

Avis, Paul, 1995. *Faith in the Fires of Criticism: Christianity in Modern Thought*. London: Darton, Longman & Todd.

Bambrough, Renford, 1990. Fools and Heretics. In: A. Phillips Griffiths ed., *Wittgenstein Centenary Essays*. Cambridge e.a.: Cambridge University Press, pp. 239–250.

Bauckham, Richard, 2003. *Bible and Mission: Christian Witness in a Postmodern World*. Carlisle: Paternoster/Grand Rapids: Baker.

Barr, James, 1961. *The Semantics of Biblical Language*. Oxford: Oxford University Press.

Barr, John, 1980. Conversion and Penitence. In: Thomas F. Torrance ed., *Belief in Science and Christian Life: The Relevance of Michael Polanyi's Thought for Christian Faith and Life*. Edinburgh: The Handsel Press, pp. 49–70.

Barth, Karl, 1924. Die Neue Welt in der Bibel. In: Karl Barth, *Das Wort Gottes und die Theologie*. München: Kaiser, pp. 18–32.

Barth, Karl, 1932–1967. *Die kirchliche Dogmatik*, 4 Bände. München: Chr. Kaiser Verlag; Zollikon/Zürich: Evangelischer Verlag.

Barth, Karl, 1934. *Nein! Antwort an Emil Brunner*. München: Kaiser.

Barth, Karl, 1946. No! Answer to Emil Brunner. In: Karl Barth & Emil Brunner, *Natural Theology: Comprising "Nature and Grace" by Professor Dr. Emil Brunner and the Reply "No!" by Dr. Karl Barth*. London: Geoffrey Bless, pp. 65–128.

Barth, Karl, 1947. *Die Protestantische Theologie im 19. Jahrhunderd: Ihre Vorgeschichte und ihre Geschichte*. Zollikon/Zürich: Evangelischer Verlag.

Barth, Karl, 1956–1975. *Church Dogmatics*, 4 vols. Edinburgh: T & T Clark.

Barth, Karl, 1957a. *Evangelische Theologie im 19. Jahrhundert*, Theologische Studien 49. Zollikon/Zürich: Evangelischer Verlag.

Barth, Karl, 1957b. The Strange New World within the Bible. In: Karl Barth, *The Word of God and the World of Man*. New York: Harper & Brothers, pp. 28–50.

Barth, Karl, 1963. *Evangelical Theology: An Introduction*. New York: Holt, Rinehart & Winston.

Barth, Karl, 1970. *Einführung in die evangelische Theologie*. Zürich: Theologischer Verlag.

Barth, Karl, 1972. *Protestant Theology in the Nineteenth Century: It's Background and History*. London: SCM.

Bauckham, Richard, 2003. *Bible and Mission: Christian Witness in a Postmodern World*. Carlisle: Paternoster; Eerdmans: Baker.

Bavinck, J.H., 1960. *An Introduction to the Science of Missions*. Philadelphia: Presbyterian and Reformed Publishing Co.

Becker, Ernest, 1973. *The Denial of Death*. New York: Simon & Schuster.

Bediako, Kwame, 1992. *Theology and Identity: The Impact of Culture upon Christian Thought in the Second Century and Modern Africa*. Oxford: Regnum Books.

Bediako, Kwame, 1995. Translatability and Cultural Incarnations of the Faith. In: Kwame Bediako, *Christianity in Africa: The Renewal of a Non-Western Religion*. New York: Orbis, pp. 109–125.

Bediako, Kwame, 2000. *Jesus in Africa: The Christian Gospel in African History and Experience*. Yaoundé: Clé; Akropong-Akuapem: Regnum Africa.

Berger, Peter L., 1963. *Invitation to Sociology: A Humanistic Perspective*. Harmondsworth: Penguin Books.

Berger, Peter L., 1969. *A Rumor of Angels: Modern Society and the Rediscovery of the Supernatural*. Garden City: Doubleday.

Berger, Peter L., 1980. *The Heretical Imperative: Contemporary Possibilities of Religious Affirmation*. Garden City: Anchor.

Berger, Peter L., 1999. The Desecularization of the World: A Global Overview. In: Peter L. Berger ed., *The Desecularization of the World: Resurgent Religion and World Politics*. Grand Rapids: Eerdmans & Washington D.C.: Ethics and Public Policy Centre, pp. 1–18.

Berger, Peter L., 2002. Introduction: The Cultural Dynamics of Globalization. In: Peter L. Berger & Samuel P. Huntington eds, *Many Globalizations: Cultural Diversity in the Contemporary World*. Oxford, New York, e.a.: Oxford University Press, pp. 1–16.

Berger, Peter L., 2006. Religion in a Globalizing World. *The Pew Forum on Religion and Public Life*. http://pewforum.org/events/?EventID=136, consulted 18/04/2010.

Berger, Peter L. & Luckmann, Thomas, 1967. *The Social Construction of Reality: A Treatise in the Sociology of Knowledge*. Harmondsworth: Penguin.

Berkhof, Hendrikus, 1985. *Christelijk geloof: Een inleiding tot de geloofsleer*, Vijfde, herziene druk. Nijkerk: Callenbach.

Berkhof, Hendrikus, 1990. *Christian Faith: An Introduction to the Study of the Faith*, revised edition. Grand Rapids: Eerdmans.

Berkouwer, G.C., 1957, De mens als beeld Gods, Series: Dogmatische studieën. Kampen: Kok.

Berkouwer, G.C., 1962. *Man: The Image of God*, Series: Studies in Dogmatics. Grand Rapids: Eerdmans.

Berlo, David K., 1960. *The Process of Communication: An Introduction to Theory and Practice*. New York e.a.: Holt, Rinehart & Winston.

Bertens, Hans, 1995. *The Idea of the Postmodern: A History*. London, New York: Routledge.

Bevans, Stephen B. 2002. *Models of Contextual Theology*, revised and expanded edition. Maryknoll: Orbis.

Blocher, Henri, 1984. *In the Beginning: The Opening Chapters of Genesis*. Leicester: IVP/ Downers Grove: IVP.

Blumenberg, Hans, 1966. *Die Legitimität der Neuzeit*. Frankfurt am Main: Suhrkamp.

Blumenberg, Hans, 1983. *The Legitimacy of the Modern Age*. Cambridge, MA: MIT Press.

Bonhoeffer, Dietrich, 1951. *Widerstand und Ergebung: Briefe und Aufzeichnungen aus der Haft*, Herausgegeben von Eberhard Bethge. München: Kaiser.

Bonhoeffer, Dietrich, 1956. *Letters and Papers from Prison*, edited by Eberhard Bethge, translated by Reginald H. Fuller, second edition. London: SCM Press.

Bosch, David J., 1991a. *Transforming Mission: Paradigm Shifts in Theology of Mission*. Maryknoll: Orbis.

Bosch, David J., 1991b. *The Vulnerability of Mission*. Birmingham: Selly Oak Colleges.

Brent, John S. & Chismar, Douglas E., 1984. Person-Centered Apologetics: An Empathic Approach. *Journal of Psychology and Christianity,* 3 (1), pp. 18–26.

Bruce, F.F., 1977. *The Defense of the Gospel in the New Testament*, revised edition. Leicester: IVP.

Brueggemann, Walter, 1982. *Genesis: A Bible Commentary for Teaching and Preaching*. Atlanta: John Knox.

Brunner, Emil, 1929. Die andere Aufgabe der Theologie. *Zwischen den Zeiten,* 7 (3), pp. 255–276.

Brunner, Emil, 1939. *Man in Revolt: A Christian Anthropology*. London: Lutterworth Press.

Brunner, Emil, 1941. *Der Mensch im Widerspruch: Die christliche Lehre vom wahren und vom wirklichen Menschen*, dritte, unveränderte Auflage. Zürich: Zwingli-Verlag.

Brunner, Emil, 1946. Nature and Grace: A Contribution to the Discussion with Karl Barth. In: Karl Barth & Emil Brunner, *Natural Theology: Comprising "Nature and Grace" by Professor Dr. Emil Brunner and the Reply "No!" by Dr. Karl Barth*. London: Geoffrey Bless, pp. 15–64.

Brümmer, Vincent, 1981. *Theology and Philosophical Inquiry*. London: MacMillan.

Buber, Martin, 1958. *I and Thou*, Second edition. New York: Charles Scribner's Sons.

Calvini, Johannis, 1559. *Institutio Christianae Religionis.* In Peter Barth, Wilhelm Niesel eds, *Johannis Calvini Opera Selecta*, vols III–V. München: Kaiser, 1926–1952. Trans. *Institutes of the Christian Religion*, translated by Henry Beveridge, 2 vols. Grand Rapids: Eerdmans, 1975.

Carson, D.A., 1996. *The Gagging of God: Christianity Confronts Pluralism*. Grand Rapids: Zondervan.

Chang, Curtis, 2000. *Engaging Unbelief: Captivating Strategies from Augustine and Aquinas*. Downers Grove: InterVarsity Press.

Chesterton, G.K., 1996 [1908]. *Orthodoxy*. London, Sydney, Auckland: Hodder & Stoughton.

Childs, Brevard S., 1993. *Biblical Theology of the Old and New Testaments: Theological Reflection on the Christian Bible*. Minneapolis: Fortress Press.

Chisholm, Roderick M., 1989. *Theory of Knowledge*, third edition. Englewood Cliffs: Prentice-Hall.

Clark, David K., 1993a. *Dialogical Apologetics: A Person-Centered Approach to Christian Defense*. Grand Rapids: Baker.

Clark, David K., 1993b. Narrative Theology and Apologetics. *Journal of the Evangelical Theological Society,* 36, pp. 499–515.

Clark, David K., 1996. Relativism, Fideism & the Promise of Postliberalism. In: Timothy R. Phillips & Dennis L. Okholm eds, *The Nature of Confession: Evangelicals and Postliberals in Conversation*. Downers Grove: IVP, pp. 107–120.

Clark, Gregory A., 1996. The Nature of Conversion: How the Rhetoric of Worldview Philosophy Can Betray Evangelicals. In: Timothy R. Phillips & Dennis L. Okholm eds, *The Nature of Confession: Evangelicals and Postliberals in Conversation*. Downers Grove: IVP, pp. 201–218.

Clark, Kelly James, 1990. *Return to Reason: A Critique of Enlightenment Evidentialism and a Defense of Reason and Belief in God*. Grand Rapids: Eerdmans.

Coady, C.A.J., 1992. *Testimony: A Philosophical Study*. Oxford: Clarendon.

Collins, Robin, 1999. A Scientific Argument for the Existence of God: The Fine-Tuning Design Argument. In: Michael J. Murray ed., *Reason for the Hope Within*. Grand Rapids: Eerdmans, pp. 47–75.

Colyer, Elmer M., 2001. *How to Read T.F. Torrance: Understanding his Trinitarian and Scientific Theology*. Downers Grove: IVP.

Comstock, Gary L., 1987. Two Types of Narrative Theology. *Journal of the American Academy of Religion,* 55, pp. 687–717.

Corner, Mark, 1986. Review of *The Nature of Doctrine. Religion and Theology in a Postliberal Age*, By George A. Lindbeck. *Modern Theology,* 3, pp. 110–113.

Covey, Stephen R., 1989. *The Seven Habits of Highly Effective People: Restoring the Character Ethic*. New York: Fireside.

Cowan, Steven B. ed., 2000. *Five Views on Apologetics*. Grand Rapids: Zondervan.

Cragg, Kenneth, 1980. Conversion and Convertibility: With Special Reference to Muslims. In: John R.W. Stott & Robert Coote eds, *Down to Earth: Studies in Christianity and Culture*, The Papers of the Lausanne Consultation on Gospel and Culture. Grand Rapids: Eerdmans, pp. 193–208.

Craig, William Lane, 1984. *Apologetics: An Introduction*. Chicago: Moody.

Craig, William Lane, 1994. *Reasonable Faith: Christian Truth and Apologetics*, revised edition. Wheaton: Crossway.

Craig, William Lane, 1995. Politically Incorrect Salvation. In: Timothy R. Phillips & Dennis L. Okholm eds, *Christian Apologetics in the Postmodern World*. Downer's Grove: IVP, pp. 75–97.

Craig, William Lane, 2000. Classical Apologetics. In: Steven B. Cowan ed., *Five Views on Apologetics*. Grand Rapids: Zondervan, pp. 26–55.

Cross, Richard, 1999. *Duns Scotus*. New York e.a., Oxford University Press.

Cullmann, Oscar, 1951. *Christ and Time*. London: SCM.

Cupitt, Don, 1982. *The World to Come*. London: SCM.

Cupitt, Don, 1984. *The Sea of Faith*. London: BBC.

Dalferth, Ingolf U., 1986. Theologischer Realismus und Realistische Theologie bei Karl Barth. *Evangelische Theologie*, 46, pp. 402–422.

Davidson, Donald, 1984. On the Very Idea of a Conceptual Scheme. In: Donald Davidson, *Inquiries into Truth and Interpretation*. Oxford: Clarendon Press. pp. 183–198.

Deddo, Gary W., 1997. Persons in Racial Reconciliation: The Contributions of a Trinitarian Theological Anthropology. In: Dennis Okholm ed., *The Gospel in Black and White: Theological Resources for Racial Reconciliation*. Downers Grove: InterVarsity Press, pp. 58–67, 168–170.

Deddo, Gary W., 1999. *Karl Barth's Theology of Relations: Trinitarian, Christological, and Human: Towards an Ethic of the Family*. New York e.a.: Peter Lang.

Deddo, Gary W., 2001. Jesus' Paradigm for Relating Human Experience and Language about God. In: William A. Demski & Jay Wesley Richards, *Unapologetic Apologetics: Meeting the Challenges of Theological Studies*. Downers Grove: InterVarsity Press, pp. 187–206.

Descartes, 1637. *Le Discours de la méthode*; trans. *Discourse on the Method of Rightly Conducting One's Reason and Seeking Truth in the Sciences*, In: *The Essential Descartes*, edited and with an introduction by Margaret D. Wilson, New York, Scarborough: Meridian, 1983, pp. 106–153.

Descartes, 1641. *Meditationes de prima philosophia*; trans. *Meditations on Forst Philosophy in Which the Existence of God and the Distinction Between Mind and Body are Demonstrated*. In: *The Essential Descartes*, edited and with an introduction by Margaret D. Wilson, New York, Scarborough: Meridian, 1983, pp. 154–223.

Dawkins, Richard, 2006. *The God Delusion*. London: Bantam Press.

Devitt, Michael, 1984. *Realism and Truth*. Oxford: Blackwell.

Dockery, David S., 1995. The Challenge of Postmodernism. In: David S. Dockery ed., *The Challenge of Postmodernism: An Evangelical Engagement*. Grand Rapids: Baker, pp. 13–18.

Dockery, David S. ed., 1995. *The Challenge of Postmodernism: An Evangelical Engagement*. Grand Rapids: Baker.

Dulles, Avery, 1971. *A History of Apologetics*. New York: Corpus.

Dulles, Avery, 1992. *Models of Revelation*, 1992 edition. Maryknoll: Orbis.

Dyrness, William A., 1982. *Christian Apologetics in a World Community*. Downers Grove: IVP.

Edgar, William, 1995. No News is Good News: Modernity, the Postmodern and Apologetics. *Westminster Theological Journal,* 57, pp. 359–382.

Edgar, William, 1996. *Reasons of the Heart: Rediscovering Christian Persuasion*. Grand Rapids: Baker.

Evans-Pritchard, E.E., 1950. *Witchcraft, Oracles and Magic among the Azande*. Oxford: Clarendon Press.

Feinberg, Paul D., 2000a. A Cumulative Case Apologist's Response [to Classical Apologetics]. In: Steven B. Cowan ed., *Five Views on Apologetics*. Grand Rapids: Zondervan, pp. 67–73.

Feinberg, Paul D., 2000b. Cumulative Case Apologetics. In: Steven B. Cowan ed., *Five Views on Apologetics*. Grand Rapids: Zondervan, pp. 148–172.

Finkielkraut, Alain, 1987. *La défaite de la pensée: Essai*. Paris: Gallimard.

Finkielkraut, Alain, 1988. *The Undoing of Thought (La Défaite de la Pensée)*. London, Lexington: The Claridge Press.

Fisher, Roger & Chry, William, 1984. *Getting to Yes: Negotiating Agreement Without Giving In*. London: Hutchinson.

Flew, Anthony ed., 1984. *A Dictionary of Philosophy*, Second revised edition. London: Pan Books.

Ford, David F., 1985. "The Best Apologetics is Good Systematics": A Proposal about the Place of Narrative in Christian Systematic Theology.

Foucault, Michel, 1975. *Surveiller et punir: Naissance de la prison*. Paris: Gallimard.

Foucault, Michel, 1977. *Discipline and Punish: The Birth of Prison*. New York: Pantheon Books.

Frame, John M., 1995. *Cornelius Van Til: An Analysis of his Thought*. Phillipsburg: Presbyterian and Reformed.

Frame, John M., 2000. Presuppositional Apologetics. In: Steven B. Cowan ed., *Five Views on Apologetics*. Grand Rapids: Zondervan, pp. 208–231.

Frei, Hans W., 1974. *The Eclipse of Biblical Narrative: A Study in Eighteenth and Nineteenth Century Hermeneutics*. New Haven: Yale University Press.

Frei, Hans W., 1975. *The Identity of Jesus Christ: The Hermeneutical Basis of Dogmatic Theology*. Philadelphia: Fortress.

Frei, Hans W., 1992. *Types of Christian Theology*, edited by George Hunsinger & William C. Placher. New Haven/London: Yale University Press.

Gaudeul, Jean-Marie, 1991. *Appelés par le Christ: Ils viennent de l'Islam*. Paris: Cerf.

Gaudeul, Jean-Marie, 1999. *Called from Islam to Christ: Why Muslims become Christians*. Oxford: Monarch.

Geertz, Clifford, 1993. *The Interpretation of Cultures*. London: Fontana Press.

Geisler, Norman, 1976. *Christian Apologetics*. Grand Rapids: Baker.

Goldingay, John, 1994. *Models for Scripture*. Grand Rapids: Eerdmans.

Grant, Robert M., 1986. *Gods and the One God*. Philadelphia: Westminster.

Green, Michael, 1992. *Evangelism through the Local Church*. Nashville: Oliver-Nelson.

Green, Roger Lancelyn & Hooper, Walter, 1988. *C. S. Lewis: A Biography*. London: Souvenir Press.

Grenz, Stanley J., 1994. *Theology for the Community of God*. Carlisle: Paternoster.

Grenz, Stanley J., 1995. Star Trek and the Next Generation: Postmodernism and the Future of Evangelical Theology. In: David S. Dockery ed., *The Challenge of Postmodernism: An Evangelical Engagement*. Grand Rapids: Baker, pp. 89–103.

Grenz, Stanley J., 1996. *A Primer on Postmodernism*. Grand Rapids: Eerdmans.

Grenz, Stanley J., 1997. *Sexual Ethics: An Evangelical Perspective*, Second Edition. Westminster John Knox Press: Louisville.

Grenz, Stanley J., 1998. *Created for Community: Connecting Christian belief with Christian Living*, Second Edition. Grand Rapids: Baker.

Grenz, Stanley J., 2001. *The Social God and the Relational Self: A Trinitarian Theology of the Imago Dei*, Series: The Matrix of Christian Theology. Louisville: Westminster John Knox.

Grenz, Stanley J. & Franke, John R., 2001. *Beyond Foundationalism: Shaping Theology in the Postmodern Context*. Louisville: Westminster John Knox Press.

Griffin, David Ray, 1989. Introduction to SUNY Series in Constructive Postmodern Thought. In: David Ray Griffin, William A. Beardslee, Joe Holland, *Varieties of Postmodern Theology*. Albany: State University of New York Press, pp. XI–XIV.

Griffiths, Paul J., 1988. An Apology for Apologetics. *Faith and Philosophy,* 5, pp. 399–420.

Griffiths, Paul J., 1991. *An Apology for Apologetics: A Study in the Logic of Interreligious Dialogue*. Maryknoll: Orbis.

Guinness, I. Oswald, 1973. *The Dust of Death: A Critique of the Establishment and Counter Culture – and a Proposal for a Third Way*. Downers Grove: IVP.

Guinness, I. Oswald, 1981. *Towards a Reappraisal of Christian Apologetics: Peter. L. Berger's Sociology of Knowledge as the Sociological Phenomenon to Christian Apologetics*. Ph.D. University of Oxford.

Guinness, I. Oswald, 1983. *The Gravedigger File: Secret Papers on the Subversion of the Modern Church*. London: Hodder & Stoughton.

Guinness, I. Oswald, 1994. Mission Modernity: Seven Checkpoints on Mission in the Modern World. In: Philip Sampson, Vinay Samuel, Chris Sugden, *Faith and Modernity*. Oxford: Regnum, pp. 322–352.

Gumbel, Nickey, 1994. *Searching Issues: Tackling Seven Common Objections to the Christian Faith*. Eastbourne: Kingsway.

Gundry, Robert H., 1993. *Mark: A Commentary on His Apology for the Cross*. Grand Rapids: Eerdmans.

Gunton, Colin E., 1997. *The Promise of Trinitarian Theology*, second edition. Edinburgh: T & T Clark.

Habermas, Gary R., 2000. Evidential Apologetics. In: Steven B. Cowan ed., *Five Views on Apologetics*. Grand Rapids: Zondervan, pp. 91–121.

Habermas, Gary & Flew, Anthony, 1987. *Did Jesus Rise from the Dead: The Resurrection Debate*. Terry L. Miethe, ed., San Francisco: Harper & Row.

Hackett, Stuart C., 1957. *The Resurrection of Theism: Prolegomena to Christian Apology*, Second Edition. Baker: Grand Rapids.

Hackett, Stuart C., 1979. *Oriental Philosophy: A Westerner's Guide to Eastern Thought.* Madison: The University of Wisconsin Press.

Handspicker, Meredith B., 1991–1992. Toward a Postliberal Apologetics. *Journal of the Academy for Evangelism in Theological Education,* 7, pp. 72–81.

Helm, Paul, 1994. *Belief Policies*. Cambridge: Cambridge University Press.

Henry, Carl F.H., 1995. Postmodernism: The New Spectre? In: David S. Dockery ed. *The Challenge of Postmodernism: An Evangelical Engagement*. Grand Rapids: Baker, pp. 34–52.

Hensley, Jeffrey, 1996. Are Postliberals Necessarily Antirealists? Reexamining the Metaphysics of Lindbeck's Postliberal Theology. In: Timothy R. Phillips & Dennis L. Okholm eds, *The Nature of Confession: Evangelicals and Postliberals in Conversation*. Downers Grove: IVP, pp. 69–80.

Herbst, Michael, 1987. *Missionarischer Gemeindeaufbau in der Volkskirche*. Stuttgart: Calwer.

Hexham, Irving, Rost, Stephen & Morehead, John W. eds, 2004. *Encountering New Religious Movements: A Holistic Approach.* Grand Rapids: Kregel.

Hick, John, 1977. *God and the Universe of Faiths: Essays in the Philosophy of Religion*. Glasgow: Collins.

Hicks, Peter, 1998. *Evangelicals and Truth: a Creative Proposal for a Postmodern Age*. Leicester: Apollos (IVP).

Hiebert, Paul G., 1999. *Missiological Implications of Epistemological Shifts: Affirming Truth in a Modern/Postmodern World.* Harrisburg: Trinity Press International.

Hoekema, Anthony A., 1994. *Created in God's Image*. Grand Rapids: Eerdmans.

Hollinger, Dennis, 1995. The Church as Apologetic: A Sociology of Knowledge Perspective. In: Timothy R. Phillips & Dennis L. Okholm, *Christian Apologetics in the Postmodern World.* Downer's Grove: IVP, pp. 182–193.

Horkheimer, Max & Theodor W. Adorno, 1969. *Dialektik der Aufklärung: Philosophische Fragmente*, Neuausgabe. Frankfurt am Main: Fischer Verlag.

Horkheimer, Max & Theodor W. Adorno, 2002. *Dialectic of the Enlightenment Philosophical Fragments*. Stanford, Stanford University Press.

Hunsinger, George, 1991. *How to Read Karl Barth: The Shape of his Theology*. New York/Oxford: Oxford University Press.

Hunsinger, George, 1992. Hans Frei as Theologian: The Quest for a Generous Orthodoxy. *Modern Theology,* 8, pp. 103–128.

Hunsinger, George, 1996. What Can Evangelicals and Postliberals Learn from Each Other? The Carl Henri – Hans Frei Exchange Reconsidered. In: Timothy R. Phillips & Dennis L. Okholm eds, *The Nature of Confession: Evangelicals and Postliberals in Conversation*. Downers Grove: IVP, pp. 134–150.

Huxley, Aldous, 1969. *Brave New World*. New York: Harper & Row.

Igenoza, Andrew Olu, 1989. Time, History and Eschatology: An Evaluation of an Aspect of Mbiti's Theology. In: Nigel M. de S. Cameron, *Issues in Faith and History: Papers presented at the second Edinburgh conference on Dogmatics, 1978*. Edinburgh: Rutherford House Books, pp. 36–47.

Iyer, Pico, 2000. *The Global Soul: Jet Lag, Shopping Malls, and the Search for Home*. New York: Alfred A. Knopf.

James, William, 1960. *The Varieties of Religious Experience: A Study in Human Nature*. London, Glasgow: Collins.

Johnson, Philip, Payne, Simeon & Wilson, Peter, 2008. Towards a Contextualized Astrological Apologetic with a Case Study for Booth Ministry Outreach. *Missiology,* 36 (2), pp. 184–200.

Kagamé, Alexis, 1976. *La Philosophie Bantu comparée*. Paris: Présence Africaine.

Kaiser, Christopher B., 1991. *Creation and the History of Science*. Grand Rapids: Eerdmans.

Kant, Immanuel, 1781. *Kritik der Reinen Vernuft*, in: Immanuel Kant, *Werke*, Band 3–4, Sonderausgabe, Darmstadt: Wissenschaftliche Buchgesellschaft, 1983; trans. Immanuel Kant, *Critique of Pure Reason*, translated by Norman Kemp Smith, 2nd impression with corrections. London: MacMillan, 1933.

Kant, Immanuel, 1783. Beantwortung der Frage: Was ist Aufklärung. In: Immanuel Kant, *Werke*, Band 9, Schriften zur Anthropologie, Geschichtsphilosophie, Politik und Pädagogik, Erster Teil, Sonderausgabe. Darmstadt: Wissenschaftliche Buchgesellschaft, 1983, pp. 53–61.

Kant, Immanuel, 1788. *Kritik der praktischen Vernunft*, in: Immanuel Kant, *Werke*, Band 6, *Schriften zur Ethik und Religionsphilosophie*, Erster Teil, Sonderausgabe (Darmstadt: Wissenschaftliche Buchgesellschaft, 1983), pp. 103–302.

Kelsey, David H., 1990. Church Discourse and Public Realm. In: Bruce D. Marshall ed., *Theology in Dialogue: Essays in Conversation with George Lindbeck*. Notre Dame: University of Notre Dame Press, pp. 7–33.

Kelsey, David H., 2009. *Eccentric Existence: A Theological Anthropology*, 2 volumes. Louisville: Westminster John Knox Press.

Kenneson, Philip D., 1995. There's No Such a Thing as Objective Truth, and It's a Good Thing, Too. In: Timothy R. Phillips & Dennis L. Okholm, *Christian Apologetics in the Postmodern World*. Downer's Grove: IVP, pp. 155–170.

Kraft, Charles H., 1996. *Anthropology for Christian Witness*. Maryknoll: Orbis.

Kraft, Charles H., 1999. *Communicating Jesus' Way*, revised edition. Pasadena: William Carey Library.

Kraft, Marguerite H., 1995. *Understanding Spiritual Power: A Forgotten Dimension of Cross-Cultural Ministry*. Maryknoll: Orbis.

Kreeft, Peter & Tacelli, Ronald K., 1994. *Handbook of Christian Apologetics: Hundreds of Answers to Crucial Questions*. Downers Grove: InterVarsity Press.

Küng, Hans, 1978. *Existiert Gott? Antwort auf die Frage der Neuzeit*. München e.a.: Piper Verlag.

Küng, Hans, 1981. *Does God Exist? An Answer for Today*. Garden City: Doubleday.

Kuhn, Thomas, 1996. *The Structure of Scientific Revolutions*, Third edition. Chicago: University of Chicago Press.

Lamb, Jonathan, 1997. *Tough Minds, Tender Minds: Holding Truth and Love Together*. Leicester: Inter-Varsity Press.

Lapide, Pinchas, 1983. *The Resurrection of Jesus Christ: A Jewish Perspective*. Minneapolis: Augsburg.

Lausanne Committee for World Evangelization, 1980. The Willowbank Report. In: John R.W. Stott & Robert Coote eds, *Down to Earth: Studies in Christianity and Culture*, The Papers of the Lausanne Consultation on Gospel and Culture. Grand Rapids: Eerdmans, pp. 308–339.

Lewis, C.S., 1955a. *Mere Christianity*. Glasgow: Collins.

Lewis, C.S., 1955b. *Surprised by Joy: The Shape of My Early Life*. London: Collins.

Lewis, C.S., 1987. Christian Apologetics. In: C.S. Lewis, *Timeless at Heart: Essays in Christian Theology.* London: Collins, pp. 13–30.

Lewis, Gordon R., 1976. *Testing Christianity's Truth Claims: Approaches to Christian Apologetics*. Chicago: Moody Press.

Lindbeck, George A., 1971. The Sectarian Future of the Church. In: Joseph P. Whelan ed., *The God Experience*. New York: Newman Press, pp. 226–243.

Lindbeck, George A., 1984. *The Nature of Doctrine: Religion and Theology in a Postliberal Age*. Philadelphia: Westminster Press.

Lindbeck, George A., 1986. Barth and Textuality. *Theology Today,* 43, pp. 361–376.

Lindbeck, George A., 1996. Atonement and the Hermeneutics of Intratextual Social Embodiment. In: Timothy R. Phillips & Dennis L. Okholm eds, *The Nature of Confession: Evangelicals and Postliberals in Conversation*. Downers Grove: IVP, pp. 221–240.

Lindbeck, George A., 1997. The Gospel's Uniqueness: Election and Untranslatability. *Modern Theology*, 13, pp. 423–450.

Lindbeck, George A., Hunsinger, George, McGrath, Alister E. & Fackre, Gabriel, 1996. A Panel Discussion. In: Timothy R. Phillips & Dennis L. Okholm eds, *The Nature of Confession: Evangelicals and Postliberals in Conversation*. Downers Grove: IVP, pp. 246–253.

Lindsley, Art, 2008. *Love the Ultimate Apologetic: The Heart of Christian Witness*. Downers Grove: IVP.

Loscalzo, Craig A., 2000. *Apologetic Preaching: Proclaiming Christ to a Postmodern World*. Downers Grove: InterVarsity Press.

Lubac, Henri de, 1991. *Surnaturel: Etudes historiques*, nouvelle édition avec la traduction intégrale des citations latines et grecques. n. p.: Desclée de Brouwer.

Lundin, Roger, 1995. The Pragmatics of Postmodernity. In: Timothy R. Phillips

& Dennis L. Okholm eds, *Christian Apologetics in the Postmodern World*. Downer's Grove: IVP, pp. 24–38.

Luther, Martin, 1523–1524. *Genesis Vorlesung*. *Luther's Works* 1: *Lectures on Genesis Chapters 1–5*, edited by Jaroslav Pelikan. Saint Louis: Concordia Publishing House, 1958.

Lyotard, Jean-François, 1979. *La Condition postmoderne: Rapport sur le savoir*. Paris: Minuit,

Lyotard, Jean-François, 1984. *The Postmodern Condition: A Report on Knowledge*. Manchester: Manchester University Press.

Lyotard, Jean-François, 1986. *Le Postmoderne expliqué aux enfants: Correspondance 1982–1985*. Paris: Galilée.

Lyotard, Jean-François, 1992. *The Postmodern Explained: Correspondence 1982–1985*. Minneapolis: University of Minnesota Press.

MacIntyre, Alasdair, 1971. Is Understanding Religion Compatible with Believing, in: Bryan R. Wilson ed., *Rationality: Key Concepts in the Social Sciences*. New York etc.: Harper & Row, pp. 62–77.

MacIntyre, Alasdair, 1980. Epistemological Crises, Dramatic Narrative, and the Philosophy of Science. In: Gary Gutting ed., *Paradigms and Revolutions: Appraisals and Applications of Thomas Kuhn's Philosophy of Science*. Notre Dame/London: University of Notre Dame Press, pp. 54–74.

MacIntyre, Alasdair, 1985. *After Virtue: A Study in Moral Theory*. Second edition, London: Duckworth.

MacIntyre, Alasdair, 1988. *Whose Justice? Which Rationality?* London: Duckworth.

Macken, John, 1990. *The Autonomy Theme in the* Church Dogmatics*: Karl Barth and his Critics*. Cambridge e.a.: Cambridge University Press.

Macquarrie, John, 1982. *In Search of Humanity: A Theological & Philosophical Approach*. London: SCM.

Macquarrie, John, 1988. *Twentieth Century Religious Thought*. Fourth edition, London: SCM.

Maharaj, Rabindranath, 2004. *Death of Guru*. London: Hodder & Stoughton.

Magesa, Laurenti, 1997. *African Religion: The Moral Traditions of Abundant Life*. Maryknoll: Orbis.

Manaranche, André, 1985. *Le Monothéisme chrétien*. Paris: Cerf.

Marshall, Bruce D., 1990. Absorbing the World: Christianity and the Universe of Truths. In: Bruce D. Marshall ed., *Theology in Dialogue: Essays in Conversation with George Lindbeck*. Notre Dame: University of Notre Dame Press, pp. 69–102.

Marshall, Bruce D., 2009. Introduction: *The Nature of Doctrine* after 25 Years. In: George A. Lindbeck, *The Nature of Doctrine: Religion and Theology in a Postliberal Age*, 25th Anniversary Edition with a New Introduction by Bruce D. Marshall and a New Afterword by the Author. Louisville: Westminster John Knox Press.

Masolo, D.A., 1994. *African Philosophy in Search of Identity*. Nairobi: East African Educational Publishers.

Mavrodes, George I., 1970. *Belief in God: A Study in the Epistemology of Religion*. New York: Random House.

Mavrodes, George I., 1983. Jerusalem and Athens Revisited. In: Alvin Plantinga & Nicholas P. Wolterstorff eds, *Faith and Rationality: Reason and Belief in God*. Notre Dame: University of Notre Dame Press, pp. 192–218.

Mbiti, John S., 1969. *African Religions and Philosophy*. Nairobi: East African Educational Publishers.

Mbiti, John S., 1971. *New Testament Eschatology in an African Background: A Study of the Encounter between New Testament Eschatology and African Traditional Concepts*. Oxford: Oxford University Press.

Mbiti, John S., 1991. *Introduction to African Religion*, Second revised edition. Nairobi: East African Educational Publishers.

McCormack, Bruce L., 1995. *Karl Barth's Critically Realistic Dialectical Theology: Its Genesis and Development: 1909–1936*. Oxford: Clarendon Press.

McCormack, Bruce L., 2008. Beyond Nonfoundational and Postmodern Readings of Barth: Critically Realist Dialectical Theology. In: Bruce L. McCormack, *Orthodox and Modern: Studies in the Theology of Karl Barth*. Grand Rapids: Baker Academic, pp. 109–165.

McCracken, David, 1994. *The Scandal of the Gospels: Jesus, Story, and Offense*. New York, Oxford: Oxford University Press.

McDowell, Josh, 1977. *More Than a Carpenter*. Wheaton: Tyndale House Publishers.

McDowell, Josh, 1979, 1981. *Evidence that Demands a Verdict: Historical Evidences for the Christian Faith*, 2 vol., revised edition. San Bernardino (Ca.): Here's Life Publisher.

McGrath, Alister E., 1990. *The Genesis of Doctrine: A Study in the Foundations of Doctrinal Criticism*. Oxford: Blackwell.

McGrath, Alister E., 1992. *Bridge-Building: Effective Christian Apologetics*. Leicester: IVP.

McGrath, Alister E., 1996a. An Evangelical Evaluation of Postliberalism. In: Timothy R. Phillips & Dennis L. Okholm eds, *The Nature of Confession: Evangelicals and Postliberals in Conversation*. Downers Grove: IVP, pp. 23–44.

McGrath, Alister E., 1996b. *A Passion for Truth: The Intellectual Coherence of Evangelicalism*. Leicester: Apollos (IVP).

McGrath, Alister E., 1998a. *The Foundations of Dialogue in Science and Religion*. Oxford: Blackwell.

McGrath, Alister E., 1998b. Biblical Models for Apologetics. *Bibliotheca Sacra* 155, pp. 3–10 ("Evangelical Apologetics"), pp. 131–138 ("Apologetis to the Jews"), pp. 259–265 ("Apologetics to the Greeks"), pp. 387–393 ("Apologetics to the Romans").

McGrath, Alister E., 1999. *Thomas F. Torrance: An Intellectual Biography*. Edinburgh: T & T Clark.

Metzger, Bruce M., 1975. *A Textual Commentary on the Greek New Testament*, Corrected edition. n.p.: United Bible Societies.

Michaelson, Gordon E. Jr., 1988. The Response to Lindbeck. *Modern Theology*, 4, pp. 107–120.

Middleton, Richard J. & Walsh, Brian, 1995a. Facing the Postmodern Scalpel: Can the Christian Faith Withstand Deconstruction? In: Timothy R. Phillips & Dennis L. Okholm eds, *Christian Apologetics in the Postmodern World*. Downer's Grove: IVP, pp. 131–154.

Middleton, Richard J. & Walsh, Brian, 1995b. *Truth is Stranger Than it Used to Be: Biblical Faith in a Postmodern Age*. Downers Grove IL: IVP.

Mohler, Jr., R. Albert, 1995. The Integrity of the Evangelical Tradition and the Challenge of the Postmodern Paradigm. In: David S. Dockery ed. *The Challenge of Postmodernism: An Evangelical Engagement*. Grand Rapids: Baker, pp. 67–88.

Montgomery, John Warwick, 1978. *Faith Founded on Fact: Essays in Evidential Apologetics*. Nashville: Thomas Nelson.

Mouw, Richard J., 1992. *Uncommon Decency: Christian Civility in an Uncivil World*. Downers Grove: InterVarsity Press.

Mudimbe, V.Y., 1988. *The Invention of Africa: Gnosis, Philosophy, and the Order of Knowledge*. Bloomington: Indiana University Press.

Mulago, Vincent, 1969. Vital Participation: The Cohesive Principle in the Bantu Community. In: Kwesi Dickson & Paul Ellingworth, *Biblical Revelation and African Beliefs*. Maryknoll: Orbis, pp. 139–158.

Murphy, Nancey, 1996. Postmodern Apologetics: Or Why Theologians *must* Pay Attention to Science. In: W. Mark Richardson & Wesley J. Wildman eds, *Religion and Science: History, Method, Dialogue*. New York: Routledge, pp. 105–120.

Murphy, Nancey, 1999. Missiology in the Postmodern West: A Radical Reformation Perspective, in: J. Andrew Kirk & Kevin J. Vanhoozer eds, *To Stake a Claim: Mission and the Western Crisis of Knowledge*. Maryknoll: Orbis, pp. 96–119.

Murphy, Nancey & McClendon, Jr., James Wm., 1989. Distinguishing Modern and Postmodern Theologies. *Modern Theology*, 5, pp. 191–214.

Murray, Michael J., 1999. Reason for Hope (in a Postmodern World). In: Michael J. Murray ed., *Reason for the Hope Within*. Grand Rapids: Eerdmans, pp. 1–19.

Nash, Ronald H., 1992. *Worldviews in Conflict: Choosing Christianity in a World of Ideas*. Grand Rapids: Zondervan.

Naugle, David K., 2002. *Worldview: The History of a Concept*. Grand Rapids: Eerdmans.

Nellas, Panayiotis, 1997. *Deification in Christ: Orthodox Perspectives on the Nature of the Human Person*. New York: St. Vladimir's Seminary Press.

Netland, Harold A., 1988. Toward Contextualized Apologetics. *Missiology,* 16, pp. 289–303.

Netland, Harold A., 1991. *Dissonant Voices: Religious Pluralism and the Question of Truth*. Grand Rapids: Eerdmans.

Netland, Harold A., 1994. Truth, Authority and Modernity: Shopping for Truth in a Supermarket of Worldviews. In: Philip Sampson, Vinay Samuel, Chris Sugden (eds.), *Faith and Modernity*. Oxford: Regnum, pp. 89–115.

Netland, Harold A., 2001. *Encountering Religious Pluralism: The Challenge to Christian Faith and Mission*. Downers Grove: IVP.

Newbigin, Lesslie, 1986. *Foolishness to the Greeks: The Gospel and Western Culture.* Grand Rapids: Eerdmans.

Newbigin, Lesslie, 1989. *The Gospel in a Pluralist Society*. London: SPCK.

Newbigin, Lesslie, 1991. *Truth to Tell: The Gospel as Public Truth.* Grand Rapids: Eerdmans.

Newbigin, Lesslie, 1994. Truth and Authority in Modernity. In: Philip Sampson, Vinay Samuel, Chris Sugden, *Faith and Modernity*. Oxford: Regnum, pp. 60–88.

Newbigin, Lesslie, 1995. *Proper Confidence: Faith, Doubt and Certainty in Christian Discipleship*. London: SPCK.

Newbigin, Lesslie, 1996. *Truth and Authority in Modernity*. Valley Forge: Trinity Press International.

Niebuhr, Reinhold, 1941. *The Nature and Destiny of Man: A Christian Interpretation*, vol. 1: Human Nature. London: Nisbet & Co.

Niebuhr, Reinhold, 1943. *The Nature and Destiny of Man: A Christian Interpretation*, vol. 2: Human Destiny. London: Nisbet & Co.

Niebuhr, H. Richard, 1951. *Christ and Culture*. New York e.a.: Harper & Row.

Nietzsche, Friedrich 1883–1884. *Also Sprach Zarathustra*, 3 Teile, Volker Gerhardt ed. Berlin: Akademie Verlag 2000. Trans. *Thus Spoke Zarathustra*, a new translation by Clancy Martin, with an introduction by Kathleen M. Higgins & Robert C. Solomon, and notes by Kathleen M. Higgins, Robert C. Solomon & Clancy Martin. New York: Barnes & Noble Classics, 2005.

Nietzsche, Friedrich, 1886. *Jenseits von Gut und Böse*. In: Nietzsche, Friedrich. *Jenseits von Gut und Böse; Zur Genealogie der Moral*, Giorgio Colli & Mazzino Montinari eds 2, durchgesehene Auflage. München: Deutscher Taschenbuch Verlag/Berlin: De Gruyter, 1988. Trans. *Beyond Good and Evil*, translated by Helen Zimmern. Buffalo: Prometheus Books 1989.

Nietzsche, Friedrich, 1894. *Der Antichrist: Fluch auf Das Christentum*. In: Friedrech Nietzsche, *Der Antichrist, Ecce Homo, Dionysos-Dithyramben*, 5. Auflage. München: Goldman Verlag 1986, pp. 7–86. Trans. *The Antichrist*, in: Friedrich Nietzsche, *Twilight of the Idols/The Antichrist*, translated by R.J. Hollingdale. London: Penguin, 1990.

Oden, Thomas C., 1995. The Death of Modernity and Postmodern Evangelical

Spirituality. In: David S. Dockery ed., *The Challenge of Postmodernism: An Evangelical Engagement*. Grand Rapids: Baker, pp. 19–33.

O'Donovan, Joan E., 1986. Man in the Image of God: The Disagreement between Barth and Brunner Reconsidered. *Scottish Journal of Theology*, 39, pp. 433–459.

O'Donovan, Oliver, 1986. *Resurrection and Moral Order: An Outline for Evangelical Ethics*. Leicester: IVP.

Orr, James, 2002. *The Christian View of God and the World: As Centring in the Incarnation*, reprinted from the third edition [1897]. Vancouver: Regent College Publishing.

Osborne, Grant R., 1991. *The Hermeneutical Spiral: A Comprehensive Introduction to Biblical Interpretation*. Downers Grove: IVP.

Paley, William, 1802. *Natural Theology: Or, Evidences of the Existence and Attributes of the Deity Collected from the Appearances of Nature*. Farnborough: Gregg, 1970.

Pannenberg, Wolfhart, 1968. *Jesus: God and Man*. London: SCM.

Pannenberg, Wolfhart, 1983. *Anthropologie in theologischer Perspektive: Religöse Implikationen anthropologischer Theorie*. Göttingen: Vandenhoeck & Ruprecht.

Pannenberg, Wolfhart, 1985. *Anthropology in Theological Perspective*. Philadelphia: Westminster.

Pannenberg, Wolfhart, 1991. *Systematic Theology*, vol. I. Grand Rapids: Eerdmans.

Pascal, Blaise, 1963. *Pensées*. In: Blaise Pascal, *Oeuvres Complètes*, Présentation et notes de Louis de Lafuma. Paris: Seuil, pp. 493–649, translated by A.J. Krailsheimer, *Pensées*. London: Penguin 1966.

Patterson, Sue, 1999. *Realist Christian Theology in a Postmodern Age*. Cambridge: Cambridge University Press.

Pénoukou, Efoé-Julien, 1984. *Eglises d'Afrique: Propositions pour l'Avenir*. Paris: Karthala.

Peterson, Eugene H., 1989. *The Contemplative Pastor: Returning to the Art of Spiritual Direction*. Grand Rapids: Eerdmans.

Phillips, Timothy R. & Okholm, Dennis L., 1995. Introduction. In: Timothy R. Phillips & Dennis L. Okholm eds, *Christian Apologetics in the Postmodern World*. Downer's Grove: IVP, pp. 9–23.

Phillips, Timothy R. & Okholm, Dennis L., 1996. The Nature of Confession: Evangelicals & Postliberals. In: Timothy R. Phillips & Dennis L. Okholm eds, *The Nature of Confession: Evangelicals & Postliberals in Conversation*. Downers Grove: IVP, pp. 7–20.

Pico della Mirandola, 1486. *On Human Dignity*. In: E. Cassirer, P.O. Kristeller & J.H. Randall, Jr. eds, *The Renaissance Philosophy of Man (Petrarca, Valla, Ficino, Pico, Pomponazzi, Vives)*. Chicago: University of Chicago Press 1948.

Placher, William C., 1985. Revisionist and Postliberal Theologies and the Public Character of Theology. *The Thomist,* 49, pp. 392–416.

Placher, William C., 1989. *Unapologetic Theology: A Christian Voice in a Pluralist Conversation*. Louisville: Westminster/John Knox.

Placher, William C., 1997. Postliberal Theology. In: David F. Ford ed., *The Modern Theologians: An Introduction to Christian Theology in the Twentieth Century*, second edition. Oxford: Blackwell, pp. 343–356.

Plantinga, Alvin, 1980. *Does God Have a Nature? The Aquinas Lecture, 1980*. Milwaukee: Marquette University Press.

Plantinga, Alvin, 1983. Reason and Belief in God. In: Alvin Plantinga & Nicholas P. Wolterstorff eds, *Faith and Rationality: Reason and Belief in God*. Notre Dame: University of Notre Dame Press, pp. 16–93.

Plantinga, Alvin, 1988. Positive Epistemic Status and Proper Function. In: James Tomberlin ed., *Philosophical Perspectives* 2: *Epistemology*. Atascadero: Ridgeview Press, pp. 1–50.

Plantinga, Alvin, 1992. Augustinian Christian Philosophy. In: *The Monist*. 75, pp. 291–320.

Plantinga, Alvin, 1993a. *Warrant: The Current Debate*. New York/Oxford: Oxford University Press.

Plantinga, Alvin, 1993b. *Warrant and Proper Function*. New York/Oxford: Oxford University Press.

Plantinga, Alvin, 1995. A Defense of Religious Exclusivism. In: T.D. Senor ed., *The rationality of Belief and the Plurality of Truth*. Ithaca/London: Cornell University Press, pp. 191–215.

Plantinga, Alvin, 2000. *Warranted Christian Belief*. New York/Oxford: Oxford University Press.

Polanyi, Michael, 1946. *Science, Faith and Society*. London: Oxford University Press.

Polanyi, Michael, 1962. *Personal Knowledge: Towards a Postcritical Philosophy*, Corrected edition. Chicago: University of Chicago Press.

Polanyi, Michael 1967. Science and Reality, *British Journal of the Philosophy of Science,* 18, pp. 177–196.

Polkinghorne, John, 1986. *One World: The Interaction of Science and Theology*. London, SPCK.

Polkinghorne, John, 1989. *Rochester Roundabout: The Story of High Energy Physics*. Harlow: Longman.

Polkinghorne, John, 1991. *Reason and Reality: The Relationship between Science and Theology*. London: SPCK.

Potter, Ronald, 1995. Christian Apologetics in African–American Grain. In: Timothy R. Phillips & Dennis L. Okholm, *Christian Apologetics in the Postmodern World*. Downer's Grove: IVP, pp. 173–181.

Poythress, Vern S., 1988. *Science and Hermeneutics*, Foundations of Contemporary Interpretation. vol. 6, Leicester: IVP.

Quine, Willard V.O., 1961. Two Dogmas of Empiricism. In: Willard V.O. Quine, *From a Logical Point of View: 9 Logico-Philosophical Essays*. Second edition, revised. Cambridge: Harvard University Press, pp. 20–46.

Quine, Willard V.O. & Ullian, J.S., 1978. *The Web of Belief*, Second edition. New York: Random House.

Ratzsch, Del, 2000. *Science and its Limits: The Natural Sciences in Christian Perspective*. Downers Grove: IVP.

Rehnman, Sebastian, 1998. Barthian Epigoni: Thomas F. Torrance's Barth-Reception. *Westminster Theological Journal*, 60, pp. 271–296.

Rendtorff, Trutz, 1986. Der Freiheitsbegriff als Ortsbestimmung neuzeitlicher Theologie am Beispiel der kirchlichen Dogmatik Karl Barths. In: Hermann Deuser e.a. (Hrsg.) *Gottes Zukunft – Zukunft der Welt: Festschrift für Jürgen Molltmann zum 60. Geburtstag*. München: Kaiser, pp. 559–577.

Richardson, Alan, 1947. *Christian Apologetics*. London: SCM.

Richardson, Kurt A., 1995. Disorientations in Christian Belief: The Problem of De-traditionalization in the Postmodern Context. In: David S. Dockery ed. *The Challenge of Postmodernism: An Evangelical Engagement*. Grand Rapids: Baker, pp. 53–66.

Rietkerk, Wim, 1993. *Ik wou dat ik kon geloven: Over psychische factoren die een belemmering vormen voor het vertrouwen op God*. Kampen: Kok Voorhoeve.

Rietkerk, Wim, 1997. *If Only I Could Believe!* Carlisle: Solway.

Rorty, Amélie Oksenberg, 1988. The Deceptive Self: Liars, Layers, and Lairs, in: Brian McLaughlin & Amélie Oksenberg Rorty eds, *Perspectives on Self-Deception*. Berkeley e.a.: University of California Press, pp. 11–28.

Rorty, Richard, 1991. Introduction: Antirepresentationalism, ethnocentrism, and liberalism. In: idem, *Objectivity, Relativism and Truth: Philosophical Papers*, vol. 1. Cambridge e.a.: Cambridge University Press, pp. 1–17.

Rothacker, E., 1979. *Das Buch der Natur: Materialien und Grundsätzliches zur Metapherngeschichte*. Bonn: Bouvier.

Samuel, Vinay, 1994. Modernity, Mission and non-Western societies. In: Philip Sampson, Vinay Samuel, Chris Sugden eds, *Faith and Modernity*. Oxford: Regnum, pp. 314–320.

Sanneh, Lamin, 1989. *Translating the Message: The Missionary Impact on Culture*. New York: Orbis.

Schaff, Philip, 1919. *The Creeds of Christendom: With a History and Critical notes*, vol. 3, The Evangelical Protestant Creeds, Fourth edition – Revised and enlarged. New York: Harper & Brothers.

Schleiermacher, Friedrich, 1830. *The Christian Faith*, English Translation of the Second German Edition. Edinburgh: T & T Clark 1989.

Schweizer, Eduard, 1971. *Jesus*. Richmond: John Knox.

Sherlock, Charles, 1996. *The Doctrine of Humanity*, Series: Contours of Christian Theology. Leicester: IVP.

Sims, John A., 1995. Postmodernism: The Apologetic Imperative. In: David S. Dockery ed., *The Challenge of Postmodernism: An Evangelical Engagement*. Grand Rapids: Baker, pp. 324–343.

Sire, James W., 1994. *Why Should Anyone Believe Anything at All?* Downers Grove: IVP.

Sire, James W., 1995. On Being a Fool for Christ and an Idiot for Nobody: Logocentricity and Modernity. In: Timothy R. Phillips & Dennis L. Okholm, *Christian Apologetics in the Postmodern World*. Downer's Grove: IVP, pp. 101–127.

Sosa, Ernest, 1980. The Pyramid and the Raft: Coherence versus Foundations in the Theory of Knowledge. In: Peter French, Theodore E. Uehling & Howard Wettstein eds, *Midwest Studies in Philosophy*, vol. V. Minneapolis: University of Minnesota Press, pp. 3–25.

Sproul, R.C., Gerstner, John & Lindsley, Arthur, 1984. *Classical Apologetics: A Rational Defence of the Faith and a Critique of Presuppositional Apologetics*. Grand Rapids: Zondervan.

Stackhouse Jr., John G., 1995. From Architecture to Argument: Historic Resources for Christian Apologetics. In: Timothy R. Phillips & Dennis L. Okholm, *Christian Apologetics in the Postmodern World*. Downer's Grove: IVP, pp. 39–55.

Stackhouse Jr., John G., 2002. *Humble Apologetics: Defending the Faith Today*. Oxford, New York, e.a.: Oxford University Press.

Storkey, Elaine, 1994. Modernity and Anthropology. In: Philip Sampson, Vinay Samuel, Chris Sugden eds, *Faith and Modernity*. Oxford: Regnum, pp. 136–150.

Stott, John R.W., 1982. *I Believe in Preaching*. London, Sydney, Auckland: Hodder & Stoughton.

Stout, Jeffrey, 1981. *The Flight from Authority: Religion, Morality, and the Quest for Autonomy*. Notre Dame: University of Notre Dame Press.

Stout, Jeffrey, 1987. A Lexicon of Postmodern Philosophy. *Religious Studies Review,* 13, pp. 18–22.

Tanner, Kathryn, 1997. *Theories of Culture: A New Agenda for Theology*. Minneapolis: Fortress Press.

Taylor, Charles, 1989. *The Sources of the Self: The Making of the Modern Identity*. Cambridge: Cambridge University Press.

Taylor, Mark C., 1984. *Erring: A Postmodern A/theology*. Chicago: The University of Chicago Press.

Taylor, Mark C., 1992. Reframing Postmodernisms. In: Phillipa Berry, Andrew Wernick eds, *Shadow of Spirit: Postmodernism and Religion*. London/New York: Routledge, pp. 11–29.

Tempels, Placide, 1945. *La Philosophie Bantoue*. Elisabethville: Présence Africaine.

Tempels, Placide, 1969. *Bantu Philosophy*. Paris: Présence Africaine.

Ter Linde, Nico, 1996. *Het verhaal gaat ...* Deel 1, De verhalen van de Thora. Amsterdam: Balans.

Ter Linde, Nico, 1999. *The Story Goes ...* 1, *The Stories of the Torah*. London: SCM.

Thiel, John A., 1994. *Nonfoundationalism*. Minneapolis: Fortress Press.

Thiemann, Ronald F., 1985. *Revelation and Theology: The Gospel as Narrated Promise*. Notre Dame: University of Notre Dame Press.

Thiemann, Ronald F., 1986. Response to George Lindbeck. *Theology Today* 43, pp. 377–382.

Theissen, G., 1999. *A Theory of Primitive Christian Religion*. London: SCM.

Thiselton, Anthony C., 1980. *The Two Horizons: New Testament Hermeneutics and Philosophical Description with Special Reference to Heidegger, Bultmann, Gadamer and Wittgenstein*. Exeter: Paternoster Press.

Tilley, Terrence W., 1988. Incommensurability, Intratextuality, and Fideism. *Modern Theology,* 5, pp. 87–111.

Tilley, Terrence W. et al., 1995. *Postmodern Theologies: The Challenge of Religious Diversity*. Maryknoll: Orbis.

Tiplady, Richard, 2003. Introduction. In: Richard Tiplady ed., *One World or Many? The Impact of Globalisation on Mission*. Pasadena: William Carey Library, pp. 1–9.

Tolkien, J.R.R., 1966. On Fairy Stories. In: Dorothy Sayers e.a., *Essays Presented to Charles Williams*. Grand Rapids: Eerdmans, pp. 38–89.

Topping, Richard R., 1991. The Anti-Foundationalist Challenge to Evangelical Apologetics. *The Evangelical Quarterly,* 63, pp. 45–60.

Torrance, Thomas F., 1962. *Karl Barth: An Introduction to his Early Theology 1910–1931*. London: SCM.

Torrance, Thomas F., 1969. *Theological Science*. London, etc.: Oxford University Press.

Torrance, Thomas F., 1971. *God and Rationality*. London e.a.: Oxford University Press.

Torrance, Thomas F., 1976. *Space, Time and Resurrection*. Edinburgh: Handsel Press.

Torrance, Thomas F., 1980. The Framework of Belief. In: Thomas F. Torrance ed., *Belief in Science and Christian Life: The Relevance of Michael Polanyi's Thought for Christian Faith and Life*. Edinburgh: Handsel Press, pp. 1–48.

Torrance, Thomas F., 1982. Theological Realism. In: Brian Hebblethwaite & Stuart Sutherland, *The Philosophical Frontiers of Christian Theology: Essays Presented to D.M. MacKinnon*. Cambridge: Cambridge University Press, pp. 169–196.

Torrance, Thomas F., 1984. Natural Theology in the Thought of Karl Barth. In: Thomas F. Torrance *Transformation and Convergence in the Frame of*

Knowledge. Explorations in the Interrelations of Scientific and Theological Enterprise. Grand Rapids: Eerdmans, pp. 285–301.

Torrance, Thomas F., 1985. *Reality and Scientific Theology*. Edinburgh: T & T Clark.

Torrance, Thomas F., 1990. *Karl Barth: Biblical and Evangelical Theologian*. Edinburgh: T & T Clark.

Torrance, Thomas F., 1992. *The Mediation of Christ*, revised edition. Edinburgh: T & T Clark.

Torrance, Thomas F., 1995. *Divine Meaning: Studies in Patristic Hermeneutics*. Edinburgh: T & T Clark.

Torrance, Thomas F., 1999. *Reality and Evangelical Theology: The Realism of Christian Theology*, With a new foreword by Kurt Anders Richardson. Downers Grove: InterVarsity Press.

Torrance, Thomas F., 2001. *The Ground and Grammar of Theology: Consonance between Theology and Science*, New edition. Edinburgh: T & T Clark.

Tracy, David, 1975. *Blessed Rage for Order: The New Pluralism in Theology*. New York: Seabury Press.

Tracy, David, 1981. *The Analogical Imagination: Christian Theology and the Culture of Pluralism*. New York: Crossroads.

Tracy, David, 1985. Lindbeck's New Program for Theology: A Reflection. *The Thomist,* 49, pp. 460–472.

Turaki, Yusufu, 1997. *The Tribal Gods of Africa: Ethnicity, Racism, Tribalism and Gospel*. Nairobi: AEA.

Van den Brink, Gijsbert, 1993. *Almighty God: A Study in the Doctrine of Divine Omnipotence*. Kampen: Pharos.

Van den Toren, Benno, 1993. A New Direction in Christian Apologetics: An Exploration with Reference to Postmodernism. *European Journal of Theology*, 2, pp. 49–64.

Van den Toren, Benno, 1995. *Breuk en brug. In gesprek met Karl Barth en postmoderne theologie over geloofsverantwoording*. Zoetermeer: Boekencentrum.

Van den Toren, Benno, 1997. Kwame Bediako's Christology in its African Evangelical Context. *Exchange,* 26, pp. 218–232.

Van den Toren, Benno, 2002. God's Purpose for Creation as the Key to Understanding the Universality and Cultural Variety of Christian Ethics. *Missiology,* 30, pp. 215–233.

Van den Toren, Benno, 2009. *A Pocket Guide to Christian Belief*. Oxford: Lion.

Van den Toren, Benno, 2010. *Reasons for my Hope: Responding to non-Christian Friends*. Oxford: Monarch.

Van der Walt, B.J., 1997. *Afrocentric or Eurocentric? Our task in a multicultural South Africa*. Potchefstroom: Potchefstroomse Universiteit vir Christelike Hoër Onderwys.

Vanhoozer, Kevin J., 1999. The Trials of Truth: Mission Martyrdom and the

Epistemology of the Cross. In: J. Andrew Kirk & Kevin J. Vanhoozer eds, *To Stake a Claim: Mission and the Western Crisis of Knowledge*. Maryknoll: Orbis, pp. 120–156.

Van Til, Cornelius, 1946. *The New Modernism: An Appraisal of the Theology of Barth and Brunner*. London: Clarke.

Van Til, Cornelius, 1962. *Christianity and Barthianism*. Phillipsburg: Presbyterian and Reformed.

Van Til, Cornelius, 1967. *The Defense of the Faith*, Third edition. Phillipsburg: Presbyterian and Reformed.

Van Til, Cornelius, 1971. Response by Cornelius Van Til" [to Gordon R. Lewis], in: E.R. Geehan, *Jerusalem and Athens: Critical Discussions on the Philosophy and Apologetics of Cornelius Van Til*. Nutley: Presbyterian and Reformed, pp. 361–368.

Veith, Jr., Gene Edward, 1994. *Postmodern Times: A Christian Guide to Contemporary Thought and Culture*. Wheaton: Crossway Books.

Von Rad, Gerhard, 1964. *Das Erste Buch Mose: Genesis*, series: Das Alte Testament Deutsch, 7. Auflage. Göttingen: Vandenhoek & Ruprecht.

Von Rad, Gerhard, 1972. *Genesis: A Commentary*, Old Testament Library. Philadelphia: Westminster.

Walgrave, J.H., n.d. [1966]. *Geloof en Theologie in de crisis*. Kasterlee: De Vroente.

Wallace, Mark I., 1987. The New Yale Theology. *Christian Scholar's Review,* 17, pp. 154–170.

Walls, Andrew F., 1996, *The Missionary Movement and in Christian History: Studies in the Transmission of Faith*. New York: Orbis/ Edinburgh: T & T Clark.

Walsh, Brian W. & Middleton, J. Richard, 1984. *The Transforming Vision: Shaping a Christian Worldview*. Downers Grove: IVP.

Ware, Timothy, 1964. *The Orthodox Church*. Reprinted with revisions. London: Penguin Books.

Wells, David F., 1993. *No Place for Truth: Or Whatever Happened to Evangelical Theology?* Grand Rapids: Eerdmans.

Webster, Douglas, 1995. Evangelizing the Church. In: Timothy R. Phillips & Dennis L. Okholm eds, *Christian Apologetics in the Postmodern World*. Downer's Grove: IVP, pp. 194–208.

Wenham, Gordon J., 1987. *Genesis 1–15*, Word Biblical Commentary, vol. 1. Dallas: Word.

Werpehowski, William, 1986. Ad Hoc Apologetics. *The Journal of Religion,* 66, pp. 282–301.

Westermann, Claus, 1994. *Genesis 1–11: A Continental Commentary*. Minneapolis: Fortress Press.

White, Graham, 1984. Karl Barth's Theological Realism. *Neue Zeischrift für Systematische Theologie und Religionsphilosophie*, 26, pp. 54–70.

Wilkinson, Loren E., 1996. Immanuel and the Purpose of Creation. In: Donald

Lewis & Alister McGrath eds, *Doing Theology for the People of God: Studies in Honour of J.I. Packer*. Leicester: Apollos (IVP), 245–261.

Williams, Paul, 2002. *The Unexpected Way: On Converting from Buddhism to Catholicism*. Edinburgh: T & T Clark.

Williams, Stephen N., 1994. Modernity and Morality. In: Philip Sampson, Vinay Samuel & Chris Sugden eds, *Faith and Modernity*. Oxford: Regnum, pp. 151–162.

Williams, Stephen N., 1995. *Revelation and Reconciliation: A Window on Modernity.* Cambridge: Cambridge University Press.

Wilson, Bryan R. ed., 1971 *Rationality: Key Concepts in the Social Sciences*. New York e.a.: Harper & Row.

Wittgenstein, Ludwig 1953. *Philosophical Investigations*, The German text, with a revised English Translation, Third edition. Oxford: Blackwell, 2001.

Wolff, Hans Walter. 1973. *Anthropologie des Alten Testaments*. München: Kaiser Verlag,

Wolff, Hans Walter, 1974. *Anthropology of the Old Testament*. Philadelphia: Fortress Press.

Wright, Chris, 1990. *What's so Unique About Jesus?* Eastbourne: Marc (Monarch Publications).

Wright, N.T., 2003. *The Resurrection of the Son of God.* Minneapolis: Fortress Press.

Zagzebski, Linda, 1993. Religious Knowledge and the Virtues of the Mind. In: Linda Zagzebski ed., *Rational Faith: Catholic Responses to Reformed Epistemology*. Notre Dame: University of Notre Dame Press, pp. 199–225.

INDEX